The
Ultimate
LABRADOR
RETRIEVER

Edited by
Heather Wiles-Fone

HOWELL
BOOK
HOUSE

Copyright 1997 and 2003 by Ringpress Books
A division of Interpet Publishing

This edition first published in the United States in 2003 by
HOWELL BOOK HOUSE
An imprint of Wiley Publishing Inc
909 Third Avenue, New York, NY 10022

Second edition
ISBN 0764526391

Library of Congress CIP data applied for.

CONTENTS

CONTRIBUTORS

HEATHER WILES-FONE (Breed Consultant) founded her Heatherbourne kennel in the late 1960s, and has since achieved considerable success in the show ring. Heather is a Championship judge of the breed and travels extensively on judging appointments.

RICHARD EDWARDS comes from a dog-showing family, and the Lasgarn affix was registered in the 1940s. Labradors first joined the kennel in the 1960s, and since then Richard has owned five show Champions.

MARIANNE FOOTE's Winroc kennel has produced multiple conformation Champions, National Specialty Show winners, FC, AFC and NAFC titled dogs, plus Hunt Test and Obedience titled Labradors at all levels.

JANE BORDERS has made up more than 30 American Champion Labradors, as well as many Field and Obedience titled dogs. She is an AKC approved judge of the breed.

MAJORIE SATTERTHWAITE has spent her life breeding, showing, trialing, and working her Labradors. She has bred a total of 10 full English Champions under her Lawnwoods prefix.

ALISON JONES BvetMed MRCVS is an expert in canine nutrition. After a spell working in general practice, she joined Hill's Pet Nutrition Ltd. as a veterinary advisor.

PENNY CARPANINI has established a highly succesful breeding programme, using her Carpenny affix. Her achievements include: Top Labrador 1993, Top Labrador Puppy 1995, and a Best in Show at Championship level.

C.C. GUARD is a highly respected trainer with wide experience in Working Trials, Obedience and Agility. She judges Obedience at Championship level, and judges Working Trials – all stakes.

DAVID CRAIG has worked closely with the Bradking kennel, and co-owned and exhibited the male CC recordholder, Ch. Bradking Hugo. David is an international Championship judge of the breed.

JANICE PRITCHARD has been involved with Labradors since the 1960s, and six British Champions and 17 overseas Champions carry her Charway affix. Janice has judged Labradors all over the world.

CAROL COODE's Warringah kennel has gained a reputation for sound stock of excellent type and temperament. All her dogs are gun-trained, and nine have become full Champions. Carole is in great demand as a judge, and has travelled to all five continents on judging appointments.

SUSAN SCALES specialised in producing Labradors that could work in the field, and were also worthy winners in the show ring. Her Manymills kennel has produced stock of the highest calibre.

DICK LANE BSC FRAGS FRCVS has spent his working life as a vet in practice, and has been employed by the Guide Dogs for the Blind Association as their consultant. He has been awarded the Fellowship of the Royal College of Veterinary Surgeons, and the Fellowship of the Royal Agricultural Society.

Other contributions have come from: Jan-Erik Ek (Sweden), Maria Sawnljung and Eeva Rautala (Finland), Anja Verbeek de Neef (The Netherlands), Dr Isabella Kraft and Dr Helmut Kamlah (Germany), and Carmen Copestake (South Africa).

FOREWORD

Since the original publication of *The Ultimate Labrador Retriever* in 1997, the Labrador has continued to gain in popularity in the United Kingdom and the United States of America. The breed's natural affection and intelligence, together with a great sense of fun, has made the Labrador a much sought after family dog and companion. As a shooting dog, the Labrador's ability in the field is unrivalled, portraying the typical obedient and eager-to-please temperament.

In the show ring, numbers have increased and it is not uncommon for Labradors to have the top entry at Championship shows. Furthermore, the breed's popularity has increased enormously in Europe, and since the introduction of the Pet Passport Scheme, many overseas exhibitors travel to the U.K. to exhibit their stock. This scheme also enables British dogs to go to other countries, and compete. International Champion Carpenny Walpole, owned by Mrs Penny Carpanini, won his full Champion title in Britain, having qualified in the field, and then went to Scandinavia where he gained his Finnish, Norwegian, and Swedish titles in the show ring, thus giving him the additional title of Nordic Champion. To become a Swedish Champion, a dog has to prove his ability at trials, and the requirements are pretty stiff. Walpole has proved himself to be one of the few modern day dual purpose Labradors – a truly outstanding achievement.

Competition is still very strong in the show world, and some of the long-established kennels are consistently to the fore in the winning stakes. It is impossible to mention them all but the world-renowned Sandylands kennel, now owned by Mr & Mrs G. Anthony and Mrs Erica Jayes, since the death of Mrs Gwen Broadley, is still producing Champions today. This is surely the most successful Labrador kennel of all time, and, at the time of writing, the total number of Champions bred or owned stands at 83, including just a few Flat Coated Retrievers, English Springers, Cockers and Pointers.

The Labrador remains a firm favourite as a fun-loving family companion.

The British breed recordholder, winning the most Challenge Certificates, is the famous yellow male Sh. Ch. Bradking Hugo, owned and bred by Mr and Mrs A. Kelly. He gained 50 CCs in total, overtaking the previous recordholder – the beautiful Sh. Ch. Croftspa Hazelnut of Foxrush, who won 45 CCs.

Throughout the USA, there are many Labrador breeders who, with their wealth of knowledge and dedication, produce top-class representatives of the breed. The strength in quality of black bitches is exceedingly impressive, and, when lined up at a Specialty show, they completely fill the eye. The Tabatha kennel, owned by Carol Heidl, is well known for producing excellent breed type with very good conformation. Another long-established kennel is Dickendall, which has owned and bred some very influential stud dogs – there can't be many pedigrees without that prefix along the line somewhere.

Specialty shows are a great event, where the cream of Labradors is exhibited. Many dogs have to travel huge distances in order to compete. Probably the club with the highest number of entries is the Labrador Retriever Club of the Potomac, where the number is in the region of 1,100.

The year 2003 marked the 100th anniversary of the Labrador being recognised as a separate breed by the Kennel Club in the UK. Prior to that, the Labrador was combined in a group with the other retriever breeds. To mark this occasion, the Labrador Club of UK held a special celebration at Belvoir Castle, in Lincolnshire, incorporating a weekend of shows and a working test, with judges from the UK, Australia and Finland.

Over the years, there have been numerous reports of remarkable achievements by Labradors, but the extraordinary devotion of a yellow male, living in the South of England, deserves a special mention. Endal was trained by Canine Partners for Independence as an assistance dog, and he has transformed the life of his owner, who was injured in the Gulf War and subsequently confined to a wheelchair. For his dedication and aptitude at assisting his

Endal, Dog of the Millennium, works the cash dispenser.

master, Endal was awarded the ultimate accolade of Dog of the Millennium.

A contrasting story, which shows the Labrador's courage and intelligence, concerns a black Labrador male, who was lost overboard from his owner's boat in the English Channel. The dog swam 10 miles to the shore, and, showing further ingenuity, he managed to find his way back home – much to his owner's amazement!

Both these stories epitomise the unique and endearing nature of the Labrador, and it is little wonder that we wish this breed to be part of our lives.

HeatherWiles-Fone. Spring 2003

1 *INTRODUCING THE LABRADOR RETRIEVER*

The Labrador, as a breed, is a friendly, happy and charming dog. Labradors are good-tempered, easy to train, eager to please, and devoted to their families. They become fond of, and attached to, other household pets, not only cats, but even hamsters and budgerigars. They will put up with almost anything from children, love their company and are tolerant to the point of saintliness, asking for nothing more in life than to be with you and your family, and to please you all. They will never growl, but new owners should always be warned not to allow their over-enthusiastic children to abuse the wonderfully benevolent temperament of a Labrador. Never forget that a young puppy is an animal, not a toy. Basically, a Labrador is a pleasure to live with and to look after. Indeed, the breed's love of, and devotion to, their families is heart-warming and endearing.

There should never be any danger of a

The hallmark of the Labrador temperament is kindliness, affection, devotion, intelligence and obedience.

Photo: Amanda Bulbeck.

In order to achieve the potential in your dog, it is important to provide a well-rounded education.

Labrador fighting with other dogs. If anything, their fault is over-friendliness. They will cheerfully and innocently run up to any other dog, tail wagging and wanting to play. However, you should always remember that not all other breeds are as friendly, and this trait can sometimes land Labradors in trouble.

Although Labradors are good house-dogs, who will give a warning if a stranger is at the door and whose deep and resonant bark will warn off possible intruders, they are in no way guard dogs. In fact, they are more likely to greet and make a fuss of visitors than attempt to ward them off in an aggressive manner. This delightful temperament is to be fostered, as a Labrador (like all other gundog breeds) should never be aggressive, although, on the other hand, never too timid or nervous in any way, shape or form.

Clearly, when selecting a Labrador as a pet, the correct temperament is a much more important factor than construction. A slight fault or failing, which may debar your Labrador puppy from becoming a top-class show dog, will not detract from his obvious qualities as a pet. A good temperament, kindliness, affection, devotion, intelligence and obedience are far more important than slightly straight shoulders, or a shortish neck!

Labradors are, on the whole, very sensitive to punishment and, generally, a stern reprimand for a misdemeanour is sufficient deterrent. The mere fact that you sound displeased will usually be punishment enough, as Labradors want nothing more than to please their owners. Far better results are gained through the use of praise and affection than harsh treatment. When I started in the breed, I was given the wise advice to 'temper justice with mercy', and I have found this approach works very well.

THE RIGHT START
If your Labrador puppy is to be a household pet, several important considerations must be borne in mind when bringing your puppy up properly so as to develop into a well-rounded, sensible, and well-behaved animal with whom it is a pleasure to live and share one's life. My first Labrador was purchased when I was twelve years old. I made several bad mistakes in

Int. Am. & Mex. Ch. JanWood's Secret Agent CD, WC:
The Labrador excels as a gundog, working on land and in water.

bringing up this puppy. Looking back, I advise you to realise that actions, which may seem extremely funny and cute in a relatively small, harmless eight-week-old puppy, can turn into firmly entrenched anti-social behavioural patterns, problematic in a mature dog. One of the first words your puppy must learn is "No!", and when the misdemeanour stops, you reward the young dog by lavishing praise. Remember, if you put yourself into the mind of the puppy, you will not go far wrong.

When exercising my own dogs, either in public places or in nearby woods, I regularly see dog owners make a dreadful mistake. They often reprimand a dog who eventually comes back to them, after running ahead and sniffing another oncoming dog. This action is senseless, serving only to reinforce to the dog that, on returning to the owner, chastisement will follow. As well as training your puppy to come when called, other useful lessons are sit and stay, and walking to heel. If this groundwork is done thoroughly and sensibly, then by the time your mature Labrador is strong and powerful, you will have in your care an obedient, well-behaved dog with whom you are proud to appear in public. A bonus is that, should you be planning extra-curricular or club activities when your Labrador is older, the foundations of basic obedience will already have been firmly established. With a dog as intelligent and biddable as a Labrador, you can indeed teach an old dog new tricks. I know of quite a few mature show dogs who, once they have gained their show championship titles, have gone on to attain Show Gundog Working Certificates, even without previous formal training in this sphere.

THE WORKING GUNDOG
Labradors are excellent as shooting dogs, the original job for which they were bred. For this reason, at the turn of the century, their numbers and popularity rose rapidly, due to gamekeepers' recognition of the breed as a gundog of great ability and versatility. In fact, the Labrador became the most popular working gundog breed. Their obedience, easy trainability, good nose and common sense qualify them as really useful gundogs.

In our modern society, there are far fewer

gamekeepers, but the Labrador still remains the most popular shooting companion, with both field triallers and rough shooters. Today, when gundog work falls into several different categories, most Labradors as gundogs are owned by people who want to shoot over them, or who wish to take their dog picking up or beating on the local shoot. Usually, these dogs are also pets of the hunter's family, once again proving how versatile the Labrador's role can be. It must also be said that this way of life is probably the most satisfactory for the dog, because a Labrador is not a kennel dog by nature. Members of the breed appreciate lots of family love and affection, and at the same time they enjoy fulfilling the purpose for which Labradors were developed in this country. Other gundog competition enthusiasts can be divided into those who enter competitive field trials, where the dog is judged under authentic shooting-day conditions and is required to make retrieves from freshly-shot game, and those who participate in gundog working tests, which feature retrieves in simulated shooting conditions, using the likes of canvas dummies or even cold game.

THE VERSATILE LABRADOR

Labradors can be trained for all sorts of useful occupations in everyday society, from fetching an owner's newspaper or slippers, to guiding the blind, working as police sniffer dogs detecting drugs and explosives, or performing mountain and water rescues. These tremendous qualities make the Labrador one of the most popular breeds worldwide, suiting practically everyone and able to fit in anywhere.

The decision to use Labradors as guide dogs is based on their solid, stoic temperament, and on their intelligence and biddability, which add up to a wonderful testament to the Labrador as a breed. Initially, the Guide Dogs for the Blind Association in the UK obtained Labradors for its organisation from show lines, and certainly several very famous show dogs from the world-renowned Sandylands kennel of Gwen Broadley were used in the early days of Guide Dogs for the Blind. Many puppies sired by Candlemas Sandylands Timber became successful guide

The decision to use Labradors as guide dogs is based on their solid, stoic temperament, their intelligence and biddability.
Photo: Peter Byron,
courtesy of Seeing Eye, USA.

dogs, which speaks volumes for the sound, sensible temperament Gwen has always strived to maintain. Today the GDBA has its own highly successful breeding programme. However, reputable Labrador breeders are still approached for either puppies or youngsters who can be incorporated. This shows not only the high regard in which the GDBA holds the breed as regards temperament and personality, but also that reputable breeders are considered to be doing a good job in maintaining the breed's temperamental virtues, which are, after all, of paramount importance, and without which a

Labrador is not a Labrador!

Dogs for the Disabled is a much younger charity than Guide Dogs for the Blind, but one which has an almost unlimited future in training dogs to help people with a wide range of physical handicaps. Based upon a Labrador's willingness to share the owner's life, skilled, positive training can produce a dog who will tremendously enhance the life of a handicapped person. Labradors have proved successful and responsive to the training necessary to produce a qualified Dog for the Disabled, and there can be no doubt that this success is largely due to the breed's inherent intelligence and the ease with which they can be trained.

Recently, I came across a new police role for the Labrador. A policeman visited the school at which I taught, in order to explain to primary-age pupils the necessity of saying "No!" to strangers, an extremely important message to get across to children. I wondered about the presence of his two impeccably-behaved Labradors, but I soon discovered their purpose. The black Labrador male was called Jet, and the yellow male Rex. When the dogs were asked "What do you say to strangers?", they both barked in reply. More than a year later, the policeman brought Rex and Jet back to school to reiterate the campaign's message. When the policeman asked if anybody knew what he was called, there was complete silence among the children. However, when he asked them if they knew the dogs' names, the children's hands shot up because nearly all of them remembered Rex and Jet. More importantly, they immediately recalled the message the dogs conveyed – that you must say "No!" to strangers, just like the two Labradors did. After this experience, I thought how wonderful was the symbol of a well-behaved Labrador who barked at the question, instilling such an important social message. Throughout the proceedings, the two dogs behaved impeccably and thoroughly enjoyed the attentions of 200 children,

converging to pat them. All this shows what a remarkable temperament and personality the breed possesses. The story is all the more heartwarming because these two Labradors were both rescued from unsuitable homes, where they had been badly treated.

CARING FOR THE LABRADOR

Another great advantage of a pet Labrador is the breed's inherent cleanliness, and ease of maintenance. Labradors have short coats that dry easily, and do not carry a lot of dirt and mud into the house. Even when they do get dirty, a thorough cleaning and quick dry with a wash-leather is enough to make them clean enough to come into the house again. If, in summertime, they go for a long walk and have a swim (a pastime that Labradors love), they are easily dried with a wash-leather, which absorbs the wetness from their coat. Having a double coat, consisting of a harsh top coat and dense undercoat, Labradors quickly dry off after getting wet. Even in rain and dirty weather, when the fields are like quagmires, these dogs can come home filthy and after a quick wash, and thorough use of the chamois leather, they are as clean as a new pin. As regards my own dogs, who are both kennel and house-dogs, once they are clean, I put them into a kennel with a good depth of fresh wood-shavings. This quickly dries wet coats, and they come out smelling nice too.

Labradors are very quick to learn their place and a routine. They are seldom a nuisance, providing you are firm when they are young, taking trouble to teach them they must behave and ensuring that they obey your wishes.

The Labrador, as a breed, is strongly and sensibly built without any exaggerated or ridiculous fancy points or frills, and with very few weaknesses in anatomy. The typical Labrador is a no-nonsense dog of sound construction and build. While such inherited defects as hip dysplasia, PRA and hereditary

'The Labrador is strongly and sensibly built without frills, and with very few weaknesses in anatomy'

A hardy, no-nonsense breed, the Labrador is easy to care for and will rarely experience major health problems.

cataract do exist, Labradors are very healthy dogs. If you buy from a reputable establishment, you will find the breed to be trouble-free throughout their lives. They do not suffer easily from cuts, serious injuries or broken bones, for they are sturdily and strongly built. Also, they have thick, dense, waterproof coats with thick skins, and are well protected, not only with muscle, but with a layer of fat. I have found that, apart from routine bills from my vet for inoculating young puppies against distemper, hardpad, parvovirus and hepatitis, and for giving boosters to my adults once a year, I visit the vet very seldom indeed. The Labrador's heavy double coat, although it is short, is dense and thick, and this seems to prevent such common injuries as minor accidents and tears. Moreover, their thick-set build stands up to bumps, knocks and abrasions that would cripple, or at least injure, a lighter-built, finer-coated, less hardy dog.

Such hardiness most likely stems from the breed's origins in Newfoundland. Labradors were expected to retrieve fish that fell out of the nets and flapped on the surface of the icy seas. They also had to carry the rope end from boat to shore in the strongest of tides and the stormiest of weather. This made them hardy, strong and healthy animals out of necessity, and I suggest this is certainly a contributory factor in the Labrador's popularity in so many spheres today.

Labradors grow into fairly large dogs, weighing between 60 and 80lbs or more, and they require quite an amount of food. However, they are what I call very good doers. That is, they seem to thrive on simple, plain, wholesome food, and do not need pampering or tempting with tidbits. When rearing puppies and young adults, you must feed them the very best of everything, if you want them to grow up into strongly-built, well-boned, healthy and handsome adults. I give much credence to the saying that "you only get out of them what you put in" when it comes to rearing youngsters. However, the main problem is keeping adult Labradors slim and fit, because they are inherently greedy and will eat all that is set before them, if given half a chance. They have voracious appetites. I have known a sensible, gentle Labrador eat his breakfast, then find a bucket of fat left in the garage after the lean meat was cut up to be frozen, and polish off the lot, until his stomach was like a balloon. Apart from a little flatulence afterwards, this fellow was perfectly all right, although he had to have very light meals for a few days.

Some smaller dogs of other breeds eat quite as much as a fully-grown Labrador, whose equivalents in size often need to eat a good deal more food. Therefore Labradors can be said to be economical feeders, compared with other dogs of their size – provided their feeder is sensible, keeps a strict eye on their waistlines, and stays impervious to blackmailing glances and hints at mealtimes.

Contrary to popular belief, I contend that Labradors as a breed do not require an enormous amount of exercise. People seem to think that they need ten, or at least four, miles a day. This is actually untrue and, as a general rule, people tend to over-exercise puppies and youngsters, and under-exercise adults. I think this is because, as puppies and youngsters, Labradors are still a novelty to the family, who cannot wait to take their puppy for a walk. Clearly, your Labrador needs to be let out as frequently as any other breed in order to stretch the legs, limber up, play and perform a regular toilet. Apart from this, however, a short, brisk morning walk and a good walk in the evening, or vice versa, will keep your dog fit and well, and with some free galloping and a small amount of walking on hard roads during these walks, the dog will be fit enough to do a full day's shooting without distress, whenever it is required, as long, of course, as the diet is correct too.

My own routine is to give my dogs an hour's free exercise over the fields in the morning, when they gallop and release their energy. In the evening, they get an hour's exercise which involves both free running and road walking. If I am away from home for a short period of time, however, the dogs are left in my father's care. They get less exercise, but they are still perfectly happy and contented. Indeed, they adjust to such changes remarkably well. In fact, that is another characteristic virtue of the breed – they are extremely adaptable and versatile.

SUMMING UP THE LABRADOR

The word that sums up my own experience of the breed is 'versatile'. This best describes the various qualities of the Labrador. If you put the correct amount of forethought into the choice of the breeder from whom you acquire your puppy, and you carry out sensible rearing and training, the dog will return your attention with a great deal of love, affection and companionship. Your Labrador will enrich your life, and that is no exaggeration. I have owned Labradors since the age of twelve, and can vouch for the fact that your life, like mine, will be made fuller and more interesting by owning one or more. Furthermore, a caring companion like a Labrador will also do much to enrich the lives of your children, who will learn a great deal about how to treat animals and care for them. Considering the multitudinous and varied virtues and qualities of the Labrador, it is hardly surprising that the breed is now the number one companion dog in both Britain and North America. This status, of course, brings with it the potential problems that over-breeding creates. However, it is as a result of the Labrador's enduring popularity with the public that this status has been achieved.

2 ORIGINS AND HISTORY

The Labrador has been in Britain for at least 170 years and, for much of that time, debate and speculation have existed as to the breed's origins. As time passes, new information on the breed seems unlikely to come to light. However, it is also a fact that some breed histories are poorly organised, and a few are more confusing than helpful. The aim of this chapter is to tease out and develop the main themes, and present the historical evidence logically and consistently.

THE NEWFOUNDLAND CONNECTION

Lord George Scott, writing in *Scott and Middleton: The Labrador Dog* (1936), opens the book with a simple but brilliant sentence: "The direct descendants of the black water dogs imported from Newfoundland are called Labradors." Much of this chapter revolves around an explanation and amplification of this sentence.

There is abundant contemporary evidence to confirm the breed's roots in Newfoundland. Colonel Hawker in *Instructions to Young Sportsmen* (1814) recalls the dogs of the island, and distinguishes between the big Newfoundland dog and the St John's breed, a smaller dog: "...by far the best for every kind of shooting, is oftener black than any other colour, and scarcely bigger than a pointer. He is made rather long in the head and nose; pretty deep in the chest; very fine in the legs, has short or smooth hair, and does not carry his tail so much curled as the other...The St John's breed of these dogs is chiefly used on their native coast by fishermen."

Sprake in *The Labrador Retriever* (1933) tells

of a W.E. Cormack who made a journey across Newfoundland in 1822 and noted a well-established breed: "dogs...admirably trained as retrievers in fowling, and otherwise useful...The smooth or short haired dog is preferred because in frosty weather the long haired kind become encumbered with ice on coming out of the water."

Blaine in the *Encyclopaedia of Rural Sports* (1840) points out those very features that have attracted many of us to the breed, good sense and great tractability: "The St John's breed is preferred by the sportsman on every account, being smaller, more easily managed, and sagacious in the extreme. His scenting powers are great. Some years ago these dogs could be readily procured at Poole, ... Indeed, gentlemen...have found them so intelligent, so faithful, and so capable of general instruction, that they have given up most sporting varieties and content themselves with these."

Youatt in *The Dog* (1845) devotes a substantial section to the dogs of the island: "Some of the true Newfoundland dogs have been brought to Europe and have been used as retrievers. They are principally valuable for the fearless manner in which they will penetrate the thickest cover. They are comparatively small, but muscular, strong and generally black. A larger variety has been bred, and is now perfectly established. He is seldom used as a sporting dog, ... but is admired on account of his stature and beauty."

It is beyond doubt that there were black water dogs, proficient at retrieving, in Newfoundland at the beginning of the 19th century. Clearly, two sorts existed: the massive, heavy-coated dog

Am. Can. Ch.
Waggin' Tails
Incredi-Bull, JH
(Am. Can. Ch. Valli-
Vue Chelons Mr.
Levi JH– Ch.
Highland Break of
Dawn) bred by
Sharon Grieves,
Waggin' Tails
Labradors, and
Lillian Knoblock,
Highland Labrador
Retrievers.
Contemporary evi-
dence that the
Labrador Retriever
has its roots in
Newfoundland.

Photo courtesy of
Sharon Grieves.

we now know as the Newfoundland, and a smaller, less substantial variety, from whom our Labradors are descended. The two types would probably have been interbred. It is very unlikely that the hard-worked inhabitants of Newfoundland would have cared much about the niceties of breed type. Nevertheless, many authors are at pains to make a distinction between the larger and the smaller variety, and this distinction is possibly more important than may at first be realised. In the period 1865 to 1870, that important chronicle of country affairs, *The Field* magazine, contained considerable correspondence about the dogs of Newfoundland. In 1869, a letter writer signing himself 'Index' noted: "that around St John's were immense numbers of close, smooth coated black dogs from 18 inches to 24 inches high, called Labradors, often admirable retrievers, which are not true Newfoundlands except by birth on the island."

In a letter to *The Field*, dated March 1870, a W.C. of Halifax, Nova Scotia, wrote: "The Labrador dog – in my opinion a distinct breed – is an animal I know and I have always been most firmly impressed with the idea that they were only to be met with on that part of the coast of Labrador which to us is known as the south shore of the mainland in the Straits of Belle Isle. Certainly it is that I never saw them in perfection but there."

Walsh, once editor of *The Field*, in his famous book *Stonehenge on the Dog* (1879), has a section devoted to the St John's or Labrador. However, his account is slightly confusing and, in part, he is talking of crosses between the St John's and Setters which provided wavy-coated, and later Flatcoated retrievers. Walsh illustrates the breed with a drawing by Earl and, yet, assuming Earl's rendering of the breed is a good likeness, this is not the dog that we recognise as a Labrador, being closer to a Flatcoated.

Earl's illustration is quite different from Buccleuch Cabot, the black dog imported into England from Newfoundland in the 1930s. The illustration is also very different from photographs of the black water dogs found living in a remote Newfoundland fishing village by Wolters in *The Labrador Retriever* (1981).

The next question is how did these black water dogs get to the island? It is possible that the original inhabitants of Newfoundland had such dogs before Europeans arrived. Cooper in *The Newfoundland* (1977) notes that the Indians of North America had dogs, but that they were Spitz in type with small ears, curled tails and wedge-shaped heads, pointed in the muzzle. Cooper quotes archaeological evidence to support this claim. It is most likely that the ancestors of the black water dogs came from Europe. Early seafarers took dogs with them on their voyages. Maintaining a supply of fresh food was a problem, so hunting dogs were useful in obtaining fresh meat on some distant shore. Once established in a colony, settlers would import cattle and sheep, and with them herding dogs. The indigenous populations of these distant lands were regularly hostile to the newcomers, so the European sailors and settlers needed guard dogs. The small sailing vessels used by these fishermen and traders would have had much in the way of nets and tackle on their decks, precious items likely to get washed overboard, in this case into a very cold and dangerous North Atlantic Ocean. No man would risk going into the sea without the certainty of getting back on board, and so a brave, good-coated, strong-swimming water dog was invaluable.

English history books generally credit John Cabot, sailing from Bristol, with the discovery of Newfoundland in 1497, but there is a mass of evidence to show that other European nations were in the area at around the same time. It is known that the Vikings, already in Greenland, had briefly settled Newfoundland as far back as AD 1000. The Vikings probably had dogs with them, which may have survived down the centuries, possibly with the Indians, but such a theory seems unlikely.

The great seafaring nations of the western European seaboard were all involved in fishing and trading with each other, and with the New World, by the early 16th century. Cooper points to the triangular trade between the south coast of Britain, Portugal and Newfoundland, particularly in fish and timber, and a trade in wine between Britain and Portugal. He speculates on the sorts of dogs these seafarers might have taken with them. The English had their guard dogs, mastiff types that had been in the country at least since Roman times, and their sheepdogs and spaniels, many of whom were black. From continental Europe, the Bretons, the Basques, the Spanish and the Portuguese would have taken their massive guard dogs, the chien-dogue of France, the Pyrenean dogs, who were both guards and herders. Traders would also have taken their Barbets, wonderful water dogs, and the black hounds of St Hubert, a breed well known in that great English seafaring county of Devon, and the Portuguese had excellent water and cattle dogs.

Thus, much as the New World was to become a melting pot of people emigrating from Europe, it is possible to think of Newfoundland as a melting pot of the canine races. We can therefore imagine the Newfoundland dogs developing, through the demands of the new land, into the dogs described by Hawker, Cormack and others.

STRENGTH OF TYPE

Clearly, the Labrador dog was manufactured, a practice that continues to the present time. The very selection process that results from the breeding of dogs in domestic conditions involves a shaping by man of both the physical and mental attributes of the dog. It is in this sense that dogs are manufactured. However, with the Labrador, unlike many other breeds, there does seem to be a strength of type that some authors have seen as evidence of ancient lineage, something that probably has little scientific basis. Nevertheless, it is a fact that if a Labrador is mated to almost any other sort of dog most of the resulting progeny look like Labradors. If one of the most Labrador-like crosses is then mated back to a pure bred Labrador, it is almost certain that the whole litter will be decent Labradors, though someone very experienced in looking at Labradors might not be fooled. It is possible that the Labrador is more than a mere medley, or some canine potpourri, of half a dozen European breeds.

IBERIAN LINKS

Mary Roslin-Williams in her influential book

The Dual-Purpose Labrador (1969), includes a photograph of a Cane di Castro Laboreiro, a breed found in Northern Portugal. She wonders whether this clearly Labrador-like dog was the solid foundation upon which the breed developed in Newfoundland. The Portuguese were a major seafaring nation. There is no reason to doubt that they took dogs to the New World. The name Laboreiro may be a coincidence, but it is a very interesting coincidence. The same picture had been used many years before in *The Working Dogs of the World* (1947) by Hubbard, who described the dog as a Portuguese Cattle Dog, of which the Cane de Castro Laboreiro was one variety.

Hubbard goes so far as to provide a detailed description of the dogs: "The head is broad ... a well defined stop ... the eyes are medium in size set rather obliquely and almond shape, dark in colour; the ears are set rather wide apart, wide at the base, triangular and carried pendant though not Hound fashion; the muzzle is of fair depth with strong level teeth. The body is typical length (rectangular rather than square) and is well muscled yet lithe, with deep chest and well coupled loins; the legs moderately boned, straight and sinewy, with round compact feet, the tail is of natural length, set low and carried low in repose or horizontal when in action. The coat is short and harsh generally, though smooth

The Portuguese Cattle Dog, featured in Hubbard's book 'The Working Dogs of the World', bears a distinct resemblance to the modern Labrador.
Photo courtesy: Richard Edwards.

on the muzzle, ears and fronts of the legs. Colours are all greys and all brindles. The height is 24 inches for dogs and 22 inches for bitches ... Weights are relatively heavy (especially for the male dogs) as 77 pounds is the ideal average for dogs, and 55 pounds that for bitches."

The evidence of the photograph is compelling. The dog is very like a modern Labrador, not as heavy, nor as finished, nor as refined as a modern show Labrador, but that is another story. Hubbard's description of the dog could be part of a Labrador Standard. There is a strong case for the Caone de Castro Laboreiro to be regarded as at least the foundation of the Labrador, maybe a foundation built upon by the addition of mastiff blood for substance, plus perhaps the black St Hubert's hound for colour, and possibly a dash of water dog for the retrieving instinct.

Mary Roslin-Williams later wrote *All About The Labrador* (1975), and returned to the idea with the comment: "I am told by someone who travels regularly through the northern border between Portugal, Spain and France that the local dogs working the cattle still look like poor specimens of Labradors, and that at first he believed them to be bad Labradors, until he found them to be the working dog of the district and of ancient descent."

More recently, Mr and Mrs G.A.O. Jenkin of Beadles Labradors were holidaying in the Algarve, southern Portugal, when they spotted an old black Labrador asleep in the sun outside a grocer's shop. They assumed it had been left by an expatriate British family and asked the grocer about the dog. He confirmed it was his dog, but insisted it was a native Portuguese breed and they would find plenty of them about. Intrigued by this, the couple spent the rest of their holiday on the look-out and saw plenty of the dogs, black, yellow and brindle. Although they noted some variations, many looked very like Labradors.

Throughout the available literature there have been allusions to an Iberian connection for the Labrador. Eley in *The History of Retrievers* (1920) was full of praise for the Labrador, insisting: "that I have today no dog of any other breed in my kennel, that I have no intention of changing allegiance. Labrador is a Spanish word meaning a workman. Evviva Labradores."

Vesey-Fitzgerald in *The Domestic Dog* (1957) reviews the dog in art, and asks the reader to consider the work of Velazquez (1599-1660) suggesting that he was a realist who could only paint from a model. Velazquez painted the Infante Don Fernando as a sportsman. Alongside the Prince is his dog: "...who has powerful jaws and a marked stop and the suggestion of width between the ears and the kindly eye giving the impression of great intelligence...I am convinced that we have the first portrait of the breed we know today as the Labrador. We are too apt to think of Labrador as a cold and inhospitable coastal province of Canada. It is as well to remember that in Spanish it simply means a workman."

Lord George Scott in *Scott and Middleton: The Labrador Dog* is clearly aware of the Iberian connection, yet he makes only a short point of this, before moving on: "The Portuguese word Lavrador means Labourer."

We may be fairly sure that the dogs of the Iberian peninsula played a major role in the development of today's Labrador.

SELECTION AND DEVELOPMENT
It is, however, certain that the black water dogs came from Newfoundland. Their ancestry is less clear, but it is possible to be more confident of one episode in their early history – an account of how one family came by the breed and found the dogs ideal for their purposes. In an article in *The Field* (February 1990), the Earl of Malmesbury wrote of his great-great-grandfather, the second Earl of Malmesbury, buying the dogs, then called little Newfoundlanders, in either 1823 or 1824. The Malmesbury estate at Hurn in Dorset was very low-lying, prone to

'We may be fairly sure that the dogs of the Iberian peninsula played a major role in the development of today's Labrador'

Brookland Mischievous Sea-Lion CDX, MH, CGC (Brookland Marshland Mikie – Brookland Corn Dancer) was bred by Nancy H. Love, Virginia, and is owned and trained by Wendy Pennington, California. The Labrador's development as a breed was based on its outstanding working ability.

Photo: Rich Bergman, courtesy of Wendy Pennington.

extensive flooding, and was the home and breeding ground for many wildfowl.

On a trip to nearby Poole, the second Earl saw dogs from the Newfoundland fishing fleet playing in the sea, retrieving so keenly and so naturally that it crossed his mind they might be ideal as retrievers of the wildfowl that comprised the shooting on his estate. The set of circumstances here is crucial. In an article for *The Field* (December 1989), Wilson Stephens argues that most of the great estates would have had little use for these excellent retrieving dogs anyway. At this time, before the development of the breech-loading shotgun, shooting was a much less hurried affair since guns had to be muzzle-loaded. Pointers or Setters or other questing dogs would be more use pushing out one or two birds at a time, which could be shot and then picked at leisure. Most of the time there was no need for a speedy, efficient game-gathering dog.

However, on the Malmesbury estate, the game was wildfowl which might fall, possibly wounded, into deep water. In these circumstances, a good, fast, fearless and strong swimmer as a retriever was an asset. The Labrador breed became firmly established with the Malmesbury family at Heron Court. Other wildfowlers, close to Poole, also acquired the dogs. Colonel Radclyffe was one whose family maintained the breed, and later helped in developing yellow Labradors.

Elsewhere in Britain, other landed families took up the breed, buying the dogs from northern ports, such as Greenock, which traded with Newfoundland. Lord George Scott writing in *Sprake: The Labrador Retriever* argues that the Dukes of Buccleuch and the Earl of Home had Labradors, but that by the latter part of the 19th century the breed had died out, except at a few estates on the south coast of England. Scott goes

on to pinpoint the resurgence of the breed: "Lord Dalkeith, afterwards the 6th Duke of Buccleuch, and the 12th Earl of Home both spent several winters at Bournemouth in the early 1880s, and when shooting at Heron Court (where wild duck shooting was first class), were amazed at the work of Lord Malmesbury's dogs, especially in water. Lord Malmesbury gave some of his breed to both."

From these gifts, the Labrador breed spread out slowly to the great houses of Britain, especially the Buccleuch estates and the Hirsel estate of Lord Home. Apparently, a keeper took dogs with him when he moved from the Hirsel to work for Sir Frederick Graham, who later let his son-in-law, the Earl of Verulam, have some specimens of the breed to set up a kennel. From these lines, the Munden kennel of the Hon. A. Holland Hibbert started.

What was especially significant was that, although the breed was spreading simply on its own merit, it was good at its work, and was singularly lucky to have as patrons rich and landed men who did not breed the dogs for money. These men were used to having quality things around them; grand houses, lovely horses and good dogs. These circumstances allowed the breed to develop quietly and privately. It would appear that one motive for Lord George Scott to write his contribution to *The Labrador Dog* was the desire to show how his family, and a few others, had maintained the Labrador as pure bred, and he researched pedigrees to prove it.

In the book's preface he is very direct in his assertion: "It will be noted that every authentic strain in the pedigrees can be traced back to the dogs described in this book as the foundations of the Labrador retriever in this country; and there is no evidence of any other early source to which the true Labrador can be traced."

Essentially all the lines went back to the dogs given as gifts by the third Earl of Malmesbury to Lord Dalkeith and Lord Home. In particular, the dog Avon 1885, bred by Lord Malmesbury, became regarded as the ancestor of the modern breed. While most pure bred Labradors can be traced back to the dogs owned by landed families in the 1880s, and while the Buccleuchs and others have kept their strains pure, it is also true that other breeds have been introduced into the Labrador breed from time to time.

NEW STATUS

While the Labrador had been steadily spreading out across Britain, the shooting scene had changed. In his article in *The Field,* Stephens notes that the style of shooting had changed dramatically with the development of the breech-loading shotgun in the 1860s. It was then possible for a shooter, with a loader, to maintain almost constant fire it such were required. On many estates, driven game became the norm. Beaters would drive game, now reared in large numbers for this very purpose, towards the guns. Many birds could be shot, though not necessarily killed outright, within a short time. This meant that a good and reliable, yet fast and keen, retriever was needed, a specialist dog who was exceptional at the work. Of course, such a dog was available in the Labrador, but it was not the Labrador who came to the fore but the Flatcoated Retriever. This was a very different sort of dog, probably a mixture of Sheepdog, Setter with (maybe) some Labrador blood. The Flatcoateds were to reign supreme throughout the whole of the last quarter of the 19th century, and they developed into efficient and handsome retrievers. The breed attracted a number of rich patrons who were prepared to pay large sums of money for good specimens. As well as a worker, the Flatcoated variety became one of the most popular show dogs in the final years of the last century. The Labrador had gone missing, and was almost forgotten – though forgotten is probably the wrong word, since few people knew about the breed in the first place.

Three developments changed the status of the Labrador for ever. One was the stuttering, but eventually inescapable, growth of field trials, another was the increasing popularity of dog

FACING PAGE: The Labrador soon gained a reputation as a strong, fast and fearless swimmer.
Photo: Graham Cox.

Yago aus Luhlsbusch. It was not long before the Labrador was recognised as the best overall retrieving breed, well-suited to working in all conditions.   *Photo: Ruth Stegemann.*

shows, and thirdly, perhaps most significantly, in part due to the concerted efforts of The Hon. A. Holland-Hibbert, the Kennel Club agreed in 1903 to recognise the Labrador as a breed.

Lord Chesterfield, Mr Portal and Mrs Quintin Dick compiled the *Stud Book and Record of Field Trial for Retrievers 1899-1922*, published by the Labrador Retriever Club. The compilers record: "It was in 1875 that the Kennel Club held its first Field Trial for Pointers and Setters but the credit of holding the first Retriever Trials belongs to the Society of the International Gun-dog League, and to that Society the gratitude of all who have the interests of the Retrievers at heart is due. The first Trial for Retrievers took place in 1899, when a mixed stake for Retrievers and Spaniels was held, and was won by Painter, a Flat Coated Retriever...

"The year 1906 will always be an important one in the history of Trials as it was in that year that the Honourable A. Holland-Hibbert ran Munden Single, the first Labrador to compete at Trials (or Bench). Up to this time the Flat Coat had held undoubted sway over the Curly, but from 1906 onwards the Labrador has gradually established the extraordinary record for work which the breed now holds."

Actually, the Stud Book records Munden Single as taking a Certificate of Merit at the International Gun-dog League's trial at Sherbourne in 1904. Slowly, but indubitably, the Labrador started to dominate field trials, so much so that in the years closely preceding the First World War, Labradors took most of the places at trials. Two dogs, Major Portal's Flapper and Captain Butter's Peter of Faskally won well and were very influential in producing trial winners. The pattern had been set. Demonstrably, the Labrador was better at field trials than other retrievers, though occasionally an exceptional Flatcoated and later an exceptional Golden Retriever would beat them. It did not take long for ordinary shooting men to adopt the Labrador as their first choice of retriever. The Flatcoated went into a decline, though in recent years the breed has seen a revival, particularly in the show ring. Later, the Golden Retriever came along and has maintained a faithful following but, as far as the shooting field is concerned, the Labrador has no close rival.

SHOWS AND COMPETITIONS

It might come as something of a shock to those who dislike dog shows, but Kennel Club recognition, which allowed the breed to be shown, was the single most important factor in stabilising type. Dog shows brought Labradors together in numbers, and direct comparison between exhibits became easy. Perhaps more than anything else, certain males started to build reputations based on their show wins and became important stud dogs. A few dogs set the type – actually the winners set the type – and so it has continued. This in itself brought certain matters to a head. Although the KC had done the world of dogs a great service by regulating activities, there was still much that the modern enthusiast might find unacceptable. There existed the practice of registering cross bred dogs as the breed they most resembled. This had been common in the Spaniel breeds, and, to a lesser extent, was happening with the retrievers. In 1916, Horton Max won two Challenge Certificates as a Labrador, including the CC at Crufts. Max had much Flatcoated blood close up in his pedigree and, while everyone involved accepted that Max was a handsome dog, he was not a pure bred

Am. Can. Ch. Wyntercreek Royal Velvet Am. Can. CDX, JH, CGC (Ch. Somersett Silent Knight CD, WC – Wyntercreek Sassy Sheena WC) ,bred by Mary Jane Sarbaugh, Wyntercreek Labradors, and Merlyn Foote, Somersett Labradors, Washington. The Kennel Club's recognition of the Labrador had a significant influence on stabilising type.

The Labradors at Winelight Farm, Oregon. The Labrador is now one of the most

Labrador. Directly because of Max's wins, senior Labrador breeders met, and decided to form a club to protect and promote the breed. Again, it was a group of influential people, people able to get things done, who formed the club.

THE LABRADOR RETRIEVER CLUB
The Labrador Retriever Club was founded in 1916 with the Hon. A. Holland Hibbert (later Lord Knutsford) as chairman, a post he held until his death in 1935, and Mrs Quintin Dick (later Lorna, Countess Howe) as secretary and treasurer, posts she held for the next 45 years. The club served as a focus for the breed, especially by organising field trials and representing the interests of the breed at the Kennel Club. The committee of the Labrador Retriever Club set about drawing up a Breed Standard for the Labrador that the KC later adopted. This Breed

Standard has been amended on a number of occasions down the years, though some people to this day prefer the original version.

The club was careful to foster the goodwill of the gamekeepers upon whom the future of the breed depended. Keepers were not required to pay membership fees at first, and were later asked to pay at concessionary rates. The club did not organise a championship show of its own until 1938, but did provide special prizes at other shows.

From the start, specials were given to dual-purpose dogs and dogs shown by gamekeepers. Over the years many other clubs have been formed to promote the Labrador, mainly by region, but there is no doubt that winning a trial organised by the Labrador Retriever Club or a CC at its championship show, is still an exclusive privilege.

popular breeds in the world.   *Photo courtesy: Pamela J. Hansen.*

COUNTESS HOWE

Some commentators have implied that it was Countess Howe who discovered the Labrador, but this was not so. The breed was firmly established, albeit on a small scale, before she became involved. However, she quite quickly became the dominant figure within the Labrador world, and anything of significance concerning the breed came to her attention. Countess Howe was co-opted on to the Field Trial Committee of the Kennel Club – remarkable, since the KC was a male preserve, and for many years Countess Howe was the only woman on any KC committee. There is no question that Countess Howe was very influential. In addition to her administrative duties, Countess Howe assembled a wonderful kennel of Labradors, which included a whole range of Champions, Field Trial Champions and dual Champions. Of the ten dual Champions to date, Countess Howe

owned four; Banchory Bolo, Banchory Painter, Banchory Sunspeck and Bramshaw Bob. Her workers won at the highest level, her famous FT Ch. Balmuto Jock winning the Retriever Championship three times. Dual Champion Bramshaw Bob went Best in Show at Crufts two years running. The Banchory kennel was at its very peak during the fifteen years before the Second World War. It did not quite recapture its pre-eminence post-War, but it did house one very famous show dog in Ch. British Justice.

Mr C. Mackay Sanderson in *The Labrador Retriever Stud Book 1949,* writes of Countess Howe: "Indisputably, the most helpful friend of the breed in the last quarter of a century, her vigorous personal propaganda on its behalf, persistent and successful exhibition and generous support of the field trials, contributed in substantial degree to the rapid ascent of the Labrador to fame and widespread popularity.

Lady Howe's bold purchasing also helped the breed enormously, and by this is meant buying for exhibition, work or propagation; and, to her, more than any other individual, is due the credit for the commanding position the Labrador occupies in the Gundog world today."

COLOUR CHANGES

The other important development in this period was the acceptance, slowly and grudgingly at first, of the yellow colour within the breed. Various colours had cropped up in litters from the very start, but most breeders thought of Labradors as black dogs, excepting the odd spot of white in the right places. Other colours would have been disposed of at birth. The Radclyffe family registered the yellow Ben of Hyde as a Labrador and, from this dog, the colour started to spread throughout the breed. Early in the development of the colour, Mrs Veronica Wormald became interested in yellows and, probably as a reaction to the early resistance she encountered, she became determined to foster and promote them. With others, but essentially through her own efforts, Mrs Wormald formed the Yellow Labrador Club in 1924, with the avowed aim of providing a sheltered haven for the colour to progress by running trials and shows limited to yellows. The colour received impetus from the highly influential yellow stud dog Golden Morn, who is to be found throughout yellow pedigrees, and from the fact that the most successful show dog of the period, the handsome Ch. Banchory Danilo, although black, carried the yellow colour. Most of the yellows of the period were descended from a combination of Golden Morn to Danilo daughters or vice versa.

The chocolate colour has gone through a similar process of doubt and resistance, and it too received a major boost when one of the most famous show dogs of the 1970s, Ch. Follytower Merrybrook Black Stormer, proved to carry the colour. From him, chocolates have progressed steadily. Note that, as far as the shooting field is concerned, the Labrador is usually a black dog. A few people prefer the yellows and they are accepted well enough, but chocolates are a very minor force.

GROWING INTEREST

By the early 1920s, the pattern on the competitive side of the Labrador world had been set. In 1920 there were 19 field trials at which Labradors could be entered, and there were 12 sets of Challenge Certificates awarded. Through the 1920s and 30s, the scene expanded slowly under the watchful eye of Countess Howe, until in 1937 there were 20 sets of CCs on offer and the trials had expanded to some 45 stakes. This

In the early days of the breed, Labradors were always thought of as black dogs. Gradually the yellow colour was accepted.

Photo: Amanda Bulbeck.

Out Of The Mist To Stoneavon, owned by Mr E. Par. The chocolate Labrador is becoming more popular, although it is rarely seen among working gundogs.

Photo: Carol Ann Johnson.

state of affairs continued in much the same way after the Second World War until the late 1950s.

Obviously, it took Europe a decade or so to recover from the War, but by 1960 Great Britain was more prosperous, and people started to use their spare cash on a whole range of pursuits and hobbies. The ownership of pedigree dogs was one such activity. The British public discovered the Labrador, not as a working dog but as a pet. All those years of careful selection to produce good gundogs had been brilliantly successful, and now the public suddenly realised that the Labrador was a calm, even-tempered dog, easily-trained, and very adaptable, whom they could trust even with a teasing child.

The numbers of Labradors escalated rapidly. In the mid-1960s entries at shows started to increase dramatically. The Labrador slowly took over from other breeds as the most popular family dog. This rapid increase in the Labrador's popularity was not welcomed by everyone. Many enthusiasts had been quite happy for the breed to be a barely open secret, known to people interested in country pursuits, but not mass-produced or popular in any way. Actually, even within the world of the working Labrador, there had been an increase in interest, and activities such as water tests and working tests had been slowly developed to satisfy the needs of Labrador owners who did not have access to shooting proper. In recent years this interest in the breed as a working dog by people who have little direct contact with the country, save through their dogs, has continued to expand significantly.

THE BREED SPREADS
Canadians, more specifically Newfoundlanders, will doubtless claim the Labrador as their own, but there can be no disputing that the breed was

developed to its present high state in Britain. Labradors from this country were sent out around the world, as ever more people came to recognise the merit of the breed.

Some of the earliest exports occurred when foreign guests at big shooting estates in England and Scotland saw the quality of the work done by Labradors, and bought some of the breed to take home with them. A number went to India. In the 1920s, several rich and powerful American families not only bought Labradors, but set up shooting of the kind to be found in Britain on their own estates, especially in the eastern states of the USA. To run these shoots in the proper manner they hired young gamekeepers, especially from Scotland, and with them came more Labradors. Warwick in *The Complete Labrador Retriever* (1964) is specific: "The greatest credit in acquainting the Americans with Retriever training is due to the Scottish trainers that came over in that period."

Rich patrons such as the Hon. F.P. Lord (Blake), the Hon. W.A. Harriman (Arden), Mr J.F. Carlisle (Wingan) and Dr S. Millbank (Earlsmore) imported top-quality British stock from Countess Howe (Banchory) and from Mr H. Saunders (Liddly), and dogs from the Whitmore bloodlines and later from the Hon. Mrs Hill-Wood (Hiwood) and Mrs Gwen Broadley (Sandylands). In the immediate post-War years, Mr and Mrs J. Warwick (Lockerbie) continued to import top-class Labradors from Britain. It is interesting to note that the breed developed in the USA in the same private manner that it had done in Britain.

Before the Second World War only the Americans were to show a real and sustained interest in the breed. After the War, especially in the 1960s, the breed conquered all the English-speaking nations; Canada, South and East Africa and Australasia. More recently, Labradors have become a firm favourite in Europe, at first in Scandinavia and later in the rest of mainland Europe. From the most private beginnings on the south coast of England, the Labrador has spread across the world and is at home with all strata of society, from royalty and heads of state to the most humble citizen.

'The Labrador has spread across the world and is at home with all strata of society, from royalty to the most humble'

3 THE LABRADOR PUPPY

You and your family may have been attracted to certain breeds of dogs and have finally decided upon a Labrador Retriever, probably because the breed has a naturally friendly disposition towards everyone. Labradors possess an inherent desire to please, great gentleness and an ability to interact with all members of the family and treat them as equals. As your Labrador grows into maturity, you will find that you have a dog who is game for everything and a very welcome addition to the family.

Of course, the addition of a dog means greater responsibilities. Any dog needs a regular daily programme which includes home comforts, good food, exercise and discipline. Due deliberation given to the question of how best to go about purchasing your puppy will be time well spent. Your Labrador's initial cost will be a tiny fraction of the overall expense of upkeep during the next 12 to 15 years of the dog's life, even though you will receive such a lot in return. You need to consider a number of essential points.

YOUR ACCOMMODATION AND LIFESTYLE

Think carefully about the day-to-day life you and your prospective dog are going to lead. Labradors are generally visualised as a country lover's companion and are associated with tweeds, wellingtons and country walks. If you do not live in the country, your town or city house must be situated within easy walking distance of local parks. A small town-house will hardly be any more suitable for a lively, active Labrador than a flat or apartment without a garden. Your home will, of course, need to be adequately fenced around the garden, with fencing at least five feet in height. All gates leading to the road must be equally high. You will probably have already given some thought to such precautions, as you do when it comes to safety and outdoor facilities for the rest of the family. Just as children need space, so does a good-sized dog. The organisation and timetable of a busy family will have to include the needs of the puppy, who will later become an adult dog. You cannot expect to be able to give your puppy breakfast, then rush off to work or school, without providing adequate supervision and attention for your new canine family member.

I am personally averse to a dog being left alone for more than four hours a day, and only if the dog has enjoyed a good early morning walk and been given the correct amount of its current diet. Your Labrador can then be left looking forward to another bout of exercise in the next few hours. After all, you would not leave a child alone all day. It also goes without saying that whoever is in charge of the dog should be fit and well, in order to cope with regular walks every day, come rain or shine.

It is no good expecting children to dedicate hours of their daily routine to the puppy, once the initial novelty has worn off. They, too, are young and developing, and will naturally take on many other commitments, meaning a change of priorities at a moment's notice. You may already have other animals in the house, which means that your dog will become yet another dependant to care for. Cats, of course, generally look after themselves.

Tiger Tiger of Carpenny, owned by Mrs P. Carpanini. Labradors possess a desire to please, a great gentleness and an ability to interact with all members of the family.

Photo: Carol Ann Johnson.

Making up your mind which puppy to choose is an almost impossible task. Be guided by the breeder who will know more about the person-ality of each individual.

Photo: Amanda Bulbeck.

A ROLE FOR YOUR DOG

Whatever role you consider that your Labrador must take, it has to be for the dog's lifetime, not just a passing fancy. If you want a companion, think in terms of the dog as a complete and important member of the household. If you have visions of a Labrador as a breeding proposition, you will have to consider many important issues in depth, and will probably come to the conclusion that such ambitions are unrealistic for most people. If you want a working dog, who can be trained for a day's shooting, you need to be in possession of a shotgun licence, plus ready-made facilities to train a dog, in the country, with adequate land and game available for that purpose. Perhaps you envisage becoming a member of a shooting syndicate, in which case it is preferable to buy a suitable puppy from a proven work-orientated Labrador breeder.

By the same token, a potential show dog is best acquired from a well-known and reputable show kennel. Only dedicated breeders can give you advice on the correct choice of Labradors with either show or work potential.

Obedience training will give you an insight into the world of really good obedience dogs in that particular sphere of competiton. The overall message is: Do your homework on Labradors, and be realistic about what you want from the dog and what you can offer in return. Bearing in mind all the potential activities outlined above, be prepared to pay a fair price for what you desire. Remember, too, that whichever sort of dog you take on must subsequently be able to enjoy the lifestyle of your choice and become the willing and fun-loving family companion that you originally planned. That is only fair to the dog.

HOLIDAYS

Most families take annual holidays, and unless you can take your Labrador with you, provision must be made for the care of your dog during your absence. The obvious solution is boarding kennels, which, these days, can be quite expensive. The good ones are popular, so you may need to visit and book up months in advance. It would be wise to make sure that the various kennels you view will be exercising your dog daily, and you need to feel quite confident that your dog will settle happily. I would not recommend leaving a puppy under six months of age, but for an older dog the experience of a well-run establishment can actually be advantageous.

THE WORKING DOG

Many people think of a Labrador as a working companion, and I too consider that almost any member of the breed can be trained for rough shooting. Often owners decide that a family dog is all they want, but, in time and after consideration, they become interested in rough shooting. Be aware that motivating a pet dog into a dog for shooting does not happen instantly! To train a dog for work means many hours of training from puppyhood. It usually involves a gundog training society, and can be a very pleasurable activity, with weekly meetings during the summer, a group of fellow members sharing the same interest, and going through various forms of obedience and retrieving training out in the country. It is a very satisfying experience to participate with your Labrador, in a line of twelve or more in a large open field, the dogs sitting and staying off the lead, then being called up to their owners in turn.

It is also very rewarding when your joint efforts result in your Labrador jumping fences, swimming rivers and returning to you with the dummy, bird or rabbit which you sent your dog to retrieve. Take the opportunity of watching gundog demonstrations at local county shows, and you cannot fail to come away with a lasting impression, and, given time, even a sense of vocation. It could be you – and may even lead to you considering a larger step forward into the field trial world. Here you can expect to undergo a much more thorough training, with lots of gundog working tests, usually performed on dead game and dummies. Your Labrador must excel in obedience, have a good nose for game and at all times be well-bonded to you as owner.

Before even beginning to think about this very high level of competititon, it is essential to read specific books, written by experienced field trial judges, and fully digest their contents. If you wish to visit a field trial, you may be allowed to 'walk up' on the side of the line of participating

ABOVE: Training for success (pictured left to right): Am. Can. Ch. Diamond's Trevor Dillon Am. Can. CD, JH, CGC; Am. Can. Bda. Ch. Diamond's Mustang Sally Am. Can. CD, JH, CGC; Am. Can. Ch. Gem Blue Bandit Am. Can. CD, JH: All three littermates achieved their multiple titles before the age of three.

Photo courtesy of Gerry Cochran, Diamond Labradors, Ohio.

LEFT: Paul Thorpe's yellow Labrador FTCh. Hamford Dee brings a cock pheasant to hand, watched by judge John Greeves; The Labrador makes a superb working gundog, but a great deal of work goes into achieving this sort of partnership.

Photo: Graham Cox.

dogs, but you must at all times place yourself under the command of the steward, carrying a flag.

If you feel that field trialling is your main consideration in acquiring a puppy, visit a kennel with a good reputation for producing field trial winning dogs – a very specialised indulgence.

THE SHOW DOG

You may have often visited a dog show, and there begun to fancy the idea of showing your own puppy. You will have noticed how well-behaved the dogs at the show seem, and you cannot be blamed for thinking how easy it all looks! I can assure you that many hours of work will have been put into a show dog long before he steps into the ring. However, most exhibitors

are willing to show you their dogs and puppies. Very understandably, they are proud of their dogs – but show dogs rarely come ready-made.

As a potential puppy owner and novice at show-going, you will notice that dogs and puppies are shown in different classes, dependent upon age and past performance. Exhibitors and officers at local canine shows are always most helpful to a newcomer, and will explain the ins and outs of what goes on. Attending ring training classes will teach you how to show your dog, using the correct nylon lead, and how to stand and gait your Labrador to bring his best assets to the attention of the judge. You will meet fellow novice exhibitors who do the rounds at a variety of local shows. This can be a most enjoyably competitive experience, provided you have managed to obtain a puppy with the

The show dog: Bryant's Mr. Manners (Clarion's Keaghan, CGC – Concho's Yellow Pages) is owned by Gerald Dzenzel DVM, AHT and shown by Autumn Davidson DVM; judge, Winnie Limbourne, Wingmaster.
It is important to decide on a role for your dog, whether it is as a show dog, a working gundog, or a much-loved companion.

Photo by Paul Boyte: courtesy of Autumn Davidson DVM, Clarion Labradors, California.

The companion dog par excellence:
The Labrador will reward you with many years of devoted companionship.

Photo:
Amanda Bulbeck.

prospect of show potential, and always assuming that you have reared the dog well and trained it properly, possibly under the guidance of the breeder.

If you decide to show your Labrador, it will certainly involve a lot of travelling – preferably in a well-equipped estate car with built-in dog cages or guards for safety. For yourself, you will need specialised clothing for rain and windy weather, plus smarter clothes for showing indoors – not to mention a sense of humour, capped with tenacity and sportsmanship.

Perhaps most importantly of all, if you really feel inclined to try showing, then go specifically to a show kennel, and explain to the breeder what you want to do. Buying a puppy without having all the risks and drawbacks pointed out could be disappointing for you if things do not turn out as well as expected.

THE COMPANION DOG

After many years of showing and working dogs, I have come to the conclusion that a good pet home is by far the best for a Labrador puppy. Be prepared to attend a three-month obedience course when the puppy is five or six months of age. In my opinion, this is essential for the ownership of a well-behaved Labrador. Do not be put off at the end of the first course if your dog is not quite the perfect model of obedience you had hoped for. In fact, young dogs often need further sessions, but by then you as an owner will, almost certainly, be thoroughly enjoying your weekly visit to training.

A well-fenced garden, mentioned earlier, and plenty of companionship are the other keys to success with a companion Labrador. Only a dog left alone and bored eventually seeks a way out of the garden looking for companionship.

Do not overlook the possibility of older puppies, who may be available for various reasons. Sometimes, prospective owners prefer to have a ready-trained youngster of about six months of age. Certainly, by this age, one can see more or less what the puppy is going to be like on maturity and, if well-reared and socialised, many problems will have been left behind. Of course, a grown-on puppy is more expensive to buy, and you would miss all the fun of watching your very young puppy grow and develop in the early weeks.

MALE OR FEMALE

An important decision you need to make is whether you want to own a dog or a bitch. Many people opt for a bitch, because they believe females are quieter and more companionable. Certainly, Labrador bitches are usually very sweet, loving and more gentle, if sometimes a little perverse in nature.

However, bitches come into season twice yearly, and have to be looked after very carefully during that particular period. You need to be vigilant in keeping a bitch away from dogs, and keeping dogs away from your home. If you decide on neutering, bear in mind that spaying a bitch is slightly more expensive than neutering a dog. Some people feel that a bitch is a better investment, particularly if she has show potential. They reason that if the bitch grows on satisfactorily and fills all the criteria, a litter could be bred off her. Remember, though, that breeding a litter is a complicated matter, and entails a great deal of work and expense on your part.

A dog will grow to be larger and more robust, but, as the years go by, he will settle down and become a very faithful companion. In fact, dogs make excellent companions for all the family. They are, of course, very lively, bouncy and active when young, but as they grow older they become less demanding and perhaps more faithful than bitches. A dog who joins a household which already includes pets will fit in well with every other creature, cats in particular. Your Labrador dog must be taught right from the start that no chasing of cats or rabbits is allowed, and thus he will learn to respect them. Certainly, dogs love the company of other animals, and are quite devastated if the time comes when they lose them.

COLOUR AND TYPE

Choice of colour when selecting your Labrador puppy is really quite personal. There is certainly no inherent difference among the members of the same litter, and indeed you may find yourself looking at a litter which contains all three colours, black, yellow and chocolate. It is what is under the skin that matters, and character is developed by the owner.

The best way to decide on colour and type of Labrador is to go to dog shows, talk to the exhibitors, look at their dogs and see what takes your fancy. Maybe you would prefer to see gundogs working, in which case gundog societies will be able to tell you where and when, as is the case with field trials.

It is far better, in your search for a really good and well-reared puppy, to be guided by the recommendations of dedicated breeders, rather than looking at advertisements in the local paper, or patronising commercial kennels where you will have no opportunity to see the parents of the pup you buy.

FINDING A BREEDER

Having settled on the Labrador as your preferred breed, you then have to find out where to look for your intended Labrador puppy. Good breeders have no need to advertise their puppies – in fact they often have long waiting lists. They also sell upon recommendation from the secretaries of breed clubs, and also those of fellow Labrador club members. Another outlet for breeders is the owner of the stud dog they have used.

VISITING A BREEDING ESTABLISHMENT

Once you have decided upon the colour, sex and type of Labrador you wish to own, you should arrange to visit the breeder of your choice. Be sure to wear clean clothes and shoes, and do not expect to be allowed to handle puppies, as infections can easily be carried unknowingly from home to home.

As a breeder myself, I prefer to meet prospective puppy owners before the puppies are born. This gives buyers the opportunity of ironing out in advance any difficulties over puppy ownership that might be worrying them. In turn, the breeder can decide whether he or she feels that the puppies are likely to be suitable for the buyers, or indeed whether the buyer is suitable to own one of the precious litter. General expenses,

ABOVE: A group of Kamrats Labradors pictured in Sweden.
Choice of colour comes down to personal preference – the character of the dog is the most important.
Photo courtesy: Jan-Erik Ek.

PHOTOGRAPHS FACING PAGE
TOP: Mandigo's Winzerhoff Heat Wave (Clarion's Keaghan CGC – Mandigo's Sweet Revenge),
owned by Karin Wickstrom and Autumn Davidson DVM.
The female Labrador is sweet and loving, with a gentle disposition.
Photo: Paul Boyte, courtesy of Autumn Davidson DVM, Clarion Labradors, California.

BELOW: Can. Ch. ShaRays Royal Heir WC, CGC (Am. Can. Ch. ShaRay's Emmanuel CD, JH, CGC
– Ch. Somersett ShaRay Magic Minx), owned by Ray and Sharon Edwards, ShaRay Labradors,
Washington. The male Labrador is stronger and more robust than the female, but he will settle down
to be a most faithful companion.
Photo courtesy: Sharon Edwards.

and costs and methods of feeding, can be explained, and the puppy's future environment discussed. Make quite sure that the breeder shows you the national Kennel Club accreditation for both parents, as well as hip scores and updated annual eye certificates.

On your first visit, also note whether the outside runs and kennels are clean, with fresh bedding, and that clean water in bowls is readily available. Check that the kennel occupants are happy, well-groomed and cheerful. Above all, state clearly what your aims and expectations are, and the breeder of your choice will be only too happy to try to accommodate you.

Finally, when you meet the breeder, you can make arrangements to view the litter when it is born, and for the eventual collection of your chosen puppy.

CHOOSING FROM THE LITTER

Puppies are usually ready to go to their new homes between seven and eight weeks of age, though their socialisation should have already begun at six weeks. I find that puppies who are born in the breeder's house, and kept indoors at least until their eyes are open and they are able to hear household noises, are far more socialised by human handling and cuddling. This is not always the case with puppies who are born and kept in an outside kennel with their mother until they are old enough to leave home.

When viewing a litter and making your final decision, be sure that the puppy's ears and teeth are clean, the eyes are clear and bright, the coat looks clean, shining and healthy, and the nails have been cut short. A puppy who scampers around full of life could just be the bundle of fun for you.

A puppy intended as a family pet should be chosen from a litter of perhaps six, and you should be looking for the one who attracts you most. This may be the first to jump out of the sleeping quarters to greet you, or even the one who is just slightly less pushy, but still comes over to you to see what is going on. A puppy who hangs back or runs into a corner is certainly not going to be an extrovert.

A Labrador pup intended as a working dog should be the lively one, who misses nothing

and wants to be out of the box first. This one can be seen picking up toys, and really making his presence felt, perhaps slightly more agile than the others and maybe not quite so good-looking. A potential working Labrador should ideally be a young handful, who needs guiding along the right lines.

DOCUMENTATION

You should be given a copy of your puppy's pedigree, relevant national kennel club registration certificate, a diet sheet, samples of the food the pup is used to, and, hopefully, the next meal (already prepared) to take away with you. You should also receive a certificate of insurance for a month, which you can then extend if you wish, a note of when the pup was last wormed, and any last-minute instructions or advice that the breeder may consider useful. After that, it is straight home to a new life for you and your very special puppy.

Breeders usually like to hear that the puppy has settled in, so a phone call from you within 48 hours, along with any queries you might have, would be much appreciated.

PREPARING YOUR HOME

Select a cosy spot in your house where you intend your puppy to sleep. If this is in a corner of the kitchen, perhaps placing the bed near a radiator would be a good idea if the weather is cold. Buy a strong fibreglass or plastic bed, and line it with an old blanket or synthetic bedding. Both are washable and will withstand some wear and tear. Alternatively you can purchase bean bags or duvets specially made for dogs, but I would advise waiting a while until your pup has stopped chewing (which may be over a year!). An unsupervised puppy can easily reduce a bean bag to a pile of polystyrene balls in no time at all, which in turn will do a canine stomach no good at all.

Cardboard boxes as sleeping quarters for very young puppies are adequate for a very short period, provided they have no staples holding them together. Again, a bored youngster will enjoy tearing the cardboard to bits in just a few minutes. This also goes for wicker baskets, which are notoriously difficult to clean. Hard

ABOVE: Puppies from a well-reared litter should be lively and inquisitive with clean coats and bright eyes.

LEFT: The breeders should have started the process of socialisation, giving the puppies a chance to explore and learn about their immediate environment. Photo: Amanda Bulbeck.

BELOW: If you are hoping to show your Labrador in the future, the breeder will help you to assess conformation and give you an opinion as to showing potential.

Photo: Keith Hawkins.

wooden boxes, so long as they are not rough, are an option, but they too attract the attentions of sharp growing teeth.

Most people prefer the kitchen or utility room as the puppy's sleeping quarters for the first few months. A washable tiled floor is ideal, even better if they are quarry tiles, or of some other purpose-made non-slip material. Linoleum is fairly good too, but beware of a very glossy surface, which can make a puppy skid while running. If possible, ensure that the room you select has fitted units throughout, thus preventing the display of tempting wires and pipes for the puppy to chew. Also ensure that the sleeping area is draught-free. The utility room often houses the central heating boiler or washing machine, which means warmth and socialising noise for your new puppy.

Wherever you choose, make sure it is near to an outside door. This means it is easier to train the puppy to go outside for toilet purposes. Meanwhile keep the floor lined with newspapers. The utility type of room is useful as it can also serve as a daytime rest room for the puppy, away from the general household activity.

THE CASE FOR CRATES
Increasingly, many dog owners like to use collapsible wire or fibreglass crates in which the puppy can sleep at night. Such crates are also useful for containing your puppy during an odd period in the day when you are busy, or you want to go shopping alone. Never leave a pup in a crate for long periods.

Remember that your little bundle of joy may be sitting angelically on your lap at two months, but by three months of age can see what is on the table, and by six months can clear the working surfaces in the kitchen – the Sunday joint would probably be his choice. By then, he may not be averse to chewing furniture legs if you leave him loose to get bored, so, unless you are into three-legged tables and chewed curtains, buy a crate!

Such crates, which have been popular in North America for many years and are now widely available in the UK, can readily be put in the rear of your car, making travel with a puppy very much safer.

Your puppy will soon look on a crate as his own personal den – a place where he feels safe and secure.
Photo courtesy: Marjorie Satterthwaite.

THE OUTSIDE ENVIRONMENT
Your garden will also require attention. Be prepared to erect a three-foot fence around the patio or outside the utility room door. Young puppies need only the minimum of exercise. Of course, you should have ensured in advance that the garden perimeter is fenced up to five feet high. Anything lower than this, and a fully-grown Labrador will view it as a great challenge. As your puppy is growing, short visits into the main garden will teach him to respect his boundary, even though he may collect a few daffodil heads on the way. A lively youngster will probably try to convert your lawn into a muddy football field if left to his own devices.

If you have a garden pond, a curious puppy must be prevented from falling into it. Your young Labrador will need constant supervision in the garden and must be taught that the pond is out of bounds. If the pond has a winter cover, make sure that it is very secure, otherwise a small puppy can wriggle inside and become trapped.

I consider Labradors to be dustbins on four legs, so you would be wise to construct a fence round any compost heap. These dogs love to eat vegetable matter, and think of horse and cow manure as great delicacies.

KENNELS AND RUNS
Other owners may like to install an outside kennel and run for the puppy, to be used for a couple of hours in the daytime. The kennel should have warm bedding inside, and the external run made secure.

Puppy buyers occasionally expect me to let them have a Labrador intended to be kept outside in a kennel and run. This is certainly not my idea of looking after a family companion. I suspect that some member of the family is rather houseproud, and cannot spare the time to train a young puppy. Of course, whenever an 'outside' dog is allowed indoors, all the pent-up energy of the day is released, and the poor animal is chastised for perfectly natural exuberance – a bit like a child let out of school. Such arrangements make it even harder to house-train the puppy, and overall, I must say I find the method rather like keeping an animal in a zoo.

Owners who like to work their dogs and want to keep them in hard conditions are going to have a different lifestyle anyway. Also, their Labradors will be getting some form of daily training and shooting at weekends, and thus have something to look forward to. If a kennel for daytime or night-time use is an absolute necessity, it needs to be five to six feet high, and at least four to five feet wide and deep, with an adequate surrounding run of chainlink or weldmesh. The building itself should be lined with zinc to prevent chewing, and must be completely waterproof. You can view these types of kennel at dog and agricultural shows but, be warned, you will need a large purse, as they are far from cheap!

COLLECTING YOUR PUPPY
The big day has arrived, and you are to take charge of your bouncing, bubbly bundle of Labrador puppyhood. If you are travelling by car, it would be wise for the puppy to miss the

Jem XLT Winroc Black Sapphire (Mex. Ch. Campbelcroft Peppermint Paddy CD, SH – Winroc XLT Onyx Injun, MH): The big moment when you take your new puppy home.

Photo courtesy: Wilma Melville.

early feed that day, so as to travel in comfort and not feel sick. Be prepared with a towel, blanket, newspapers and a damp cloth. When your puppy is put into your arms, give support under the chest, rump and back legs.

In the car, travel with the puppy on your lap, and let someone else drive. Otherwise, ask a helper to accompany you, to be responsible for holding the puppy on the back seat. *Never* put a puppy alone in the back of the car. Minor roads make the car sway from side to side, and can knock the puppy off balance. If your new puppy rolls about in the back of the car during that first journey, the experience will not be forgotten in a hurry, and future car travel may be traumatic. So it is in your own interests to plan this first journey sensibly.

ARRIVING HOME
Upon arrival at your home, put the puppy down in the kitchen, and give lots of affection to banish the memory of the travel trauma. Show your puppy where his bed is, and take him into the garden to relieve himself. After this opportunity for an inquisitive look around, offer the puppy the ready-prepared meal, which may or may not be eaten. Then take your puppy outside again to

make sure that he is comfortable. If and when he performs, give lots of praise and tell the pup he is a good dog. Inside again, let your new arrival run around the kitchen and get to know these new surroundings.

Naturally, children will be longing to play with the puppy, but do not let them fuss too much at this stage. Children must learn to treat a young dog gently, not to tease and never to grab any animal from behind. Always call the puppy towards you and make a fuss when the pup comes. Make sure that your children know exactly how to handle your young Labrador.

After a little while, show your puppy, who will by now be tired, the bed you have prepared, and try to arrange to leave the newest member of your family alone to have a welcome sleep.

Basic commands, such as "No" or "Leave" must be understood by the puppy as soon as possible, and all human members of the household must keep to the house rules, so that the puppy learns immediately what is and is not allowed. Likewise, the whole family will have chosen a name for its new member, and the pup will be quick to learn it and respond to it. Whatever command is given, make sure the human issuing it always finishes by praising the

Most puppies will take a little time to settle into a new home.

Photo: Amanda Bulbeck.

Provide your puppy with his own toys that he is allowed to play with – and substitute one of these if he is chewing something that is not allowed.

Photo: Keith Hawkins.

dog as soon as the action is performed. Remember, "No" must always really mean No.

HOUSE TRAINING

When the puppy wakes of his own accord, take him gently outside and say "Clean dog," or whatever command you have decided to use. Remember to praise again when the puppy has performed. During early house training, your most important function is to always stay with the puppy, and never scold after a mistake in the house. Designate a special spot in the garden for use as a toilet. Absolute consistency, and patient training with love and understanding, should pay dividends within a couple of weeks.

Overnight, your puppy will sleep for a few hours after the 10pm feed, and naturally will feel very strange waking up in the night with no littermates for company and warmth Go and comfort the puppy, who should be taken outside to perform, then go straight back to bed again, leaving the dog alone. As the first week goes by, your puppy will become more settled, and will manage to wait until the morning. Remember, however, a puppy needs to be put out immediately on waking up. A Labrador sleeping in a crate will probably cry to go out, because puppies, young as they are, rarely soil the beds they sleep in.

Gradually, on growing older, your puppy will regard the crate as a bedroom, and will voluntarily get into it whenever tiredness dictates.

THE UNSETTLED PUPPY

Human comfort is of great help to puppies who cannot settle at night, but, on the other hand, do not let the pup make a habit of demanding it. Providing such comfort for an unsettled puppy may mean early rising for a few days, to reassure the pup so that real unhappiness does not occur. With good management, the unsettled puppy will improve.

Sometimes I have to suggest to new owners that the puppy sleeps in the dog bed placed beside their bed, so that comfort is available is the middle of the night. Be prepared for the occasional excursion outside when the pup's bladder dictates. As with all training, both puppies and children respond well to tender, loving care.

For the most part, Labradors are excellent feeders, but they can also become spoilt and occasionally fussy eaters. Offer your puppy food, and 99 per cent of the time it will be eaten almost before you have taken your hand away from the bowl. If the puppy really does not want the meal, take it away and offer fresh food at the following feeding time. If this is still refused and you are feeding a complete feed soaked, try serving it dry instead, but make sure that there is plenty of water available to the dog.

A further refusal could signal an impending tummy upset, in which case do not offer any food for 24 hours, just honey and water. After 24 hours, you will know if the pup has eaten anything untoward, indicated either by sickness or unusual motions. At this point, a quick visit to the vet will usually sort things out. If your puppy seems fine, offer chicken and rice, or fish and rice for the next 24 hours, then return to the normal diet. Do not offer any other sort of food.

FEEDING
In the last few years, great scientific strides have been made in the manufacture of dog and cat foods. For example, there is a great assortment of biscuit meal to choose from. Some types include dehydrated meat. Others are flaky types of meal which consist of a base of wheat, corn and maize, to which different manufacturers add dried vegetables and dried meat, resulting in a complete maintenance food. Other feeds are similar, but are expanded. Servings are small nut-like biscuits, which comprise a complete feed containing every imaginable additive for the growing puppy or the adult dog. They are very easy to feed three or four times daily, either dry or with water to pre-soak. It is important to bear in mind that fresh water must be available at all times. Some breeders prefer the traditional regime of feeding two meals a day of meat/tripe and biscuit, and two meals of Weetabix or similar cereal, and milk or rice pudding. Meat can be obtained canned, as can tripe, or, alternatively, one pound weight frozen packs are available. Although breeders usually suggest exact amounts of food for the correct growth of your puppy at certain ages, these amounts are calculated on conditions at the particular breeding establishment. If you give the same quantity of food and, at the same time, unwisely subject your puppy to a great deal more exercise than he is used to, body and bone growth will suffer. At the end of 12 months, the young dog, although maturing, may look thinner than most and may in turn not have sufficient bone. Once lost, good bone can never be replaced.

To begin with, adhere to the feeding regime advocated by the puppy's breeder.
Photo: Keith Hawkins.

DIET SHEET
For the first few months, try to keep exactly to the diet and feeding times that your puppy was used to, according to the diet sheet that you were given. It must be quite disturbing for a puppy to change homes, missing littermates and coping with a change of food as well. Later on, if you feel you do want to change, the golden rule is to try changing one meal at a time over a few days, and watching to see the results. Puppies' stomachs have all the usual digestive enzymes necessary for the diet they are accustomed to. If you change suddenly, your puppy may react and have diarrhoea or be sick. If you change abruptly from a complete food to meat and biscuit, you may get the balance wrong and it will probably take a few days for the puppy's gastric juices to acclimatize. Meanwhile, you panic and change again, and then you are really in trouble.

Complete foods are manufactured to the differing needs of growing or adult dogs, as we saw above. They are usually of the expanded, or flaky, variety (rather like muesli) and an adult dog needs about one pound in weight per day, either soaked in water or fed dry. Puppies up to six months need about half as much again, although of course they will be eating 'Puppy' or 'Junior' brands of the same food. Recommended amounts are always on the packages. It might be as well to study the cost of such food when you are researching the economics of keeping one or more Labradors.

An alternative diet is beef or (green) tripe, fed with good terrier wholemeal. This can be bought in convenient frozen packs. Quantities for a puppy would be about 1lb or 450g (either meat or tripe with meal) each day. At eight weeks of age, this would be split into two meals, plus two milk and Weetabix meals daily.

If a puppy or adult dog suddenly refuses to eat the food offered, there is always a very good reason. Nature is telling the dog to lay off eating, so you must take great care. For this reason, I personally prefer an excellent quality complete feed and advise new owners to keep the puppy on that food for at least six months. Of course, if your puppy is sick or has loose motions, withold food for 24 hours, leaving an adequate quantity of honey and water available to drink. After 24 hours, offer fish and cooked rice, or scrambled egg.

A further 24 hours later, your puppy can be restored to the original diet. Incidentally, I never use cow's milk for puppies under three months of age. I find goat's milk an excellent food, but only if the puppy has been used to it, and I never mix it with complete feeds.

TRAVELLING BY CAR

Get your puppy used to travelling in the car as soon as possible. Never let your pup wander or jump about in the car, and teach the puppy from the start to Sit and Stay, particularly when you are about to open a car door. Get ready with the lead, and only then call the pup out of the car.

If, unfortunately, your puppy has had a bad experience and is travel-sick, try encouraging the youngster to sit in the car when it is parked in the driveway. Otherwise, confine the puppy's travel to very short daily drives to a local park, which provide the opportunity for running and

Most Labradors love travelling by car. Start off with short journeys to the park so your puppy will associate the experience with something pleasurable.   *Photo: Carol Ann Johnson.*

enjoyment. This will encourage the puppy to think of car trips as enjoyable events. Do not let your Labrador jump up steps or climb into a car until over eight months old, as much damage can be done by jumping and stair-climbing while the bones in a dog's limbs are still calcifying.

VISITING THE VET
Some owners like to take a puppy to their own vet for a check-up when they arrive home. If you do decide to do this, make sure you keep the puppy in your arms at all times. *Never* put a young pup on the floor, inside or outdoors, and preferably stay in the car until it is your time to see the vet. You may even find a vet who is prepared to check over your puppy in your car. After all, you will otherwise be exposing the pup to the possibility of infection in the veterinary surgery's waiting room.

IMMUNISATION
A newborn puppy has a natural immunity to disease, passed on through antibodies in the maternal bloodstream, which will last for the first three months of life. This immunity slowly diminishes from six weeks onwards until the puppy becomes vulnerable to infection. This is the best time to inoculate against four specific diseases – hepatitis, leptospirosis, canine distemper and canine parvovirus. Your veterinary surgeon will advise.

WORMING
You can expect that your puppy will have been wormed two or three times before leaving the breeder. The worms we are talking about here are roundworms, or toxocara canis. This level of worming is usually enough, but just occasionally one or two worms may be seen in the faeces. If this is the case, call in at your veterinary surgery after weighing the puppy, and ask for the appropriate dosage. I usually suggest that a puppy is wormed again anyway when inoculations are finished, and then once every six

months. When children have been playing with the puppy, get them into the habit of washing their hands frequently after touching the dog. Do the same after they have been playing outside.

GROOMING
Labradors require very little grooming, but it is just as well that the puppy gets used to being handled, brushed and combed daily. You will need some basic equipment: a brush (scrubbing brush texture), a steel comb, two steel dog bowls, nail clippers and a chamois leather. During grooming, your Labrador puppy will encounter a useful discipline, part of general training, which is to stand still for a short time every day to be brushed. Your pup will actually enjoy it. Also check eyes and ears, and teach the puppy to have the teeth brushed with canine toothpaste and a special brush. This will help to avoid obnoxious bad breath in later years. All these small lessons pay off if taught from a very early age, particularly handling, because if the need to be seen by a vet should arise, the dog will be easy to handle.

A young puppy's toenails grow quickly, because of the absence of running on hard ground like tarmac or concrete. To clip the nails, look at each in turn and cut with clippers where the hook grows over. If done carefully, avoiding the quick, the procedure will be painless, and, if done each week, the puppy will accept it as routine.

A Labrador has short hair with a dense undercoat, so mud and water will be shaken off within an hour. Rubbing down with a chamois leather will help, particularly if your puppy indulges in a favourite pastime, rolling in water and mud. As the pup grows older of course, swimming is an excellent form of exercise. Surprisingly enough, your puppy will not have the same enthusiasm for a domestic bath full of soapy water! In fact, Labradors seldom require bathing, especially since it destroys the natural oil in their coats, which helps to make the

'A Labrador has short hair with a dense undercoat, so mud and water will be shaken off within an hour'

A Labrador puppy is willing to learn, so make sure you teach good manners right from the start.

Photo: Amanda Bulbeck.

Labrador coat waterproof. Some owners like to hose down dogs when they are muddy, but I strongly disapprove because water directed on to the skin and legs can, I feel, cause rheumatism in later years. During summertime, we have a tub full of water outside, and on hot days our dogs love to jump in and out to cool off. But this particular bath does not contain soapy water!

Labradors have the easiest coats in the world to keep clean. The only time I envisage a proper bath being necessary is if your pup has rolled in fox dirt – a favourite pastime! If a sponge and a bucket of water fail to do the trick, then a bath is the only solution. Do not attempt this alone, unless you want a good soaking. Your Labrador might jump straight into the bath the first time you ask, in which case you are very lucky. Mostly it is a lift-in job for two people. Praise the puppy for being clever, and give a command to stand still. Cotton-wool in the pup's ears is important, as are lukewarm water and a good canine shampoo. Use a shower spray to rinse

out the soap completely, roughly towel away surplus water, then carry your Labrador outside before the shaking starts and you become drenched. Within an hour your pup will be reasonably dry, but it is a good idea to keep a close watch in the garden – your nice clean Labrador will probably think it a splendid idea to roll in the soil as soon as possible!

SOCIALISATION
Training to become a pleasant and enjoyable member of the household, and to fit in with society at large, is essential. A dog must know exactly where it stands in the hierarchy. Your puppy has already learnt from the natural mother what can and cannot be done, and you must take over as master (or mistress) and pack leader. Good manners in a dog are absolutely vital and, like feeding, the quality and quantity of your efforts while your Labrador is very young and willing to learn, will certainly pay dividends later.

Already, by teaching your Labrador to sit

before getting a meal, or a biscuit, you are making the young dog begin to realise that a reward is forthcoming when a command is obeyed. You may feel, on reading such a statement, that it amounts to bribery and corruption, but this certainly plays a big part in a Labrador's life. These dogs will do anything for food!

JUMPING UP

The most common complaint about Labradors is that they jump up to welcome everybody who approaches. Personally, I do not discourage this sort of welcome in the early days, because it is one way of encouraging a lot of animation in a show dog. But for the average house-dog, jumping up can be a nuisance. One method of breaking the habit that seems to work is to teach your puppy, right from the start, to fetch a favourite toy from the toybox. When someone comes to the door, your puppy will obviously come too but just send the pup back for the toy. Pleasure in returning to you proudly carrying the toy will make your puppy forget all about jumping up. If jumping up continues to be a problem, just shut the puppy in another room behind a closed door.

Of course, meeting people outside in the street is a little different. In this situation you must anticipate that the puppy is going to jump up, pull smartly back on the collar saying "Sit," and then crouch down to hold the dog in the Sit position while your fellow dog lover greets your Labrador enthusiastically. When in the house, try to get children and other members of the household to tell the puppy to fetch a toy. Say "Down" firmly, and *never* make a fuss of the puppy unless in the sitting position. Eventually, this will become a good habit and friends will not be deterred from visiting you. Never allow children to play tug of war with the dog and toy.

HOUSE RULES

Without some lessons in obedience, your dog cannot be expected to behave well in the house. Greeting people at the door will perhaps be someone's first introduction to both you and your dog, and I think we all agree that first impressions are both valuable and lasting.

For everyday living, we prefer to keep our dogs in the kitchen or garden. It is important to me to have one room where visitors can be entertained without the dog being the main attraction. Stairgates are very useful for preventing Labradors climbing the stairs, and I also use them between the lounge, dining room, and kitchen. My dogs can thus see who has arrived, without charging in and jumping all over the unsuspecting visitor.

At this point, I should stress that it is preferable for one person to do all the early training with the puppy, and to ask everybody else to keep to the house rules. Children would love to be included in training exercises, but you cannot put old heads on young shoulders and, in my opinion, they usually manage to wind the puppy up. In fact, I have to say that, as a breeder, I prefer potential owners and their families to visit me long before the puppies are born. If the children are very lively and badly-behaved, I see no reason why I should add to the parents' problem by letting them have one of my puppies.

I also feel strongly that dogs should not be encouraged to sit around the table during mealtimes. Many a Labrador has enjoyed sitting by when a toddler is eating, and has thus become grossly overweight.

If you have followed my suggestions for the accommodation of your puppy in the kitchen or similar, the puppy will readily understand its place in society when you have visitors, and will retire to bed. Once your Labrador has become obedient and less exuberant, you may allow the puppy into the room with visitors. After an initial greeting, a well-socialised puppy will go away into a corner of the room and lie down. To let a very young, bouncy dog loose upon an unsuspecting visitor could be a mini-disaster, involving coffee cups toppling off the table and cakes landing in somebody's lap. But this will not happen to you, because you are now able to introduce your new family member as a lovable, gentle dog of character.

DAILY LIFE WITH A YOUNG LABRADOR

As with children, it is a good idea to establish a regular daily routine with your Labrador puppy. Personally, I recommend the following. First thing in the morning, go to your puppy immediately on waking. The pup will be longing to see

It is a good idea to establish a daily routine with your puppy. This will help general development and education.

Photo: Carol Ann Johnson.

you, and will then want to go out for toilet purposes. You then give the first meal of the day. After half an hour running around, the puppy will be ready for a rest. Once the family has departed for work and school, there will be time for some socialising play.

Set aside two hours in the morning for the puppy to sleep quietly in the designated room or crate, after which allow the youngster out to perform toilet functions. Your Labrador will then be looking forward to the next feed. Once again, playtime around the house with toys will be enjoyed, and another period of rest should follow.

With restored energies, the puppy is ready to play with the children when they come home from school, then will look forward to teatime, the third meal of the day. Just before everybody

retires for the night, your puppy will need to be taken out again into the garden, settling down for the night after a fourth feed, around 10 p.m. Hopefully, within a month the puppy should be house-trained, and, at three months of age, will be down to three feeds daily. Obviously, increased quantities of food will be consumed at each meal, so split the total fed into three feeds instead of four.

You will watch your Labrador growing daily, and learning lots of new things that will both amuse you, and sometimes make you feel less patient. You must remember, as the puppy grows, to keep all important things out of reach, particularly children's toys, which would be better kept in their bedrooms. Clothes hanging near radiators are attractive to puppies, but, after all, you did decide to buy a retriever! If you throw anything for your puppy to retrieve, always encourage the young dog to bring it back to you and very gently take it, remembering to say "Good dog" or whatever. As Labradors get older, they will love to bring sticks back to you, and I recommend you continue to follow the same method. Sticks can so easily split in their mouths and stick in their throats unless removed gently.

For early training in the garden, and later sessions in the wide open spaces, acquire either a large solid rubber ball or a green stuffed dummy for your puppy to retrieve. Always encourage a return to you with a biscuit or tidbit.

Walking properly to heel at all times, without being allowed to pull, is a lesson well-learned for your dog at a very early age. How many times do we see an owner being pulled along by their pet dog? The bigger and stronger the dog grows, the worse the problems become. If you get matters right from the start, the bond you forge between you and your dog at a very early age will save you hours of heartache later.

The command "Sit" can also prove very useful in the house. Some dogs believe it is their divine right to barge in front of you when you are opening a door and wanting to go through it. Simply insist upon the dog sitting and staying before you open the door. Such demands made on your puppy will lead to politeness and respect in the long run. Likewise, train your puppy to refrain from jumping up and sitting on furniture. This is an asset, especially if you take your dog with you when visiting other people's homes.

Believe me, a well-trained Labrador is a joy to everybody, not least to the proud owner. You will immediately gain respect from all around, and will find that your growing puppy is even more lovable if well-behaved and obedient.

Ch. Saddlehill Hemingway CD, JH (Am. Can. Ch. Monarch's Black Arrogance CD – Ch. Saddlehill Promise WC) and Saddlehill Annie Oakley, bred by Susan and Bill Eberhardt, Saddlehill Labradors, California.
With time and patience, you will be rewarded with a well-socialised, well-behaved dog who will be a pleasure to own.

Photo: Beverly Kulp, courtesy of Susan and Bill Eberhardt.

4 TRAINING YOUR LABRADOR

Congratulations! You are the owner of a Labrador, a breed of dog that makes a wonderful pet. The Labrador is a happy family dog who enjoys life to the full, loves people and other dogs, is healthy, easy to feed, easy to groom and capable of being taken anywhere – except perhaps china shops, as that otter-like tail can clear a low table with one wag. What could be better? But, leave your puppy untrained, and you could end up with an over-sexed dustbin on legs. A Labrador left to its own devices will become self-employed. In other words, your puppy needs a leader, and that leader must be you! You will achieve the level of training you deserve. A Labrador is as good as any dog at pulling on the lead, jumping up, stealing food and picking up all the bad habits that you deplore in other people's dogs. Take the time and effort needed to train your Labrador, and you will have a wonderful companion, and a dog that everyone else will covet.

EARLY LESSONS FOR THE PUPPY
Training starts as soon as you get your puppy. You may think: "What? It's only a puppy. I'll let him settle in for a few weeks." But you would

A new puppy ready to start training: At this stage a pup can absorb new information like a sponge.

Photo: Amanda Bulbeck.

be wrong – a puppy's mind is like a sponge and can absorb an amazing amount of information. Your Labrador might as well learn from the start the behaviour that you require, rather than write the preface of his own book of canine life, which he will do, given the chance. Puppies are amazingly good at training humans.

TRAINING COMMANDS

COMING WHEN CALLED: This is the most important command in any dog's life. You have a Labrador who loves food, and from day one you can use this fact. Your puppy will be under your feet whenever you prepare his meal. Move away and call the puppy. I promise he will come. Hold the bowl just above the pup's head, and he will most probably sit. There, you have achieved two commands already! Unfortunately, I must be honest, and admit that your Labrador is mesmerised by the food bowl. The words of command you are using may not yet be engraving themselves in your puppy's mind. Not to worry, you have had a success and can build on it. Keep a few food treats handy, some in a small tin that rattles, to reward successes at other times during the day.

Call your pup to you when he is not engrossed in some other pastime. Squat down if necessary, and reward your puppy with praise, stroking and a food-treat. The rattle of the tin will work, even if the pup is preoccupied. Do not worry – your puppy is not going to need food bribes for the rest of his life, as long as you always remember to use verbal praise and stroking when you reward with a food-treat.

Call your dog even when you do not want him. This sounds nonsensical, but it means that the puppy learns in a relaxed manner. It is a good idea to call the puppy sometimes if you are in another room, or out of sight. This helps to establish the command. If you get fraught, which is all too easy when you need your puppy in a hurry, the puppy will feel your tension.

RETRIEVE: With a Labrador, the Retrieve naturally follows on from coming when called. The Labrador instinct is to have something in the mouth. Just squat down and call the puppy. Always try to take the object or toy from the puppy's mouth gently, rather than letting the puppy drop it or race past you with it. You never know, you may want to have a go at some form of competition in the future. A dog that drops a retrieve in the early stages develops a habit that is very difficult to cure.

WALKING ON A LOOSE LEAD: Take this in easy stages. Try it at home, before you think you are going to need it. Walk a few steps at a time, then play with the toy or give the puppy a food-treat that is in your hand. You are getting your puppy's attention on you, not on sniffs on the ground or what the pup thinks may be round the next corner. An even easier way is to mask a food-treat in your hand and hold it out in front of the puppy's nose. A Labrador's nose will be glued to food and it is a happy way to start, especially if the puppy does not like the lead.

DOWN POSITION: Otherwise known as lying down when told. This is one of the easiest movements to teach the smallest of Labradors, and the most spectacular as far as outsiders are concerned. With the puppy in the Sit position, take the food-treat from in front of the nose down to the ground about six inches in front of the puppy's toes. The puppy will lie down to eat the food-treat. By always using the command "Down", with plenty of praise, you can dispense with the food very quickly and keep the pup in the Down position for a little longer each time. There is nothing cruel about making a puppy lie down. After all, it does it for at least eight hours every night. You have already taught your puppy to sit for dinner. You can build on this, with the use of a food-treat above the head to begin with, until just a command and hand signal are sufficent.

'Call your dog even when you do not want him...it means that the puppy learns in a relaxed manner'

ORGANISED SCHOOLING

Some readers may be thinking: "Surely it is too soon to be thinking about this with my young puppy. My baby only needs to be at home with me." As you have discovered, training began on Day One. Socialisation in the early days stops many hang-ups that can appear later. Get your pup out and about as soon as possible. Check with your vet if you are worried for health reasons.

PUPPY PLAYGROUPS: Such groups will not formally train your puppy – you have already started that in an easy way at home – but they are a great way of meeting people. Other puppies and children, indeed whole families, go to classes. Try to attend a class without your pup the first time. You will have to book in advance anyway, as these classes are very popular. Your gut feeling will tell you if the class is any good. If you do not like it, look for another, since nothing is too much trouble for you on behalf of your Labrador puppy. Take your puppy out with you at every opportunity, but do not lose friends by insisting you take him into their homes – he is not yet reliably trained. An awful lot of people do not like dogs, but will stomach a well-trained one, murmuring "I wish all dogs were like yours."

DOG TRAINING CLASSES: Socialising and training do not end with puppy classes. If the puppy classes are held at a dog training club, you will be told about the next step. Otherwise, you will probably find details of local training classes at your vet. When you go to new classes, again check in advance. Are the classes enjoyable? Are the people smiling? Are owners simply obeying a sergeant major, jerking their dogs round on choke-chains and doing set exercises? Assess the situation, and if necessary vote with your feet. There is no need nowadays for any form of harsh training. Gentle persuasion is so much better. At a good class, your pup will meet dogs of all ages, and of different inclinations, discovering that the world is made up of all sorts of dogs, some nice, some not. Just like the real world! A good training class should be a source of knowledge on general care. It will also help solve training troubles.

Homework sheets, or help sheets, are usually handed out each week. Study them carefully. It always shows if you have not worked with your puppy between classes, no matter how clever you think he is! Problems are usually given a specific slot in every class. If the trainer has not got time during the class, or feels the problem is not a general one, there is probably time for discussion after class, or a handout that will help you.

TRAINING AIDS

You have four major aids to help you with your training at all stages. Food (or a toy), the lead, touch and, above all, your voice. As your puppy gets the message, you can gradually drop continual food rewards, but still use commands, praise and stroking. Once you have taken the puppy off the lead and created distance between you and your Labrador, all you have left is your voice, with all its various pitches and tones. A puppy will listen to a whisper, but the use of a shout is always a last resort – you can only shout so loud, and eventually the puppy will learn to ignore you. The other pitfall of using your voice is the constant repetition of a command: "Down, Down, Down, Down." The puppy hears the first one and thinks: "In a minute. Oh, she's said it again, and again. Now she's getting annoyed. I'll still think about it." This is a recipe for trouble. Your puppy must learn that the command comes only once and must be obeyed instantly.

Having said all that, do not forget that you originally got your puppy to enjoy life with a Labrador. Play with your dog, invent games, have fun. Life is not all training. Let there be times when your puppy can just be a dog.

BASIC EXERCISES

In the language of dog training, the basic exercises are the Sit Stay, the Down Stay, the Heel on Lead, the Recall and the Retrieve. I have already covered these, except the Stays, in the first steps with your Labrador outlined above.

THE STAY

This means staying in the position in which the

TRAINING EXERCISES Demonstrated by Carol Gaunt, with Cherry and Chloe.

ABOVE LEFT: Food is a highly effective training aid – particularly with Labradors. Cherry has learnt to sit when a tidbit is held above her head. This reaction is quickly associated with the command "Sit."

ABOVE RIGHT: This exercise is taken a step further when teaching the Down. To begin with, a tidbit is held at ground level to encourage the correct response.

BELOW: Training exercises should always be interspersed with play sessions. If your dog believes that training is fun, you have achieved a major goal.

THE STAY

ABOVE: When teaching the stay, do not be tempted to progress too swiftly. Give the command backed up with a hand signal, and leave your dog a short distance before returning.

BELOW: Cherry now has the confidence to stay in the Down. This exercise can be built up until your dog is steady in the Down-Stay for an extended period.

HEELWORK

LEFT: Every dog owner wants to be able to walk with their dog on a loose lead. Carol has taught Chloe this exercise in the garden, where it is free of distractions.

RIGHT: For competition-style heelwork, the dog has to be glued to the left side with attention fixed on the handler.

THE RECALL

LEFT: The recall involves stringing together a series of exercises. The dog must sit on command, be steady in the stay, come when called, and then finish on command. Here, Cherry is being given the command "Wait", backed up with a hand signal.

RIGHT: Cherry stays in the Sit while Carol walks away.

BELOW: Carol turns to face Cherry before giving the next command.

ABOVE: On the command "Come", Cherry returns to Carol.

LEFT: Cherry returns in a straight line, and sits in front of Carol.

RIGHT: Carol gives the command "Heel" or "Finish".

BELOW LEFT: Cherry circles round the back of Carol's legs to return to her left hand-side.

BELOW RIGHT: Exercise finished: Cherry ends up in the position he started from.

1

2

3

THE RETRIEVE

1. Labradors love to retrieve, so teaching this exercise is a matter of curbing enthusiasm and imposing formal discipline.

2. Cherry is taught to take the dumb-bell on the command "Hold".

3. The dumb-bell must be held in the mouth without chewing or mouthing.

4. Chloe demonstates the full Retrieve exercise. Like the Recall, this is a matter of stringing a number of exercises together. It starts with the command "Wait".

5. Carol throws the dumb-bell.

6. Chloe must wait in position until given the next command.

7. On the command "Fetch" or "Hold", Chloe runs out to pick up the dumb-bell.

8. After picking up the dumb-bell, Chloe must return in a straight line to Carol.

9. Chloe sits in the Present, still holding the dumb-bell.

10. On the command "Give" Chloe lets go of the dumb-bell.

11. Carol takes the dumb-bell, and the exercise is complete. For competition purposes, the handler will also have to 'finish' their dog.

Photography: John Sellers

dog is placed until the handler returns. A Stay, be it Sit, Stand or the most useful one, Down, is always taught with the puppy on the lead. A Stay is a confidence exercise, and your Labrador should always know you will return before releasing him from the given position. Until the puppy will stay for at least two minutes, do not attempt to move away, but reassure the pup with the word you are teaching, thus: "That's a good Down. Clever dog. Down."

EVERYDAY TRAINING
Your puppy should understand all the key words you use before you go to Training Classes. There you can learn the technique that turns these actions into formal exercises. Continue to practise at home and on your walks. Teach your puppy to respect all livestock, and to follow the Country Code. Although you may not live in a town, teach your dog about noisy traffic, and temptations that appear constantly, in the form of other people, their shopping baskets and their children. A 16-month, completely untrained Labrador that I inherited became most worried about a man who descended from a telegraph pole in the middle of a local town centre. I asked the man to climb up again, to show my dog that it was neither magic nor anything to be afraid of. Not only did that co-operative man go up again, but as an added bonus he made a fuss of Cuillan when he returned to earth. Result? One confident dog.

All training or 'shaping' (the new dog training term) is really just a set of tricks that turn into canine good manners. You will be able to think of all sorts of tricks to teach your puppy, like giving a paw, lying down and rolling over (useful at the veterinary surgery), walking backwards, and picking up anything you may drop. Labradors can even beg, but please, not while still a puppy, because the bones are too soft. Anything your puppy learns to do will increase the bond between you, and make all future training far easier.

CORRECTING PROBLEM BEHAVIOUR
The famous master of Obedience training, Charlie Wyant, would always say: "Never let it happen." That is all very well for experienced

dog people. Often it is too late for the new owner. The first time a problem occurs, it is a one-off; the second is becoming a habit. Never be afraid to go back to page one. Your basics have probably slipped, and you need to start at the beginning again. It happens at some time or other to everyone training a dog, if they are truthful. Training your Labrador is mostly common sense, but there are plenty of short cuts. There are also plenty of people available to help you, especially if you go to classes. Canine behaviourists cost a fortune, and are usually a last resort for really severe problems.

If your puppy does destroy something, or has an accident when you are out, do not punish immediately on your return. It is too late. The puppy, delighted that you are home, will see nothing but an angry face and hear only a stern voice. He has forgotten about the tea towel left temptingly hanging over the side of the kitchen unit. Pick up the pieces, clear up the mess and take the puppy away from the scene of the crime; then you can return to being your usual loving self. Labradors turn their slapdash humans into tidy people.

MOUTHING: Mouthing is just another word for biting. Do not let it start. A dog that bites humans nowadays goes on a one-way trip to the vet under the Dangerous Dogs Act. There is no longer such a thing as 'being allowed one bite'. Show your puppy that biting hurts, and that all games and cuddles stop immediately when it happens. Withdraw and turn away. Aggressive possession over food bowls, toys or a particular area of the house or garden must never be allowed, right from the start.

CAR SICKNESS: Travel sickness is a bore, and sometimes the puppy is scared of even sitting in a car, thinking "I wasn't at all well in there last time. I'd rather stay outside." Most dogs these days have to be able to travel. If your puppy hates the car, try feeding dinner in the stationary vehicle. Sit in the car with the puppy when you are not going out, and read the paper, or do the crossword. Turn on the engine, turn it off and get out together. Soon the car will become merely another part of the puppy's home. It sometimes helps to make sure the pup cannot see out of the car windows. In bad cases of sickness, the only answer is to persevere. All the drooling etc. will get better in time, but make sure the puppy goes on all your journeys if at all possible. Things will not improve if your puppy is always left at home, nor will he magically grow out of it.

OVER-SEXED LABRADORS: This problem is not uncommon. Rescue societies will tell you that nearly all mongrels are part Labrador. Most males adjust to a celibate life, but some do not, and the worst thing you can do is let your young male dog have a taste of mating with a friend's Labrador up the road, and then say never again. That is the ultimate cruelty. Some male Labradors mount everything in sight; cushions, children, your leg, the curtains, and every bitch he sees, ready or not. These dogs will certainly be happier if they are castrated. I can almost hear some readers asking "How could you be so cruel?" Castration is not cruel. It involves the dog's everyday happiness. A male Labrador is in season 365 days of the year. Every guide dog (except breeding stock) is castrated or spayed, before going to live with their blind owner, and all are very happy with their way of life.

THE LABRADOR BITCH: Bitches are another matter. Can you cope with three weeks incarceration twice a year? If you can, splendid, but remember there is never such a thing as a safe time. I have had bitches tied on the second day of showing colour, and on the 23rd day at the end of the season. You may be convinced that you have the most beautiful Labrador bitch in the world, but think carefully before you get her mated. She will have to have her hips X-rayed and her eyes tested, and you will need at least six people on your waiting list for her puppies. Carbon copies do not happen in dogs. Family characteristics sometimes reappear, but, like humans, the puppies could inherit most of their dominant father's ways, instead of their mother's sweetness. Having a litter does not prevent health problems in the future. That is an old wives' tale.

HOLIDAYS WITH LABRADORS
Hotels can be a bit of a bore, even if the proprietor allows your dog in the communal rooms. As a responsible dog owner – even of a well-behaved Labrador – you should not inflict your treasure on other guests. A number of hotels take dogs, but use your common sense, and think of others. A hotel owner was heard to

A well-behaved dog is a pleasure to take on holiday – and they can also lend a paw!
Photo: C.C. Guard.

remark: "I've never had a dog yet that smoked in bed, set fire to the mattress or stole the towels and ashtrays!"

Walking holidays are ideal. When you are prepared to relax at the end of the day, your Labrador has a full tummy, and is more than ready to sleep, in preparation for the next day's adventure. My favourite form of holiday with my Labradors is on a canal boat. Endless walks, getting on and off, helping with the locks, living in another world of peace and quiet where the speed limit is four miles an hour. One piece of advice is to take plenty of towels with you. My Labrador Brodie was fooled when we tied up on the opposite bank the second night. First thing in the morning he led the way as usual, and jumped straight into the canal!

If you only consider going abroad for your holidays, you will need to make arrangements well in advance. A good friend is well worth cultivating, either to live in or to have your Labrador as a house guest. There are firms that will look after your house and all your pets. You will have peace of mind, but also need a deep pocket. If you are happy with the idea of kennelling, check the establishment first to make sure your dog will be exercised, fed correctly and not have to share a kennel with a dog of uncertain temperament. Book well in advance, as good kennels are booked up year after year.

NEW CHALLENGES

Once you have trained your Labrador in all the basics, other people may remark how intelligent and well-behaved a dog you possess. Perhaps you feel your Labrador needs something extra to occupy his mind, and you have discovered that you really enjoy teaching your dog. There are three further disciplines for you to try, which are open to all breeds: Working Trials, Obedience and Agility.

WORKING TRIALS

Working Trials were started in 1923, designed for German Shepherd Dogs. They are the canine equivalent of the horse world's three-day eventing. Trials have gradually evolved to include all breeds.

You need to be able to travel if you are going

Brodie, trained by C.C. Guard tackles the scale – one of the exercises required in the Agility section of Working Trials.
Photo courtesy: C.C. Guard.

to take Working Trials seriously, but great fun can be had qualifying your dog at a leisurely pace at Trials held within a reasonable travelling distance of your home. It is a lonely sport, as 90 per cent of training is usually done alone. However, it is useful to belong to a club or group that hold training sessions, to see whether the results you have attained training by yourself can be achieved in public. Your dog training class will usually be able to put you in touch with local owners who work their dogs in Trials.

Working Trials score over other disciplines because it is qualifying against a standard that counts, not coming first. By qualifying at a Championship Trial, letters are added to the

A training group with the unofficial name of 'Camp Run Amuck.' 'Campers' are (from left to right) back row: Brooklands Mischievous Sea Lion CDX, MH; Sam Sea Lion Diver CDX, SH; Saddlehill Drummer Boy UD, MH; Kobi's King Murphy (Chesapeake). The front row are all Chesapeake Bay Retrievers.

dog's Kennel Club registered name. In order to qualify, the dog must get at least 70 per cent in all three sections, with an overall mark of at least 80 per cent. My first dog ended up as Elsa of Philkindy, CDEx, UDEx, WDEx, TDEx. If she had managed to win the top stake twice, she would have been able to put WT Ch. in front of her name.

These letters need translation as follows:

CD Stake = Companion Dog Stake = CD Ex
UD Stake = Utility Dog Stake = UD Ex
WD Stake = Working Dog Stake = WD Ex
TD Stake = Tracking Dog Stake = TD Ex
WT Ch = Working Trial Champion

US WORKING TRIALS

In the US similar titles are competed for under the umbrella of Obedience Trials. The titles are: CD, CDX, UD and UDX. The title of Working Trial Champion is not recognised. Despite the continued popularity of the Labrador as a breed, participation in advanced obedience has not grown with that popularity. In 1995 statistics show a sharp contrast in number of titles earned in advanced classes as opposed to Novice titles: 523 CD, 139 CDX, 51 UD, and 12 UDX.

In addition, the Amerian Kennel Club offers three separate tracking titles: Tracking Dog (TD), Tracking Dog Excellent (TDX) and the Variable Surface Tracking (VST) title. Like obedience titles these accomplishments are added as a suffix to the dog's registered name. Entries at tracking tests are often limited to four to six dogs because track laying requires large land areas. Participation is at the whim of the draw.

In 1995 the American Kennel Club approved the rules and regulations for a Variable Surface Tracking (VST) title. As indicated by its name, the track is laid over a variety of surfaces, with and without vegetation. To be eligible for a VST test a dog must have earned a TD or TDX. Labradors love tracking and it is a training regimen that can be started with a very young dog. A number of Labradors have passed the novice Tracking Test and earned TD titles at just over six months of age. The title of Champion

*Ch. Saddlehill Hemingway CD, JH; Saddlehill Annie Oakley WC; Ch. Saddlehill O'Brien's Rapparee JH;
Saddlehill Markflite Melody CD, JH; Ch. Saddlehill Driftwood CD, JH; Saddlehill Petty Girl CDX, SH and
Photo: Beverly Kulp, courtesy of Susan Eberhardt, Saddlehill Labradors, California.*

Tracker (CT) will be awarded to any dog completing all three tracking titles, TD, TDX and VST, and may be used as a prefix on the dog's official name. This is a non-competitive title.

NOSEWORK

The Nosework Section of a Working Trial is made up of a half-mile track and a search. The track is laid by a person walking normally in a pattern designed by the judge. Articles (for example, a cartridge, a piece of wood or metal, a cork, or a piece of string) are placed on the track by the tracklayer, and are then recovered by the dog. The search takes place in a 25-yard square marked by four poles. Four articles are placed in the square, and the dog must retrieve at least two to qualify. Labradors excel in the Nosework Section. Both tracking and searching appear to come naturally to them, although a little bit of expertise from their human partner can help. Extra marks gained in Nosework can help to pad out marks in the other sections.

CONTROL SECTION

Control is the obedience part of Working Trials. CD Stake has no track, but more Obedience, including Heelwork on and off lead, a Recall and a two-minute Sit Stay out of sight of the handler, in addition to most of the the other Control exercises in the higher stakes. Heel off lead in the higher stakes is worked at normal, fast and slow pace, without talking to the dog, as is retrieving a dumb-bell. There is a Sendaway in the direction decided by the judge (with re-direction in the top stake) and a 10-minute Down Stay out of sight of the handler. Speak (bark) on command is substituted for the dumb-bell retrieve in TD Stake. Steadiness to Gunshot comes under the Control Section, but is usually carried out after the tracking and searching. To be honest, the Control Section is the most difficult part of Working Trials for Labradors, and needs very careful training to ensure that the dog does not switch off or become bored.

AGILITY SECTION

Agility is composed of a three-foot hurdle, a nine-foot long jump and a six-foot scale (usually like a door). Control has to be shown on the other side of the jumps, and the dog has to wait and then return over the scale. Taught carefully and not too early, the Agility Section is a piece of cake for your Labrador.

PATROL DOG STAKE

The only Stake I have not mentioned is the Patrol Dog Stake, or PD, which is equivalent to the TD Stake, but includes biting and chasing, and is not recommended for a pet dog. Numbers are very small in PD Stake, and no longer include a police entry.

WORKING TRIAL CHAMPIONSHIPS

Any dog that wins a Championship TD Stake in the current year is invited to the Crufts of Working Trials. This is hosted by a different Championship Society each year in the third week of October. The first two Kennel Club Working Trial Championships ever held were won by WT Ch. Linnifold Black Magic CD Ex, UDEx, WDEx, TDEx, a black Labrador bitch, owned by Susan Hodson (now Wood).

Working Trials produce a dog that, in the Nosework Section, has to make all the decisions, but in the Control and Agility Sections must be completely compliant to the owner. A dominant breed of dog finds this difficult, whereas a Labrador is always happy to use his nose and still be obedient in the other two sections.

A WORKING TRIAL STAR

In 1995, a Labrador did it again. WT Ch. Karl of Killerby, CDEx, UDEx, WDEx, TDEx, owned by Pete Hodgkins, won the Kennel Club WT Championships held by Midland Counties German Shepherd Association at Ollerton in Derbyshire, England.

Jet, as he is called by the Hodgkins family, qualified to go to the KC Championships by winning the Championship TD Stake at Scarborough out of an entry of 115 dogs (no ballot is ever allowed in the top stake), and qualified for the KC Working Trial Championships in 1995. This was Jet's third appearance at the KC Championships.

Although Jet's Nosework was excellent, he was lying third at the beginning of the final day. The two dogs in front of Jet broke their ten-minute out of sight Down Stays, and Jet won the most prestigious Working Trial of the year. This is why a dog's ability to qualify in all sections wins the day. Jet was bred by Mr M.K. Standard. His pedigree carries many famous names including FT Ch. Berrystead Bob, FT Ch. Sandringham Sydney, FT Ch. Holdgate Willie, and FT Ch. Sherry of Biteabout.

In everyday life, Jet is very laid back. He tol-

Ears flying – Jet takes off for the long jump.   *Photo courtesy: C.C. Guard.*

erates visitors, lives happily with the Collies in the family, and sleeps on a blanket on the sofa. His best trick every day is to fetch his food bowl when he thinks a meal is due. Mention anything to do with work, and he comes alive. Owner Pete feels that Labradors take longer to learn, but when they have mastered an exercise, it is there for good. His advice is to take small methodical steps, while making sure the dog thinks of it all as a game.

Pete often tracks Jet in the dark, as it is the only free time Pete gets during the week in the winter. It made Pete trust Jet on the track, and improved his casting on corners. When Jet was one year old, Pete took him to a fair. After watching the Gundog Scurry, Pete thought he would have a go with Jet. Although Jet had never retrieved a dummy before, and did not mark it the first time, Pete used his Sendaway training, and Jet won the Scurry after a run-off.

Pete said: "I am very proud of Jet's great achievements in Working Trials, but first and foremost he is a family pet who lives in the house. Jet is my constant companion, and a real pleasure to own and train. We are both looking forward to defending our title at the Kennel Club Working Trial Championships to be held at Lauder in 1996."

OBEDIENCE
In the UK Obedience developed as a separate discipline from Working Trials, supported by people who found the long hours, access to a large acreage and the isolated training involved in Working Trials too demanding. The style of work has changed drastically over the past 15 years, and it has become a form of dedicated dressage, where every whisker has to be in place. Unfortunately, this does not suit Labradors. Having won out of the lower classes, progress is more difficult when the handler is no longer allowed to talk to the dog. Border Collies can be taught by constant repetition, whereas a Labrador's attitude is: "I've done that five times already. What am I doing wrong?"

In the UK Obedience Champions earn their titles after winning out of the lower classes, and then winning three Championship C Classes. In the US the Obedience Trial Championship (OTCh.) is a showcase for outstanding workers. Only those Labradors that have achieved a Utility Dog title are eligible to vie for an Obedience Trial Championship and competition is keen. Professional trainers and skilled amateur trainers compete regularly.

The Obedience classes vary in detail from country to country, but the exercises, ascending in order of difficulty, are very much the same. In the UK the format is:

Pre-Beginners: Heel on Lead and Heel Free, Recall and Finish, Sit Stay, Down Stay.

Pictured left to right: OTCh. Shakespeare's Trixie UDT, WC; OTCh. Shadow Glen's Autumn Gold UDT, JH; and Ch. Beechcroft Wren of Shadow Glen UD, JH (pictured at three months). 'Trixie' defeated over 3,000 dogs during her obedience career and earned multiple All Breed High Combined and High in Trial awards.

Photo courtesy: Margaret S. Wilson, Shadow Glen Labradors, Maryland.

Beginners: As Pre-Beginners, plus a Retrieve.

Novice: As Beginners, plus a Temperament Test, but the Retrieve must be a Dumb-bell.

In these three classes you can talk to your dog all the time you are working, except during the Stays.

Class A: As Novice, but the Recall is to Heel, the Down Stay is five minutes out of sight, and Scent on cloths is introduced.

Simultaneous command and signal are allowed at the beginning of each exercise, but no encouragement after that.

Class B : Heel Free at three paces, Sendaway and Recall, Retrieve Judge's Article, Stand Stay, Sit Stay, and Down Stay out of sight and a more difficult Scent on cloths.

Either a command or a signal are allowed during most of the exercises.

Class C: As Class B, but with the Stand, Sit and Down position included in the three-pace Heelwork. Also Distant Control, again the Stand, Sit, and Down positions with the dog at a distance. The Scent test is done with cloths and the dog has to find the Judge's scent.

THE ROAD TO SUCCESS
Sue Potter lives near Chester-le-Street, County Durham, England. Sue has made up Obedience Champions with Border Collies and German Shepherd Dogs, so has all the necessary Obedience training knowledge at her finger tips.

Oscar, or Oscar Centurion, actually belongs to Malcolm Sutherland, managing director of Barbour. Oscar is a Labrador from a working background and has several FT Champions in his pedigree. He appeared at Sue's training club at seven months of age, exuberantly dragging his owner's wife into the hall on the end of his lead. Oscar was big, bouncy and very strong.

Sue took him over for three minutes to show his handler how to cope. A bond for life was formed in that short time, and Oscar showed Sue that he had great potential and would do anything for her.

After four weeks, Sue was certain that Oscar was competition material. The proud owner asked Sue if she would train Oscar. Sue had never trained another person's dog for competition, but was completely won over by Oscar, so agreed to work him in Obedience competitions. Tuesdays and Thursdays were spent being a dog at Sue's home, mixing with her dogs, cats and ducks, going for walks and learning competition work. Although very boisterous, Oscar never tried to challenge Sue's dogs. He behaved like an angel on roller-skates, immediately obeying every command, sharing sleeping quarters with her dogs and even going on holiday with Sue to the Isle of Man. A typical Labrador, Oscar always had something in his mouth and would rifle through the dogs' toy box as soon as he came into the house. His temperament was superb. In his own home he was a different character, still a loving dog, but taking his time to think about obeying commands. He lolled about on his own leather settee and slept upstairs for comfort.

Oscar was 11 months old when he went to his first show with Sue, where he came 2nd in Novice. Within the month, he had won three Novice classes and had come second again. His progress through the classes was meteoric. Very soon he was in Championship C Class, where his best place was a third. He did have a bit of trouble in training when he first started Class A Scent and Class B Sendaways. He did not want to go away from Sue, but by carefully building up his confidence step by step, success was soon assured. His love of work and of Sue knew no bounds.

I have already mentioned how hard it is to do well with any breed other than a Collie in Obedience. Sue summed up Oscar as: "A dog of a lifetime. My bond with Oscar was extraordi-

'Sue took him over for three minutes to show his owner how to cope... a bond for life was formed in that short time'

Pictured left to right, four Utility Dog titled Labradors, three with American and Canadian conformation titles and two with Tracking Dog titles: Am. Can. Ch. Sunnybrook Acres Black Star UD, TDX, Can. CDX, WC; Am. Can. Ch. Springwind's Pot O'Honey UD, TD, JH, Can. CDX; Am. Can. Ch. Beechcroft Springwind's Jet UD, JH, Can. CDX; and Springwind's Mr. Billy Boy UD – all owned and trained by Sheri Walsh, Springwind's Labradors, Fairbanks, Alaska.

nary, and I would never have believed I could love working a Labrador so much. If I could get another Lab like Oscar, I would have one tomorrow."

OBEDIENCE TRAINERS IN THE US
Nancy Pollock, Las Cruces, New Mexico has been a Labrador owner and an AKC Obedience Trial judge for many years. She says:

"I believe that the Labrador's intelligence and natural independence – a quality that enhances its performance as a hunting companion or gundog – has discouraged many Labrador owners from moving to the advanced level to compete against the two high-scoring breeds in today's Obedience Trials, the Golden Retriever and the Border Collie.

"In addition, not all Labradors are natural jumpers and some may need to be taught the timing and balance required for jumping, much as a horse does. Training methods must be adapted to maintain a Labrador's interest and attain the desired precision required for high scores at the advanced level. I have found that playing with a tennis ball has worked well as a motivating reward, especially in teaching the drop on recall and in straightening the dog's broad jump."

Sue Luebbert, an Obedience trainer since the 1970s in Fremont, California, has similar obser-

Saddlehill Drummer Boy UD, MH, CGC was bred by Susan Eberhardt, Saddlehill Labradors, California, and is owned and trained by Wendy Pennington, California. 'Drummer' competes in Scent Hurdles, Flyball and Agility.

Photo: Beverly Kulp, courtesy of Wendy Pennington.

1. *Figgis of Frensham clears the hurdles with ease.*
   Photo courtesy: C.C. Guard.

2. *ATCh. Can. OTCh. Ramapo's Medicine Man WC – Agility titles, AAD, AX, NAC, OAC, OGC; Obedience titles UDX, Can. UD, U-CDX, aged eleven years, tackles the A-frame on the Agility course.*
   Photo courtesy: Marietta Huber, Ramapo Retrievers, Illinois.

3. *ATCh. Can. OTCh. Ramapo's Medicine Man jumps the tyre on the Agility course.*
   Photo courtesy: Marietta Huber, Ramapo Retrievers, Illinois.

4. *ATCh. Can. OTCh. Ramapo's Medicine Man negotiates the weave poles.*
   Photo courtesy: Marietta Huber, Ramapo Retrievers, Illinois.

vations. Sue works with all breeds and has trained her own Labradors and Border Collies to advanced degrees.

"I find that a Labrador quickly tires of the repetitive training and precision required for today's Advanced Obedience competition. It is therefore important to avoid repeating exercises in the same environment and in the same order. I advise trainers to practice heeling exercises in unlikely spots, and encourage them not to allow themselves to become static in their training methods. Stimulating a Labrador's interest becomes the task."

Luane Vidak is a trainer and an AKC Obedience judge at all levels and resides in Watsonville, California. She judged her first Obedience match in the early 1970s and has been judging ever since. Luane is a multiple breed owner and has won a UD and an Agility title with her Sheltie; a CDX with her Miniature Schnauzer; and UD and JH titles with her Labradors. She also hunts with her Labradors. In addition to judging, Luane teaches puppy socialising classes and Open work.

"I believe that bonding is the first step to developing a competitive team in Obedience. It is essential to start training as early as possible.

"The advent of the Obedience Trial Championship refined Obedience work, requiring greater precision in performing the exercises. To have a Labrador that is competitive in Advanced Obedience it should be athletic and co-ordinated enough to handle repetitive jumping on a variety of surfaces, and have a willingness-to-please attitude. The overweight Labradors that can be seen in some conformation rings handicap the breed."

AGILITY

Agility is the youngest of the the disciplines. It came to public notice in 1980. Everybody has their own theory as to who started it, and where it originated. I can remember, in the 1970s, having an obstacle race for fun with all the Working Trial agility equipment, tracking poles, straw bales and anything else that came to hand. It helped pass the time while all the certificates were written out in preparation for the prizegiving. The Metropolitan Police used to have Obstacle Races as part of their Open Day at Keston Training School.

Agility first appeared at Crufts as a demonstration, between two teams from Working Trial Clubs. The Kennel Club soon realised that this was going to be a popular sport, with great spectator appeal, and rules were drawn up. In the UK there is no such thing as an Agility Champion, as Agility is still considered to be a fun sport. But it will not be too long before Agility Champions are added to the KC rules. Several European countries have Agility Champions already, although it was we British who taught them what Agility was all about!

Agility titles were first recognised by the American Kennel Club in 1995. Courses, obstacles and times are adjusted to the dog's height and experience, and classes are Novice, Open and Excellent. Three separate qualifying scores are required for a title. Corresponding titles are Novice Agility Dog (NAD), Open Agility Dog (OAD) and Agility Dog Excellent (ADX). Titles are non-competitive. Forty-five Labrador Retrievers earned titles in this sport during its inaugural year.

Agility courses are composed of: hurdles, a long jump, a suspended tyre, a table, two types of tunnel (a soft canvas one and a solid pipe type) are some of the obstacles used. It is obvious how the dog is intended to cope with them. The contact equipment is a dog walk, an 'A' frame and a see-saw. These are painted a different colour three feet from either end, and the dog must put at least one paw on the contact area. The weave poles have to be negotiated in a special way and any mistake must be corrected before continuing the round. Points are lost for knock-downs, refusals, not making a contact point and incorrectly negotiating the weave. Like horses, dogs can be eliminated for taking the wrong course.

> *'Bonding is the first step to developing a competitive team in Obedience...it is essential to start training as early as possible'*

THE AGILITY STAR

A regular competitor in Agility, with her black Labrador bitch, is Carol Goodes, who comes from Loughborough in Leicestershire, England. Her partner trains Labradors as gundogs. With her own bitch Black Astoria (pet name Cass), Carol decided to do something different. Cass came from a working background, so Carol thought she would try Agility.

Carol bought Cass from a friend for £25 – the best £25 Carol ever spent. Cass is very even-tempered, enjoys human company and, as most Labradors do, always carries something in her mouth. Her favourite position is flat on her back on her bean bag with her legs in the air. Cass also likes to help at bathtime, and will dry Carol given half a chance. Although Cass likes to please, constant repetition bores her, so Carol has to keep training fun. Cass had trouble with the tyre. If it was held in place on the frame by chains, Cass would often jump through the gaps. Her natural exuberance used to make her skid off the table.

For two years Carol and Cass attended Derby and District Dog Training Club, helped by Dave Blackshaw, a very well-known Collie competitor. Cass could not produce the turn of speed of the Collies, but won out of Starters in 1990. She also qualified for the Royal Canine Masters Final. The top six finalists from this competition are invited to compete in Europe – using European dogs, naturally. In 1995, Cass qualified at Packington to go to the Agility Allstars at the Horse of the Year Show. This is a new venture, bringing other breeds to the most prestigious Agility finals of the year, with the added attraction of TV coverage.

Allstars were scheduled for their first appearance at Olympia on the popular Monday evening and the packed house was left shouting for more. All the handlers and their dogs were presented to Prince Michael of Kent. The judge said in his written report: "Unfortunately, the brakes didn't quite work at the table and Cass skidded off causing five faults, with another five faults for a pole off a jump." He finished by saying that all the dogs and handlers gave 101 per cent, and the crowd rewarded the Allstars with the biggest cheer of all four days. This type of competition is here to stay.

Although Carol and Cass had trouble with the table, they would love to qualify again. Next time, Carol hopes not to feel so nervous and to be able to enjoy the attention of the thousands of spectators.

5 KEEPING YOUR LABRADOR FIT

Nutrition has never been the sole domain of the medical practitioner or of the veterinary surgeon. It is relatively recently that the medical profession has developed clinical nutrition to the point that there are professors in the subject, and that veterinary surgeons in companion animal practice have realised that they have an expertise to offer in this area of pet health care. This is curious because even the earliest medical and veterinary texts refer to the importance of correct diet, and for many years veterinary surgeons working with production animals such as cattle, pigs and sheep have been deluged with information about the most appro-

Tureel Just a Joy, bred by Mrs C.E. Turner. Good bone development can only be achieved if dogs are fed on a balanced diet which is suited to their individual needs.

Photo: Carol Ann Johnson.

priate nutrition for those species. Traditionally, of course, the breeder, neighbours, friends, relatives, the pet shop owner and even the local supermarket have been the main sources of advice on feeding for many pet owners. Over the past fifteen years there has been a great increase in public awareness about the relationships between diet and disease, thanks mainly to media interest in the subject (which has at times bordered on hysteria), but also to marketing tactics by major manufacturing companies. Few people will not have heard about the alleged health benefits of 'high-fibre', 'low-fat', 'low-cholesterol', 'high in polyunsaturates', 'low in saturates' and 'oat bran' diets. While there are usually some data to support the use of these types of diets in certain situations, the benefits are frequently overstated, if they exist at all.

Breeders have always actively debated the best way to feed dogs. Most Labrador owners are aware of the importance of good bone development and the role of nutrition in achieving optimal skeletal characteristics. However, as a veterinary surgeon in practice, I was constantly amazed and bewildered at the menus given to new puppy owners by breeders. These all too frequently consisted of complex home-made recipes, usually based on large amounts of fresh meat, goat's milk, and a vast array of mineral supplements. These diets were often very unbalanced and could easily result in skeletal and other growth abnormalities.

Domesticated dogs usually have little opportunity to select their own diet, so it is important to realise that they are solely dependent upon their owners to provide all the nourishment that they need. In this chapter, I aim to explain what those needs are, in the process dispel a few myths, and hopefully give some guidance as to how to select the most appropriate diet for your dog.

ESSENTIAL NUTRITION
Dogs have a common ancestry with, and are still often classified as, carnivores, although from a nutritional point of view they are actually omnivores. This means that dogs can obtain all the essential nutrients that they need from dietary sources consisting of either animal or plant material. As far as we know, dogs can survive on food derived solely from plants – that is, they can be fed a 'vegetarian diet'. The same is not true for domesticated cats, which are still obligate carnivores, and whose nutritional needs cannot be met by an exclusively vegetarian diet.

ENERGY
All living cells require energy, and the more active they are the more energy they burn up. Individual dogs have their own energy needs, which can vary, even between dogs of the same breed, age, sex and activity level. Breeders will recognise the scenario in which some littermates develop differently, one tending towards obesity, another on the lean side, even when they are fed exactly the same amount of food. For adult maintenance a Labrador will need an energy intake of approximately 30 kcal/lb body weight (or 65 kcal/kg body weight). If you know the energy density of the food that you are giving, you can work out how much your dog needs; but you must remember that this is only an approximation, and you will need to adjust the amount you feed to suit each individual dog. This is best achieved by regular weighing of your dog and then maintaining an optimum body weight.

If you are feeding a commercially-prepared food, you should be aware that the feeding guide recommended by the manufacturer is also based on average energy needs, and therefore you may need to increase or decrease the amount you give to meet your own individual dog's requirements. In some countries (such as those within the European Community) legislation may not allow the energy content to appear on the label of a prepared pet food; however, reputable manufacturing companies can and will provide this information upon request.

'I was constantly amazed and bewildered at the menus given to new puppy owners by breeders'

When considering different foods it is important to compare the metabolisable energy, which is the amount of energy in the food that is *available* to a dog. Some companies will provide you with figures for the gross energy, which are not as useful, because some of that energy (sometimes a substantial amount) will not be digested, absorbed and utilised.

There are many circumstances in which your dog's energy requirement may change from its basic adult maintenance energy requirement (MER):

WORK

Light	1.1 - 1.5 x MER
Heavy	2 - 4 x MER
Inactivity	0.8 x MER

PREGNANCY

First 6 weeks	1 x MER
Last 3 weeks	1.1 - 1.3 x MER
Peak lactation	2 - 4 x MER
Growth	1.2 - 2 x MER

ENVIRONMENT

Cold	1.25 - 1.75 x MER
Heat	Up to 2.5 x MER

Light to moderate activity (work) barely increases energy needs, and it is only when dogs are doing heavy work, such as pulling sleds, that energy requirements are significantly increased. Note that there is no increased energy requirement during pregnancy, except in the last three weeks, and the main need for high energy intake is during the lactation period. If a bitch is getting sufficient energy, she should not lose weight or condition during pregnancy and lactation. Because the energy requirement is so great during lactation (up to 4 x MER), it can sometimes be impossible to meet this need by feeding conventional adult maintenance diets, because the bitch cannot physically eat enough food. As a result she will lose weight and condition. Switching to a high-energy diet is usually necessary to avoid this.

As dogs get older their energy needs usually decrease. This is due in large part to being less active caused by getting less exercise, e.g. if their owner is elderly, or enforced by locomotor problems such as arthritis, but there are also changes in the metabolism of older animals that reduce the amount of energy they need. The aim should be to maintain body weight throughout old age, and regular exercise can play an important part in this. If there is any tendency to decrease or increase weight this should be countered by increasing or decreasing energy intake accordingly. If the body weight changes by more than ten per cent from usual, veterinary attention should be sought, in case there is a medical problem causing the weight change.

Changes in environmental conditions and all forms of stress (including showing), which particularly affects dogs with nervous temperaments, can increase energy needs. Some dogs, when kennelled for long periods, lose weight due to a stress-related increase in energy requirements which cannot easily be met by a maintenance diet. A high-energy food containing at least 1900 kcal of metabolisable energy/lb dry matter (4.2 kcal/gram) may be needed in order to maintain body weight under these circumstances. Excessive energy intake, on the other hand, results in obesity which can have very serious effects on health.

Orthopaedic problems such as rupture of the cruciate ligaments is more likely to occur in overweight dogs. This condition, which often requires surgical intervention, is very common in the older Labrador and may present as a sudden-onset complete lameness, or a gradually-worsening hind leg lameness. Dogs frequently develop heart disease in old age, and obesity puts significant extra demands on the cardiovascular system, with potentially serious consequences. Obesity is also a predisposing cause of non-insulin dependent diabetes mellitus, and has many other detrimental effects on health, including reducing resistance to infection and increasing anaesthetic and surgical risks. Once obesity is present, activity tends to decrease and it becomes even more necessary to decrease energy intake; otherwise more body weight is gained and the situation is made worse.

Labrador puppies are genetically predisposed to the development of juvenile obesity. This is often made much worse by the public image of the roly-poly Labrador puppy encouraged by the media. These overweight puppies are more prone to the development of skeletal problems such as hip dysplasia and osteochondritis. They also then have a lifelong predisposition to adult obesity with the multitude of risks this brings. Labradors, especially bitches, are also more likely to develop diabetes mellitus if they are overweight.

Prevention of obesity in the Labrador is essential to avoid such conditions as described above, but can be a constant challenge for the owner of a dog born thinking the whole world is edible.

Energy is only available from the fat, carbohydrate and protein in a dog's diet. A gram of fat provides 2 1/4 times as much energy as a gram of carbohydrate or protein and so high energy requirements are best met by feeding a relatively high-fat diet. Dogs rarely develop the cardiovascular conditions, such as atherosclerosis and coronary artery disease, that have been associated with high fat intake in humans.

Owners may think that protein is the source of energy needed for exercise and performance, but this is not true. Protein is a relatively poor source of energy because a large amount of the energy theoretically available from it is lost in 'meal-induced heat'. Meal-induced heat is the metabolic heat 'wasted' in the digestion, absorption and utilisation of the protein. Fat and carbohydrates are better sources of energy for performance.

For obese or obesity-prone dogs a low energy

Ch. Harbortop's Redwick Valhalla MH (Am. Can. Ch. Harbortops August Knight– Mallard's Norwegian Sweet) pictured at two and half years. He is a conformation champion, a Master Hunter and a super hunting companion. The energy needs of a working dog must be considered when planning a diet. *Photo courtesy: Steve and Julie Kirk.*

intake is indicated, and there are now specially prepared diets that have a very low energy density; those which are most effective have a high fibre content. Your veterinary surgeon will advise you about the most appropriate type of diet if you have such a problem dog. Incidentally, if you do have an overweight Labrador it is important to seek veterinary advice in case it is associated with some other medical condition.

CHOOSING A DIET

The first important consideration to make when selecting a maintenance diet, is that it should meet the energy requirements of your dog. In some situations, specially formulated high-energy, or low-energy diets will be needed to achieve this. Other nutrients that must be provided in the diet include essential amino acids (from dietary protein), essential fatty acids (from dietary fat), minerals and vitamins. Carbohydrates are not an essential dietary component for dogs, because they can synthesise sufficient glucose from other sources.

Do not fall into the trap of thinking that if a diet is good for a human it must be good for a dog. There are many differences between a human's nutritional needs and those of the dog. For example, humans need a supply of vitamin C in the diet, but under normal circumstances a dog can synthesise its own vitamin C, and so a dietary source is not essential. The amount of nutrients that a dog needs will vary according to its stage of life, environment and activity level. For the rest of this section, life-cycle feeding will be discussed.

FEEDING FOR GROWTH

Growing animals have tissues that are actively developing and growing in size, and so it is not surprising that they have a relatively higher requirement for energy, protein, vitamins and minerals than their adult counterparts (based on the daily intake of these nutrients per kg of body weight).

Birth weight usually doubles in seven to ten days and puppies should gain 1-2 grams/day/lb (2-4 grams/day/kg) of anticipated adult weight. An important key to the successful rearing of neonates is to reduce the puppies' energy loss by maintaining their environmental temperature, as well as by ensuring sufficient energy intake. Bitch's milk is of particular importance to the puppy during the first few hours of life, as this early milk (called colostrum) provides some passive immunity to the puppy because of the maternal antibodies it contains. These will help to protect the puppy until it can produce its own immune response to any challenge from infectious agents.

Survival rate is greatly decreased in puppies who do not get colostrum from their mother. Orphaned puppies are best fed a proprietary milk replacer, according to the manufacturer's recommendations, unless a foster mother can be found. Your veterinary surgeon will be able to help if you find yourself in such a situation.

Obesity must be avoided during puppyhood, as so-called juvenile obesity will increase the number of fat cells in the body, and so predispose the animal to obesity for the rest of its life. Overeating is most likely to occur when puppies are fed free choice (ad lib) throughout the day, particularly if there is competition between littermates. A better method is to feed a puppy a daily ration appropriate to its body weight divided into two to four meals per day – the number decreasing as it gets older. Any food remaining after twenty minutes should be removed.

In 1987 growth studies were carried out using two groups of Labrador puppies, one group fed free-choice and the other group fed twice daily for 30 minutes. This showed that the time-restricted group consumed less food but still achieved similar adult size to the group fed ad lib. By consuming less food the puppies were less likely to develop diseases of over-nutrition. Limiting food intake in growing Labrador retriever puppies has also been associated with fewer signs of hip dysplasia.

> **'If you do have an overweight Labrador, it is important to seek veterinary advice'**

Labradors seem to be born with a love of food, and you will rarely come across picky feeder.

Photo: Amanda Bulbeck.

It is best to feed a growing puppy on a proprietary pet food that has been specially formulated to meet its growing needs.

Photo: Amanda Bulbeck.

Proper growth and development is dependent upon a sufficient intake of essential nutrients, and if you consider how rapidly a puppy grows, usually achieving half its adult weight by four months of age, it is not surprising that nutritional deficiencies, excesses or imbalances can have disastrous results, especially in the larger breeds of dog. Deficiency diseases are rarely seen in veterinary practice nowadays, mainly because proprietary pet foods contain more than sufficient amounts of the essential nutrients. When a deficiency disease is diagnosed it is usually associated with an unbalanced home-made diet. A classical example of this is dogs fed on an all-meat diet. Meat is very low in calcium but high in phosphorus, and demineralisation of bones occurs on this type of diet. This leads to very thin bones that fracture easily, frequently resulting in folding fractures caused simply by weight-bearing.

Development of a good skeleton results from an interaction of genetic, environmental, and nutritional influences. The genetic component can be influenced by the breeder in a desire to improve the breed. Environmental influences, including housing and activity level, can be controlled by the new puppy owner with good advice from the breeder. However, nutrition is one of the most important factors influencing correct development of the puppy's bones and muscles.

In growing puppies it is particularly important to provide minerals, but in the correct proportions to each other. The calcium:phosphorus ratio should ideally be 1.2-1.4:1, and certainly within the wider range of 1-2:1. If there is more phosphorus than calcium in the diet (i.e. an inverse calcium:phosphorus ratio), normal bone development may be affected. Care also has to be taken to avoid feeding too much mineral. A diet for growing puppies should not contain more than two per cent calcium. Excessive calcium intake actually causes stunting of growth, and an intake of 3.3 per cent calcium has been shown to result in serious skeletal deformities, including deformities of the carpus, osteochondritis dissecans (OCD), wobbler syndrome and hip dysplasia. These are common diseases, and while other factors such as genetic inheritance may also be involved, excessive mineral intake should be considered a risk factor in all cases.

If a diet already contains sufficient calcium, it is dangerously easy to increase the calcium content to well over three per cent if you give mineral supplements as well. Some commercially available treats and snacks are very high in salt, protein and calories. They can significantly upset a carefully-balanced diet, and it is advisable to ask your veterinary surgeon's opinion of the various treats available and to use them only very occasionally.

A growing puppy is best fed a proprietary pet food that has been specifically formulated to meet its nutritional needs. Those that are available both tinned and dry are especially suitable to rear even the youngest of puppies. Homemade diets may theoretically be adequate, but it is difficult to ensure that all the nutrients are provided in an available form. The only way to be sure about the adequacy of a diet is to

have it analysed for its nutritional content *and* to put it through controlled feeding trials.

Supplements should only be used with rations that are known to be deficient, in order to provide whatever is missing from the diet. With a complete balanced diet *nothing* should be missing. If you use supplements with an already balanced diet, you could create an imbalance, and/or provide excessive amounts of nutrients, particularly minerals.

Nutritional management alone is not sufficient to prevent developmental bone disease. However, we can prevent some skeletal disease by feeding appropriate amounts of a good-quality balanced diet. Dietary deficiencies are of minimal concern with the ever-increasing range of commercial diets specifically prepared for young growing dogs. The potential for harm is in overnutrition from excess consumption and supplementation.

FEEDING FOR PREGNANCY
AND LACTATION
There is no need to increase the amount of food being fed to a bitch during early and mid-pregnancy, but there will be an increased demand for energy (i.e. carbohydrates and fats collectively), protein, minerals and vitamins during the *last* three weeks. A bitch's nutritional requirements will be maximum during lactation, particularly if she has a large litter to feed. Avoid giving calcium supplementation during pregnancy, as a high intake can frustrate calcium availability during milk production, and can increase the chances of eclampsia (also called 'milk fever' or puerperal tetany) occurring.

During pregnancy a bitch should maintain her body weight and condition. If she loses weight her energy intake needs to be increased. A specifically formulated growth-type diet is recommended to meet her nutritional needs at this time. If a bitch is on a diet formulated for this stage of her life, and she develops eclampsia, or has had previous episodes of the disease, your veterinary surgeon may advise calcium supplementation. If given during pregnancy, this is

'Nutritional management alone is not sufficient to prevent developmental bone disease'

A bitch's nutritional needs will be maximum during lactation, particularly if she has a large litter to feed.

Photo: Carol Ann Johnson.

only advisable during the very last few days of pregnancy when milk let-down is occurring, and preferably is given only during lactation (i.e. *after* whelping).

FEEDING FOR MAINTENANCE AND OLD AGE

The objective of good nutrition is to provide all the energy and essential nutrients that a dog needs in sufficient amounts to avoid deficiency, and at the same time to limit their supply so as not to cause over-nutrition or toxicity. Some nutrients are known to play a role in disease processes, and it is prudent to avoid unnecessarily high intakes of these whenever possible. The veterinary surgeons at Hill's Science and Technology Centre in Topeka, Kansas, are specialists in canine clinical nutrition and they are particularly concerned about the potential health risks associated with too high an intake of Protein, Sodium (salt) and Phosphorus during a dog's adult life.

These nutrients are thought to have an important and serious impact once disease is present, particularly in heart and kidney diseases. Kidney failure and heart failure are very common in older dogs and it is believed to be important to avoid feeding diets high in these nutrients to such an 'at risk' group of dogs. Furthermore, these nutrients may be detrimental to dogs even before there is any evidence of disease. It is known that salt, for example, can be retained in dogs with subclinical heart disease, before there

is any outward evidence of illness. Salt retention is an important contributing factor in the development of fluid retention (congestion), swelling of the limbs (oedema) and dropsy (ascites).

A leading veterinary cardiologist in the USA has claimed that 40 per cent of dogs over five years of age, and 80 per cent of dogs over ten years have some change in the heart – either endocardiosis and myocardial fibrosis (or both). Both of these lesions may reduce heart function. Phosphorus retention is an important consequence of advancing kidney disease which encourages mineral deposition in the soft tissues of the body, including the kidneys themselves, a condition known as nephrocalcinosis. Such deposits damage the kidneys even more, and hasten the onset of kidney failure.

As a dog ages there are two major factors that determine its nutritional needs:

1. The dog's changing nutritional requirements due to the effects of age on organ function and metabolism
2. The increased likelihood of the presence of subclinical diseases, many of which have a protracted course during which nutrient intake may influence progression of the condition.

Many Labrador owners are aware of a condition called gastric dilatation and torsion, commonly known as 'bloat'. This potentially life-threatening condition was previously thought to

Am. Can. Ch. McDerry's Midwatch Starkist Am. Can CDX, AWC, pictured at eleven years of age. As a dog gets older, diet should be reassessed.

Photo courtesy: Marion Lyons.

be due to the ingestion of a high-fat or carbohydrate meal. Current thinking is that bloat is due to aerophagia (the intake of large amounts of air with a meal), common in greedy individuals, and the predisposing factors may be:

Genetic make-up
Competitive feeding
Strenuous exercise around meal times
Excitement at feeding time.

The last three factors encourage rapid eating.

Special highly digestible diets are available from veterinary surgeons to feed to at-risk indi-

viduals. Energy requirements usually decrease with increasing age, and food intake should be adjusted accordingly. Also the dietary intake of some nutrients needs to be minimised – in particular, protein, phosphorus, sodium and total energy intake. Dietary intake of other nutrients may need to be increased to meet the needs of some older dogs, notably essential fatty acids, some vitamins, some specific amino acids and zinc. Unlike humans, calcium and phosphorus do not need to be supplemented in ageing dogs – indeed to do so may prove detrimental.

INTERPRETATION OF LABELLING ON PET FOODS

Labelling laws differ from one country to the next. For example, pet foods sold in the USA must carry a Guaranteed Analysis, which states a maximum or a minimum amount for the various nutrients in the food. Pet foods sold in Europe must carry a Typical (as fed) Analysis, which is a declaration of the average amount of nutrients found from analysis of the product.

'COMPLETE' VERSUS 'COMPLEMENTARY'

In the UK a pet food must declare whether it is 'complete' or 'complementary'. A 'complete' pet food must provide all the nutrients required to satisfy the needs of the group of pet animals for which it is recommended. At the time of writing there is no obligation for a manufacturer to submit such a diet to feeding trials to ensure that it is adequate.

In the USA some manufacturers submit their pet foods to the feeding trials approved by the Association of American Feed Control Officials (AAFCO) to ensure that they meet the nutritional requirements of the National Research Council (e.g. the Hill's Pet Nutrition range of Science Diet products). A 'complementary' pet food needs to be fed with some other foodstuff in order to meet the needs of the animal. Anyone feeding a complementary food as a substantial part of a dog's ration is obliged to find out what it should be fed with, in order to balance the ration. Failure to do so could result in serious deficiency or imbalance of nutrients.

DRY MATTER

The water content of pet foods varies greatly, particularly in canned products. In the USA there is a legal maximum limit (78 per cent) which cannot be exceeded, but no such limit is in force in Europe and some European canned petfoods contain as much as 86 per cent water. Legislation now makes it compulsory for the water content to be declared on the label and this is important, because to compare one pet food with another, one should consider the percentage of a nutrient in the dry matter of food.

For example, two pet foods may declare the protein content to be 10 per cent in the Typical Analysis printed on the label. If one product contains 75 per cent water it has 25 per cent dry matter, so the protein content is actually 10/25 x 100 = 40 per cent. If the other product contains 85 per cent water, the protein content is 10/15 x 100 = 66.6 per cent. This type of calculation (called Dry Weight Analysis) becomes even more important when comparing canned with dry products, as the water content of dry food is usually only 7.5-12 per cent.

You can only effectively compare pet foods if you know:

1. The food's energy density
2. The dry weight analysis of the individual nutrients.

COST

The only valid way to compare the cost of one food against another is to compare the daily feeding costs to meet all the needs of your dog. A high-energy, nutritionally-concentrated type of diet might cost more to buy per kilogram of food, but it could be cheaper to feed on a cost per day basis. Conversely, a poor quality, poorly digestible diet may be cheaper per kilogram to buy, but actually cost more per day to feed, because you need to feed much more food to meet the dog's requirements. The only valid reason for feeding a food is that it meets the nutri-

tional requirements of your dog. To do that, you need to read between the marketing strategies of the manufacturers and select a diet that you know provides your dog with what it needs.

HOME-MADE DIETS

What about home-made recipes? Well, theoretically it is possible to make a home-made diet that will meet all the nutritional requirements of a dog, and all foodstuffs have some nutritional value, *but* not all published recipes may actually achieve what they claim. The reason is that there is no strict quality control of ingredients, and the bioavailability of nutrients may vary from one ingredient source to another. If you feed a correctly balanced home-made diet, meals are often time-consuming to prepare, usually need the addition of a vitamin/mineral supplement, and if prepared accurately can be expensive. Variations in raw ingredients will cause fluctuations in nutritional value.

The only way to be absolutely sure that a home-made diet has the nutritional profile that you want is to mix *all* the food ingredients plus supplements, treats, snacks, scraps etc. in a large pot, homogenise them and have a sample analysed chemically (this costs well over £100 (US$160) for a partial analysis). Compare this analytical content with the published levels for nutrient requirements.

You may feel that feeding an existing home-made recipe passed on to you, or developed over a number of years is adequate. But how do you know? What is the phosphorus level of the diet that you are feeding? An undesirably high level of intake may take a long time before it results in obvious problems.

Sometimes the condition of your dog(s) will give you an idea that all is not well with the diet you are feeding. One of the most common questions asked by breeders at dog shows is: "Can you recommend a diet that will keep weight on my dogs?" Unless there is a medical problem (and in such cases you should always seek vet-

'Sometimes the condition of your dog(s) will give you an idea that all is not well with the diet you are feeding'

erinary attention first), the only reason dogs usually have difficulty maintaining their weight is simply that they have an inadequate energy intake. This does not mean that they are not eating well – they could be eating like a horse, but if the food is relatively low in energy content, and if it is poorly digestible, your dog may be unable to eat sufficient food to meet its energy needs. Large bulky faeces are an indicator of low digestibility. A poor-looking, dull, dry or scurfy coat, poor skin and other external signs of unthriftiness may also be an indicator of poor nutrition. How many 'poor-doers' and dogs with recurrent infections are on a diet with a marginal nutritional level of adequacy?

SUMMARY

The importance of nutrition has been known for many years and yet, sadly, it is still surrounded by too many old wives' tales, myths and unsubstantiated claims. The emergence of clinical nutrition as a subject in its own right has set the stage for the future. Hopefully, in the future we shall hear about the benefits and dangers of different feeding practices from scientists who can base their statements on fact, not merely opinion. Already we know that an ill dog has different nutritional requirements to a healthy dog. In some cases, dietary management can even offer an alternative way to manage clinical cases. For example, we currently have the ability to dissolve struvite stones in the urinary bladder simply by manipulating dietary intake instead of having to resort to surgery.

Please note, dietary management is not 'alternative medicine'. Proper nutrition is the key to everything that a living animal has to do, be it work, play, or repairing tissues after an injury. It is not an option; it is a crucial part of looking after an animal properly. If you own a dog then you should at least ensure that the food you give supplies all his/her needs and avoids the excessive intake of energy or nutrients that may play a role in diseases which your pet could develop.

6 THE BREED STANDARDS

So far as the history of the breed is concerned, first came the dog, then came the breed custodians, then the Kennel Club, then The Labrador Retriever Club and with it the Breed Standard(s) – the written blueprint for the breed!

The chapter on the origins and history of the breed discusses in more detail the early possible ancestors of the modern Labrador Retriever, which were first imported into Britain early in the 19th century. In his introduction to *The Popular Retrievers* the Hon. Arthur Holland-Hibbert, later Lord Knutsford, contended that the modern Labrador is mainly a pure descendant of the St John's Newfoundland. He admits that when imported "he was as freely crossed as those that produced the flat-coated sort."

It is worth looking at the old breed points describing the now extinct St John's Newfoundland or Labrador Dog. This Standard description has many points in common with that for the modern Labrador Retriever, and also some differences, notably the coat and tail.

BREED POINTS FOR THE ST JOHN'S NEWFOUNDLAND OR LABRADOR DOG

The following is an extract from the third edition, published in 1879, of *The Dog, in health and disease* by Stonehenge (Editor of *The Field*).

POINTS	VALUE
Skull	15
Nose and Jaws	5
Ears and Eyes	5
Neck	5
Shoulder and Chest	10
Loins and Back	10
Quarters and Stifles	10
Legs, knees and hocks	10
Feet	5
Tail	5
Coat	5
Colour	5
Symmetry	5
Temperament	5
Total	**100**

The St John's or Labrador Dog. Reproduced from The Dog in Health and Disease by Stonehenge, 1879. Courtesy of Richard Edwards.

SKULL is wide, but not so much as in the larger variety; flat at the top, but with a slight furrow down the middle; moderately long, with a brow only just rising from the straight line; a very high occipital protuberance.

NOSE AND JAWS These must be long enough to carry a hare, and wide enough for the development of the nasal organ of scent, with open nostrils. Teeth level.

EARS AND EYES The ears are small and pendant close to the head. The hair short and a very slight fringe at the edge. Eyes of medium size, intelligent and soft.

NECK Moderately long, that is to say, as long as it can be got; imported and pure Labradors being often too short to stoop for a scent without difficulty.

SHOULDERS AND CHEST The chest is apt to be barrel-like, but it is better somewhat narrow and deep, giving lodgement for more oblique shoulders, and rendering the dog able to stoop.

BACK AND LOINS Should be strong and well coupled, with deep back ribs.

QUARTERS AND STIFLES Bent stifles are seldom met within this breed, but they should not be confined in width. The quarters are generally straight, but a slight slope is by no means a disadvantage.

LEGS, KNEES AND HOCKS These ought always to be straight, muscular and strong in bone.

FEET are large, and should be specially attended to, as they are apt to be flat and thin-soled.

TAIL is bushy without setter feather. It is carried high during excitement, but should not be curled over the back.

COAT is moderately short, but wavy, from its length being too great for absolute smoothness. It is glossy and close, admitting wet with difficulty to the skin, owing to its oiliness, but possessing no under-coat.

COLOUR is a rich jet black without rustiness. No quantity of white is admissible, but the best bred puppies often have a white toe or star.

SYMMETRY is of some importance, as indicating adaption to the work this dog has to do. It is often considerable.

TEMPERAMENT Without a good disposition and temper, no dog can be made into a good retriever, and therefore this point should be carefully examined in it.

THE EARLY BREED CUSTODIANS

As we read in the chapter on the origins and history of the breed, the breed's earliest custodians were male aristocrats and gentry: the Earls of Malmesbury (Malmesbury), the Dukes of Buccleugh and their brother Lord George Scott (Buccleugh), Lord Knutsford (Munden), the Earl of Home and Mr Radclyffe (Zelstone). All of these men owned early imported dogs. By 1913 the breed's greatest benefactress, and its most influential lady, came on to the scene. This was Mrs Quintin Dick, later Lorna, Countess Howe (Banchory). During this time the breed was in the hands of devoted breeders and guardians, yet still there was no Breed Standard, just an 'understanding' among a small, select group.

Today, over a century and a half later, the Labrador has become this country's most popular breed and is owned by everyone from lords to labourers. In 1995 for instance, over 32,000 Labradors were KC registered in Britain. However, although the breed is no longer the private preserve of a small nucleus of sporting gentlemen, its custodianship by today's modern breeders still remains vital.

THE ESTABLISHMENT OF THE KENNEL CLUB

The publication, *The History of the Kennel Club,* states that in the middle of the 19th century the prosperous and leisured Victorians had a passion for exhibitions and instructive entertainment. This was the era of the dog show and, later on, field trials. Inevitably, as these competitive events gained momentum there arose a need to organise a controlling body to legislate on canine matters.

On April 4th 1873, the Kennel Club was founded in London by a team of 12 gentlemen led by S.E. Shirley M.P. Their first task was to compile a KC stud book of show records, dating from 1859. Ten simple rules relating to dog shows were written which, if adopted by societies, meant that the societies would be 'recognised' by the KC and their winners would be eligible for stud book entry. Next, the monthly *Kennel Gazette* was published, and in 1880 the controversial 'Universal Registration' system followed. It was in 1903 that the Labrador first had separate classes, in the KC show at Crystal Palace. According to the stud book, Challenge Certificates were on offer but none were awarded.

The Labrador first appeared in the KC's classification of separate breeds in 1904, and in that same year breed history was made, by the man who had probably made it possible, when the Hon. A. Holland-Hibbert's Munden Single became the first Labrador bitch to win a CC. Mrs H.C. Palmer's Dunboyne was the first dog to win a CC (both at the KC show at Crystal Palace). In 1904 Single was also the first Labrador to compete in a field trial, winning a Certificate of Merit and attracting much admiration.

Since then the breed has, in one sense, never looked back. Numbers competing at shows and in trials are now enormous. Sadly, however, the breed is now split, by and large, into two populations, competing separately for success in the field or in the show ring.

THE LABRADOR RETRIEVER BREED CLUB

On April 5th 1916, the Labrador Retriever Club was formed. The inaugural meeting took place in London at the Ladies' Kennel Association rooms, Belfast Chambers in Regent Street. Nine of the most influential Labrador people of that time attended the meeting. The club's first elected chairman was the Hon. Arthur Holland-Hibbert, and Mrs Quintin Dick was elected secretary and treasurer. Both held these posts for a considerable length of time, giving the club the stability and commitment it needed. The actual committee read like Burke's Peerage!

One of the main factors that influenced the formation of the club was the fact that the Kennel Club allowed inter-bred Retrievers to be registered under whatever breed they most resembled. This unsatisfactory arrangement came to a head at Crufts in 1915, when the black Labrador Horton Max, exhibited by Alan

Shuter, won the CC. Max was by a purebred Flatcoated Retriever named Ch. Darenth, and his relatives were also winning in the Flatcoat ring.

A meeting was subsequently held and attended by interested parties from both breeds. They sent a petition to the KC which asked that none other than purebred Labradors should compete in Labrador classes in shows. The desired change eventually came by simply altering the conditions of registration. However, it was still permissible to register and trial inter-bred Retrievers and, for that matter, cross-bred Retrievers. The last inter-bred registration at the KC appears to have been as late as 1971.

After the aforementioned episode The Labrador Retriever Club was 'born'. Lorna, Countess Howe wrote: "The main object of the club was to encourage and protect the breed which had proved so eminently successful for work and which was rapidly coming to the fore as a force to be reckoned with in the judging for Best in Show at Championship Shows."

Two of the club's first duties were to draw up a set of rules and a standard of points, i.e. the first Breed Standard for the Labrador Retriever. At last the chapter proper can begin!

THE FIRST BREED STANDARD (1916)

The Breed Standard drawn up by the committee of the Labrador Retriever Club in 1916 was accepted by the Kennel Club and remained unchanged until 1950. At trials, special prizes were offered to encourage breeders of working dogs to aim for the Breed Standard. Indeed, the club specials and trophies were awarded on condition that: "Pedigrees must be produced if required, to prove that the winners' parents and grandparents were Labrador Retrievers."

The first Standard was written by a team who had the working abilities of the breed very much in mind and at heart. Certain aspects of the Standard indicate that the writers were at pains to clarify the differences between the Labrador, its relative the Flatcoated Retriever, and the old Wavy-coated Retriever. This is the wording used by the committee of The Labrador Retriever Club, 1916 (Extract from *The Labrador Retriever Club Year Book 1985*):

GENERAL APPEARANCE

The general appearance of the Labrador should be that of a strongly built, short coupled, very active dog. Compared with the Wavy or Flat-coated Retriever he should be wider in the head, wider through the chest and ribs, wider and stronger over the loins and hindquarters. The coat should be close, short, dense and free from feather.

DETAILED DESCRIPTION

Head: The skull should be wide, giving brain room; there should be a slight 'stop', i.e. the brow should be slightly pronounced so that the skull is not in a straight line with the nose. The head should be clean cut and free from fleshy cheeks. The jaws should be long and powerful and quite free from snipiness or exaggeration in length; the nose should be wide and the nostrils well developed. The ears should hang moderately close to the head, rather far back, should be set somewhat low and not be large and heavy. The eyes should be of a medium size, expressing great intelligence and good temper, and can be brown, yellow or black.

Neck and chest: The neck should be long and powerful and the shoulders long and sloping. The chest must be of good width and depth, the ribs well sprung, and the loin wide and strong, stifles well turned, and the hindquarters well developed and of great power.

Legs and feet: The legs must be straight from the shoulder to the ground, and the feet compact with toes well arched and pads well developed; the hocks should be well bent, and the dog must be neither cow-hocked nor move too wide behind; he must stand and move true all round on legs and feet.

Tail: The tail is a distinctive feature of the breed; it should be very thick towards the base, gradually tapering towards the tip, of medium length and should be practically free from any feathering, but should be clothed thickly all round with the Labrador's short thick dense coat, thus giving that peculiar 'rounded' appearance, which has been described as the 'otter' tail. The tail may be carried gaily, but should not curl too far over the back.

Coat: The coat is another very distinctive feature of the breed; it should be short, very dense and without wave, and should give a fairly hard feeling to the hand.

Colour: The coat is generally black, free from any rustiness and any white markings, except possibly a small spot on the chest. Other whole colours are permissible.

The first Standard was comprehensive and concise, with the exception of the sections on the Labrador's head and distinctive tail, where we are treated to more detail in order to contrast the breed with the Flatcoated Retriever. In the years that followed, the suggested heights of 22 to 22.5 inches for dogs and 21.5 to 22 inches for bitches were in use, but these were not officially part of the 1916 Standard.

THE YELLOW LABRADOR BREED STANDARD (1925)

The Labrador Retriever in Britain did at one time almost split into two separate varieties (of the same breed), namely yellows and blacks! If separate registration had been granted then the two colours (chocolates/livers were not even under consideration at that time, even though they existed) would have competed apart from one another for CCs, something which today seems absurd. In 1925, The Yellow Labrador Retriever Club was founded and its own Yellow Standard was drawn up. In her classic book, *The Complete Labrador Retriever,* Helen Warwick writes:

"A Yellow standard was drawn up as any standard has to be, to list the correct points and draw attention to the undesirable features prevalent at the time of setting up a standard. There was such a divergence of type, make and shape in those days that it became imperative to establish it for the sake of the colour's future; for uniformity of type and the elimination of as many structural evils as possible.

"The following points were supereminent: ears badly carried, often too large, sometimes near prick and poorly set; overly short necks and upright shoulder placement, resulting in a stilted paddling front gait, topaz eyes, which, even if they did upon occasion harmonise with the coat had an ill-disposed look that is alien to the breed. Colours were uneven; there was great flecking or patches of darker on lighter or vice versa; large white patches on the most unconventional places. There were poor feet and other flaws."

Fortunately the two colours were not divided. The unofficial Yellow Standard was written in 1925, abandoned as obsolete in 1959, and thereafter the 'Black' Standard was followed. It is particularly interesting to note that the Yellow Standard actually endorsed 'throatiness', a feature otherwise regarded as a flaw.

In a review from the weekly Labrador column of the *Kennel Gazette* in 1936, Richard Anderton argued that there was no good reason to tolerate throatiness in the yellows any more than in the blacks, nor does he believe throatiness was limited to that colour, having seen many throaty blacks. Today, throatiness is not a common fault in the show Labrador at all and is a rarity in the working Labrador. Nowadays, when throatiness is evident, it shows no colour prejudice!

THE YELLOW LABRADOR STANDARD (1925)

GENERAL APPEARANCE: The general appearance of the Yellow Labrador should be that of a short coupled, strongly built and active dog, deep through the heart and well ribbed up, with strong loins and hindquarters.
COAT: The coat should be short, thick without wave, and practically a double coat, the undercoat being thick and woolly, the overcoat being smooth.
COLOUR: May vary from fox red to cream, without white except on chest or the extreme tips of the toes. The coat should be of a whole colour and not of a flaked appearance.
HEAD: The skull should be broad, with brow slightly pronounced, with long and powerful jaws, but free from snipiness. The nose should be wide and the nostrils well developed, black in colour, or may harmonise with the coat. The eyes should be dark brown in colour or to match the coat, with dark rims. The ears small and slightly elevated, and should hang close to the

head; in colour they should be darker than, or the same as, the coat.
NECK AND CHEST: The neck should be stocky and should be inclined to be throaty. The chest wide and of good depth. Shoulders square in front and running well back from the point.
LEGS AND FEET: Legs should be short and straight from the shoulder with plenty of bone, and not back at the knee. The feet compact, circular and strongly made, with well developed pads.
TAIL: The tail should be thick towards the base, gradually tapering, round or otterlike in appearance, and may curl slightly, or droop.

THE BREED STANDARD (1950)

The 1916 Standard was the official 'word picture' of the breed until 1950, when it was revised and subsequently adopted by the Kennel Club. This later document gives a fuller description of the breed points, yet it is still essentially a version of the original Standard.

The most notable differences are those of eye colour and stop; from brown, yellow or black we go to brown or hazel, from slight stop we go to pronounced stop. Additions include reference to all three colours, with shades of yellow also being described. The undercoat is now referred to as being weather-resisting, desired heights are now formally included, bite is described for the first time and a list of faults appears, to help keep breeders and judges 'in line'. No regularised weight was included, but 56 to 65 pounds is sometimes quoted in dog books of this time.

THE 1950 BREED STANDARD
GENERAL APPEARANCE: The general appearance of the Labrador should be that of a strongly built, short coupled, very active dog, broad in the skull, broad and deep through the chest and ribs, broad and strong over the loins and hindquarters. The coat close, short with dense undercoat and free from feather. The dog must move neither too wide in front or close behind; he must stand and move true all round on legs and feet.
HEAD AND SKULL: The skull should be broad with a pronounced stop so that the skull is

not in a straight line with the nose. The head should be clean cut without fleshy cheeks. The jaws should be medium length and powerful and free from snipiness. The nose wide and the nostrils well developed.

EYES: The eyes of medium size expressing intelligence and good temper, should be brown or hazel.

EARS: Should not be large and heavy and should hang close to the head and set rather far back.

MOUTH: Teeth should be sound and strong. The lower teeth just behind but touching the upper.

NECK: Should be clean, strong and powerful and set into well placed shoulders.

FOREQUARTERS: The shoulders should be long and sloping. The forelegs well boned and straight from the shoulder to the ground when viewed from either the front or the side. The dog must move neither too wide nor too close in front.

BODY: The chest must be of good width and depth with well spring ribs. The back should be short coupled.

HINDQUARTERS: The loins must be wide and strong with well turned stifles; hindquarters well developed and not sloping to the tail. The hocks should be slightly bent and the dog must neither be cow-hocked nor move too close behind.

FEET: Should be round and compact with well arched toes and well developed pads.

TAIL: The tail is a distinctive feature of the breed; it should be very thick towards the base gradually tapering towards the tip, of medium length and practically free from any feathering, but clothed thickly all round with the Labrador's short thick dense coat, thus giving that peculiar 'rounded' appearance which has been described as the 'otter' tail. The tail may be carried gaily, but should not curl over the back.

COAT: The coat is another distinctive feature of the breed, it should be short and dense and without wave, with a weather-resisting undercoat, and should give a fairly hard feeling to the hand.

COLOUR: The colour is generally black, chocolate or yellow, which may vary from fox-red to cream, free from any white markings. A small white spot on the chest is allowable, the coat should be of a whole colour and not of a flecked appearance.

WEIGHT AND SIZE: Desired height for dogs 22 to 22.5 inches; bitches 21.5 to 22 inches.

FAULTS: Under or overshot mouth; no undercoat; bad action; feathering; snipiness on the head; large or heavy ears; cow-hocked; tail curved over back.

THE 1982 AND 1986 REVISIONS

The 1950 Breed Standard was later updated, but only in very minor ways. In 1982 the heights were converted to centimetres to comply with metrication. The heights for dogs were now desired at 56 to 57 cm and bitches 54 to 56 cms. A clause on testicles was added, and males were required to have two, both apparently normal and fully descended into the scrotum.

In 1986 the Kennel Club requested that Breed Standards should conform to a set layout and use uniform terminology. This Breed Standard is currently in use, and is the one which I shall later use for discussion alongside the current American Standard. In 1986 the words "Weight and" were finally dropped, as weight had never been included, only height. The section on faults was removed and replaced with a blanket statement which appears in all Breed Standards. It reads:

"Any departure from the foregoing points should be considered a fault and the seriousness with which the fault should be regarded should be in exact proportion to its degree."

This is rather a perplexing and quantitative statement if taken literally. Does it give greater freedom for a more balanced evaluation, as opposed to fault judging? Or is it a pathetic evasion? It avoids the task of referring to specific faults, but probably does not help those who wish to learn about the breed.

THE FCI LABRADOR STANDARD

The British Labrador Retriever Breed Standard is the source for all others, because Britain is considered to be the breed's country of origin, certainly its country of development. The Federation Cynologique Internationale (FCI) is a huge international body to which many countries' Kennel Clubs are aligned. The FCI regards the Labrador as a British breed and uses the current British KC approved Standard. (See the 1986 version discussed below.)

THE AMERICAN BREED STANDARDS
The American Kennel Club (AKC) was founded in 1884, and first recognised the Labrador Retriever as a separate breed in the late 1920s. Previously they had been classified merely as 'retrievers' along with the other varieties. Only a small number of Labradors had been imported into the USA prior to the First World War, and they were used for shooting.

The American Labrador Retriever Club Inc. was established at the beginning of the 1930s. Mrs Marshall Field was its first president, serving from 1931 to 1935, Franklin B. Lord and Robert Goelet were the vice-presidents, the treasurer/secretary was Wilton Lloyd-Smith and the board of directors included Marshall Field, William J. Hutchinson and Paul C. Pennoyer.

Initially the US Standard was exactly the same as the British (except for the spelling of the word 'colour'!). Neither included a desired height clause. However, when revisions followed, the differences between the two began to appear. Both Standards were revised in the 1950s. (See the 1950 British Breed Standard.) The official AKC Standard was approved on April 9th 1957, and contained a number of differences compared to that of the home country. These included:

Head: Slight stop (cf. pronounced stop in the British Standard). Jaws long (cf. jaws of medium length).
Mouth: Level mouth (cf. lower teeth just behind but touching the upper).
Eyes: Brown, yellow or black, but brown or black preferred (cf. brown or hazel).
Coat: Short, dense without wave and should give a fairly hard feeling to the hand (cf. Short, dense, without wave with weather-resisting undercoat and should give a fairly hard feeling to the hand).
Weight: Dogs: 60 to 75 lbs, Bitches: 55 to 70 lbs (cf. nil).
Height: Dogs: 22.5 to 24.5 inches, Bitches: 21.5

to 23.5 inches (cf. desired height Dogs: 22 to 22.5 inches, Bitches: 21.5 inches).
Faults: Nil (cf. Undershot or overshot mouth, no undercoat, feathering, snipiness on the head, large or heavy ears, cow-hocked, tail curled over back).

Here for the first time we see some significant deviations, notably height, as the American dogs were now expected to be generally taller than everywhere else in the world. No emphasis was placed on undercoat, one of the breed's most distinctive features, and the variations in head and eye colour describe a slightly different head type. One could also infer that the scissor bite was incorrect in USA since their Standard asked for a level bite.

However, during the 1990s the USA was to see its most controversial revision ever, a move that was finally endorsed by the AKC on March 31st 1994. This current Standard was proposed by the parent club, The Labrador Retriever Club Inc. It was opposed by many judges and breeders who considered it too long and wordy, but most of all it was disliked because it contained disqualifications. In her book *The Versatile Labrador Retriever*, published in 1994, Nancy Martin writes:

"I feel that some parts of this (the 1994) Standard are very good, but as a member of the parent club I voted against it for several reasons. It is too long, and I think it should be edited down to retain the pertinent points, striking out passages that are either unnecessary or redundant. One highly respected English Labrador authority has said: "What are they trying to do, write a book?" In comparing the British and American Standards, the former is short and to the point, covering everything briefly and concisely, and it is recognised by Labrador clubs and breeders throughout the world as the standard for the breed.

"It is unclear to me why our American Standard should be different from virtually all the other countries in the world. Dissimilar hunting conditions have been cited as an explanation for allowing a much taller dog in the US, but what about Australia, South Africa, Sweden

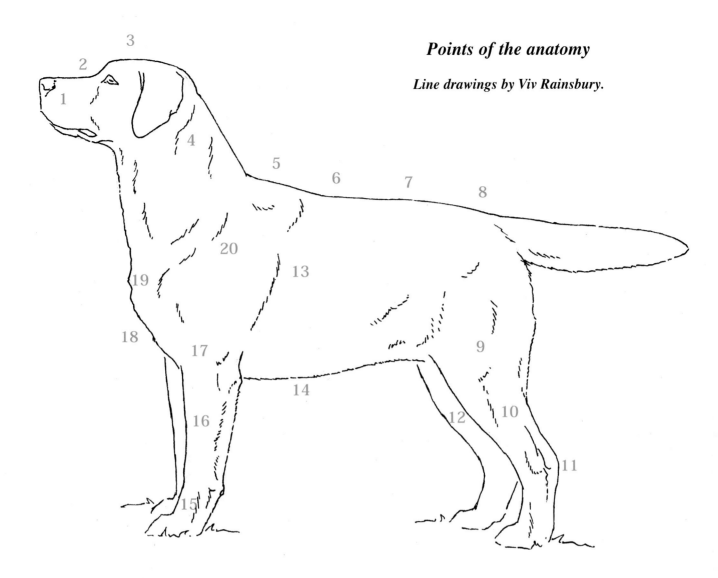

1. Muzzle
2. Stop
3. Skull
4. Neck
5. Withers
6. Back
7. Loin
8. Croup
9. Thigh
10 Second/Lower thigh

11. Hock
12. Stifle
13. Ribs
14. Brisket
15. Pastern
16. Forearm
17. Upper arm
18. Chest
19. Point of shoulder
20. Shoulder

or Finland? Surely they do not have the same hunting conditions as the UK, but each of these countries retains the Standard of the country that developed the breed. Does anyone seriously think that a Labrador that stands 24.5 inches can retrieve better than one that is 22 inches, or succeed better in the show ring?"

COMPARISON OF BREED STANDARDS
I propose to compare and discuss the world's two main Breed Standards, the British (revised in 1986) and the American (revised in 1994), by quoting the relevant section from each, followed by some personal comments. To do this it has been necessary to rearrange the order of some parts of the Standard, but all are included.

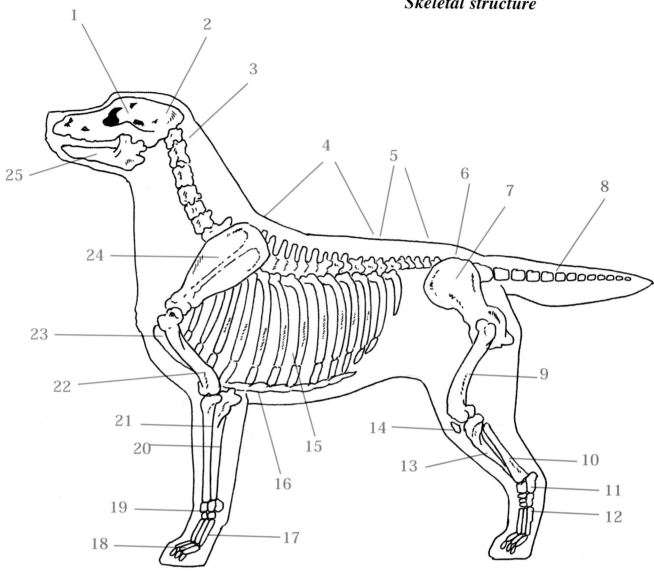

1. Cranium
2. Occiput
3. Cervical vertebrae (7)
4. Thoracic vertebrae (13)
5. Lumbar vertebrae (7)
6. Sacrum
7. Pelvis
8. Caudal/Coccygeal vertebrae
9. Femur
10. Fibula
11. Tarsals
12. Metatarsals
13. Tibia
14. Patella
15. Ribs
16. Sternum
17. Metacarpals
18. Phalanges
19. Carpals
20. Ulna
21. Radius
22. Humerus
23. Prosternum
24. Scapula
25. Mandible

GENERAL APPEARANCE

BRITISH: Strongly built, short coupled, very active; broad in skull; broad and deep through the chest and ribs; broad and strong over loins and hindquarters.

AKC: The Labrador Retriever is a strongly built, medium sized, short coupled dog, possessing a sound, athletic, well balanced conformation that enables it to function as a retrieving gun dog; the substance and soundness to hunt waterfowl or upland game for long hours under difficult conditions; the character and quality to win in the show ring; and the temperament to be a family companion.

Physical features and mental characteristics should denote a dog bred to perform as an efficient Retriever of game with a stable temperament suitable for a variety of pursuits beyond the hunting environment.

The most distinguishing characteristics of the Labrador Retriever are its short dense, weather-resistant coat; an 'otter' tail; a clean cut head with broad back-skull and moderate stop; powerful jaws; and its 'kind' friendly eyes, expressing character, intelligence and good temperament. Above all, the Labrador Retriever must be well balanced enabling it to move in the show ring or work in the field with little or no effort. The typical Labrador possesses style and quality without over refinement, and substance without lumber or cloddiness. The Labrador is bred primarily as a working gun dog; structure and soundness are of great importance.

In one glance we can see that the American section is verbose and repetitive. However, if it was pruned, I think it would be better than the British equivalent for the following reasons.

It refers to balance, an omission from the British Standard; it emphasises the hunting and retrieving functions of the breed, which amazingly the British standard does not; it clarifies right at the start the breed's classical distinguishing features – its coat, otter tail, head and expression; it refers to the need for substance without lumber or cloddiness, and any contem-

porary revision of the Standard does, I feel, need to make this very clear. In the show ring there is a tendency towards 'overdone' Labradors (more size and weight does not make a better Labrador); similarly at field trials there are many lightly built whippety-looking Labradors, built for speed rather than hours of steady work. Neither of these extremes are typical of the Breed Standard, but they are common in the breed today.

In her book *Labradors Today* Carole Coode writes: "Those that tend towards breeding Labradors too far either side of this desirable norm will have dogs that do not have the staying power, because they have no reserves of strength, or are so heavily or badly constructed that they tire too easily. We must always remember that the Breed Standard was drawn up by people who used the Labrador as a working dog ... even if we know that our dogs may never have the opportunity of fulfilling their role as retriever in the field."

CHARACTERISTICS AND TEMPERAMENT

BRITISH

Characteristics: Good tempered, very agile. Excellent nose, soft mouth, keen love of water. Adaptable, devoted companion. Temperament: Intelligent, keen and biddable, with a strong will to please. Kindly nature, with no trace of aggression, or undue shyness.

AKC

Temperament: True Labrador temperament is as much a hallmark of the breed as the 'otter' tail. The ideal disposition is one of a kindly outgoing tractable nature; eager to please and non-aggressive towards man or animal. The Labrador has much to appeal to people; his gentle ways, intelligence and adaptability make him an ideal dog. Aggressiveness towards humans or other animals, or any evidence of shyness in an adult, should be severely penalised.

The two British sections on Characteristics

and Temperment overlap. Perhaps if the breed's distinguishing features and working functions could have been included under 'characteristics' it might have read better. Use of the words 'very agile' always perplexes me. I associate the word with the meaning 'nimble', and fail to see how a sturdy, strongly built working dog could properly be described as being very agile. Athletic or active yes, but not 'very agile'.

However, both Standards describe Labrador temperament with deep understanding and both are admirable. Without doubt the good, kind, biddable and intelligent temperament of the Labrador is its greatest attribute. Such a marvellous nature makes the breed a pleasure to own and has enabled it to become so popular and so versatile. On the subject of bad temperament, I am reminded of what was written in the Standard for the old St. John's Newfoundland breed: "Without a good disposition and temper, no dog can be made into a good retriever." One only need add the words "or companion" and the statement remains true for the modern Labrador Retriever.

HEAD AND SKULL: EYES, EARS AND MOUTH

BRITISH
Skull: Broad with defined stop; clean cut without fleshy cheeks. Jaws of medium length, powerful, not snipey. Nose wide, nostrils well developed.
Eyes: Medium size expressing intelligence and good temper, brown or hazel.
Ears: Not large or heavy, hanging close to the head and set rather far back.
Mouth: Jaws and teeth strong, with perfect regular and complete scissor bite, i.e. the upper teeth closely overlapping the lower teeth and set square to the jaws.

AKC
The skull should be wide; well developed, but without exaggeration. The skull and foreface should be on parallel planes and of approximately equal length. There should be a moderate stop, the brow slightly pronounced so that the skull is not absolutely in a straight line with the nose. The brow ridges aid in defining the stop. The head should be clean cut and free from fleshy cheeks; the bony structure of the skull chiselled beneath the eye with no prominence in the cheek. The skull may show some median line; the occipital bone is not conspicuous in mature dogs. Lips should not be squared off or pendulous, but fall away in a curve towards the throat. A wedge-shaped head, or a head long and narrow in muzzle and back-skull is incorrect, as are massive, cheeky heads. The jaws are powerful and free from snipiness, the muzzle neither long and narrow nor short and stubby. The nose should be wide and the nostrils well developed. The nose should be black on black or yellow dogs, and brown on chocolates. Nose colour fading to a lighter shade is not a fault. A thoroughly pink nose or one lacking in any pigment is a disqualification.
Teeth: The teeth should be strong and regular with a scissor bite, the lower teeth just behind but touching the inner side of the upper incisors. A level bite is acceptable, but not desirable. Undershot, overshot or misaligned teeth are serious faults. Full dentition is preferred. Missing molars or pre-molars are serious faults.
Ears: The ears should hang moderately close to the head, set rather far back, and somewhat low on the skull, slightly above eye level. Ears should not be large and heavy but in proportion with the skull and reach to the inside of the eye when pulled forward.
Eyes: Kind friendly eyes imparting good temperament, intelligence and alertness are a hallmark of the breed. They should be of medium size, set well apart, and neither protruding nor deep set. Eye color should be brown in black and yellow Labradors, and brown or hazel in chocolates. Black or yellow eyes give a harsh expression and are undesirable.
Small eyes set close together, or round prominent eyes are not typical of the breed. Eye rims are black in black and yellow Labradors, and brown in chocolates. Eye rims without pigmentation is a disqualification.

THE HEAD

LEFT: Correct head: A well-balanced and typical head, with a kind expression.

BELOW: Incorrect: The head is overdone, with full cheeks and short in the muzzle. The eyes are round. It is similar to a Rottweiler's head.

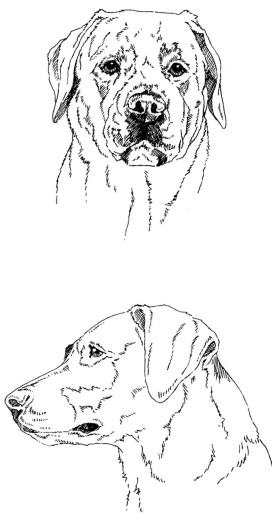

ABOVE: Incorrect: The head is too houndy in type and expression. The features are plain, the ears are heavy, and the eyes are wide-set.

RIGHT: Incorrect: The head is too fine and narrow. It lacks stop and the ears are too high.

It is the Labrador head which shows more variation than probably any other feature. Judges' show critiques repeatedly state that heads vary a lot. So which of these two descriptions is the better? Is it the brief British one or the longer American one?

A Labrador with a poor head is nondescript, while a good head completes the picture. Personally, I feel that including negatives in a Standard can be helpful, because a feature which may not be understood when describing the ideal may become clearer when compared to undesirable alternatives.

The late Mary Roslin-Williams was a sage when it came to coining a phrase, and she wrote: "A typical Labrador looks like a Labrador and nothing else. If he reminds you of any other breed then he is not typical." If one applies this to the head, then if it reminds you of a Rottweiler (and unfortunately some of the show types do) or of a fine-headed Foxhound or snipey Whippet (and unfortunately some of the working types do), it is not a typical Labrador head. In recent years some of the heads seen in the show ring have been too short and deep in muzzle, too pronounced in stop, too domed in skull, too cheeky, too filled in below the cheek bone, too round in eye or haw-eyed. All make for a foreign look.

At the other extreme, some of the working type heads are far too fine and snipey, while some are too flat in stop, with high-set ears and lacking the lovely soft expression known to the breed. All of these features also make for a foreign head. The American and British Standards do still differ slightly on their definitions of the stop (moderate, cf. defined), and my interpretation of the former would be that it describes a lesser stop. The need for a wide nose and well-developed nostrils is to help the Labrador's scenting ability.

Details of the eye are far better covered in the AKC standard. However, the hazel eye is still not acceptable to the AKC, other than in chocolates. This seems strange when it previously accepted black and yellow eyes. Labradors with a black eye look blank and without expression, while a light eye gives a hard, staring look.

Above all the Labrador should have a kind,

good-natured expression, sometimes romantically described as a melting expression. Also, I would disagree with the AKC's requirements for black eye rims in yellow. Surely they mean dark? Black eye rims are only seen in some yellows, more often than not the creams and reds. Dark rims are the norm in other shades of yellow.

As a matter of principle, many Americans take exception to the disqualification on eye rims lacking pigment, although this colour, seen in the 'yellow livers' for instance (with the 'bbee' genotype), is most peculiar and unattractive. I think that poor pigment spoils expression a great deal, and is certainly undesirable.

After years of subscribing to a level bite, the AKC now requests the scissor bite, but it is hardly surprising that the level bite is still regarded as acceptable, though not now desirable. The AKC now states that missing molars or pre-molars are serious faults. When judging the whole Labrador, I am not convinced that such an omission could ever be regarded as serious. The statement "full dentition is preferred" would have done nicely.

Both Standards end up saying similar things on ears, bearing in mind that high-set ears give the Labrador an untypical terrier-like look. In her book *The Dual-Purpose Labrador* Mary Roslin-Williams argues that ears should not be so small that they stand away in a bit of wind, letting draughts and water into the ear! Indeed, throughout her chapter on conformation, Mary links every feature of the Labrador to its working function, so it is well worth reading.

NECK, TOPLINE AND BODY

BRITISH
Neck: Clean, strong, powerful, set into well-placed shoulders.
Body: Chest of good width and depth, with well-sprung barrel ribs. Level topline. Loins wide, short coupled and strong.

AKC
Neck: The neck should be of proper length to allow the dog to retrieve game easily. It should be muscular and free from throati-

THE NECK

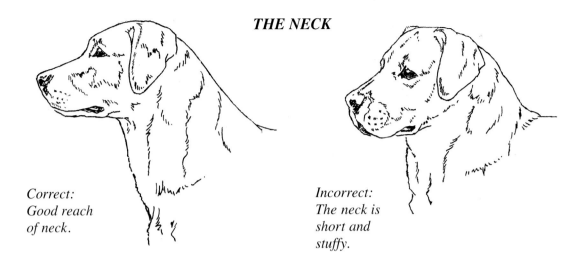

*Correct:
Good reach
of neck.*

*Incorrect:
The neck is
short and
stuffy.*

ness. The neck should rise strongly from the shoulders with moderate arch. A short thick neck or a 'ewe' neck are incorrect.
Topline: The back is strong and the topline is level from the withers to the croup when standing or moving. However, the loin should show evidence of flexibility for athletic endeavour.
Body: The Labrador should be short coupled, with good spring of ribs tapering to a moderately wide chest. The Labrador should not be narrow chested, giving the appearance of hollowness between the front legs, nor should it have a wide, spreading, bulldog-like front. Correct chest conformation will result in tapering between the front legs that allows unrestricted forelimb movement. Chest breadth that is either too wide or too narrow for efficient movement and stamina is incorrect. Slab sided individuals are not typical of the breed; equally objectionable are rotund or barrel chested specimens. The underline is almost straight, with little or no tuck up in mature animals. Loins should be short, wide and strong, extending to well developed, powerful hindquarters. When viewed from the side the Labrador Retriever shows a well developed, but not exaggerated fore chest.

In the section on topline, the Standard is actually describing the backline, the region from behind the withers to the junction of the loins

and croup. Labradors as swimming dogs should not have a flat backline. The withers should show slope, but thereafter the back should be level. A low tail-set with a steep or rounded croup is probably the commonest cause of poor backlines in Labradors, and this spoils the dog's general outline and balance.

Toplines which dip behind the withers and roach backs are unmistakable faults, and unfortunately they are not rare in the field trial bred dogs. A clean, strong neck with sufficient length is needed for picking up game. One is unlikely to see a working bred dog which is short and stuffy in the neck, since the dog would be too badly restricted for doing his work. We cannot consider the neck without also looking at front construction as a whole. If the forequarters are badly assembled, this affects how the dog moves and manoeuvres at work (and in the show ring). Labradors are short coupled dogs with strong muscular backs and wide loins, which means they can take the strain out of their work. Viewed from above, the body should not be narrow or long behind the ribcage and over the loins. It should, however, have a waist and not a back like a table top, as seen in far too many show dogs.

Unfortunately, too many working dogs are very shelly and tucked up in the body. The Breed Standard does not describe this at all. The AKC Standard's request for mature adults to have an almost straight underline, with little or

THE BODY

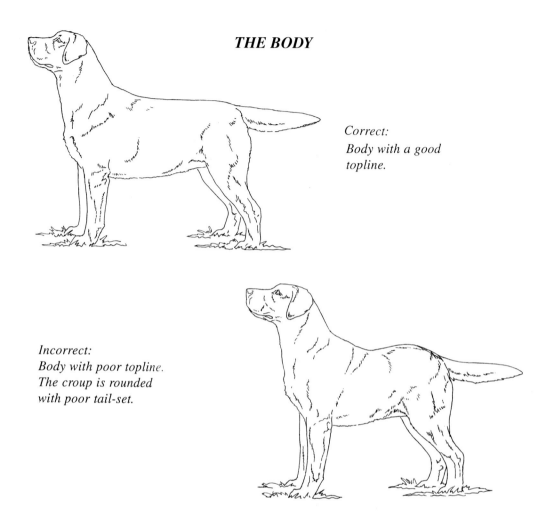

Correct:
Body with a good
topline.

Incorrect:
Body with poor topline.
The croup is rounded
with poor tail-set.

no tuck up, gives cause for concern. When this sort of level belly is seen, the Labrador is usually overweight, out of shape or in whelp. I think this requirement contradicts others in the Standard, certainly as regards the request for working condition.

Labradors need a broad deep chest and well sprung ribs so that they have plenty of heart and lung room to support their active work. If the shoulders are loaded and the chest is wider than the hindquarters, the dog will have difficulty swimming and galloping. Standing in the show ring such dogs look unbalanced, and loaded or built-up in front.

Some judges feel for a hand's width across the front chest, and this is a useful guide. Similarly, looking for chest depth to elbow level is a useful pointer, as an over-deep chest makes a dog look shorter in the leg and unbalances the over-

all picture. Shallow-chested dogs are seldom seen in the show ring, but surprisingly such chests are not uncommon in working dogs bred for 'sprinting retrieves'.

FOREQUARTERS

BRITISH
Shoulders long and sloping. Forelegs well boned and straight from elbow to ground when viewed from either front or side.

AKC
Forequarters: Should be muscular, well co-ordinated and balanced with the hindquarters. Shoulders: The shoulders are well laid back, long and sloping, forming an angle with the upperarm of approximately 90 degrees that permits the dog to move his forelegs in

FOREQUARTERS

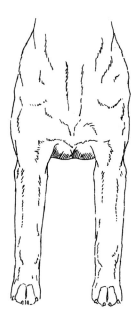

Correct front.

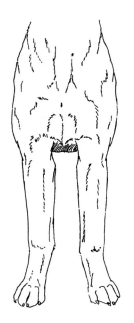

Incorrect: Narrow chest, with turned out feet and long pasterns.

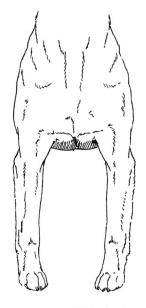

Incorrect: Wide in front with bowed legs, out at elbow and the feet turn inwards.

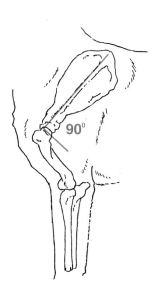

90 degrees front: 'Ideal' angulation between shoulder blade (scapula) and upperarm (humerus). This allows for good reach of stride.

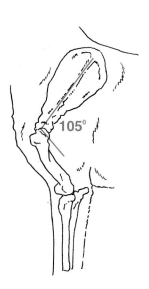

105 degrees front: The wider angulation is probably more typical of the breed.

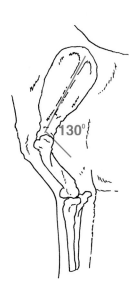

130 degrees front: This shows a shorter, steeper shoulder blade, and shorter, upright upperarm. This restricts the length of stride.

an easy manner with strong forward reach. Ideally the length of the shoulder blade should equal the length of the upperarm. Straight shoulder blades, short upperarms or heavily muscled or loaded shoulders, all restricting free movement, are incorrect. Front legs: When viewed from the front, the legs should be straight with good strong bone. Too much bone is as undesirable as too little bone, and short legged heavy boned individuals are not typical of the breed. Viewed from the side, the elbows should be directly under the withers, and the front legs should be perpendicular to the ground and well under the body. The elbows should be close to the ribs without looseness. Tied in elbows or being 'out at the elbows' interfere with free movement and are serious faults. Pasterns should be strong and short and should slope slightly from the perpendicular line of the leg.

Here again we see a great deal of difference in length and detail between the two Standards. It is a widely-held view (both sides of the Atlantic!) that one of the commonest conformational faults in the show Labrador is its front, due to insufficient length and lay-back of the shoulder blades and/or short steep upperarms. An incorrect front can still be produced with a long and sloping shoulder if the upperarm is too short and straight. In view of this, it is an omission that the British Standard makes no reference to the upperarm (humerus). Anatomically, I understand that the most commonly seen shoul-

der angulation in the dog is 105 degrees, rather than the 'classical' 90 degrees quoted in the AKC Standard.

Even in 1969 Mary Roslin-Williams was at pains to emphasise these points in her writing. Incorrect shoulders were often found in well-known winners at that time, and the same is true today. I think that if the AKC version on forequarters could be amended slightly, it would be even more helpful to judges and breeders.

Similarly, on the subject of leg bone, the AKC Standard hits the nail on the head. In striving for a 'dual-purpose' type (and therefore a correct type), the contrast in the two extremes of bone is excellent and worth emphasising in the Standard. If there is one major difference between 'show' and 'working' types (how I hate to categorise them like this), it is in bone/substance/build. At the extremes, they compare as heavyweights to flyweights, and neither is correct. While both Standards do ask for a strongly built, active dog, I think it is worth emphasising the incorrectness of the two extremes, since both are so often seen. Labrador bone should be strong and round, not fine and tapering in the pasterns or hocks. In other words, it should be good bone right down to the feet.

FEET

BRITISH
Round, compact; well arched toes and well developed pads.

FEET

Correct: 'Cat' feet, round and compact, with toes well arched and thick pads.

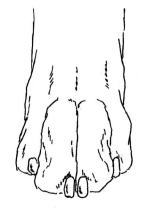

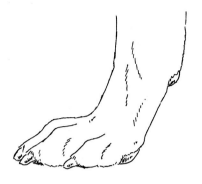

Incorrect: 'Hare' feet.

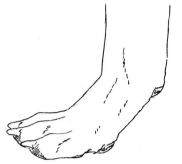

Incorrect: Flat feet.

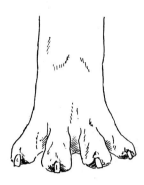

Incorrect: Splayed feet.

AKC
Feet are strong and compact with well arched toes and well developed pads. Dew claws may be removed. Splay feet, hare feet, knuckling over, or feet turning in or out are serious faults.

The British Standard describes forelegs which are straight from elbow to ground, and this implies that the pasterns should also be straight rather than very slightly sloping and thus having spring or 'give'. Very upright pasterns are a weakness, as they can knuckle over at the joint and do not make good shock-absorbers when running or landing from a jump. Perhaps the American Standard could qualify what degree of out- or in-turned feet constitutes a serious fault. The feet described in the Standards are designed not to be easily damaged, and so suit a working dog.

HINDQUARTERS

BRITISH
Well developed, not sloping to tail; well turned stifle. Hocks well let down, cow hocks highly undesirable.

AKC
The Labrador hindquarters are broad, muscular and well developed from the hip to the hock, with well turned stifles and short strong hocks. Viewed from the rear, the hind legs are straight and parallel. Viewed from the side, the angulation of the rear legs is in balance with the front. The hind legs are strongly boned, muscled with moderate angulation at the stifle, and powerful, clearly defined thighs. The stifle is strong and there is no slippage of the patellae while in motion or when standing. The hock joints are strong and well let down and do not slip or hyperextend while in motion or when standing. Angulation of both stifle and hock joint is such as to achieve the optimal balance of drive and traction. When standing, the rear toes are only slightly behind the point of the rump. Over angulation produces a sloping topline not typical of the breed. Feet are strong and compact, with well arched toes and well developed pads. Cow hocks, spread hocks, sickle hocks and over angulation are serious structural defects and are to be faulted.

Looking at old photographs of Labradors, it is noticeable that they were generally lighter and straighter in hindquarters than many shown today. Well turned stifles and well developed hindquarters are now more common. Strong, well angulated hindquarters give the Labrador a driving hind action. Well turned, short hocks can take a lot of strain, and help power the dog forward and on the turn. Straight, 'Chow' hocks are inclined to knuckle inwards, like a double joint, and together with straight stifles and sickle or cow-hocks they are a source of great hind weakness.

Cow-hocks reduce forward thrust and slow a dog down. Over-angulated, sweeping hindquar-

HINDQUARTERS

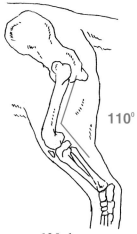

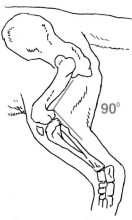

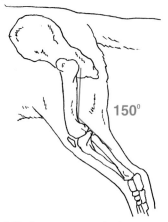

Correct: 120 degrees angulation: A normal construction, ideally giving good hind action.

90 degrees angulation: Over-angulation, may incline to cow or sickle hocks. Produces poor hind action.

150 degrees angulation: Showing a straight stifle, also illustrates a straight hock. The produces poor hind action, with insufficient reach of stride and propulsion.

ters, which can look very showy when standing, are often accompanied by cow-hocks. As with forequarters, it is difficult to write about hindquarters without also referring to movement. Reference to slipping patellae and hocks will come as a surprise to British readers. Are these points necessary in the Breed Standard?

TAIL

BRITISH
Distinctive feature, very thick towards the base, gradually tapering towards tip, medium length, free from feathering, but clothed thickly all round with short, thick dense coat, thus giving rounded appearance described as 'otter' tail. May be carried gaily, but should not curl over back.

AKC
The tail is a distinguishing feature of the breed. It should be very thick at the base, gradually tapering toward the tip, of medium length, and extending to no longer than to the hock. The tail should be free from feathering

and clothed thickly all round with the Labrador's short dense coat, thus having that peculiar rounded appearance that has been described as the 'otter' tail. The tail should follow the topline in repose or when in motion. It may be carried gaily, but should not curl over the back. Extremely short tails or long thin tails are serious faults. The tail completes the balance of the Labrador by giving it a flowing line from the top of the head to the tip of the tail. Docking or otherwise altering the length or natural carriage of the tail is a disqualification.

The Standards both tell us exactly what is required, although the more detailed American version includes useful information on length. A Labrador's otter tail is quite distinctive and is there for a purpose, to act as a rudder when swimming and to help balance the dog when standing or moving. Tail set has already been mentioned along with topline, and the tail should flow in line with the backline. In the show ring a wagging tail held almost level with the back when standing and moving looks very

TAIL

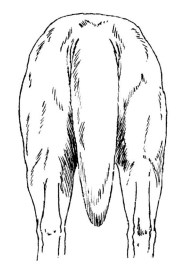

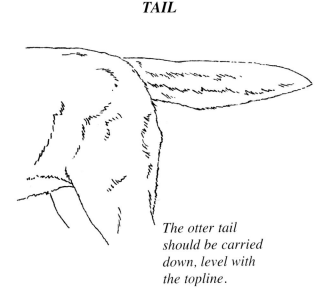

Correct: The otter tail should be thick and tapering.

The otter tail should be carried down, level with the topline.

Incorrect: Tail carried over the back.

Incorrect: gay tail.

attractive and balanced, but this is not a requirement. The Standard also allows for tails to be carried upright, so long as they do not bend over the back. Again a quote from Mary Roslin-Williams sets the mind at rest: "A dog with a really typical tail is nearly always a really typical Labrador right through and, oddly enough, usually has the right character." A really good otter tail is a joy to behold, and the Breed Standards leave us in no doubt about this characteristic. The American disqualifications seem bizarre, since I understand these are not prob-

lems particular to the breed. Also, they are covered by other AKC general rules.

MOVEMENT

BRITISH
Free, covering adequate ground; straight and true front and rear.

AKC
Movement of the Labrador Retriever should be free and effortless. When watching a dog

MOVEMENT

Incorrect: The stride is too short.

Incorrect: Moving too close behind and brushing.

Incorrect: Cow-hocked.

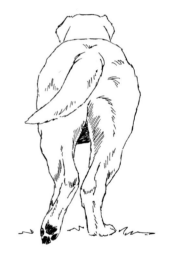

Incorrect: Moving out at elbows.

Incorrect: Toeing out at front.

move toward oneself, there should be no sign of elbows out. Rather the elbows should be held neatly to the body with the legs not too close together. Moving straight forward without pacing or weaving, the legs should form straight lines, with all parts moving in the same plane. Upon viewing the dog from the rear, one should have the impression that the hind legs move as near as possible in a parallel line with the front legs. The hocks should do their full share of the work, flexing well, giving the appearance of power and strength. When viewed from the side, the shoulders move freely and effortlessly, and the foreleg should reach forward close to the ground with extension. A short choppy movement or high knee action indicates a straight shoulder; paddling indicates long weak pasterns; and short stilted rear gait indicates a straight rear assembly; all are serious faults. Movement faults interfering with performance including weaving, side winding, crossing over, high knee action, paddling, and short choppy movement, should be severely penalised.

The British requirements are simple and concise, but I am not happy with them. In a working breed more is needed. The word 'adequate' in the English language has a number of meanings, and one of them condones what we so often see in the show ring: movement which is 'only satisfactory', or 'barely sufficient'. The AKC section is far more inspiring, and leaves judges and breeders in no doubt as to what they are looking for. Dare I say that I have noticed better movement in the American show ring?

COAT

BRITISH
Distinctive feature; short, dense without wave or feathering, giving fairly hard feel to the touch; weather-resisting undercoat.

AKC
The coat is a distinctive feature of the Labrador Retriever. It should be short, straight and very dense, giving a fairly hard

feeling to the hand. The Labrador should have a soft weather-resistant undercoat that provides protection from water, cold and all types of ground cover. A slight wave down the back is permissible. Woolly coats, soft silky coats, and sparse slick coats are not typical of the breed, and should be severely penalised.

Correct coat is one of the points which denote correct type. A Labrador without a good double coat, as described so well in the Standards, would soak up water and fail to have the protection and warmth it needs when working in dense cover or freezing cold water. The dense, water-shedding Labrador coat is not likely to get wet to the skin, so is a positive asset for a working dog. It perplexes me that so many field trial bred dogs, who would benefit from this characteristic, lack the correct type of coat. They are often very sparse in undercoat, virtually single-coated and with thin poor tails to match. The colour of the undercoat is generally lighter than the topcoat, more a browny or greyish black in the blacks. I know that some of our most experienced British Labrador breeders consider that a slight wave is no sin, often accompanying a really good Labrador coat.

COLOUR

BRITISH
Wholly black, yellow or liver/chocolate. Yellows range from light cream to red fox. Small white spot on chest permissible.

AKC
The Labrador Retriever coat colors are black, yellow and chocolate. Any other color or combination of colours is a disqualification. A small white spot on the chest is permissible, but not desirable. White hairs from ageing or scarring are not be be misinterpreted as brindling.
BLACKS: are all black. A black with brindle marking or a black with tan markings is a disqualification.
YELLOWS: may range in color from fox-red to light cream with variations in shading on

ABOVE: The chocolate Labrador: Int. Fin. Est. Ch. WW-94 Bubbling Bedouine, bred by Maria Swanljung, owned by L. Bergh.

BELOW: The black Labrador: Sh Ch. Toplict Tintagel's Tagel Moon.
Photo courtesy: A. Verbeek-de Neef.

the ears, back and underparts of the dog. **CHOCOLATES: Chocolates can vary in shade from light to dark chocolate. Chocolate with brindle or tan markings is a disqualification.**

The AKC references to mis-marking, shading and disqualifications abound in this section. Also use of the word 'brindling' when referring to white hairs is unusual, as brindling normally relates to black hairs. I think that use of the word 'wholly' negates the need to go into details about mis-marking. Here in Britain, there has been much open debate about what constitutes the shade 'red fox', since foxes come in many shades! Some yellows have darker shading on the face, like a mask, and this alters the expression a lot, making it look harder. I suppose the AKC would technically count this as a shading disqualification?

Both Standards point out that a small white chest spot is permissible, but no mention is made of 'Bolo pads', the white pads and heels seen on some blacks. White hairs in the undercoat is another feature which is not mentioned, and some blacks and chocolates have white roots to their undercoat. The white ring at the base of the hair one third of the way down the tail is a well recognised trait in many good-coated chocolates. It is interesting that the American Standard confirms the range of shades in chocolates, from light to dark. Many judges and breeders do prefer the darker, richer shade, but light chocolate is not incorrect in either Standard.

SIZE, PROPORTION AND SUBSTANCE

BRITISH
Ideal height at withers: Dogs 56-57 cm (22-22.5 ins.). Bitches: 54-56 cm (21.5-22 ins.).

AKC
Size: The height at the withers for a dog is 22.5 to 24.5 ins; for a bitch 21.5 to 23.5 ins. Any variation greater than 0.5 inch above or below these heights is a disqualification. Approximate weight of dogs and bitches in working condition: dogs 65 to 80 lbs; bitches

55 to 70 lbs. (The minimum height ranges set forth shall not apply to dogs or bitches under 12 months of age.) Proportion: Short-coupled; length from the point of shoulder to the point of the rump is equal to or slightly longer than the distance from the withers to the ground. Distance from the elbow to the ground should be equal to one half of the height at the withers. The brisket should extend to the elbows, but not perceptibly deeper. The body must be of sufficient length to permit a straight, free and efficient stride; but the dog should never appear low and long or tall and leggy in outline. Substance: Substance and bone proportionate to the overall dog. Light, 'weedy' individuals are definitely incorrect; equally objectionable are cloddy lumbering specimens. Labradors shall be shown in working condition, well-muscled and without excess fat.

The 1916 British Standard did not specify a height, but with the revisions came the measurements given above. However, our Standard has never said, 'must be'. First it was 'desired height', now it is 'ideal height', and this gives room for use of common sense when judging the whole Labrador. I think it a tragedy that deviations from the height can lead to disqualification in USA. Use of the height wicket to confirm a Labrador's height, with a view to disqualifying it, is to my mind quite ridiculous.

Most of the other points raised in this section of the AKC standard have been commented on elsewhere. However, should measuring length from the point of shoulder read point of withers? Otherwise a square dog is being described, and very short square dogs would not be able to move and work with sufficient free length of stride. I am in favour of the Standard asking for show dogs to be shown in well-muscled condition, without excess fat, but do not agree that they should be in working condition, as working Labradors are invariably very lean.

FAULTS AND DISQUALIFICATIONS

BRITISH
Faults: Any departure from the foregoing

Can. OT Ch. & Ch. Redsky's Divine Designate WCX: The correct thick double coat, which is water-shedding.

points should be considered a fault and the seriousness with which the fault should be regarded should be in exact proportion to its degree. NOTE: Male animals should have two apparently normal testicles fully descended into the scrotum.

AKC
DISQUALIFICATIONS:
1. Any deviation from the height prescribed in the Standard.
2. A thoroughly pink nose or one lacking in any pigment.
3. Eye rims without pigment.
4. Docking or otherwise altering the length or natural carriage of the tail.
5. Any colour or a combination of colours other than black, yellow or chocolate as described in the Standard.

I have discussed the British Standard on faults already. It is interesting that the AKC Standard makes no mention of male entirety. The American disqualifications, especially as regards height, are disliked by so many that it seems unfair and undemocratic to have introduced them in 1994 after so many years without disqualifications. They will not improve the breed, and are not needed if the Standard is otherwise well written.

CONCLUSION
The Labrador Retriever Breed Standard is neither universal, nor has it been left unchanged since the original British Breed Standard was written in 1916. So what is the philosophy behind a Breed Standard, and what are its purposes? First and foremost, a Breed Standard is a word picture to describe the ideal dog of a particular breed. A number of questions come to mind. How open should it be to interpretation? Can a Standard be over-prescribed? When revised, should it take into account breed weaknesses of that time? Should it contain negatives?

Or disqualifications? Should it help breeders/judges to recognise the qualities of a dual-purpose Labrador? What do we mean by a dual-purpose Labrador? And is the Standard going to help us produce more of them? Can people ever agree?

Stonehenge, writing in the 19th century about judging the old St John's Newfoundland or Labrador Dog, stated: "Fancy dogs may be measured by any rule, however artificial, but a shooting dog should only be judged by points which are relevant to his work." This statement was written before the first proper Labrador Breed Standard was published, ironically by men and a woman who sincerely believed in the working function of the breed. Yet, to this day, over a hundred years on, the cynicism in this quote still applies in many quarters.

It is very easy to criticise the work done by others in writing the Standards (actually it is not that easy!). However, in this chapter it has been my task to comment and criticise, and I have done that. My conclusions are that the British Standard is a useful snapshot, clear, concise and quick to retain. If brevity is a virtue, the British Standard is positively saintly. I have discussed many points which I feel could be added to the British Standard to improve it. If I had to choose only one, it would definitely be a re-write of the section on movement, as this is so sadly lacking.

The American Standard is more like a detailed oil painting where too much oil paint has been used, and the frame is faulty. If it was cleaned up/pruned down and the frame removed, it could be made into a masterpiece. Judges and breeders will always vary in the emphasis they place on particular features, and it is always necessary to judge the dog as a whole, not as a series of parts with faults. My advice would be to seriously consider both of these Standards, the long and the short. While one lacks content and detail, the other contains verbiage and disqualifications. They are both like the proverbial curate's egg, good in parts. Together they could make a whole.

7 THE JUDGE'S VIEW

When you have been involved in the dog showing world for a number of years, you may well feel ready to take on the task of judging. It may be that you have enjoyed a considerable degree of success, and you feel you have something to contribute. Or perhaps you have not been as lucky as you think you should have been, and you see judging as a way of redressing the balance. Whatever your reasons for wanting to judge, you will soon find out that it is not as easy as it looks! It is all too easy to criticise the judge's placings, it is quite another matter to stand in the centre of a busy ring and make calm, rational decisions, based on an in-depth knowledge of the breed, and, most importantly, the ability to make a clear interpretation of the Breed Standard when assessing living specimens.

JUDGING IN THE USA

In the USA, becoming an AKC licensed judge for any breed is a lengthy process. The AKC is constantly changing their stipulated requirements, seeking to improve the selection of judges with the implied intent of improving the quality of new judges.

An aspiring judge applying to AKC for the first time must meet the following minimum prerequisites: (1) have ten years' documented experience in the sport; (2) have owned or exhibited several dogs of the initial breed(s) requested; (3) have bred or raised at least four litters in any one breed; (4) have produced two champions out of a minimum of four litters; (5) have five stewarding assignments at AKC Member or Licensed Shows; (6) have judged six Sanctioned matches, Sweepstakes or Futurities; (7) must meet the occupational eligibility requirements under AKC Rules; (8) must pass a comprehensive 'open book' examination demonstrating understanding of AKC Rules, Policies and Judging Procedures; (9) must pass a test on the Standard of each breed requested; (10) must be interviewed; (11) must provide two references. To satisfy these and additional requirements requires time, effort, and money on the part of the would-be judge. It is unnecessary to further detail all the convoluted arrangements whereby an applicant is finally approved to judge initially on a Provisional basis, and, after a specified number of assignments, to become a Regular Judge.

The American Kennel Club publishes *Guidelines for Dog Show Judges* which details, in general terms, the required judging procedures. All judges must physically examine each dog, i.e. must open the dog's mouth (or have the handler do so) to check dentition and bite and must check that every male has two normally descended testicles. He/she must go over the dog to determine soundness of back, hocks and coat condition. Some judges do an extensive 'hands on' examination, while others do as little as possible with a Rottweiler! For example, one well-known judge *gently* holds the left ear of an Open Class male while doing her routine examination, as if to reassure him. Actually, she is really controlling that dog until she has moved back from his head area. The judge is required to individually gait each dog to determine soundness, always using the same ring pattern to ensure impartiality.

The interpretation of the Standard is the sole responsibility of the judge. A judge can adjudicate only those dogs which are presented in the conformation ring on a particular day.

JUDGING IN THE UK

In Britain, the Kennel Club does not give rules and regulations regarding an individual's qualifications to judge. It is a matter of acquiring experience in a breed, achieving success in the show ring and in a breeding programme, and generally serving an apprenticeship in the breed. The Kennel Club has a list of approved Championship judges, which is based on levels of previous judging experience.

In most cases, the would-be judge will serve an apprenticeship of around five years, during which time they should be reasonably successful at Championship Shows, and their home-bred litters should display soundness and type. During this pre-judging period, the aspiring judge should learn as much as possible about the breed, reading books and attending seminars, and also studying the Breed Standard in great detail, working on a personal interpretation of it. It is a useful exercise to watch leading judges at work in the ring, studying their methods and working out why certain selections have been made.

A JUDGING EXERCISE

All Labrador Retrievers must be judged by the Breed Standard which has been adopted in the country where the breed is being judged. This is the guide that all judges must follow, regardless of whether the type of Labrador varies from country to country. The British and American Breed Standards vary slightly (see Chapter Six: the Breed Standards), and obviously, all judges form their own interpretation of the Standard. As an academic exercise, three Championship judges – Jane Borders (USA), Heather Wiles-Fone (UK) and Dr Helmut Kamlah (Germany) – were asked to assess three dogs and three bitches from a series of photographs, showing head, profile, forequarters, and hindquarters. The dogs were not named, the judges were merely told their ages.

Clearly, it is impossible to make an accurate evaluation of a dog from photographs alone, as the essential areas of temperament and movement cannot be brought into the balance. Heather Wiles-Fone says: "Obviously it is impossible to make an absolutely accurate assessment of a dog from a photograph. The main difficulties are with regard to evaluating size and movement, and knowing whether the dog has a correct double coat. Temperament has to come out of the equation, and when judging a Labrador, this is possibly the highest priority of all. However, the photos are of excellent quality, and although the grass means that the feet cannot always be seen clearly, we can get a good, overall impression of the six Labradors selected for this exercise. The head studies are particularly good, showing the eye-colour and capturing expression."

Dr Kamlah comments: "Judging dogs from pictures is always a risky exercise as there are limitations with regard to the dog's expression and personality with a photo that freezes a single moment in time. This may result in a more favourable or less favourable assessment of the dog's quality. Perhaps most significant is the exclusion of movement when judging dogs from photographs. It is of the utmost importance to see the anatomical correctness of the animal, which proves its hunting and working capabilities – a criterion which should never be neglected, even with pure-bred show lines.

"A good dog or bitch should satisfy our idea of a typical, working Labrador, which, of course, differs in individual perception. I always like to see that body size and strength, and length of legs and sound feet, are supporting a straight, forward movement, both in slow paces and at full speed. The strong neck is necessary for the retrievers of heavier game, and the mouth should be big enough to carry game properly. The 'otter tail' gives balance on the move, both on land and in water. But all in all, our Labrador should have a most beautiful face which gives evokes an emotional response – it the unspoken plea, impossible to resist – which says: 'Let's do something together.'"

Labrador A: Dog (21 months old)

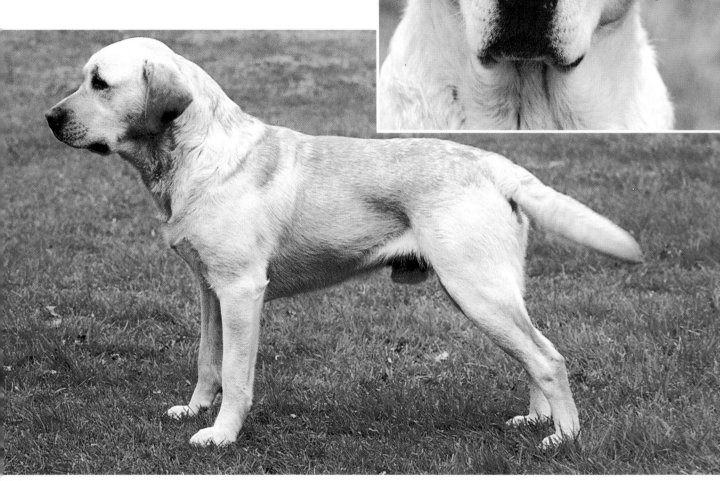

HEAD STUDY

Heather Wiles-Fone (UK): "A dog with a well-shaped head, with a wide skull which allows plenty of room for the brain. The ears are neat and well set. His almond-shaped eyes have a gentle expression, with good pigmentation around the rims A quality, typical head.

Jane Borders (USA): "This dog has a lovely head type, with a kindly expression. He has a good balance of muzzle and skull, with complementary head planes and breadth. The ears could use a little more leather as they are a bit small, but not so that they spoil the look of the head."

Dr Helmut Kamlah (Germany): "This dog shows the kind expression you would expect from a Labrador. He has a little less pigment than I would like to see, but he has good colour."

PROFILE

Heather Wiles-Fone (UK): "A short-coupled body with level topline. From this angle, you can see his good length of foreface and sloping shoulders. The front legs are strong-boned, but appear to be a little weak in pasterns. Personally, I would like to see more development in the hindquarters and greater depth of body. This could come with maturity.

Jane Borders (USA): "The coat character of this dog is good with nice colour overlay. The body shows less maturity than you would expect in a dog of this age, with lack of body depth, but this may come as he matures. I would expect this dog to look his best at four years of age."

Dr Helmut Kamlah (Germany): "Looking from the profile, the ears seem to be a little low-set. The head seems to belong to a heavier dog. A good, level back, but unbalanced in the hindquarters. It could be that he will develop with maturity."

FOREQUARTERS

Heather Wiles-Fone (UK): A strong wide chest with well-boned legs. This shot suggests that he also has well-developed shoulders."

Jane Borders (USA): "This yellow has excellent breadth of chest, with a correctly placed front assembly. The front angles appear to be balanced."

Dr Helmut Kamlah (Germany): "Good front, with correct angulation of the forehand. He stands a little too open."

HINDQUARTERS

Heather Wiles-Fone (UK): "The hocks are nice and straight, but I would prefer more muscle development, particularly in the second thigh."

Jane Borders (USA): "He appears to have a somewhat long second thigh, but this could be actuated by the leg placement in the photo. Looking at the front and rear assembly, I would expect this dog to move correctly."

Dr Helmut Kamlah (Germany): "The hindquarters are under-developed and out of balance with the rest of the dog. He is stretched out too far, making it difficult to judge, but it looks as though he is straight in the stifles."

A JUDGING EXERCISE

Labrador B: Dog (13 months old)

HEAD STUDY

Heather Wiles-Fone (UK): "A very masculine head, with an alert expression and a strong foreface. The eyes are rather light in colour. This is also true of the coat colour, thus making his expression rather hard. The ears are well set on. There is no pigmentation on the lips, and the flews are somewhat loose. My main reservation is that his head is very strong, bearing in mind his age of 13 months.

Jane Borders (USA): "This dog appears very mature for his age, but lacks the head type that I prefer. The expression is coarse, the skull lacks depth, and the muzzle is long."

Dr Helmut Kamlah (Germany): "This youngster has a nice head and a good ear-set. He is a little lighter in the eye than I would like to see, and he is short in the mouth for a retriever who has to pick up game. He does not appear to have the Labrador's typically kind expression, but this may be due to the photographic situation."

PROFILE

Heather Wiles-Fone (UK): "This male gives an overall impression of balance. The short-coupled body has a strong topline and a good tail-set. The coat is a good, dark colour."

Jane Borders (USA): "The topline is good, but he appears to be straight-shouldered. From this angle, he appears to stand 'east-west'."

Dr Helmut Kamlah (Germany): "This is a promising dog with a good lay of shoulders, a straight back, and good tail-set."

FOREQUARTERS

Heather Wiles-Fone (UK): "The boning is good and the legs are straight. However, I would like to see more width between the legs From this angle, he appears a little straight in the upper arm."

Jane Borders (USA): "Again, this photo gives the impression that the dog stands 'east-west'. He looks steep in the shoulder."

Dr Helmut Kamlah (Germany): "The front appears to be correct, with nice, straight legs."

HINDQUARTERS

Heather Wiles-Fone (UK): "A well-balanced rear end with good angulation. The tail is the correct shape, but perhaps looks a shade feathery."

Jane Borders (USA): " The rear assembly is nicely put together, with a good second thigh."

Dr Helmut Kamlah (Germany): "Well-muscled quarters with sufficient angulation. He has the correct 'otter tail' – a hallmark of the breed."

A JUDGING EXERCISE

Labrador C: Dog (8 years old)

HEAD STUDY

Heather Wiles-Fone (UK): "*A well-defined head showing no signs of coarseness. The almond-shaped eyes depict honesty in his expression. The ears are correctly set. There is a good length of foreface and plenty of depth to the muzzle, which would enable him to pick up a bird with ease.*"

Jane Borders (USA): "*This dog has a classic head, totally Labrador, with a kind expression and correct eye colour. The skull and muzzle are beautifully balanced, with perfect ear placement. The ear leather is good, which softens and frames the head.*"

Dr Helmut Kamlah (Germany): "*Looking at this dog's face, he sems to be saying: 'I am the one you love!' He has the typical Labrador expression, with hazelnut-coloured eyes, good ear-set and nice nostrils.*"

PROFILE

Heather Wiles-Fone (UK): "*A substantially built male, but he appears to be heavy in front, therefore presenting a rather unbalanced outline. There is plenty of forechest, though he is rather long in the back. Good tail-set and nicely turned stifles. He appears to have the correct, dense coat.*"

Jane Borders (USA): "*Unfortunately, this dog appears out of balance. He has a ewe neck and a poor shoulder set.*"

Dr Helmut Kamlah (Germany): "*His head study is beautiful, but looking at the profile, this dog does not seem so impressive. He has a good neck and shoulders, a deep body, and good quarters – all the requirements for an excellent dog – but he seems a little unbalanced. It could be that he is too heavy or too straight in front. He has the correct coat texture, and shows the relaxed calmness the breed is known for.*"

FOREQUARTERS

Heather Wiles-Fone (UK): "*This dog is deep through the chest, with plenty of heart-room. Ample bone. He could possibly do with a fraction more length of leg, which would result in a more balanced picture.*"

Jane Borders (USA): "*A disappointing front assembly. The dog appears to have a pigeon front.*"

Dr Helmut Kamlah (Germany): "*Looking straight on, the front appears to be correct, but, this does not match my impression when looking at the profile. I believe this male is too heavy in the forehand assembly which makes him appear unbalanced.*"

HINDQUARTERS

Heather Wiles-Fone (UK): "*A pleasing rear with well-developed second thigh. In this shot, the right hock is turned in slightly. He obviously lies on hard ground, as calluses are visible on both legs.*"

Jane Borders (USA): "*The rear assembly appears to be lacking in substance, and he has a long second thigh.*"

Dr Helmut Kamlah (Germany): "*This male has good quarters, with plenty of substance.*"

A JUDGING EXERCISE

Labrador D: Bitch (4 years old)

HEAD STUDY

Heather Wiles-Fone (UK): "This bitch has a most beautiful head, where everything is well proportioned. Her eyes exude gentleness and honesty, and she looks as though she is waiting for the next command. A truly exquisite Labrador head, full of quality."

Jane Borders (USA): "This bitch has a stunning head, with lovely mascara enhancing her beautiful expression and correct eye colour. The head is very feminine with good planes, and nice ear size.

Dr Helmut Kamlah (Germany): "A nice portrait, showing a typical head with dark eyes, and good ear-set. She has a little less pigment than I would like to see."

PROFILE

Heather Wiles-Fone (UK): "This angle shows a classical outline excelling in good shoulder placement, with a deep, well-sprung body and strong bone. The coat appears to be correct, and the quarters are nicely angulated."

Jane Borders (USA): "The body style looks a little long, although the topline is good. She appears to be a fine representative of the breed."

Dr Helmut Kamlah (Germany): This bitch has a good neck and a level topline. She appears to have sufficient angulation front and rear. I would say that this was an excellent bitch without major faults. She is very light in colour."

FOREQUARTERS

Heather Wiles-Fone (UK): "Her front is absolutely straight. The legs are perpendicular to the ground, with well-knuckled feet. There is ample width of chest."

Jane Borders (USA): "The front assembly appears to be correctly balanced."

Dr Helmut Kamlah (Germany): "A good front, with very good feet."

HINDQUARTERS

Heather Wiles-Fone (UK): "A strong, well-muscled rear, with straight hocks. She has a typical tail, rounded in shape, which is known as an 'otter tail'. It is clothed thickly all round with short, dense coat – thick towards the base and gradually tapering to the tip. No signs of any feathering."

Jane Borders (USA): "She could use a little more angle on the rear-end to balance the front assembly. The 'otter tail' is correctly coated."

Dr Helmut Kamlah (Germany): "The rear end is well put together, and she appears to have the correct tail-set."

A JUDGING EXERCISE

Labrador E: Bitch (2 years 6 months old)

HEAD STUDY

Heather Wiles-Fone (UK): *"This shows a wide skull but, in my opinion, the head looks rather masculine – a bit too heavy for a bitch. The lower eyelids appear somewhat slack, and the flews are also loose. The eye colour is reasonable for a chocolate."*

Jane Borders (USA): *"This bitch's head is a bit heavy, but she has a kindly eye. She has good planes of skull and muzzle with a proper stop.*

Dr Helmut Kamlah (Germany): *"A nice head, with good eye-shape and good eye-colour. She is a little shorter in the muzzle than I would like to see for hunting purposes. She has neat ears."*

PROFILE

Heather Wiles-Fone (UK): *"Beautifully balanced and well-constructed, with a lovely, clean neck. The shoulders are long, and sloping deep through the brisket. A short-coupled body with level topline, and the tail coming straight off the back. The coat appears to be correct, and is a good, dark colour. Well-angulated quarters."*

Jane Borders (USA): *"This is a very lovely over-all bitch. She is slightly longer than tall, but she has a good, hard topline, and excellent shoulder set. Again, this is one fine representative of the breed."*

Dr Helmut Kamlah (Germany): *"A fully developed young bitch, with well-angulated shoulders, an excellent back and a good tail-set. She is well-balanced throughout"*

FOREQUARTERS

Heather Wiles-Fone (UK): *"She has a good front with a deep chest. The elbows are tucked well in. The legs are strong and well-boned, with neat, tight, cat-like feet. This angle indicates well-developed shoulders."*

Jane Borders (USA): *"Good overall balance of front assembly. The elbows appear to be very slightly tied, but the general make-up of this girl is so good that minor faults must be forgiven."*

Dr Helmut Kamlah (Germany): *"Looking at the front view, this bitch is well put together."*

HINDQUARTERS

Heather Wiles-Fone (UK): *"Excellent, powerful back-end, with very good second thigh. Typical 'otter tail', wide at the base and tapering to the tip. This shot gives the appearance of the tail being rather short, but this could be due to the angle of the photo. The left hock appears to be turned in."*

Jane Borders (USA): *Excellent rear assembly, with good balance between the front and the rear. The angulation is correct, and she has a very good tail-set."*

Dr Helmut Kamlah (Germany): *"Excellent rear angulation and good hindquarters. She has a fine 'otter tail'".*

Labrador F: Bitch (3 years old)

HEAD STUDY

Heather Wiles-Fone (UK): *"I like this bitch's intelligent and alert expression. She is feminine in outlook, with medium-brown, almond-shaped eyes. There is a nice length of foreface, although the ears are perhaps a shade too heavy. She appears to be carrying loose skin under the jaw and neck area."*

Jane Borders (USA): *"This bitch has a rather ordinary head. It is the right shape and make, but lacking the kindly expression that is so typical of the breed."*

Dr Helmut Kamlah (Germany): *"This lady seems to show sound temperament, and she is interested in other things than the photographer. Unfortunately, the head is disturbing in the overall expression. I believe this can be attributed to a slightly masculine expression. However, she has a pleasing head shape, with dark eyes, and good ear-set."*

PROFILE

Heather Wiles-Fone (UK): *"This bitch presents a smart, well-balanced outline. She has a good reach of neck, but appears rather throaty. Excellent lay-back of shoulder, and plenty of forechest. Compact in body, and well-turned stifles. Typical of the breed.*

Jane Borders (USA): *"Her body style appears to be out of balance with an over-angulated shoulder. However, the topline is good, the tail-set is correct, and she appears to have proper coat."*

Dr Helmut Kamlah (Germany): *"In profile, the muzzle appears a little too pronounced and she has a rather throaty neck. She is relatively light in build."*

FOREQUARTERS

Heather Wiles-Fone (UK): *"A straight front, with strong-boned legs which are tucked neatly under the chest. This angle reveals good shoulder placement and a well-sprung body."*

Jane Borders (USA): *"She appears to be slightly pigeon-fronted. The front assembly looks as though it is over-angulated."*

Dr Helmut Kamlah (Germany): *"The front is correct, with straight legs showing good bone."*

HINDQUARTERS

Heather Wiles-Fone (UK): *"A nicely developed back-end, with strong, straight hocks, standing neither too wide nor too close. She could possibly do with more muscling on the second thigh."*

Jane Borders (USA): *"The rear assembly lacks angulation, and therefore appears out of balance with the front assembly."*

Dr Helmut Kamlah (Germany): *"Angulation of the rear assembly is sufficient, and she has good hindquarters."*

8 THE COMPLETE GUNDOG

The Labrador is a specialist at retrieving, rather than an all-round gundog. A shooter requiring a dog which does everything should consider a Spaniel or one of the hunt, point and retrieve breeds. However, as a retrieving dog for land or water, the Labrador stands supreme.

The Labrador is, or should be, first and foremost a working dog. If a specimen of the breed is of the wrong temperament or constructed in such a way as to be unable to work well and efficiently, that dog is no true Labrador, even if he wins in the show ring under judges ignorant of how a Labrador capable of fulfilling its function should be built.

CHOOSING A WORKING PUPPY

A Labrador puppy intended as a gundog should be carefully chosen from mainly working stock. I would be the last person to say that the pedigree should contain no show blood, but it should also contain genuine workers including Field Trial Champions. Plenty of dogs work well without ever winning, or indeed running in, a field trial, but trials remain the only guide to and measurement of working ability at the puppy buyer's disposal.

BREEDERS: It is always better to buy a puppy from a litter which the breeder has bred in order to keep a puppy, rather than one which has been produced merely to make money. The best puppies come either from dedicated breeders who do not churn out too many and have a reputation to keep up, or from owners of a good working bitch who wish to breed a litter to continue the line and to satisfy their friends who want puppies. The advantage of the latter scenario is that the litter will be a novelty, and thus will come in for a lot of attention and humanisation. The disadvantage is that the breeder will be in no position to supply advice and after-sales service, and it is not unknown for there to be difficulties in the way of incomplete paperwork, inaccurate pedigrees and late registrations. It is of course essential to insist that parents and grandparents should have had their hips X-rayed and scored. The scores of the parents should add up to not much more than 20. Their eyes should also have been tested by a BVA/KC panellist (or your national equivalent) and passed clear, within a year prior to the birth of the litter.

TIMING: Working bred puppies are mainly available from about March to September. The reason for this is that no-one with a genuinely useful working bitch is likely to want her out of action between October and January. Sporting magazines, during the summer, are full of advertisements for gundog puppies, but well-known breeders usually have waiting lists (especially for bitch puppies) and have no need to advertise.

DOG OR BITCH: It is much easier to find a good dog puppy than a bitch, because the demand for bitches is so much greater. People have the idea (true in part) that bitches are gentler, quieter and easier to train. However, *some* dogs are easier than *some* bitches. Remember too that bitches have a way of coming in season at the most inconvenient times. Equally, some dogs are oversexed and constitute a nuisance all the year round, unless castrated, which is a perfectly sensible and reasonable option. Other male domestic animals are castrated as a matter of course.

COLOUR: The question of colour is to my mind the least important factor, but many buyers will be quite determined to have one colour and not another. There is no difference in the working abilities of any of the colours, except that there are more working blacks available than yellows, because for some reason most shooting people prefer blacks to yellows. There are as yet few working chocolates, since chocolate genes have come down through show rather than working lines. I am sure this situation will change as the chocolate genes become more widespread, but at the moment, if someone tries to sell you a chocolate puppy for work, you should examine its pedigree very carefully.

THE FINAL SELECTION: Having decided upon the right litter from which to buy the puppy, and the sex and colour desired, the next problem is the actual choice of puppy. Obviously, not everyone can have first pick of the litter and to the breeder this is a real headache as everyone wants and expects to be able to choose. I try as far as possible to allot puppies according to how I think they will suit the purchaser. Unfortunately, many people refuse to take advice and, instead of going off with a quiet, gentle puppy, they insist on taking

the bold, dominant one, who will be difficult to control and who will need an expert trainer.

It is acceptable for a puppy to be quiet and even retiring, but not a nervous wreck. If the puppies have never been out of their kennel, never been socialised and never been exposed to strangers or to noise, they are likely to be very nervous, and would not be a sensible buy. I try to get my puppies used to the sound of a starting pistol before selling age, and I also have them retrieving to hand. This takes a little time, but it is time well spent. I find that if they retrieve to hand at seven or eight weeks, they continue to do so if neither the new owner nor the children of the family do anything ill-advised. The puppies should be well grown, with strong bone and good thick coats. They should be clean and sweet-smelling, and so should their kennel. Their nails should be short (either from being clipped or through exercise on hard ground) and their ears should be clean. They should have been wormed at least two or three times prior to sale.

If a puppy is going to live in the house, I see no reason why it should not leave the breeder at seven weeks, or even a day or two earlier. The Guide Dogs for the Blind Association likes to get its puppies into the homes of puppy walkers at six and a half weeks. However, many people prefer to take a puppy at eight weeks, which is the traditional age. As a breeder, I always find I have to keep a number of puppies beyond that age. Some I am keeping for myself, perhaps one or two are going abroad and cannot go until they are a bit older, plus there will be the inevitable person going on holiday, having a family wedding or some other excuse for not collecting their puppy!

THE HOME SITUATION
I am in favour of the future gundog being kept in the house, receiving humanisation and mental stimulation. Dogs are pack animals and, in my opinion, it is unkind to keep one alone in a kennel. Where two or more dogs are kept it is a different matter. However, it is essential for all the family to treat the pup sensibly and do nothing to damage future gundog training. An example is scolding or punishing the puppy for picking

up or chewing a slipper or child's toy, which could create inhibitions about retrieving. If the husband is going to train the puppy and eventually use it as a gundog, he need have no fears about his wife feeding and looking after it, and vice versa. It is the person who takes the dog out and provides the fun of hunting and retrieving who will be the one the dog looks upon as master or mistress.

EARLY TRAINING

The early training of the working puppy should consist of house-training, coming when called, walking on a lead, and (in my opinion) retrieving to hand.

HOUSE-TRAINING: House-training is based on the primitive instinct to keep the den clean, and the smaller the space the puppy is kept in at first, the easier this will be. It will also be much simpler if your puppy was frequently let out of the kennel by the breeder and encouraged to perform on grass, rather than in the kennel or run.

COMING WHEN CALLED: Coming when called is entirely a matter of making it more pleasant for the puppy to come than not to come. This is accomplished by making a big fuss of the puppy whenever he comes, and by calling him just before something pleasant is about to happen (e.g. feeding). The use of tidbits in this context is not a bad idea.

WALKING ON THE LEAD: Walking on the lead is usually quite easy to teach a young puppy. Labradors are intelligent enough to find out fairly quickly that it is much more comfortable to follow than otherwise, and that trying to hang themselves is uncomfortable and pointless.

RETRIEVING TO HAND: Retrieving to hand is something which is quite easily taught to a young puppy of working breeding and, once taught, it remains. This means that when serious training starts, at between six months and a year, the problem of the dog refusing to bring the dummy is one that just does not arise. Almost any puppy of the correct breeding will rush out

and pick up an article it sees thrown. A suitable dummy for a very young puppy is a sock, or pair of socks, knotted together to make a firm but soft parcel of a suitable size. One of the puppy's own toys should definitely not be used. Many puppies will bring the article back the first once or twice it is thrown, particularly if they are good at coming when called. However, sooner or later, the puppy will decide it is more fun to run away with the article than bring it and give it up. If the puppy does bring the dummy, either straightaway or with persuasion, the owner should praise and caress him for quite a long time before attempting to take the retrieve. If the puppy drops the dummy it is not a serious matter at this stage. However, if and when he starts running away, my method is to put him on a check cord, which usually consists of a couple of lengths of binder twine with a noose at one end for the puppy's neck. The advantage of doing this with a small puppy, rather than an older one, is that the whole thing is on a more manageable scale. The puppy is smaller so the distance of the retrieve, and therefore the cord, are both shorter. Take care not to frighten the puppy, as you may put him off retrieving altogether. In most cases, the battle will be won after a few days of the pup discovering that running away with the dummy is no longer possible because each attempt will be met with a gentle hauling-in, followed by praise and caresses for coming. I do not usually advise tidbits in any retrieving situation, because of the danger of the puppy learning to spit out the retrieve in order to eat the food.

TEACHING STEADINESS

Once the puppy is retrieving nicely to hand (and care should be taken not to dispense with the cord until a habit has been established), nothing much more in the way of serious training can be done until the puppy is old enough to be taught steadiness, which to my mind is when serious training starts. With a very bold, keen puppy this could be as early as six months, but a quieter, more diffident individual is probably best left until nine or ten months of age. One year old is not too late. In the meantime, the puppy can be walked through cover, over shallow

TOP LEFT: *Take time teaching your Labrador to 'hold' the dummy carefully. It is important that he does not get into bad habits such as mouthing.*

ABOVE: *Most Labradors will be only too happy to retrieve – the key is teaching steadiness so the dog responds only on command.*

LEFT: *Do not fall into the trap of over-training – your Labrador must retain his enthusiasm for work.*

Photos: Carol Ann Johnson.

streams and so on, to get him used to his future working environment.

SIT AND STAY: Up until now, the puppy has been allowed to run in and pick up his retrieve as soon as it is thrown. Now he has to learn to wait, which is probably the most important thing he will ever be taught. The first step is to teach the sit, by pushing or persuading the puppy into position at the same time as using the word "Sit", so that action and word are associated. Some pups learn this in one lesson, some take longer.

Once he is sitting on command, the puppy has to learn to stay until given permission to move. The most important thing to remember at this stage to praise him for staying, and not to call him up (and thus praise him for not staying).

The puppy should be told to sit, then the trainer should walk away one step and immediately return and praise him for staying. Of course, if he has moved, replace him smartly on the exact spot that he left.

Eventually, by gradually increasing the distance, the trainer will be able to leave the pup several yards away and will be able to walk about and around him and he will not try to get up. Every time the pup gets up without permission, he must be firmly replaced. Once the puppy is reasonably reliable at this exercise, you should put him on the lead, say "Sit", and throw the dummy. In all probability, the pup will try to run in but can be stopped by the lead. With most puppies, one lesson will be enough to achieve reasonable steadiness. When the pup is reliable on the lead, remove it and try the exercise with the puppy free. It is sensible, the first time or two, to throw the dummy behind you so you are in a position to intervene if the puppy tries to run in. A sensitive puppy may indeed refuse to retrieve when next asked to do so. As trainer, you need to be aware of the degree of sensitivity of your puppy and choose the right moment to allow a retrieve. However, in general, you should leave the puppy sitting while you collect the dummy yourself, more often than you send him for a retrieve.

Steadiness is something which has to be worked on for the rest of the dog's life. The shooting field is so much more tempting than anything which can be staged with dummies, which means that the pup has to be 110 per cent steady before being taken out shooting.

WALKING AT HEEL
A retriever also has to be taught to walk at heel. Some take to it with very little training, others have to be worked on quite hard and for a fairly long time. It is easiest to start with the pup on a lead, on the left except in the case of a left-handed shooter who would find it more convenient to have the dog walking on the right. The pup should be encouraged to stay roughly level with the handler's knee. If he gets too far ahead, you should do a smart about-turn to bring him behind you, rather than jerking back with the lead, although a combination of both these

actions can be used. Some trainers walk their dogs down a narrow lane (if one is available) carrying a switch with which to administer a tap on the nose if the dog forges ahead. There are more ways than one of achieving results.

DIRECTIONAL CONTROL
Once the pupil is walking nicely to heel off the lead and is steady to thrown dummies, the next important lesson is directional control. Field trial handlers spend hours teaching their dogs to be handled virtually anywhere. It is impossible to win trials without being able to put a dog exactly where you want him within a distance of 200 yards or so. The ordinary shooting owner

Am. Can. Ch. Waggin' Tails Incredi-Bull JH (Am. Can. Ch. Valli-Vue Chelons Mr Levi JH – Ch. Highland Break of Dawn), bred by Sharon Grieves.

Photo courtesy: Sharon Grieves.

has less need of this skill, but it is still extremely useful to be able to get a dog where you want him, especially if the bird is down on the far side of a river. It is also highly desirable to be able to stop the dog going for one bird in order to send him for a different one, which may be a runner, whereas the bird the dog has in mind is dead and there is less urgency to collect it.

USE OF THE WHISTLE: Before starting to teach directional control, the young dog must stop to a short blast on the whistle within a distance of about 15 or 20 yards. This is accomplished first of all by using the whistle instead of the command "Sit" when the dog is close by, or even on the lead. When the dog has learnt to sit to the whistle in this way, he should be allowed to run about at a few yards distance from the handler, who should then blow the whistle, cover the ground to reach the dog in double-quick time, and give the command to sit. Practice, combined with very gradually increasing the distances, will eventually have the desired effect. The dog must always be made to stop and sit in the place occupied when the whistle was first blown.

DUMMIES: Directional control can be started by making the dog sit and then throwing two dummies in opposite directions. Give the dog a clear signal by pointing to the dummy desired (the first one thrown) and then order him to retrieve. Most amenable puppies will go for the correct dummy first time, but if yours does not, it is essential to be able to stop the pup (by blowing the whistle) before the wrong one is picked. If the correct dummy is selected, it should be thrown back before sending him for the other. Eventually, this should teach the left and right signals, but it is equally important to be able to get the dog straight back, or closer in. It is a good idea, particularly with a sensitive puppy, to start on the 'getting back' with only one dummy, so there is no possibility of a mistake. The pup should be seated, a dummy thrown beyond him, then the handler should retreat a few yards leaving the pup in exact line between handler and dummy. The pup should then be sent for the retrieve with the normal

word of command, plus "Get out" or "Back" or whatever command has been chosen, and an appropriate signal.

Later on, the technique is to seat the pup and throw out three dummies, one behind and one to each side, and with the appropriate command and signal him to pick them in any order. Remember, the pup must be capable of being stopped if he goes for the wrong one. However, even when a dog is doing this perfectly, it does not mean that handling at a distance on strange ground will automatically follow. More and yet more practice is needed for this.

'UNSEEN' PRACTICE: It is often difficult with some dogs to get them to come closer to the handler when hunting. A good way of teaching this is to send the dog for a retrieve, and while he is out hunting for it, throw another unseen dummy closer in. Then blow the recall whistle and manoeuvre the dog into the correct position to find the closer dummy.

A gundog has to be capable of being sent for game he has not marked, i.e. 'unseens'. It is useful in this context if your pup will go out in the direction sent. Therefore, when sending my dogs for a marked dummy, I always give them an arm signal in the direction of the dummy before sending them. It is an additional exercise in steadiness as the upraised arm is not a signal to go. The dog has to await the command.

Some puppies are very reluctant to go out and hunt for something they have not seen thrown. There are several ways of overcoming this, such as throwing out three or four dummies in the same direction, and sending the pup for one after another. The puppy will rush out for the first, but may have difficulty remembering the others. As with all other training, practice makes perfect. Another idea is to put out a dummy in long grass or other light cover and send the pup only a very short distance, and always into the wind, so that he can find the dummy almost as soon as he gets to his feet and starts hunting. The pup needs to learn that if he obeys the handler and hunts in the direction indicated, he is certain to find a retrieve.

NEW CHALLENGES

Gradually the lessons should take place somewhere other than on short grass, although the early directional control training can with advantage be done on a lawn, so that the pupil sees the dummy immediately on turning in the right direction. A trained gundog also has to be able to jump, swim and face punishing cover. None of these things (except possibly jumping) can be achieved overnight. Few young dogs are happy to face brambles etc. until they have had the pleasure of working on real game, and discovering that cover is where game is mainly to be found.

JUMPING: If there is no suitable low fence available for the dog to jump over, it is not difficult to make one. It should be not more than about two feet in height so that, if necessary, you can step over with the dog on a lead. Most dogs love jumping once they get the idea.

WATER WORK: Water work is easy with most Labradors, especially if a start is made in hot weather, and if other water-loving dogs are available to set an example. A shallow stream which the handler can wade across and persuade the dog to follow (on a lead if necessary) is ideal, rather than a lake or pond where the dog has to swim out for a dummy. However, if the latter is all that is available, a place with a gradual rather than a steep entry should be chosen and the dummy thrown no more than a couple of feet from the bank. Most dogs will quickly gain the confidence to go further, but you should resist the temptation to throw the dummy too far, too soon. If the dog fails, his confidence is undermined and, unless there is another dog available, the result is a lost dummy!

Some dogs will leap into water, others tend to a more cautious and gradual entry. In Britain we rather prefer the latter, because for one thing it is quieter, so is less likely to frighten away other

RIGHT: Am. Can. Ch. Candid's Character Witness CD, JH (Am. Can. Ch. Rainell's Dynasty – Ch. Ebonylane's Hand in Hand), owned by Tom and Eileen Schmidt, bred by Janet Bottoroff.
Photo: Tom Schmidt.

BELOW: Most Labradors take to water-work with great zest. The 'double retrieve' – Solberg's Giddeon by Choice CD, MH (FC/AFC Riverbend's Bojangles – Sunnyburke Moonshine Mishaka), Master National finalist, and his daughter out of Ransom's Perpetual Pursuit CD, MH, Ransom's Perpetual Praise CD, SH. Both are owned and trained by Bernadette Brown.
Photo courtesy: Bernadette Brown.

Canadian Triple Champion Whistlnwings Kitty Magee WCX (Am. Can. Ch. Monach's Black Arrogance CD, WC – Canadian Triple Champion Kenosee Jim Dandy WCX), bred, owned and trained by Lori, Curran, Whistlnwings, Alberta, Canada.

Photo courtesy: Lori Curran.

waterfowl, and for another there is always the possibility of a submerged stake or other hazard on which the dog might be injured. However, Americans prefer a flying leap and, I am told, go to considerable lengths to try and achieve it.

Later on, the dog can be taught to go out on command for something he has not seen thrown, and also to take directions on water.

COPING WITH NOISE

Young puppies should be exposed to a certain amount of noise and taken out in the car and among people, in order to accustom them to sights and sounds other than those they

encounter at home. However, even with the boldest puppy, a tactful introduction to gunfire is advisable. Most people nowadays use a dummy launcher for training retrievers but, there again, it is most unwise to fire one close to a puppy which is unused to it. The first shot, from starting pistol, dummy launcher or gun, should be fired by someone else at a considerable distance. If the puppy shows any apprehension at all, he can be helped by your giving him a tidbit every time the gun is fired. The gun should be brought no closer until the dog is completely happy.

I have often had young dogs which were none

too keen on the dummy launcher, or on any shot fired close at hand, and did not get over this completely before they were taken into the shooting field. I do not myself shoot, and therefore, when picking up, it is easy for me to position myself a long way from the guns. In fact, for a picker-up the best and most useful position is usually a long way back, out of shot. The young dog therefore gets used to gunfire at a distance and learns that it means fun and work. The next step is to be in line, but between two guns rather than actually with one of them. I have never known a slightly gun-nervous dog, treated sensibly, not to get over it in time. However, this is quite different from real gun-shyness which, although now very rare among working strains, is incurable.

HARD MOUTH
Hard mouth is another bugbear which can crop up, although it rarely does. Some dogs can be made hard mouthed by being scratched by a lively cock pheasant, or by another dog snatching a retrieve from their mouths, but a really good mouth is virtually unspoilable. Hard-mouthed dogs damage game and render it inedible, which is why it is an eliminating fault in a field trial.

WHINING
Another eliminating fault is whining. Whiners tend to get worse rather than better, and we have all seen (or heard) the dog on a shoot which gives tongue loudly as soon as a bird is shot. Dogs like this are a perfect nuisance. Anyone who could guarantee a cure for whining would make a fortune, and probably the best that can be done is to watch for it and nip it in the bud as soon as the first squeak is heard.

INTRODUCTION TO THE FIELD
A critical part of gundog training is the introduction to the shooting field. Most pups, having been born between March and July, will be too young to take out at all in the season following their birth, but can be trained during the ensuing summer and started the following season, when they will be about 15-18 months of age. A pup born at the 'wrong' time of year is more diffi-

cult and, in general, I would say that no dog should be taken shooting before twelve months of age, and only then if under good control and of a fairly calm disposition. There are few more foolish actions than to take a young puppy out on a shoot "to get used to it" or "to see what it is all about". The youngster will only learn bad habits, start whining or get cold, bored and possibly frightened.

A young dog should be trained on dummies, progress eventually to cold, clean game shot a day or two previously, and then dead warm game. Live game and runners should come much later. Many young dogs are diffident about picking up live game, but I have never known one not get over it. Some will refuse to pick the first cold bird they are asked to retrieve, although most will do so if it is thrown in full view and the dog is sent quickly or even allowed to run in. If there is any difficulty, it is often helpful to enclose the bird in a sock or thin nylon stocking.

FIELD TRAINING IN NORTH AMERICA
By Marianne Foote

WORKING CERTIFICATES
The American Kennel Club does not require any sporting dog to pass breed specific performance tests before awarding a Championship title. However, the US parent club, The Labrador Retriever Club, Inc. requires members' dogs with a conformation championship, to obtain a Working Certificate (WC) before using the title of Champion.

The Working Certificate Test involves a bird retrieve on the land and two water retrieves in succession with birds. The dog need not be steady or deliver to hand (the area of the handler will do), and it must not be gun shy. The LRC, Inc. Working Certificate is not recognised by the AKC as a title, so it is not an official part of the dog's registered name.

FIELD TRIALS
The English Field Trial was imported to America in the early 1930s. Those trials fre-

ABOVE: Am. Can. Ch. Jolly Captain
Gibson (Am. Can. CD, JH Wyntercreek
Autumn Tyee – Keelcroft's Charisma) is
owned by Rick Mullen and Cindy King,
Bakerbay Labradors.
Photo courtesy: Rick Mullen and Cindy
King.

RIGHT: Ch. Willcare's Masterpiece CD,
JH (Ch. Hennings Mills Master Blend –
Sandlewood Tapestry CD), owned and
bred by Susan Willumsen and John
Valentine, Willcare Labradors, New
Hampshire.

quently included walk-ups, live decoys and multiple dogs on line. However, in the past half century US field trials have developed into very
different events from the English trials. These
differences reflect a much greater emphasis on
water retrieves, a wide variety of hunting conditions, the absence of grounds on which retrievers can be worked on wild game, and the development of training techniques that produce
retrievers capable of responding accurately to
hand and whistle signals at extreme distances.

Field Trial entries are not limited and it is not
uncommon to have over 70 retrievers in Open
or Amateur stakes. These entries posed a challenge for judges who, faced with time con-
straints and limited grounds, must set up
demanding tests that clearly separate the dogs

and the top four placements in a trial. The performance of these retrievers is quite extraordinary to behold. Any Open or Amateur stake will
feature competing dogs who demonstrate a combination of pinpoint marking of multiple shot
birds, precise responses to whistle and hand signals, and a level of intensity and desire that is
hard to describe. While some criticize US trials
for no longer resembling the conditions encountered in an ordinary day of hunting, the fact is
that duplicating a normal hunting situation
would not permit the judges to fairly evaluate
the comparative skills of competing dogs. Many
field trial dogs are superb hunting companions
capable of performing all the ordinary tasks of
the hunting retriever and also capable of that
long and difficult retrieve not infrequently

required when the hunter cripples game—a retriever well beyond the skills of the average canine hunting companion.

Retrievers acquire points toward a Field Championship or an Amateur Field Championship by winning or placing in the top four in an Open, Special, Limited or Amateur All-Age Stakes. Dogs compete against existing field champions for points. To become a Field Champion (FC) a Labrador must earn ten points in Open All-Age competition, including a five point win. The handler of the dog can be a professional trainer or an amateur—no distinction is made. An Amateur title (AFC) requires 15 points including a five point win earned in Open or Amateur stakes and the dog must be handled by an amateur. However, a retriever needs only ten points for an AFC if those points are acquired in Open competition with an amateur handler.

Two minor stakes make up the balance of field trial competition—the Derby, for dogs under two years of age; and the Qualifying Stake, for dogs in transition from Derby to Open competition. In the United States in 1995 there were 214 Open and Amateur All-Age stakes for retrievers and Irish Water Spaniels. The Open Stakes averaged 57 starters and the Amateur Stakes 43 starters. The AKC awarded 60 Field Champion and 38 Amateur Field Champion titles to Labradors in 1995.

NATIONAL RETRIEVING CHAMPIONSHIPS

Winning a National Championship title is a great honour and requires a supremely talented retriever. Approximately 100 retrievers qualify yearly for each of the two National Championship Stakes: the National Amateur Championship in June and the National Retriever Championship in November. The sites for championship stakes are rotated between time zones each year. Both championships have three judges and are made up of ten series, or tests, that extend over a week—a grueling undertaking for dog and handler. Labradors dominate the list of National title holders; however, only a handful have ever repeated National Championship wins and only two in the history of the breed have achieved triple wins. Dual Ch.

Shed of Arden, a black dog, won the National title in 1942, 1943 and 1946. NFC/AFC Candlewood's Tanks A Lot, a black female, won the National title in 1990, 1991 and 1994 (her sire won the title in 1992). Four Labradors have succeeded in winning both the National Championship and the National Amateur Championship.

HUNTING TESTS FOR RETRIEVERS

AKC Hunting Tests were designed for retriever owners with a primary interest in hunting, and little time or money to compete in field trials. The program has a format similar to Obedience. Titles are achieved in a non-competitive manner and tests are open to all retrievers and Irish Water Spaniels. A retriever must pass four tests at the novice level to earn the Junior Hunter (JH) title. If the trainer wishes to continue to the next level four more tests must be passed for a Senior Hunter (SH) title, and four more at the Master level for the Master Hunter (MH) title. In 1995 the AKC awarded 889 Junior titles, 362 Senior titles and 243 Master Hunter titles.

MASTER NATIONAL

For the owner who wishes to continue to qualify at the Master level an annual Master National has been added to the AKC's fall calendar. The Master National is a week-long event presided over by three judges. Dog and handler must complete six hunt scenarios to finish the event. A retriever must pass six Master level tests within the calendar year to be eligible for the Master National. In 1995 one hundred and seventy-nine dogs started in the Master National and seventy-five dogs earned qualifying scores. Among the qualifiers, a chocolate Labrador female, Am./Can. Ch. Plantier's Ruthless Ruthie CD, MH — the first of her sex and color to accomplish this.

PLUIS DAVERN, SUNDOWNER KENNELS, CALIFORNIA

Pluis Davern is a professional handler for conformation dogs, an Obedience trainer, a Search and Rescue dog trainer, and a trainer of retrievers for Hunting Tests. She also judges to the Master level at Hunting Tests for Retrievers, as

Bo-Jays Privileged Character (FC/AFC Riverbend's Bo-Jangles – Argonaut's Dixie-Mac), owned by Steve R. Deckard.

Photo: Steve R. Deckard – Sulphur Springs Photo.

FC/AFC Hightest CC Waterback MH (Castlebay's on the Double – World Famous Sweet Pea) was bred by Debra Folsom, Hightest Kennels, California and is owned and trained by Gary Ahlgren and Mary Williams, California.

Photo courtesy: Mary Williams.

well as performance events for other sporting dogs. She has bred or trained Labrador Retrievers, Golden Retrievers, German Shorthaired Pointers and Sussex Spaniels. In addition to conformation titles, many of her dogs have advanced Obedience degrees and advanced Hunting Test titles.

Pluis agrees with the observations of all the Obedience specialists – the Labrador's independence and intelligence can be a challenge in repetitive training. "It is important for an owner interested in advanced Obedience or field training to establish concentration and motivation early in their dog," she said. "Both of these sports require agility, so physical conditioning and conformation contribute to having a competitive animal.

"I think that the AKC Hunting Test Program for Retrievers has had a very positive affect on breeding programs. Many conformation exhibitors who would be unable to attend a field trial with their Labrador, now find that they can enter it in Hunting Tests with a degree of confidence. Observing marking ability and perseverance at a Hunt Test has helped in evaluating potential breeding stock – and breeders are now enhancing the hunting aptitudes of the animals they produce. The program has also provided a 'meeting place' for conformation and performance owners and they are beginning to share knowledge.

"When assessing a puppy to train for hunting or for Hunting Tests, I am looking for a strong 'chase' instinct coupled with a desire-to-please. Teamwork is the key to outstanding performances, so the latter quality is an important consideration for any trainer. My training program is firmly rooted in early motivational training."

BARBARA AND PAUL GENTHER, TEALBROOK KENNELS, FLORIDA.
Paul Genther began training and handling Labradors in 1947. His wife, Barbara, joined him in this endeavour in 1965. They have shown in Conformation, Obedience, Field Trials and Hunting Tests for Retrievers, as well as breeding Labradors. Their present facilities are in Florida and they specialise in training hunting dogs that are also family companions.

"Our idea of the ideal Labrador temperament is a dog that settles comfortably into a home routine, but has a focus and a willingness to retrieve, said Barbara. "We like a dog that is more sensitive and responsive to a handler's correction, eliminating the need for mechanical control. I also like a Labrador to resemble the dog described in the Standard.

"Lack of delivery, or not returning to the handler when called, is probably the most consistent problem we see in Labradors brought to us for training. I believe that most owners could prevent this dilemma if they could avoid 'the puppy lapse.' Too many new puppy owners fail to give a puppy all the attention it needs. This is the time to teach the dog to work for you, and not for himself. The dog needs to learn the game – to return the object to the handler.

"All too often as a puppy grows and becomes rambunctious, it is relegated to the isolation of the backyard. For a Labrador, isolation is neglect and the ensuing behavior– hysterical greetings, jumping on you, barking, digging – is all associated with this form of neglect."

The Genthers were enthusiastic about the non-competitive Hunting Retriever Test program, especially after competing in Field Trials for many years and observing the changes in those trials. They hoped Hunt Tests would provide an opportunity for those owners with neither the time nor the money to compete in Field Trials to be given a chance to test their Labrador against a standard of competence. However, some of their enthusiasm has cooled.

"We feel that many Master level tests are oriented toward success for those Retrievers that have been trained to override their natural hunting instincts and only take directions from their handler. Many of these dogs have a toughness that the average dog owner cannot cope with."

9 THE LABRADOR AT WORK

The versatility of the Labrador Retriever is demonstrated in the multiple uses that have been found for the breed beyond the hunting field and hearth. Labradors dominate most of the guide dog programmes in the United States, in the UK and in other parts of the world. They also excel as drug, arson and bomb detection dogs, as assistance dogs and as therapy dogs.

GUIDE DOGS

THE RIGHT BREED FOR THE JOB

When guide dog training was in its infancy, German Shepherd Dogs were the favoured breed. However, it was swiftly discovered that the Retriever breeds – the Labrador Retriever in particular – were supremely suited to this type of work. The Labrador's short coat is easy to care for, the dog is a suitable height for working in harness, has the intelligence to respond to training without showing too much initiative, and creates a good impression as it goes about its work. The only disadvantages to be countered are the Labrador's tendency to scavenge, and to use its nose. In fact, dogs rejected for guide dog work for the latter reason have been passed on to be trained as sniffer dogs.

As the demand for guide dogs has grown, the need to consistently produce dogs suitable for training became paramount. A breeding programme was launched, and with skilful management, the best lines for each breed used were developed. Today the Guide Dogs for the Blind Association in the UK manages a breeding stock of some 250 dogs and raises 900 puppies each year. There is a total of 4,000 working guide dogs in the UK.

It is interesting to look at the success rates of the various breeds used:

BREED	SUCCESS RATE (percentage)	NUMBER IN SURVEY
Labrador Retriever	72	4640
Golden Retriever	73	1119
German Shepherd Dog	61	908
Border Collie	65	79
Lab/Golden Ret.	82	1927
Lab/Curly Coat Ret.	82	112
Golden Ret/Collie	79	96

'As the demand for guide dogs has grown, the need to consistently produce dogs suitable for training became paramount'

The Labrador has proved its worth as a guide dog worldwide.
> *Photo: Ed Smith courtesy of Guide Dogs for the Blind Inc.*

The willing temperament of the Labrador, combined with its pleasing disposition, makes the breed ideally suited to guide dog work.

In the USA, the Seeing Eye also has its own breeding programme. As in the UK, German Shepherd Dogs were the first Seeing Eye Dogs, but in the 1970s the use of retriever breeds increased enormously. The breakdown of breeds used in the successive years was:
Labrador Retrievers: 120

German Shepherd Dogs: 116
Golden Retrievers: 16.
   The following year the figures were:
Labrador Retrievers: 136
German Shepherd Dogs: 92
Golden Retrievers 44.
   The total success rate with dogs bred by The

Seeing Eye is 65-70 per cent.

In the UK, the high success rate among first crosses, which are the product of a mating of two pure, but different, breeds was first noted when adult dogs were brought in through the approval system – dogs obtained from sources other than the Association's breeding programme. It was therefore decided to experiment with first crosses within the breeding programme. By crossing the Labrador Retriever with the Golden Retriever it was hoped to combine the best qualities of both breeds. The Golden Retriever's coat is a little more difficult to care for, and it has been found that Goldens can become a little worried when working. This, coupled with a streak of stubbornness, which can even result in a refusal to work, makes the Golden a complex breed. Cross-breeding the Labrador Retriever with the Golden Retriever has proved enormously successful, producing dogs that combine the tolerance of the Labrador with some of the sensitivity of the Golden Retriever.

However, it was found that the success rate dropped when attempts were made to breed from two cross-breeds, i.e. a Lab/Golden crossed with a Lab/Golden, and so breeding is now restricted to first crosses.

The Association has found that the ideal dog should be:
Stable.
Of a pleasing disposition.
Not neurotic, shy or frightened.
Reasonably energetic.
Not hyperactive.
Not aggressive (pure, apprehensive or protective).
Of low chasing instinct.
Able to concentrate for long periods.
Not easily distracted.
Willing.
Confident with and tolerant of children.
Confident with and tolerant of other animals.
Responsive to the human voice.
Not sound-shy.
Able to show reasonable initiative.
Not too dominant or self-interested.
Able to change environment and/or handler without undue stress.

Within the limits of body sensitivity.
As free as possible from hereditary defects (physical).

Labradors are a popular choice for most of the guide dog training programmes in the United States. Guide Dogs for the Blind, Inc., a non-profit-making charitable organisation established in 1942, provides training and guide dogs to visually impaired men and women in the USA and Canada. Their programme uses pure-bred German Shepherds, Golden Retrievers and Labrador Retrievers. Current statistics indicate that 45 per cent of their graduating guides are Labradors, a higher percentage than their other two breeds. Guide Dogs cites the hardiness of the breed, plus its even temperament and general good health as some of the reasons for the Labrador's success in this work. There are many guide dog schools in different parts of the USA. The Seeing Eye, based in New York, has recently started experimenting with German Shepherd Dog/Labrador Retriever crosses, but it is still too early to evaluate the results. Golden Retriever/Labrador crosses are also being used for guide dog work, but again, it is too early to generalise about the success of this project.

THE TRAINING PROCESS
The puppy walking scheme is an essential ingredient in producing successful guide dogs, and both the Guide Dogs for the Blind Association and The Seeing Eye operate similar programmes. In the UK, puppies are taken from the litter at six weeks of age to be placed in a family home. In the USA, the Puppy Raising Program waits until the pups are eight weeks before they are placed in homes. The aim is for the puppy to grow up in a normal family environment, and to become thoroughly socialised, encountering a variety of different situations. The puppy must get used to traffic of all kinds, and learn to walk slightly ahead, ignoring all distractions. Basic obedience exercises are also taught at this stage. The puppies are supervised throughout the time they are at walk, and then they are assessed for further training. In the UK, the dogs are brought in for training when they are around twelve months of age, while The

The puppy walking scheme serves to educate and socialise young puppies within the home, preparing them for further training.
Photo courtesy: Guide Dogs for the Blind Association.

Seeing Eye prefers to wait until dogs are 16 months old. Both dogs and bitches accepted for guide dog training are neutered. With bitches, this is done after their first season (about 14 months) to ensure physical and mental maturity. Males are neutered at around 12 months, before

the onset of dominant characteristics.

Training at one of the Guide Dog for the Blind centres in the UK usually takes around seven months. The Seeing Eye training course takes around four months. As with all forms of dog training, the work is based on basic obedience and response to commands. The training programme consists of developing a dog's concentration, along with a willingness to work for a handler. The dog is exposed to a wide range of environmental conditions, with particular emphasis on the conditions it would meet as a working guide dog, whether in a busy city or a rural environment. The dog must learn to walk at an acceptable pace for a blind owner, on a straight line, down the centre of the pavement, stopping at down kerbs. The dog is taught to avoid obstacles on the pavement, including other pedestrians, and to negotiate obstacles that block the whole pavement, returning to the pavement once the problem is by-passed.

Training in traffic is a crucial aspect of the programme. The dog is trained to develop a 'critical' area. If a vehicle comes inside the critical area, the dog would disobey a command to proceed. The critical area varies in size depending on the speed of the approaching vehicle, i.e. the faster the vehicle, the greater the critical area, and the earlier the dog should make the decision to disobey any command to proceed.

The dog would also be trained to work in all environmental circumstances, such as public transport, car travel, supermarkets, shops, locating road-crossings, finding doors, going in lifts, etc.

THE PARTNERSHIP
Blind students are individually assessed to match the right dog to suit each individual. Labrador Retrievers have been found to be the most adaptable, suiting a wide variety of differing needs and circumstances.

In the first instance, the breed of dog is chosen, and this is often influenced by physical circumstances, such as the age and height of the student, as well as any other physical disability they may have. The lifestyle of the student is taken into consideration, taking account of the family situation and the work environment. The personality of each student is also evaluated with the aim of finding a dog with the most suitable temperament. For example, some students would work better with a more sensitive dog, while others would get on better with a more tolerant, laid-back animal.

Training with the student takes four weeks on a residential course but this can depend on the aptitude and understanding of the owner, and the dog's acceptance of its change of circumstances. The new blind owner experiences the same circumstances as a dog in training, but in a more condensed form. A gradual build-up from quiet to busy city conditions will take place during the training period. The owner is given instruction on training methods and understanding dog psychology, as well as practical advice on feeding, grooming and general care of the dog.

After the course has been completed, the new blind owners are visited in their homes to check that each dog is working successfully in its new environment. These visits may vary depending on individual needs, and if necessary, the dog and owner will undergo a further week of residential training. Thereafter, guide dog owners are visited on a six-monthly basis, but more frequents visits are made if necessary.

DAWN AND DEBBIE – A WORKING FRIENDSHIP

Debbie Harris, aged 28, is now working with her second guide dog. Her first dog, a black Labrador bitch called Lucy, was retired at ten years of age.

"Lucy was slowing down a bit and was developing cataracts, so it was decided to retire her as soon as a suitable replacement was available. To begin with I was not very happy about giving up working with Lucy, but luckily, I live with my parents and they agreed to keep her. I could not bear to part with her."

Debbie's new dog, Dawn, is a yellow Labrador bitch. Debbie is under five feet in height, so one of the first criteria was selecting a dog of the right height, and not too strong for her. She also has a quiet voice, and needed a dog who would respond to sensitive handling.

"In many ways Dawn is quite similar to Lucy," said Debbie. "She is only two years old and so she tends to be more excitable, but Lucy can still be quite puppy-like – I think that kind of playfulness is one of the nice things about Labradors."

One of the most difficult problems a guide dog has to face is the constant changes of allegiance during the training period. To begin with the dog responds to the puppy-walker. When advanced training begins, the instructor becomes the focal person in the dog's life. Finally, the dog is matched with a student, and must learn to respond to its new owner.

"I was quite surprised how quickly Dawn started to respond to me," said Debbie. "The first time I met her was when the instructor brought her to my home. This was to see if we are both suited to each other. Then, when we went to the centre we were given a couple of days to settle in, and then the instructor brought the dogs to us in our own rooms. To begin with, Dawn whined a bit when she was left on her own with me. But she soon settled down. When I started to feed her, she seemed to realise I was important! To begin with, when we started working together she kept listening for the instructor's voice, but by the end of the first week she was responding to my voice."

The students take over full responsibility for their dogs within a couple of days, and this obviously helps to form a bond. They feed and groom their dogs and are responsible for taking them out to the grass runs. The training course becomes increasingly complex as the students gain confidence working with their dogs. To begin with they go on short walks in fairly quiet areas graduating to going into the city centre, travelling on a bus and a train, negotiating an obstacle course, and going on a night walk. The student must learn to give the correct commands so that the dog is given clear directions in a logical sequence. This is particularly important when negotiating complicated obstacles, when the dog may have to guide his owner off the kerb, around the obstacle and then back on to the kerb again. The dog also has to assess the height of the obstacle so that there is sufficient room for his owner to pass through.

Although Debbie had completed the training

Debbie Harris and her guide dog, Dawn, newly qualified from the training course and ready to start their working life together.

Photo courtesy: Guide Dogs for the Blind Association.

course only eight years previously with Lucy, she was surprised how tough she found it.

"It is very tiring," she said. "The work is very intensive and it demands a lot of concentration. I suppose I was slightly more relaxed than first-time guide dog owners as I had done it before – but it is hard work. You may have a very well-trained dog, but that is not enough. The handler has to work with the dog and respond to the dog in order for the partnership to work. The training course is just the start of it. The real work starts when you get home."

Debbie works as a civil servant and her journey to work involves a ten-minute walk to the bus stop, a fifteen-minute ride on the bus, and then a twenty-minute walk to her office, where she works on the thirteenth floor.

"It is important to have a dog who can cope with the journey and who will go up and down in lifts," said Debbie. "However, when I am at work, I need a dog who is prepared to settle down quietly and not demand attention from everyone. I think Dawn is quite a laid-back dog and she enjoys her comforts. She enjoys being made a fuss of, but she understands that she must not be a nuisance.

"Lucy was loved by everyone at work, and there was always someone to help me with her if necessary. Her biggest temptation was when people ate snacks at their desks – and it took a strong will to resist her pleading looks! My colleagues were all sad when Lucy came to work for the last time, and they presented her with a beautiful card, signed by everyone.

"I am confident that Dawn will cope as well as Lucy. But it takes time to build up a good working relationship. It may take as long as six months, or even a year, before we really understand each other. The important thing is we have made a good start and we have got plenty of time to build on that.

"When I heard that I was getting a new guide dog, my main worry was how Lucy would react. But she is very fond of my parents and will be content to stay at home with them during the day. After all those years of hard work, I think she deserves an easy retirement."

A TRIBUTE TO JENNA
Nothing illustrates the Labrador's versatility better than the following account by Brechie van Rooyan, a courageous blind woman living in South Africa, whose trust in her guide dog probably saved her life.

"I was working as head switchboard operator in Pretoria and Jenna, my guide dog, always slept between my table and the door, approximately three metres away from me. One day something strange happened to me. I was totally aware of everything that was taking place around me, but I could not respond. Although I showed no outwards signs that anything was amiss, Jenna suddenly jumped up and ran over to me and with little crying sounds, bumped and nudged me. One of my colleagues suggested that Jenna wanted to go out. I could not react. She spoke to me again. I again could not acknowledge her. A little while later, although I did not feel quite myself, I took Jenna out to the park three blocks away. I could not give her the usual commands, but she led me safely to the park and back through some busy traffic.

"She always felt hot at night during the summer months and would keep me awake by putting her front paws on the bed to tell me this. There was a cool spot at the front door, but she would not stay there without me. As a result, I would bench her and then she would be quite happy to stay in the coolness. That evening after chatting to a friend on the phone, I benched Jenna at the front door and went to bed.

"Shortly after midnight I got up to go to the bathroom, and I collapsed. I had had a stroke. Although Jenna could not see me from where she was lying, she immediately started barking frantically. With great difficulty, I managed to crawl towards the phone and press the re-dial button. My friend answered, but I could not speak. Fortunately, she recognised the frenzied high-pitched bark of Jenna in the background and, realising that I was in trouble, assured me that she was coming over straightaway.

"I knew that I would have to unlock the front door, but by this stage I had lost my sense of direction totally. I lay still and listened for Jenna. Then I slowly pulled myself towards the sound of barking. As soon as Jenna saw me, she stopped barking and she just cried and whimpered softly. I kept passing out, but then Jenna barked so loudly that the noise penetrated my consciousness. Again, I continued crawling towards her. On reaching her she started nudging me, trying in her way to help me up.

"At last my friend arrived. Jenna resumed her loud barking. I managed to push the key under the door and when my friend entered, Jenna lay down and, uncharacteristically, made no sound.

"As a result of this stroke, it was nine months before I could walk again and then only with a walking ring. I wanted to regain my independence, like making trips to the hairdresser, bank or supermarket on my own. So I contacted the South African Guide Dogs Association to ask them to teach Jenna to guide me with the walking ring. They were willing to help, but said that a dog would find it very difficult to guide a person in this situation and that I was possibly asking too much of Jenna. However, a trainer came to see me to try a test run with her.

"Again she showed what a remarkable dog she was. On the trial run she immediately stood on my left hand side, next to my walking ring. On my command she walked forward – not her normal walking speed, but tiny step by tiny step. Because of my weakened left side, and because I had to hold on to her harness and the ring simultaneously, the handle of the harness would slip out of my hand. When this happened, she immediately would stand still and wait for me to find the handle again.

So she guided me, walking ring and all, around every obstacle in our path. For instance, when we reached a step she would stand and wait until I had lifted the walking ring and pulled myself up. Then she would proceed sedately. Even though it took me an hour to do what we had always done in ten minutes, she never once tried to increase her speed, nor lost concentration. There was no need to train her. She instinctively knew what to do!

"Jenna, now over 14 years old, has retired. She is living in a loving home where she spends her retirement sleeping in the sun and enjoying her favourite pastime – eating!"

ASSISTANCE DOGS

Perhaps one of the Labrador's most unique adaptations is as an Assistance Dog. Assistance dog organisations train dogs to help people with physical disabilities other than blindness. Schemes to train dogs to alert people with hearing loss started in the United States, and by 1980 several programmes were operating such as the American Humane Association in Colorado in 1981. As a result of close co-operation, Hearing Dogs for the Deaf was started in the UK. Hearing Dogs are generally of mixed

breed and selected from animal shelters. They are trained to make physical contact with a paw to alert their deaf owners, and then lead them to the source of the sound such as a doorbell, telephone, smoke alarm – or even to tell a deaf mother when her baby is crying. Again, the Labrador's willing and steady temperament has been ideally suited to this work.

Canine Companions for Independence (CCI) in Santa Rosa, California is now celebrating its twenty-first anniversary. CCI's programme divides assistance dogs into three categories: service dogs, hearing dogs and social dogs. Labradors are especially helpful as service dogs, increasing the independence of the handler and

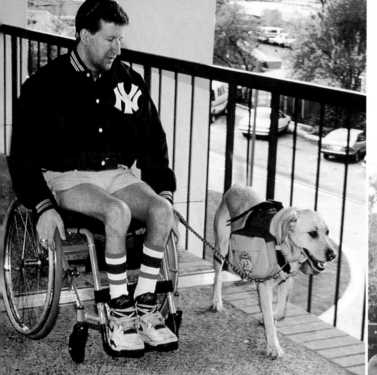

LEFT: A Canine Companions for Independence Team Training session. The disabled owner can enjoy greater independence with the help of a trained dog.

Photo: R.R. Crockett, courtesy of Canine Companions for Independence, Santa Rosa, California.

RIGHT: Whisper fetches and carries parcels, opens doors, and hands over money for his master, Barry Edy. In South Africa, Guide Dogs also provide a service to the disabled, the deaf and children with developmental difficulties. These dogs are fully trained and then matched with a suitable owner.

Photo: Rose Chamberlain, S.A. Guide Dogs for the Blind Association.

performing tasks such as turning on and off light switches, pushing elevator buttons, retrieving items and pulling a wheelchair. Canine Support Teams, Inc. in Perris, California also uses a number of Labradors as service dogs. These dogs respond to more than 50 commands, and provide an additional aid as an 'ice breaker' removing barriers that may prevent social contact and conversation.

In the UK, Dogs for the Disabled is becoming a growing force, working in close co-operation with the Guide Dogs for the Blind Association. Many of the dogs used are those who have been rejected from the guide dog training programme. This is usually due to a problem that makes them unsuitable for guiding work in stressful traffic situations, but the dogs, many of them Labradors, can happily adapt to working in a different situation.

THERAPY DOGS
By Lesley Scott-Ordish

RECOGNISING THE NEED
Early in 1974, B.M. Levinson, a professor of psychology from New York, bravely presented a paper at a symposium held in London. In it, he attempted to forecast how life would be by the year 2000. Twenty-two years on and just short of the turn of the century, it is interesting to check his forecasts. Over-fanciful in some respects, the professor nevertheless clearly spotted the trend. He predicted that man will become aware of the importance of companion animals as a source of mental health and stability in increasingly strained and unhappy family relationships. He foresaw an animal-lending service on prescription for sick and disabled people, charged for with appropriate bills.

With no knowledge of this, but greatly influenced by an international conference on the bond between people and animals held in Philadelphia in 1981, the Pets As Therapy charity was started in England in 1983. This programme offers animals, mostly dogs, who have all been carefully tested for good temperament. The animals and their owners regularly visit hospices, hospitals and homes for children and elderly people. Labradors figure high on the list for suitability as therapy dogs, because of their friendly personalities and willingness to please. They need to be past their rather boisterous puppy days, and it is the mature Labrador who is needed for therapy schemes.

In the USA, pioneering work was started in 1980 by the American Humane Association on the first bibliography of Pets Facilitated Therapy to assist societies with an interest in this new field. Subsequently, a Pet Partners programme was started by the Delta Society which has now spread to 45 states with nearly 2,000 Pet Partner teams. Michael McCulloch of Oregon State and Sam Corson of Ohio State were just two of the early and influential exponents of the benefits which animals can bring to lonely and depressed people.

Back in England, Pets As Therapy got off to a sticky start, with no takers but plenty of kindly dog-and-owner teams. The organisation had much work to do in raising the acceptability of dogs in such an environment, and in changing the perception of dogs as a danger to human health. Medical consultants agreed that the risk to patients was far greater from the humans accompanying the dog than from the dog. But after several years, the tide started to turn. The charity, which provides the visiting scheme free of charge thanks to willing dog owners, now has 9,000 friendly PAT Dogs registered. It has a considerable grateful following among many thousands of people who seriously miss contact with animals in their lives.

THERAPY IN ACTION
Hilda had not spoken an intelligible word to anyone for more than a year. But you could tell she was cross, and very unhappy. Hilda was distressed with a world which had shut her up in a care unit, away from her rather scruffy but familiar home of so many years, and the dog and chickens she had loved. No one visited Hilda. If they had, they would either have been ignored or rebuffed. She would sit for hours muttering angrily or rocking backwards and forwards, her bony body hunched up, seeking solace and comfort. Hilda was a prisoner in a society which thought it knew better than Hilda herself what was good for her.

But then PAT Dogs were invited to the home. Hilda was sitting in her usual chair when a friendly, gentle PAT Labrador Retriever bounced happily into the room. Residents looked interested at once and their faces lit up with pleasure. A lot of patting began. Suddenly the blank, unseeing expression seemed to melt away from Hilda's face. "I had a dog like that once," she said slowly and distinctly. "That's the first time I have ever been able to hear and understand what Hilda said," remarked a member of the nursing staff in amazement. "It's a little miracle."

The little miracle continued to work on Hilda as the visits progressed each week. Hilda talked to the dog, though she still ignored the kindly PAT Dog owner. But as she stroked and cuddled the Labrador, everyone could see the therapy working. Hilda learned to become a person again through the animal contact which she had missed more than anyone had recognised.

A different kind of help was provided by a PAT Dog visiting a fretful three-year-old child in hospital in Suffolk. The little girl was waiting for an operation. Nurses were having a difficult time in getting her to accept her treatment, but when the visiting PAT Dog was allowed on the cot, the child's face changed to pure delight and she accepted injections calmly as she cuddled the dog.

There is also a demand for therapy dogs who can help both children and adults to overcome a phobia or fear of dogs. Labradors are particularly well-suited to this task, as their calm and gentle temperament poses no threat. Important work is now being carried out at many clinics with therapy dogs helping desensitize people and reduce their terror.

SEARCH AND RESCUE

Labradors proved their worth as search or 'sniffer' dogs in the 1960s and 1970s when they were used to find drugs. It was in the 1980s that the police recognised the need for specialist explosive-finding dogs, and turned to Labradors because of the success they had achieved in searching for drugs. They were a known quantity with a reputation for steadiness, excellent retrieving instincts, acute scenting ability and a keenness to work. Later it was realised just how good gundogs in general were for sniffer work, and breeds other than Labradors started to be used. The Spaniel breeds have proved to be useful in situations where a lighter, more agile dog has been needed – particularly when a handler has had to lift the dog to work in high, inaccessible places.

However, the Labrador remains a popular choice for this type of work. In the UK, there are well over 100 Labradors working as search dogs with police forces. This figure does not include those working for the Armed Services, Customs and Excise, the Prison Service and the Ports Authorities. In the USA, Labradors are widely used as arson, drug and bomb-detection dogs. The breed has also proved its worth working in Wilderness and Disaster situations. Of the 16 Federal Emergency Management Agency (FEMA) advanced certified Disaster dogs, five are Labrador Retrievers. Search and Rescue training requires a dog who is fearless in strange situations, athletic and focused in its search quest, as well as having a dedicated trainer and handler. Dogs are taught to move with care through rubble and to 'alert', indicating to their handlers the presence of another person. The handlers of FEMA-certified dogs must keep in touch by bleeper with a central office so that they may be reached in an emergency.

Although training methods vary according to the task the dog is required to carry out, the general principles remain the same, relying on the working ability of each individual dog, and the partnership between dog and handler.

Tom Bowles has been handling dogs for 25 years with the Police Force and has specialised in bomb-detection work. His first dog was a Golden Retriever. He currently works with a Springer Spaniel and an eight-year-old black Labrador Retriever, whom he picked out as a six-week-old puppy. He called the Labrador Dino – a play on the French word for dynamite.

Tom considers that Labradors are the best dogs for explosives work. "They are steady and level-headed," he says. "It is essential that bomb dogs can work systematically. If, for example, they are searching a house, they have to make

The Labrador's sense of smell, coupled with its ability to work under instruction, has led to its use as a 'sniffer dog' trained to search for drugs and explosives.

Photos courtesy: Metropolitan Police.

sure one room is clean before moving on to the next, so they will make sure the hall is clear, then the front room, then the next room, and so on through the building."

Whether explosives are actually suspected, or whether an area or building is being searched as a preventative measure, the Labrador and the handler are the first to go in – and they are on their own. "We work as a team," says Tom, "and I keep Dino in my line of sight all the time so that as soon as he finds anything, I know about it."

Dino is an expert at what is called the passive indication. "This means that if he finds any explosives he will back off, then freeze," says Tom. "He will then turn his head, look at me, and then look back at the suspect place. There is no barking and there is a definite 'no touch' policy. Once Dino has done his work and given this signal, I then indicate with my hands that he must come back to me – and we leave, quickly! It's time for the human experts to go in."

When sniffing for drugs, the method is slightly different. "The dog is allowed more freedom to search independently and out of sight," says Tom. "Again, using the example of searching a house, the drugs dog is allowed to examine the ground floor at random before moving upstairs. He can dig for the substance, or go through a black plastic bag full of rubbish and can indicate a find by barking." And, as Tom points out, there is another difference between the two methods: "When searching for drugs, we have good reasons for being fairly certain that they are somewhere on the premises. With explosives we have no idea whether they are there, or not."

FINDING SUITABLE DOGS
Obviously, it is essential to find the right type of dog for training. In some instances, there may be breeders who produce dogs of the correct type and temperament. Alternatively, people often ring the police and offer dogs, usually because their circumstances have changed and they have a young, active dog they can no longer keep, or who has proved to be too much for them to handle. When this happens, an experienced handler, such as Tom Bowles, goes to the house to inspect the dog, who needs to be between ten and 18 months of age. "First impressions are very important," he says. "The dog must come to me without hesitation. If he holds back, or shows any reserve or shyness, then the chances are I will not take that dog. What I am looking for is an out-going, enthusiastic personality."

A dog who looks promising is taken away and placed into a police environment, initially just

This yellow Labrador exhibits intensity and persistence at the buried tube during 'bark alert' training for disaster search.

Photo courtesy: Wilma Melville.

Dino, a highly successful 'sniffer' dog specialising in bomb detection, is an expert in passive indication. Here, he has clearly located the place to search. A swift response confirms the presence of explosives.

Photo courtesy: Tom Bowles.

for one day and then returned home. "Some dogs dislike this," says Tom, "so they are not going to be suitable. But if the dog enjoys the experience, then the periods away from home are extended, while we continue to assess the animal. When we decide the dog really is suitable, it is allocated to a handler, and the real training begins."

TRAINING

Training depends on the breed used, but more importantly, it depends on the personality of each individual dog. "The training has to be geared to each individual dog," said Tom. "It is very much a question of instinct, experience and the gut feeling of the handler. Every dog learns at a different rate, so you cannot be hard and fast about when the dog should have reached a particular point in its training. Some are incredibly quick learners, some are much slower, but you just know they are going to get there in the end." The failure rate is high, averaging about 50 per cent, but this ensures that only the very best dogs are put to work in situations which may well be life-threatening to both dog and handler. Initially both drug and explosive dogs are trained in the same way, and all training is based on the essential principles of play and reward. "For me," says Tom, "the most useful

training aid is a tennis ball!"

The Labradors are taught to play and retrieve – the tennis ball is thrown and the dog brings it back. At first the dog can see where the ball lands. Later, the ball is hidden. "It is repetitive," admits Tom "but the object is to make the dog's desire for the ball greater than the instinct to play with anything else retrieved. In the case of drug dogs, when drugs are substituted for the ball, the dog will bring the drugs back to the handler because it wants the reward – having the ball back." The tennis ball can also be used to counteract the potential problem of a dog swallowing the drugs found. As soon as the dog has made a find, the handler throws the ball and off goes the dog after it, totally forgetting about the newly-found drugs.

This is the point at which the bomb dog training branches off on to a separate track. The aim now is to train the dog to seek, find and then retire. "This is the difficult part," Tom explains. "Having done all this encouraging to get the dog to find and retrieve, you then have to keep the dog keen on searching, but stop the actual retrieve. Again, you have to make the dog want the ball more than the stuff found." When the point is reached in training when actual explosives are substituted for the ball, the dog will find them but will back off, or freeze. "The dog will do this," says Tom, "because it knows if it does so, I will give a reward – the tennis ball."

Tom is due to retire next year. His Springer Spaniel, who is still young, will go to another handler. "But Dino stays with me," he says. "He can retire as well – I think he has earned it."

HEROIC DOGS

Our understanding of the many ways in which dogs provide assistance and therapy for humans is growing all the time. There is no other animal so responsive, willing and able to please. To celebrate this, the British charity PRO Dogs rewards dogs who have given particular service to their owners or to the community. Labradors have featured in the awards on many occasions. This breed is among the bravest, most devoted and trainable of dogs, and since the presentation of the PRO Dog of the Year Gold Medal Awards started in 1979, Labradors have won medals on nine occasions.

There was Emma, the chocolate Labrador, trained as a guide dog for Sheila Hocken, who continued her work bravely until it was discovered that the dog herself was going blind. The keen scenting ability of the breed is illustrated by the persistent work of Brumby, a black Labrador drug detection dog, who won the Award in 1982 and, more recently, in 1995, by Jake, a six-year-old yellow Labrador drug detection dog, based at the ferry port of Rosslare in Ireland. Drug smugglers planned to end Jake's successful career after he rooted out hidden drugs worth more then £9million. He was captured, but fortunately found before he was killed. Jake has a great personality and clearly enjoyed himself throughout the awards celebration.

Jason, a black Labrador, won the award in 1989. The frenzied wagging of his tail was the signal he made when he detected and sniffed out lethal bombing devices planted by the IRA in Northern Ireland. On one occasion, the dog detected explosives hidden in a dustbin and gave the warning in time to save the life of four soldiers. The dog was blown into the air and injured, but, fortunately, made a good recovery.

The scenting and tracking abilities of the breed are typified by Jet, another black Labrador, who won a medal in 1983. He saved the lives of children at four o'clock one morning, when they were found in intensely cold conditions in a crevice on a mountain peak in Wales. Jet is a trained Search and Rescue Dog, regularly called out on mountain rescue work. A yellow Labrador called Mutley won an award in 1993 for raising a fire alarm and saving the life of his elderly owner.

A rescue of a different kind resulted in an award for Tark, a chocolate Labrador, in 1995. She dived into a fast-running river on command and retrieved a drowning Yorkshire Terrier puppy, although for a time it appeared that the dangerous current would account for two canine lives. On another occasion, a 17-year-old young man went for a swim without being aware of the treacherous corkscrew currents in that part of the river. His friend dived in to help, but was soon in similar difficulties and sucked under the water too. An elderly man, Osmond Sambrook, was out walking with Sandy, his yellow Labrador, and saw what was happening. He dived in to help, followed by Sandy. After a struggle, Mr Sambrook managed to get one young man out, while the other was saved by putting an arm around the dog's neck, eventually reaching the safety of the bank.

Labradors are, of course, noted for their gameness and are highly-valued by the sporting enthusiast. The following award story illustrates bravery, plus a guarding and defending instinct not generally seen in gundogs. One day, farmer Kenneth Parr, was attacked by a large Charolais bull. The bull charged at Kenneth and rammed him in the back. He was left pinned against a fence, his pelvis broken in three places and the angry bull standing over him. The animal would certainly have trampled him to death if it had not been for the bravery of Wotsit, Kenneth's yellow Labrador. Wotsit managed to manoeuvre herself between the animal and her master, and angrily barked and bit at the bull's legs and nose. This succeeded in keeping the bull at bay so that Kenneth was able to crawl painfully backwards, through the hedge, to safety.

10 BREEDING LABRADORS

If you are considering breeding a litter, the first and most important thing to do is to try and assess your bitch honestly, not through rose-coloured spectacles. Is she truly good enough – in other words, does she conform strongly to the Breed Standard, without too many failings. Every litter should be approached with the goal of improving your stock or, if it has already reached a high level, maintaining the present standard. Your motives must be good.

Do not be railroaded into breeding from your bitch. She might be your first, and well-meaning people, in some cases even your vet, may be insisting that she "needs" a litter. No bitch needs a litter – what she has not had, she will not miss. I am a firm believer in spaying or castrating, if the animal is not to be used for breeding and will remain purely a family companion. This should be done when maturity has been reached, and not before. Spaying eliminates the problem of seasons in the bitch, while castration takes the sex drive out of the dog and makes him a little more easy to handle. I have worked

Heatherbourne Promise and offspring. Breeding dogs is a big responsibility and should never be undertaken lightly.

Photo: R. Willbie.

Trenow Minuet: An invaluable brood bitch, producing numerous Champions and CC winners.

Photo courtesy: Mr and Mrs R.A. Floyd.

for the Guide Dogs for the Blind Association, which has a policy of across-the-board spaying and castration. I know it is a fallacy that such Labradors "go to fat," and overweight guide dogs are not evident on the streets. Cutting down the food intake slightly balances out the lower sex drive.

COMMON HEREDITARY DEFECTS

You have ascertained that you have a good bitch, with no major failings, either in breed type or structure. This also means using Kennel Club accredited schemes to check eyes and hips, and possibly screening elbows. Labradors have a few hereditary defects that must be checked. Those affecting the eyes include: hereditary

cataract, posterior pole cataract, retinal dysplasia, retinal fold (or tears), entropion, central progressive retinal atrophy and generalised progressive retinal atrophy. Other breed-associated diseases include hip dysplasia, osteochondrosis dissecans (OCD) and epilepsy. (All these conditions are dealt with in detail in Chapter Sixteen.)

BREEDING METHODS

Let us consider your potential brood bitch. She is fit and healthy, sound and a good example of the breed, clean, wormed and in the peak of health, not too young (under two years) nor too old (over five years) for a first litter. There are three methods of breeding we can use.

IN BREEDING
In breeding should only be used by breeders who know their lines over many generations. The main mating combinations are mother/son, daughter/father, brother/sister. Such close breeding will bring out all the very good, but also all the very bad, points. Some wonderful animals have been bred this way – but you do not tend to hear about the bad ones. In breeding is not something that I have used, as yet, in 30 years.

LINE BREEDING
This tends to be what most successful kennels use. We go a further generation at least from in breeding for tight line breeding, i.e. grand-daughter/grandfather, grandson/grandmother, uncle/niece, aunt/nephew, and cousins/cousins, plus a further generation back for continued line breeding. It is hard to convey to the general public that this is good practice. The advantages are that you, and those behind you in the line, hopefully recognise problem areas where the faults lie and try to stay clear of them. At the same time, the virtues of the previous generations will be carried down to your stock, as well as bringing in a little more new blood. You will know what size the animals should reach, the type of temperament to expect and the Labrador type you will breed in your litter. If you have bought in a good bitch from a successful line, why undo all the good her breeder has achieved by outcrossing her? The resulting pups may never resemble their mother, but countless other dogs mish-mashed in the outcross history. Go back to the bitch's breeder and take some advice. The kennel's good name is at stake, so you will be advised correctly.

OUTCROSSING
This method certainly has its uses. A line that has been kept very tight needs new blood introduced from time to time. You must use it wisely, and try to find out as much as you can about the new line you are going into. You can often get a particular point you badly wanted, but spend the next two generations breeding out something else that you certainly did not want. Beware the one spectacular dog from mediocre parents or lines. Use him and you will be very lucky

indeed to get all his points in your litter. The pups will more likely resemble his siblings or parents.

SELECTING A STUD DOG
What a great many people do when beginning their breeding career is to go to the 'top dog' of the moment. He is obviously a good dog or he would not be where he is, but he is not going to suit all the bitches brought to him. He will suit some down to the ground, but on others he will be far less successful, because the lines or types do not click. It will not be his fault, but it will be yours for not choosing the right dog for your bitch.

Before you make any breeding decisions, talk to lots of Labrador people – hopefully the successful ones. Listen and take advice, but remember that the bottom line is that it must be you who takes the decision about which stud dog to use on your bitch. You need to be able to to live with this responsibility later, should the mating prove to be not all you had hoped for.

YOUR DOG AS POTENTIAL STUD
We have been concentrating on the bitch, but what of those people (mostly men in my experience) who want to use their dog at stud? The opportunities for your dog to be used at stud are very slim, unless he has proved himself successful in the show ring, in field trials or in obedience. If he is merely your companion and the owner of a bitch down the road wants to use him, think very hard before you agree. You will have to have his eyes checked and hips X-rayed, not a small sum to outlay. When it gets to the actual mating, does he know what to do, and do you know how to help him? Also ask yourself the question "If you had sex just once would you want to stop?", because that is what you are asking your dog to do. It usually brings home to the owner just what they are considering putting the dog through. What he does not know about will not hurt him, but, once tried, the stud experiment could turn him into a pest.

COLOUR GENES
As well as health and type, colour plays a big part in breeding Labradors. We have three

colours, black, yellow (from pale cream through to fox red) and chocolate.

BLACK AND YELLOW

Black and yellow colour inheritance is reasonably simple to explain and follows the simple Mendelian principle of dominant (black) and recessive (yellow). Dominant black Labradors when mated together will only produce dominant black puppies. Dominant black mated to an impure black (i.e. carrying the colour yellow) will produce all black puppies, but half will carry the (recessive) yellow gene.

Two impure blacks mated together will produce approximately two yellow pups in a litter of eight. Of the remaining six pups, two will be dominant black and four will be impure blacks carrying the yellow gene. An impure black mated to a yellow will produce four impure blacks and four yellow pups. A dominant black mated to yellow will produce a litter of blacks, but all will carry the recessive yellow gene. Yellow mated to yellow will not produce any blacks at all.

The above proportions are based on an average sample of 100 puppies. Obviously the bigger the litter, the nearer you will be to the expected ratio; small litters can be inconclusive.

CHOCOLATE/LIVER

The colour inheritance pattern that produces the chocolate colour is more complicated than the black/yellow inheritance patterns. Up to now, we have been using the accurate but simplified genetics of B = dominant black and Y = recessive yellow. To understand the relationship of chocolate/liver, it is necessary to understand the slightly more advanced genetic principles, as follows:

B = black.
b = brown (in Labradors we say chocolate or liver).
E = the ability to express pigment or coat colour.
e = the inability to express dark pigment or coat colour, i.e. can only express light colour such as yellow.

Dominant genes are always written as a capital letter, and recessive genes (or genes which

SIRE/DAM	PUPPIES		
	DOMINANT BLACK	BLACK CARRYING YELLOW	YELLOW
BB x BB	●●●●		
BY x BB	●●	◐◐	
BY x BY	●	◐◐	○
Y x BY		◐◐	○○
BB x Y		◐◐◐◐	
Y x Y			○○○○

Colour inheritance in Labradors.

can have their effect masked by the corresponding capital letter of the alphabet) are always written as a small letter. For example, B is dominant over b, therefore the dog carrying Bb is black, but the dog carrying bb is chocolate. However, the e gene (represented by a small letter) is not necessarily recessive to other letters of the alphabet, only to a capital E. Therefore, when ee is present in the Labrador it masks the effect of Bs or bs, and the dog (being unable to express black or chocolate) is yellow in appearance.

In other words, the E or e sequence has the ability to affect the B or b sequence. The effect is called epistasis. Therefore, for a dog to be black or chocolate, it must also carry at least one E gene. If the dog only carries e genes then it cannot express black or chocolate (even if it is carrying B or b), and will be yellow. Dogs inherit one colour gene, of a pair, from each parent, one of the pair being present in the sperm and the other in the egg. When the egg and sperm fuse the result is two genes representing each given characteristic in the progeny (puppies).

The possible genetic make-ups of the Labrador are as follows:

BBEE = BLACK: Double dominant black (BB) and double dominant expression (EE) means black appearance and can only pass on black appearance.

BBEe = BLACK: Will be black in appearance (BBE), but the small e means that the dog can pass on the non-expression gene. If it mates with another dog carrying the non-expression (little e) gene, yellow pups can be born.

BbEE = BLACK: Black gene masking the effect of the chocolate (small b) gene, and double dominant expression (EE) means the dog will be black, but has the ability to pass on the chocolate (small b) gene. If it mates with another dog which carries the chocolate gene (small b), chocolate pups will be born.

BbEe = BLACK: Black gene masking the effect of the chocolate gene (small b), and expression gene (E) masking the effect of little e (non-expression of dark colour) gene. However, if this dog is mated to another dog carrying a little e, yellow pups can be produced, and if mated to a dog carrying little b, chocolate pups can be produced.

bbEE = CHOCOLATE: The two chocolate genes (bb) and the two expression genes (EE) means the dog can express dark (in this case chocolate) colour, and is chocolate. This dog

Clarion's Barley of Lorey (Huchu's Parker – Lorey's Bellamora Sandy), owned by Cara Bradley and Autumn Davidson DVM.
Breeders of chocolate Labradors strive for a dark eye colour to complement the coat colour.
Photo by Paul Boyte, courtesy of Autumn Davidson DVM, Clarion Labradors, California.

can only produce chocolate, unless it is mated to a dog which carries a B gene, when black can be produced.

bbEe = CHOCOLATE: The two chocolate genes (bb), plus one expression gene (E), means the dog can express chocolate and will be chocolate. However, the dog also carries a small e (non-expression gene), which means that if mated to another dog carrying the small e, yellow could be produced. Likewise, if this dog was mated to a black dog, the black dog's capital B would override the small b, and black could be produced. And, of course, if mated to another dog carrying a small b, chocolate could be produced. In other words, all three colours could be produced with the right mating. However, mating to a yellow dog or one carrying yellow is not advised, as the skin pigment may be very pale or pink.

bbee = YELLOW (with pink skin pigment): This dog (ee) cannot express dark pigment; this combined with the double chocolate genes (bb), results in a yellow dog with very pale skin pigment. This is not desirable.

Bbee = YELLOW (with normal skin pigment): The two small e genes mean the dog is unable to express the capital B gene which it carries, or the small chocolate gene which it carries, and will therefore be yellow. However, because it carries a B gene, this somehow manages to influence a darker skin pigment, which results in a normal yellow dog. If mated to a dog carrying an expression gene (E), black or chocolate could be produced. However, if mated to a dog carrying a small b (chocolate) gene, the possibility of producing a bbee type yellow exists. Remember, normal yellows can hide small b (chocolate) genes.

BBee = YELLOW (with normal skin pigment): The two small e genes (non-expression of dark colour) mean that the effect of the BB genes is masked, and a yellow dog is produced. Skin pigment will be normal because of the influence of BB.

It is not possible for two yellows mated together to throw any colour other than yellow – even though they may hide B or b influences. This point is illustrated below:

SIZE

Please do not take a small bitch to a large dog expecting the pups to come out a good, medium size. You will get some small, some medium

The Farbourne Labradors pictured in the Netherlands bred by Anja Verbeek-de Neef.
Consistency of type is the key to success when breeding pedigree dogs.

Photo courtesy: Anja Verbeek-de Neef.

and some large offspring. If you choose a stud of a good medium size, you will hopefully get pups, some of whom will be medium and some of whom will be smaller like your bitch – in other words, a more balanced litter. Do remember, of course, to check back in the pedigree of both your bitch and the stud dog, because you are not dealing with just two animals, but the hundreds of canine ancestors who went to make them up.

CORRECTING FAULTS OR FAILINGS
If your bitch has a failing (for example, in need of better front angulation) make sure that the dog you have chosen does not carry the same fault. Otherwise, you will be 'setting' the fault, not correcting it. In my own kennel, I could stand to gain a plainer head on my dogs, knowing that I could get them back in a generation, but I would not compromise and risk losing the existing good shoulders, excellent rear ends and good bone and feet. These features take generations to get back, and can be so easily lost.

PLANNING THE MATING
Let the stud dog owner know that you would like to bring your bitch to be mated, and give some idea of when her next season is expected. Once the owner has agreed, make sure you know what the stud fee is, and be prepared to pay it at the mating. In Britain, we pay for the mating not for puppies produced. If puppies do not ensue from the mating, the stud dog owner will normally give you another free mating at a following season of your choice. Some countries have a small initial stud fee, then so much per live puppy born. Such a transaction works out very much in the favour of the stud dog owner.

GETTING THE TIMING RIGHT
The first day that your bitch shows colour, i.e. bleeding, let the stud owner know, so that your bitch can be booked in. It is no good phoning up the day before she needs mating, and expecting to be fitted in the next day. About 70-80 per cent of bitches come into season over the same six-to-eight week period twice a year, so the dog of your choice could be very busy at the time you need to use him. Get your name down the first day she shows colour, so the stud kennel knows to expect you some time within the next 10-15 days and will keep space for your bitch.

By about the tenth day of the season, you should be able to check for 'strictures' on a maiden bitch. Insert a clean finger, covered with Vaseline, into your bitch's vagina. Strictures may occur down the sides of the vagina, making it hard to insert your finger, even down the middle. A quick trip to the vet and a few snips will solve the problem, which is unusual, but worth checking for in a maiden bitch. This simple precautionary procedure is better than feeling a fool when the stud dog owner finds strictures when checking her prior to mating, or when the stud dog has difficulty trying to mate her.

Once the mating is over, your bitch is still in season and receptive to other dogs. Please make sure you keep her safe until at least three weeks after the first show of colour, and longer if she is still interesting to other dogs. Most experienced breeders have horror stories about mis-matings. Mine was two eleven-month animals on the twenty-third day of the bitch's first season (bad enough in itself), but the fact that they were of two different breeds put an even harsher light on it. The bitch was Ch. Warringah's Flinders and the German Shorthaired Pointer dog was Sh. Ch. Warringah's Frith – who always had a particular fancy for black Labrador bitches after that!

THE SEASON
Bitches tend to come into season every six months on average. Some vary, with seasons every four to five months or stretching out to eight to nine months, or even yearly as they would in the wild. Having always kept records, I find that once a bitch has developed a pattern she tends to stick to it.

A bitch's season has three stages:-

1. The show of blood starts. The vulva tends to swell prior to this, so you can usually be on hand to check every morning with a clean tissue to see whether your bitch is 'showing colour'. I count this as Day 1. The blood lessens in amount and colour as the season progresses.

2. By days 10-12, the discharge is usually pale pink to straw-coloured, and the amount of the flow is lessening. At the same time, the swollen vulva is softening. The bitch will not let a dog mate her while the vulva is still swollen and hard, so a gentle prod to see if it is softening will help to ascertain the correct day to mate her. If you scratch her on the back where the tail joins, she should start to swing it around to one side, exposing and tipping up the vulva ready for mating. If you have other bitches around, they will often be allowed to 'mate' a receptive bitch, a day or two prior to her being ready for the dog. Once these signs are coming together, it is time to call the stud owner to let him know this stage has been reached. You usually have at least two to three days to mate her at this point.

3. After the mating, your bitch will still be able to accept another dog. She must be kept safe from other males for at least a further ten days.

THE MATING

Make sure that you are on time at the stud owner's premises, as the personnel will probably have altered their day to accommodate your visit. The dog will also have been prevented from eating a meal (he will either be turned off by a full stomach, or will regurgitate his food prior to the mating). Ensure that your bitch has urinated prior to her arrival. Have a strong leather collar fitted snugly around her neck. I like to let the dog and bitch have time to run together and get to know each other. I feel that it relaxes the bitch after her journey, and makes her more amenable to the mating. Every stud owner has an individual way of going about the mating. Some, like me, encourage the dog and bitch to run together, but this should not go on for more than 15 minutes. Otherwise there is the risk of the stud dog becoming worn out too early. If the bitch is receptive (i.e. swinging her tail round, and presenting her vulva) but the dog is getting nowhere, either because the vulva is a little too low or high or the bitch moves off quickly when he enters her, human assistance may become necessary. A natural mating is preferable, but an experienced stud dog owner can engineer a mating with a few tricks of the trade, provided the bitch is ready.

The first 30 seconds or so of the ejaculation contains seminal fluid, the next minute or two is the sperm and the remainder of the 'tie' is seminal fluid to help the sperm on its long journey to the uterine horns. If the dog is held and not allowed to turn for those three to four minutes, everything will be deposited where it needs to go. This practice also ensures that the bulb at the base of the penis, which effects the tie, has time to reach its full size. Often a dog will try to turn as he stops pumping, but before the tie is complete, and will thus cause a 'slip mating'. The semen is wasted on the ground, and it may be a long wait before the dog can perform again, possibly a matter of hours or even the next day.

As soon as the tie has been achieved, hold the bitch tightly. As the tie develops, it can be uncomfortable for her and she may try to struggle. This will only last for 30 seconds to a minute, then your bitch will settle down quietly and you can relax your hold. Some bitches do not make a sound while tied, others mutter and grumble all the way through. Very occasionally, one may be a 'screamer' and there is nothing you can do to quieten her. I am sure our neighbours must wonder what we get up to!

After holding the pair together for three to four minutes, I let the dog's front legs slide down to one side, then help his back leg over the bitch's back so that the two dogs are tail to tail. The procedure is not uncomfortable for the dog, and does have a purpose, leaving both heads free to defend themselves if necessary. The tie can last from five to forty-five minutes – each dog is different, and can vary at each mating.

REPEAT MATINGS

Usually one mating is enough, but if a bitch's owners have travelled a long way and are staying overnight, I usually mate the dogs in the evening and again the next morning. It seems a politeness, and an extra safeguard given the long distance involved. If my stud dog is young and inexperienced, and provided the bitch has co-operated well, I often like to do another mating. This helps the dog to get firmly embedded in his mind what is expected of him when females visit. I will generally use a more elderly dog a couple of times if possible – just in case his sperm are not so active as they were when he was younger.

DISPELLING MYTHS

No matter how many times one says it, some novice owners never completely believe: "A tie is not necessary to produce pups." Having had a stud dog who did not tie a third of his bitches, I do know what I am saying. As long as the dog is in the correct place for a couple of minutes, things should be fine, as all the sperm will have been deposited.

In my opinion, holding a bitch's back legs up in the air for a couple of minutes after the tie breaks does no real good. A bitch's vagina is very long, as are the uterine horns, and most of the fluid will reach them in the course of the tie. Only seminal fluid will be noticed coming out. At this stage, by all means put her on a lead and get her straight into the car to settle down in her own place while the paperwork is completed.

Do not be the type of person who says "I will be with you on the twelfth day." Your bitch may well have been ready for mating on the twelfth day of her last season, but the way each season unfolds can be different. Make sure the day you go to the stud dog is the right one for your bitch, and not what is most convenient for you. The majority of bitches are mated around the eleventh, twelfth or thirteenth day, but matings have taken place as early as the first couple of days of a season, as well as being successful after the twentieth.

AFTER THE MATING

Before you leave the stud dog owner's premises, you should have paid your stud fee and been given a receipt, have a signed and completed stud dog section of the Kennel Club form to register your litter on, plus a copy of his pedigree. I also like to have a copy of his KC/BVA hip score and his current KC/BVA eye certificate. This lasts only one year, and should carry you past the date of the puppies leaving you. I suggest giving each new puppy owner photostat copies of both the hip and eye certificates of both parents, so they can see you have done the very best possible for their new puppy.

THE IN-WHELP BITCH

The first few weeks of pregnancy pass with few outward signs. Remember your mated bitch is still in season for another ten days or so. Keep her safe from other males – it is possible to have pups sired by two different dogs in one litter – since you do not want any hiccups after all the trouble you have taken.

WORMING

Worm your bitch again while she is in whelp. Worm larvae lie dormant in the tissues of dogs, and the onset of pregnancy wakes them up. The larvae make their way back to the gut, so three to four weeks into the pregnancy a bitch should be wormed. Recent articles in the dog papers have identified the worming of in-whelp bitches as the cause of many abnormalities, a view I do not share.

SIGNS OF PREGNANCY

Some bitches will let you know very early that they are pregnant. They become 'precious' and are unwilling to do things that were commonplace prior to mating. Such bitches get a certain faraway look in their eyes and are very fey. I have known of bitches suffering from pregnancy sickness in the early weeks, and have had others who really 'blow' their ribs out before any other sign is noted. Most, however, sail through these early weeks with no outward evidence at all, except that the vulva tends not to go down to the pre-season size.

By three to four weeks, you can usually see pinker and more prominent teats especially in a maiden bitch, and a loss of hair from around the teats, making room for the pups to suckle. By five weeks, the flanks tend to fill in and she loses her waistline (I am assuming that your bitch had one to start with. A fit, slimmer bitch

'Some bitches will let you know very early that they are pregnant. They become precious...'

161

will become pregnant, and certainly whelp more easily, than a fat one.)

By six weeks, the teats tend to drop down more and the sides take on a definite bulge. This continues through seven and eight weeks, by which time the bitch may be having trouble lying down comfortably. Her reproachful looks seem to say "You did this to me," and they can certainly make an owner feel somewhat guilty. During the last week of pregnancy, the uterine horns straighten out, and the pups drop even lower in the last four to five days. This is a good indication to watch for.

PRECAUTIONS
During the pregnancy, maintain regular walks of two to three miles most days of the week. If the bitch is a real tomboy and charging around, consider putting her on a lead for the last couple of weeks. Change to shorter walks during the last two weeks, about one mile on level ground. It is most important that your bitch remains fit and active as this will make for an easier whelping.

From five weeks in whelp, I give my bitches a calcium supplement, either bone-meal or a palatable tablet, and keep this going until lactation is complete. It is important not to over-dose – though dogs will take only so much calcium and excrete the rest – but a little extra calcium will not hurt and may ward off eclampsia. A lack of calcium at any time during the lactation period must be dealt with as an emergency by your vet if you do not want to lose your bitch. The affected bitch has violent tremors, is most distressed and tries to hide away. She can even become comatose. If you suspect her symptoms indicate eclampsia, call the vet at once.

FEEDING YOUR IN-WHELP BITCH
I am a meat and biscuit person. At six weeks in whelp, I split the bitch's one meal a day into two smaller meals; at seven weeks, I increase the biscuit and double the meat ration, going from 12oz biscuit and 12oz of meat to 16oz of biscuit and 24oz of meat split over two meals.

If you feed an all-in-one or complete food, you must make sure that you upgrade your usual feed to one suitable for an in-whelp and lactating bitch. She will need to change to this early in the pregnancy, upping the content a little and splitting into two meals. Most good-quality complete foods carry a range covering puppy, junior, maintenance, high yield, and veteran diets, so you should not have to change brands.

PREPARING FOR THE BIRTH
WHELPING BOX
During the last few weeks of pregnancy you should get the whelping box into place and accustom your bitch to using it. For a Labrador bitch you will need a wooden box about four feet long by three feet wide, with sides about one foot deep. The front area should have one board that can be removed, leaving a height of about six inches so that the bitch can step in easily and not land on any whelps. This board can be put back when the pups start staggering around and trying to climb out of the box. When all the puppies need to get out at three weeks of age, both boards can be removed for an easy exit from the box.

LOCATION
Choose the proposed whelping area carefully. I whelp my bitches in the study, which is warm and cosy, has comfy chairs and a TV. To protect the carpets (your bitch will usually have a discharge from the uterus for a few weeks after whelping) I cover the floor with a plastic decorating sheet. Put lots of newspapers in the box, for the bitch to tear up when whelping starts, and place a piece of synthetic bedding on top of them. The purpose-made synthetic and washable canine bedding material is a wonderful invention. It keeps the pups warm and dry, not soggy and cold as they used to be on wet newspaper or blankets.

TEMPERATURE
The temperature needs to be a steady 70 degrees Fahrenheit (or 21 degrees Centigrade). Any hotter is uncomfortable for the bitch, and with the high sides of the box, plus the bedding and closeness of the dam, the pups are the few degrees warmer that they need to be. For the first ten days they cannot shiver, and so cannot conserve their body heat. If you cannot provide this constant background heat, you will need a

heat lamp suspended over the whelping box about three to four feet above the bitch. You do not want to make her uncomfortable so that she will leave her pups and not feed them. If the pups are all pressed around the sides of the box, it means the heat lamp is too low and they are trying to get away from it. If the pups are all in a heap, they are cold and snuggling together for warmth. If they are in a nice jumble around the box, you have got it just right.

EQUIPMENT
You will need to have your whelping 'tool-kit' ready and to hand. A strong cardboard box to take the pups, and a hot-water bottle ready to go in the bottom beneath a strip of bedding; half a dozen towels to rub the pups dry as they are born and one for the top of the cardboard box to make a snug warm place for the pups if it is necessary to remove them from the box while mum concentrates on the next birth; a bottle of antiseptic; small scissors and a bowl to put them in; 'Dopran' drops or similar, which are available from your vet and are marvellous for reviving a newborn pup who is perhaps having trouble getting going; a tube of lubricating jelly; weighing scales and a birth chart; glucose powder for the bitch; a black plastic sack for the rubbish; small tin of Lactol (or similar bitch's milk substitute); and a Belcroy tube feeder, by far the best bottle to use for pups should it be necessary to feed them due to lack of milk from the mother. Finally, invest in a powerful torch, and clean Vet Bed for when whelping is over.

LAST WEEK OF THE PREGNANCY
A pregnancy normally lasts 63 days, but a few days early or late is quite normal. I have had whelpings seven days early and four days late, and all the litters were viable. During the last week, take your bitch's temperature every day. It is a good indication of an imminent birth. The bitch's normal temperature is 101.7 Fahrenheit, a puppy's will be at least one degree higher. As the time for delivery approaches, your bitch's temperature will start to drop, possibly sticking on 100 F for a few days, but indicating that the time is very near when it reaches 99 or 98 F.

FIRST STAGE SIGNS
The outward signs to watch for are a refusal of food or reluctant eating, or frequent regurgitation. Panting, general restlessness, and starting to tear up the paper in her box are sure signs that the bitch is about to go into labour. This is called the first stage, and we are certainly on our way. It can last anything from an hour or so to twenty-four hours and can even be longer. During this time the bitch may keep asking to go outside, in which case go with her, keep her on a lead and, if it is dark, take your torch. She will be asking to go out every few minutes, but once every couple of hours will be enough to let her empty bladder and bowels. Do not let her escape to her own secret pre-dug hole under a shed or bush in the garden. Pregnant bitches can be very cunning.

THE WHELPING
Once the first stage has started, let your veterinary surgery know. Ascertain who is on duty and what number to ring should you need to call in an emergency. Occasionally a bitch will whelp during the day, but it usually happens during the night.

STAGE TWO
Labrador bitches are, on the whole, easy whelpers. The litter's average weight is 14-16oz (390-450gms). Below that figure is a little light, and above is heavy. The smallest puppy I have bred was eight ounces (225gms), and the biggest 22oz (620gms).

Once good hard contractions begin, place the bedding under the bitch. Switch your oven on to 200 degrees F, prepare a baking tray with a cloth in it, and if you have a pup who is not coming round, pop the pup on the tray, put in the oven (*with the door open*) and the hot dry air might just result in the first big breath. I have saved a few puppies in this way over the years.

Do not let contractions continue for more than one hour of straining at any time before ringing the vet, if the bitch has not produced a pup. A puppy can get wedged across the top of the uterine horns, with the other pups pressing down from both sides. If the bitch has been straining for an hour, contact the vet and meet at the surgery. An emergency Caesarian may be needed to save the pups before they all die. This has happened to me twice with the same bitch – not her fault in the least – both times after producing some of the litter. I never attempted a third litter just in case we had a third Caesar, which would not have been fair on her. I had her spayed once the pups had been taken out and before she was sewn up from her second operation. Some vets say the milk fails to come in after a Caesarian, but in my own experience of four bitches who underwent Caesars and spaying, plenty of milk came through.

Do not worry unduly if contractions stop for anything up to one hour between puppies. Bitches tend to have a short rest and start again as the pups move down the horns. Two or three pups may be delivered within just a few minutes, then she might rest for an hour. I have had litters of eight pups arriving in two hours, and a litter of six that took twelve hours. This range is quite normal.

UTERINE INERTIA
Uterine inertia occurs when your bitch seems quite happy to sleep or look after her pups for hours, and nothing at all is happening. Yet it is quite obvious to an onlooker that there are pups still inside waiting to be born, because of the size of her bulging flanks. Call the vet and meet him at the surgery. It is pointless for you to call him out, only to find that you need to go to the surgery, thus wasting even more time. Try to make sure that you have someone with you in the car to keep an eye on the bitch should she deliver more pups on the way there. Put the other pups in their box and take them along with you, or the bitch will fret. Remember to take a few more towels to deal with any pups arriving in the car or at the surgery. The vet will probably administer Oxytocin, which causes strong contractions almost immediately. If the pups are not produced, a Caesarian becomes a strong possibility. Uterine inertia tends to run in families, so is not a very good breeding prospect.

HELPING THE BITCH
From the start of stage one, stay with your bitch, as she will take comfort from having you near.

Try not to fuss, as you will only agitate her as well. I give drinks of glucose and water, which gives the bitch added energy. If it is a long whelping, take her out to relieve herself during a rest period, but keep her on a lead.

Experienced bitches will get all the pups out of the bags, cut the cords etc. – in other words cope with everything themselves. Others express obvious distaste and leave you to do it for them. Break the bag quickly and clear any mucus from the puppy's mouth and nose. Either cut the cord or tear it with your fingernails three inches from the pup, squeezing the cord on the side nearest the pup with your fingers as you do so.

Give each pup a brisk rub with the towel to dry it out and get the circulation going well. If there is a lot of mucus around the mouth, hold the puppy firmly in the towel between your hands, raise it above your head and bring it down swiftly – thus getting rid of the mucus. Check with a finger inside the mouth that there is no cleft palate (if there is, the pup is best put down by the vet on a post-whelping visit). Weigh each pup, note sex, colour, what time it was born, how long since the previous pup, the type of delivery and whether each placenta was also delivered.

BREECH BIRTHS
True breeches – just the tail presenting – are very rare. It is possible to deliver by hooking one back leg down and then the other, then pulling at a 45-degree angle with both feet held firmly in damp cotton wool as the bitch has a contraction. However, rear presentation (tail and back legs) is very normal. One of my bitches delivered 52 per cent of her pups this way.

AFTERBIRTHS
Check all the afterbirths, and let the bitch consume some of them, as they are rich in nutrients. Too many will, however, make her sick. Wrap the others in the soggy newspaper and pop them in the plastic sack. Your vet should check out the bitch and the litter within twenty-four hours of the birth. It is important to be able to account for all of the afterbirths. This is where the birth chart comes in useful.

CLEARING UP

When you think all is finished, get someone to take the bitch out to relieve herself. Meanwhile, clean up the whelping box by wiping it out with an antiseptic cloth. Put down clean paper four to five sheets thick, with clean Vet Bed on top, and place all the pups back in their new bed. Tidy up the bitch, washing her rear quarters and tail, then let her back into the whelping box with the pups. Ideally, try to sleep down near the bitch for the first couple of days until she has got over the whelping and regained her strength. Then, if a pup gets away from the rest and is crying, you can easily pick it up and put it back without her having to get up and disturb the rest of the litter. It is also a good way of making sure that she stays with her pups and bonds with them.

THE LACTATING BITCH

After all the excitement of the birth, a light meal for your bitch is in order. Eggs beaten in milk and glucose go down well, sometimes with brown bread added for a little bulk. Most bitches will take a few days to get up to full strength in the eating stakes. To tempt them, buy a couple of chickens, cook them in the microwave and finish them off in a big pot with all the juices, plus water and rice. De-bone the cold chicken and dish up rice and chicken over the next few days – lots of fresh water with glucose added is a help. Remember, good food and plenty of water make milk; do not offer lots of milky drinks which will only tend to make her stools more loose. This is also caused by eating the afterbirth that is rich with nutrients. In the wild, consuming the placentas would have got her over the first few days when she would not have been able to hunt. Also by clearing away all the traces of the birth, she was removing any smell that could encourage predators. This instinct is still strong in bitches today. You might find that you have to feed your bitch with the pups for the first few days, and put a lead on her to go out to be clean. She will not want to leave her babies.

FEEDING

Not all bitches take days to get back to normal feeding. Some want their red meat and biscuits as soon as they finish whelping. Resign yourself to being flexible and reading your own bitch correctly. Lactating bitches should ideally be on four meals a day. For convenience, I use 8oz (225gms) of biscuit and powdered milk for breakfast and a can of rice pudding for supper. This is constant, no matter what the size of the litter. The two meat meals (lunch and tea) vary in size with the size of the litter.
Four pups: give your bitch 8oz (225gms) biscuit and 12oz (350gms) meat for each meat meal.
Six pups: give 12oz (350gms) biscuit and 18oz (525gms) meat for each meat meal.
Eight pups: give16oz (475gms) biscuit and 24oz (700gms) meat for each meat meal.

This regime continues until the pups are four weeks old, when you can cut out supper. At five weeks, lose breakfast, and by six weeks put her on one big meal a day and shortly after on to her normal maintenance diet. Gradual reduction will help her milk dry up slowly as the pups become fully weaned. I am not suggesting that the above must be adhered to at all costs. In my last litter, the bitch had little milk and I was starting to wean the pups at two weeks. Consequently, the bitch's food was cut down quicker than recommended as the food was going on to her back, not into the pups – you could clearly see her putting on weight.

THE POST-WHELP BITCH

It is worth worming your bitch just about every time you worm the pups, as she is cleaning up after them all the time. I find that when the pups are four to five weeks old the bitch is quite happy to leave them at night. Nevertheless, try to keep her with them quite a lot during the day since puppies learn so much from their mother at this stage.

When the pups are approaching six weeks, your bitch will usually go in to them a couple of times a day to play and drain off her milk. Make sure this happens before she eats or at least three hours afterwards, otherwise she will regurgitate her food for the pups. This is how she would have weaned them in the wild. Let your bitch dictate how much she wants to be with the pups and for how long. As soon as the bitch indicates that she wants to go out on walks again, allow her to do so. Take things easy at first, and remember to wipe off her undercarriage with an antiseptic cloth before she rejoins the pups.

Also check twice a day for mastitis by running your hands over the teats, looking for hard swollen teats. I tend to treat these myself by applying lots of hot compresses and expressing the milk, but unless she responds rapidly you must obtain antibiotics from the vet, though continuing to apply hot compresses will do no harm. The antibiotics are a two-edged sword, as they go straight through to the pups and give them the runs. Keep an eye out constantly for eclampsia, which can happen even after your bitch has weaned the pups. As I said before, if you notice the symptoms, waste no time in calling the vet.

THE DEVELOPING PUPPIES

I use pig rails in my whelping box for the first couple of weeks to ensure the pups do not get crushed behind their dam. These can be broom handles slotted into round holes cut out of the box five to six inches above the base, and four to five inches in from the side. They are easy to remove one by one as the pups get bigger and stronger. They have small screws in the ends to make sure they stay in place.

SUPPLEMENTARY FEEDS

The first three weeks can be a doddle with your bitch doing all the work and you doing little more than gazing at the puppies and watching them grow. Sometimes a bitch will have insufficient milk and you have to take over with supplementary feeds every few hours. There are a few good bitch milk substitutes on sale at pet shops. Get some in – it will not go to waste because you can use it on the pups' cereal when they are being weaned.

The table below shows that to get the correct fat and protein levels, you would have to feed three times the amount of cow's milk, which would mean five times too much lactose – not good for the pups at all.

BIRTH TO THREE WEEKS

Pups cannot shiver for the first ten days, so need to be kept warm and cosy. It is fascinating that in a mixed litter (i.e. more than one colour) the colours tend to stick together at mum's milk bar, even before the eyes are open. Why and how this happens is a mystery. By ten to 12 days, the eyes are beginning to open, the smallest pups often being first, and at the same time the ears unseal. Not that the puppies are seeing clearly or hearing too much at this stage. By three weeks, the pups are starting to stagger about in the box, not so much playing as throwing themselves at their litter mates. They are certainly starting to socialise. At the three week stage, teeth are coming through the gums, as screams from the pups testify when they are dragged around by an ear. At three weeks, the pups should ideally move out to a puppy kennel. Such a kennel should be well-insulated and cosy. At this stage, the front of the whelping box is removed so the pups can come out and have access to the rest of the kennel, which is covered in newspapers. They use this to relieve themselves. A shelf can be fixed four feet above the box and should cover its entire width, with a heat lamp and shade cut into the centre, so the heat goes down to the pups and does not dissipate upwards. If it is a winter litter, I also cover part of the front with a thick cloth to make a good warm nest for the bitch and her pups. The large shelf above the box is useful for storing the never-ending piles of newspaper you will need for your litter.

THREE TO SIX WEEKS

By four weeks the pups will come to the door of the kennel and look out. They are fast develop-

	Protein	Fat	Lactose	Total Solids	Cal per 100g
Cow	3.5 %	3.7 %	4.9 %	12.7 %	66
Goat	3.6 %	4.2 %	4.3 %	13.0 %	68
Pig	5.2 %	4.5 %	3.2 %	16.0 %	73
Dog	8.5 %	9.6 %	3.5 %	21.6 %	30

ing in both character and appearance and, within a few days, all the pups will use their outside paved run to play and evacuate in rather than the kennel area, so they are learning to be clean.

Cleanliness in the whelping box and puppy kennel is most important at all times. Put paper under the Vet Bed and on the floor. Change the bedding as often as necessary, sometimes every other day, sometimes twice a day. Pick up in and clean the run and the inside kennel whenever the puppies make a mess, and make sure that the run is hosed down at least once a day.

Give the pups good, solid toys to play with – knotted ropes, solid balls (not too small), or plastic drinks bottles (remove anything loose). For a real treat, a cardboard box makes a won-

derful toy. The pups climb in it, on it, and then tear it to tiny shreds, so be prepared to pick up hundreds of little pieces. I find my Labradors demolish plastic squeaky toys very quickly. I bought one of those soft stuffed toys for one litter. It had a hole within half an hour, so I sewed it back up twice thinking mum was destroying it, only to find the culprits were the little thugs whose angelic faces adorn this chapter.

Nails need cutting from an early age – even by three days old they are pretty long and should be trimmed to save the bitch from their needle-sharp points. I trim puppies' nails every week until they are outside wearing them down in the run, then I trim them twice-weekly until the pups leave home. Your worming regime

It is a good policy to weigh puppies at birth and then on a weekly basis thereafter. This will help you to monitor development, checking that all the puppies are growing at a reasonable rate. At four weeks Warringah's Possum, a bitch, weighed 5lbs. At birth, she weighed 16ozs.　*Photo: Keith Hawkins.*

ABOVE: First assessment at four weeks. Warringah's Possum has good bone and topline. She is nice and short-Backed, but slightly lacking in shoulder angulation. Good tail-set.

BELOW: Warringah's Coolibah, a dog, now weighing 5lbs 8oz. He was 16oz at birth. He is short-backed with excellent shoulder angulation. Excellent hindquarters, with well-turned stifles, good second thigh an long hocks. he has well-boned legs and good feet.
Photos: Keith Hawkins.

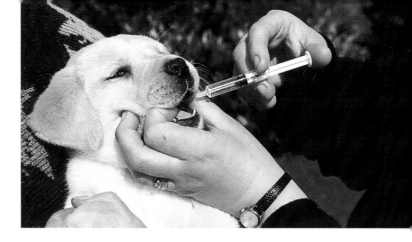

ABOVE: Some breeders prefer to use a syringe when worming puppies.

LEFT: Nails should be trimmed, or the bitch will soon be scratched and sore.

Photos: Amanda Bulbeck.

should normally start at three weeks. My advice is to then repeat every ten days (the time it takes for any leftover eggs to grow to a full-size worm). So my puppies are wormed at three, four-and-a-half, six, seven-and-a-half and nine weeks. The pups' new vet can give the 12-week worming when inoculations are being done. I usually advise my litters' new owners to worm every three months for the rest of the first year, and keep on that regime if the pup is in constant contact with children. If not, six-monthly, from one year old is adequate. I make sure the new owners know when I have wormed the pups and the preparation used so this information can be passed to the new vet.

By six weeks, I have the pups out of the run and into the garden and paddock while I feed them, and I let them run around for five, ten, or 15 minutes afterwards, depending on the weather. This gives them a chance to explore, learn about grass and earth, and get into bad habits like digging holes. The last few weeks before they leave, I bring them back into the kitchen for periods of time to get re-accustomed to the noises of the house – the washing machine, vacuum cleaner, telephone, people around, and the different feel of the floor – so it is not all frighteningly new when they leave.

Pups should get used to humans as soon as they are tumbling about. I go and sit in the puppy kennel with them, so they can climb all over me and be petted. I also chat to them when I feed them twice a day, and run my hands over them all the time. For my own guidance in assessing the litter, I stand them up and judge them at five, seven, and nine weeks, so I can write a critique on each pup.

WEANING

When you start weaning at three weeks, put your pups straight on to the very best beef possible, made into meatballs. Your bitch still has plenty of milk at this time, so I think it pointless giving puppies more milk to lap. Start off with a meatball as big as a large marble twice a day, increasing to the size of a walnut by the end of the week. After three days of meatballs, add in two milky meals, milk powder and Weetabix for breakfast and supper, one Weetabix biscuit each to begin with. By four weeks, give rice pudding for supper and keep Weetabix for breakfast. Do not introduce too many new things at once. Let the pups' tummies get used to one new food before introducing another.

By four weeks, you can use a slightly lower grade meat, and at five weeks a cheaper grade of beef with more fat content, but still the sort that humans eat. At six weeks, switch to the best pet mince, and start to add biscuit and stock.

TYPICAL DIET PER PUP
Three weeks: Lunch and tea. Give one meatball (large marble to walnut size).
Three and a half weeks: Add breakfast and supper of Weetabix plus milk powder, made sloppy to encourage lapping.
Four weeks: Breakfast of one Weetabix or one ounce cereal plus milk powder.
Lunch/tea of one meatball (walnut-sized, approx. one ounce).

LEFT: Weigh-in at six weeks. Warringah's Possum is now 7½ lbs. She is one of the lightest bitches of the litter – her sisters weighing around 8½ lbs.

RIGHT: Warringah's Coolibah now weighs 9lbs – 1½lbs more than Warringah's Possum, but only ½lb heavier than the biggest bitch in the litter.

Photos: Keith Hawkins.

At six weeks Warringah's Possum still looks good in overall shape with a good topline and a nice crest to her neck. The rear end is fine, but the front angulation is under-developed.

Warringah's Coolibah has a very pleasing shape, with a good neck, a balanced outline, and excellent front and rear angulatiuon. He has a good spring of rib and short, strong loins.

Supper of one-sixth of 14oz can of rice pudding plus a little milk.
Five weeks: Breakfast of one and a half Weetabix plus milk powder.
Lunch/tea of meatball (one to one and a half ounce).
Supper of a quarter can of rice pudding plus a little milk.
Six weeks: Breakfast of two Weetabix plus milk powder.
Lunch/tea of two ounces of meat plus half an ounce of biscuit and stock to moisten.

Supper of a quarter can of rice pudding plus a little milk.
Seven weeks: Breakfast of two Weetabix plus milk powder.
Lunch/tea of three ounces meat plus one ounce biscuit and stock.
Supper of a quarter can of rice pudding plus a little milk.
Eight weeks: Breakfast of two Weetabix plus milk powder.
Lunch/tea of four ounces meat plus one and a half ounces biscuit and stock.

As the puppies develop, they play more complicated games. It is at this time that relationships between the puppies are decided.

Photo: Keith Hawkins.

Supper of one third can of rice pudding plus a little milk.

Nine weeks: Breakfast of two or three Weetabix plus milk powder.
Lunch/tea of four ounces meat plus two ounces biscuit and stock.
Supper of one third can of rice pudding plus a little milk.

TIPS ON FEEDING THE LITTER

When you first start to feed cereal and milk the pups will wade through it, sit in it, lick it off each other, anything but actually lap it up. This might take them a couple of days to get the hang of. You will need to clean off the pups with a damp cloth after their attempts.

You can let the whole litter have breakfast and supper together from a suitable large, shallow dish. With the lunch and tea meatballs, hold each pup and spend time stroking and talking to them as you feed each one in turn. At six weeks, when you add biscuit and stock to the meat meals you can let the litter eat from the same shallow dish. I like to moisten the biscuit but not soak it. I always feed raw meat, making sure in the winter that the meat is not too chilled.

When my pups leave home at nine weeks, they go with at least four days food and I do try to encourage the new owners to stick with the diet. All ingredients are easily available from supermarkets and pet shops. Many vets will advocate the expensive all-in-one feed that they stock themselves. I have found my feeding regime has produced good dogs consistently over the past 30 years, sound, healthy and not overweight, so perhaps these vets will admit that breeders do know how to raise and feed good stock. It is interesting to note that many of the top show kennels in the country use similar feeding regimes. Having said all that, the all-in-one foods are also good, well-balanced, and dogs enjoy them. I do find that some people tend to feed too much, resulting in overweight pups and dogs, which puts an additional strain on joints and bones that do not need it, especially those of the Labrador.

You do not want a skinny Labrador puppy, so thin that you can see the ribs. Aim for a covering from a quarter to a half inch of fat, so the puppies have something to fall back on if illness strikes. I have seen pups so fat that they waddle, with full, distended bellies dragging down their toplines. This does not do them any good. You want them to thrive, and must not restrict their food during the growing months, but to have an overweight pup will injure it in the long run.

If you are going to change the pups' diet then you must do it slowly, introducing the new food gradually. It is important to impress this on the new owners of your litter. A puppy's tummy can be upset just by coming into a new home, where the water may be different or it could be colder in the kitchen (the place where most pups have their bed). Equally, missing siblings and mother is a trauma. The diet – the one thing that can be kept the same – should therefore not be changed.

SELLING THE PUPPIES

For novice breeders, I can only offer advice based on my personal experience of breeding Labradors and finding homes for the litters. We tend to have most of the pups spoken for before the litter is born. I have to let prospective buyers know that number one on the list is me. We do not tend to breed excessively, and so each litter is very special and planned carefully with the intention of keeping one or two pups to run on.

LEFT: At eight weeks Waringah's Possum weighs 12lbs 12oz. She is not one of the smallest bitches in the litter, but she is nicely covered.

RIGHT: At eight weeks, Waringah's Coolibah weighs 15lbs 2oz – he is nicely covered but not fat. He weighed the same as Warringah's Possum at birth, but at the eight week stage he is 3lbs heavier.

Photos: Keith Hawkins.

Final assessment: Warringah's Possum has a very pretty head and has a nice overall shape. However, she lacks in front angulation and is therefore unlikely to come up to standard as a prospective show dog. She went to a pet home and has become a much-loved companion.

Final assessment: Warringah's Coolibah has a pleasing depth to the muzzle. He has a good topline and tail-set. The forehand is well-angulated with good bone and tight feet. He has well-sprung ribs, short, strong loins and good hindquarters with good second thigh. He was retained at the Warringah kennels as a show prospect.

Although I let potential buyers come out and view the puppies from three weeks (not earlier as it may upset the mother), the pups have no personalities and are not up on their feet before then. I tell them they can come as many times as they like, but until I have made my choice at about seven to nine weeks they will not be able to make theirs. As we breed infrequently, we also have a list of people waiting for show pups, and they are often on the list for a couple of years. Potential show prospects, if there are any, can usually be identified by seven to eight weeks. I can then let the others know what pups I have left to sell as companion dogs.

11 *RING TRAINING AND HANDLING*

What do I look for in a show puppy? Obviously, the answer is everything set out in the Breed Standard. I make my choice at about eight weeks, when youngsters are as near a miniature of the finished adult as they will ever be. Personality counts for a lot with me. To make up a Champion is difficult. Competition these days is tough, and you have to have a good dog even to make the 'cut'. To stand a chance, a dog needs just that little bit extra, a touch of star quality that will lift your Labrador above all the others.

I like a square-looking puppy who stands correctly quite naturally. The pup should be balanced all through from muzzle to tail, preferably short coupled with a deep rib cage, the sternum well down, below or level with the elbows at this age. I look for the length of second thigh (stifle to hock) to be longer than the length of the femur (hip to stifle), with the hocks well let down. I do like to see neat feet, and really dislike wide-splayed feet on any dog. I look for a strong top line, but do not set much store on tail carriage at this age, as it will alter. Just make sure the tail set is good, and not high or low.

The puppy must have a good length of neck and long sloping shoulders with an obvious length of upper arm. When viewed from the front and back, the legs must fall perpendicularly, not outwards like the base of a triangle. Correctly-made puppies move well right from the start. The Labrador made its name on coat quality and otter tail, which is a must. Lastly, I like a prettily moulded head to set the whole thing off.

AT SIX MONTHS

By six months all the above features must be there, though the puppy may at first sight appear to be leggy in relation to the body. I look for a scissor bite, and probably would not continue with a borderline bite at this age. A male dog must be entire by now, but I would expect to have palpated the evidence at eight to ten weeks. Very often a puppy at six months is really not ready for the show ring. Never mind, if he was worth running on at eight weeks, have faith! It will all come together again in time.

HANDLING

Handling a dog in the ring is the way you present or 'show' your dog to the judge for an assessment of breed type, quality and soundness. The judge will judge your dog according to the blueprint of the breed as set out in the official Breed Standard and assess his quality against the ideal in that standard, if in a mixed breed or variety class, or, in a breed class, against the other exhibits in the ring.

In the opinion of the judge, the best dog on any given day is the winner. Judgment is made without reference to past performance or to a crystal ball for what might happen in the future. So if your dog has an off day, performing badly so the judge cannot assess him, this will be reflected in the placing he will get.

Anyone who has tried to handle a dog in the show ring for the first time will know that it is not nearly as easy as it looks when watched from the ring side! Contrary to what is too commonly practised at the growing number of junior handling competitions, good handling should

Mardas Play Away, bred by M. and D. Hepper. A promising show prospect, pictured at six months.

Photo: Lynn Kipps.

not be obvious, clever or intrusive at all. The dog should appear to be presenting himself to his best advantage, looking quite natural, alert and intelligently responsive to the handler. Ideally, the handler should melt into the background so that the onlooker and the judge will focus their attention on the gorgeous-looking dog and hardly be aware a handler is there at all.

Presentation varies according to the traditions of the country. The British method is to 'free stand' the exhibit. This more natural mode of presentation is also generally adopted in Scandinavia and Europe. 'Stacking', when the dog is held in a fixed standing pose, is often favoured in North America and Australia, especially by all-rounder judges.

The reason we usually 'free stand' our show Labradors is probably because the Breed Standard calls for a "strongly built....very active" dog, and a judge's brief is always to judge to the Standard. However, there is all the difference in the world between "very active" and unruly.

AT THE DOG SHOW

The day of the show is approaching, so what should you do in preparation? With a Labrador, surprisingly little. If he is dirty or socially undesirable on the personal hygiene front, you may need to bath him, but not unless it is really necessary and at least three days before the show if you must. Too much bathing can alter the texture of the coat, softening it and reducing its water-resistant properties. You only need to trim the twizzle off the tip of the tail to neaten its outline and you are done! I am assuming that you attend to daily grooming and regular health maintenance of your dog as a matter of course, which means that nails are trim and teeth and ears are clean.

On the day before your departure for the show, make quite sure there are no abnormal signs of weeping eyes or coughing and retching, or your dog may not be fit enough for showing. Not only is it very bad form to take an infectious dog to a show and against the rules and regulations which have been laid down to protect us all, but it could be very risky to expose your own dog to further germs while he is vulnerable. It is really not worth the risk just for one show.

Remember to take water and a bowl with you, something for him to lie on, grooming equipment and an emergency first aid kit. You will need a show lead, a number clip or rubber band to secure your ring number card to your person and a benching chain to tether your dog to the bench when he is not being shown. Not all shows have benching, but in Britain we are lucky enough to have these facilities at all our big Championship shows.

Take wet weather gear for yourself if the show is scheduled outside, or hot weather standbys to keep you and your dog cool. Wear clothing suitable for an active sport. Avoid loose jackets and skirts that could distract the dog by flapping in his face. Remember, you will be bending over your dog, so avoid wearing anything too revealing. Everything seems to be recorded on video these days!

At the show, the ring steward will call entrants for the class to assemble in the designated ring. You will receive a ring number which identifies your dog to the judge. No names are revealed to the judge beforehand, and talking to the judge is forbidden in the ring except to give the dog's age if asked.

Once assembled, all the handlers will stand their exhibits round the sides of the ring or where indicated by the ring steward. In many countries, exhibits are lined up in numerical order, but this is seldom the case in Britain. When your turn comes to be seen by the judge, walk your dog to the spot indicated and pose him. The judge will examine the dog from head to toe, including mouth, teeth and coat texture. A male dog will also be checked to see whether he is entire (two normally descended testicles) or not. Then you will be asked to move your dog up and down or in a triangle, or both. On completion of the examination you will join the others at the side of the ring until all entrants have been seen. The judge usually makes a final tour of inspection before placing the winners: first to fourth in many countries but in Britain usually first to fifth. A Champion is made up after winning the requisite number of CCs, CACs, CACIBs, Green Stars or Major Points,

The only trimming you need to do for a show Labrador is to neaten the twizzle at the end of the tail.

Photo: Clare Maiden.

depending on where in the world you are competing.

BASIC RING TRAINING

You want to try your dog at a show and he will not even stand still. How do you start? Inevitably, there will be two approaches to ring training. One is to train up a young puppy from scratch, and the other is to try and instil some ring discipline into an already grown and over-boisterous young adult, possibly also correcting existing handling faults.

Ideally, I try to start handling a puppy in the nest, thus training right from the very beginning. With a young puppy you are on virgin territory,

The aim of good handling is to present your exhibit to the best advantage for the judge's assessment. Sh. Ch. Covetwood Elouise of Carpenny, handled by Penny Carpanini, is standing four-square with a loose lead. Her attention is fixed on the handler, and she is wagging her tail, showing an easy-going, equable temperament. Showing should always look natural and easy.
Photo: Claire Maiden.

starting to train an uncluttered mind free of any previously learnt experiences. Theoretically, everything the puppy learns about life is because you, the owner/breeder, have allowed it to happen. Ideally, this unformed canine mind will be shielded from all negative, harmful and frightening experiences so that your puppy will come to regard you, and hopefully all humans, as the most wonderful, exciting and stimulating elements in his young life. Sometimes you may become even more important than food! This trust and devotion is the basis upon which all dog training is built. To achieve any kind of a rapport with your dog, he must regard you as the most important thing in his life and trust you implicitly. You cannot expect results without commitment on your part, and that takes time.

A dog's natural instincts, if they develop spontaneously without your awareness and supervision, will lead him to learn to be wary of strangers and unknown surroundings. A show dog is expected to be able to take both in his stride and subject himself to minute scrutiny and hands-on examination by a complete stranger in unfamiliar surroundings. All of which gives the lie to the frequent but ignorant comment that show dogs are brainless beauties, over-strung and good for nothing. Brainless beauties and good-for-nothing they may be, if this is all you have allowed them to become, but they cannot be over-strung and by implication nervous, if they are show dogs. It is quite useless even to try to show a dog exhibiting these traits. By and large, show dogs make the very best family pets and companion dogs simply because they have to exhibit placidity and tolerance towards people, unlike exclusively working dogs who only relate to one master.

LEARNING THE SHOW STANCE
Have the puppy standing squarely on a non-slippery surface. An old rubber-backed bath mat is useful for this. Think of the Labrador puppy profile as a box shape, with the legs set straight underneath it, naturally balanced, with a leg at each corner.

Try not to loom over your puppy or you could intimidate him. Stand beside him, not too close, with your arms slightly extended. Gently place a steadying hand under the chin extending the neck very slightly forwards, and carefully hold the tip of the tail. With a very wriggly puppy you may need to start by placing a steadying hand underneath the tummy. I have found that it is sometimes better to use the back of the hand for this or one can be tempted to grab the puppy causing him to resist and struggle more. A few soothing words might help: "Sta-aaa-nd. What a good dog!" Begin the association of word and action like this.

Stack the puppy in the show pose for only a very short time to start with, and as he gets more used to it, you can remove one steadying hand at a time and use it to stroke all down the back and legs with a firm but gentle touch. You are getting the puppy used to being closely and intimately handled all over. If your puppy is a male, remember to include his nether regions, as they are always checked by the judge in the ring to ascertain whether the dog is entire on not.

When training your very young puppy, select your moment carefully because there is little likelihood of puppy co-operation if he needs to go to relieve himself or would much rather just go to sleep. There will be plenty of opportunities during a normal day to practise, and your puppy will not even be aware that he is being trained, because all the caressing and attention will be pleasurable and standing up so close to master or mistress will be lovely.

Training, such as it is at this age, is all geared to gaining your dog's trust and confidence and teaching him to watch you, paying attention to your every move but especially to your hands and face. You may find that little things can distract your puppy's attention. In the early weeks and months I do most of this training in my kitchen where I deliberately have the radio on. The telephone is constantly ringing or some other loud distraction such as a washing machine is providing a noisy background to the lessons. The potential show puppy needs to learn to cope as early as possible with noise and distractions, because it will certainly meet both in abundance at a show. Your puppy should become completely confident in you and relaxed when you handle him, pick him up, turn him on to his back and cradle him like a baby. He will

Mardas Bayleaf, aged fifteen weeks, learning the show stance. Keep training sessions short, and make sure your puppy enjoys them.

Photo: Lynn Kipps.

run to you for comfort if frightened. Only at this stage should you entrust your baby to anyone other than regularly encountered members of the immediate household who have the same aspirations as you do for the puppy.

Anxieties acquired early in a puppy's life can lead to deep-seated problems later on that may not seem to have a rational basis unless you can relate them back. If a link cannot be traced, these 'hang-ups' can have a detrimental effect on your dog's potential show career. Potential hazards in this category to monitor most closely are the unsupervised attentions of children who can undo months of 'hands are beautiful' training at a stroke, without knowing what they are doing. Heavy-handed 'know-it-all' dog trainers can do similar damage and, for this reason, I am extremely wary of ring craft classes for puppies when you are also a novice handler or owner. If you have been advised to attend such classes, go without your puppy to start with to learn the ropes.

Other dogs outside the home pack and other animals need watching too. If the young show dog learns to be wary of other animals in the vicinity and the anxiety goes unrecognised for too long so that the circumstances of the unfortunate encounter have been forgotten, a train of events may lead your dog to turn his attention more to the potential danger (as he perceives it) than towards you.

An important point for the new handler or

trainer to bear in mind is that dogs do not rationalise, even the wisest and most intelligent of them. Learning, for a dog, is based on cause and effect. The older and more experienced a dog becomes, the more it can relate cause to effect. The more experience gained, the more there are to draw on. Your puppy, who has a mind like a blank page, is not going to be able to rationalise when he meets a bad experience. He may think more along these lines, for example: "My trainer pinched my lip when he looked at my teeth and a wasp was buzzing round my head at the time, so every time I hear a wasp I must expect to have a hurt mouth." Cause and effect.

Naturally you cannot think of everything, but wherever possible try to set up your ring training in a situation over which you have some control, certainly until your youngster has built up quite a firm body of good experiences upon which to draw for the future. If your puppy does suffer a setback, always try to analyse what triggered off that specific behaviour pattern. If you can track it back to the source, it will be a lot easier to deal with. The method will be firstly diagnosis, then re-establishing the dog's confidence in you while confronting the same or a similar situation. If trust was established in the early learning experiences, you can draw on this bond whenever necessary in the future.

EXAMINATION OF THE DENTITION
I make it a rule not to examine the mouth, teeth

and bite more than is necessary all the time a puppy is teething, in order not to risk a negative response. Ample opportunities to examine the progress of the teeth will present themselves when the puppy mouths your hand with a wide open mouth during playtime. Examination of the dentition should be left till quite late in the training programme, when your puppy has already learned to stand quietly on command. It is never taught in conjunction with food preparation or mealtimes.

Examination of the teeth is best approached quite casually and uneventfully as far as the puppy is concerned, as part of his general everyday caressing or grooming. Your own manner needs to be calm and matter-of-fact. With a confident, no-nonsense approach and the dog standing on your left side, gently cradle the lower jaw with the right hand and briefly lift the lips to expose the front teeth, with the mouth closed, with your left hand. (Reverse right and left hands if you have the dog on the other side.) Many people like to reinforce this training with a verbal command such as "Teeth", followed by praise and encouragement.

Success depends on repeated easy experiences over many weeks, never making an issue of this part of the training. Little and often is the watchword. Remember to praise the dog when the lesson has been done. Do not reinforce this training with a food reward, or the dog will come to associate teeth examination with an edible reward and salivate in anticipation. This has to be one of my pet hates when I am judging, for obvious reasons!

LEAD TRAINING
All the previously mentioned training can be started at a very young age (the sooner the better) and can be incorporated into routine maintenance and upbringing of a normal Labrador puppy during feeding, grooming and playtime. The disciplines learned are just as useful to the pet dog as to the show prospect. Lead training does require a more formal approach, but similarly the basic task is just as essential to the companion as to the show dog, and much the same principles apply.

Introduction to a collar and lead can begin

before the puppy goes out into the wide world on completion of the course of inoculations. However, lead training should not be started too young, and certainly not before the neck and legs have acquired a little tone and strength. It is a good idea to start introducing a leash when the puppy is in familiar surroundings, the kennel or the kitchen. Most puppies hate the restraint round their necks to start with but quickly learn, with the reinforcement of tidbits or a meal, that it is not such a bad thing after all.

In the show ring, by convention, we use a long slip lead (a length of strong cord or fine woven rope with a ring at one end through which the lead passes to form a noose, and loop handle at the other), but I do not advocate starting lead training with one of these. You can progress to this later. It is far less frightening for an inexperienced youngster to wear a soft snugly-fitting collar with lead attached. It is too tightly fitting if you cannot slip two fingers underneath the collar when it is fastened, and probably too loose if more than three fingers can be accommodated, allowing the puppy an opportunity to double back on himself and wriggle out of the collar if he objects too strongly.

If the introduction to walking on the lead has been broached before the puppy is taken into the outside world, he will only have one new experience to overcome at a time, which is far less traumatic for a baby. Puppies should be taught to walk on your left hand side at all times, in order not to trip you up or be trodden underfoot. The same methods are employed as for basic obedience training. However, heelwork differs between obedience and show training, in that the former prizes closeness of the dog walking at the handler's side, which is not practical for a beauty competition.

For beauty or conformation competition, great store is set on a free, effortless, driving action as the dog goes round the ring. This can only be achieved by the dog striding out freely, slightly away from the handler's side, at the best pace for that particular animal. The judge does not want to see the handler, but the dog. Do not expect to be able to achieve good show movement right away. This can always be tidied up and perfected once the puppy can move at a

Wynfaul Tamarisk for Glenorrell, handled by Sheila Saunt. Photos: Lynn Kipps.
As you progress in training, your Labrador must learn to move fluently alongside you, showing off the quality and soundness of his movement. The judge will also assess the movement from the front and from behind.

brisk trot, comfortably at your side, not pulling forward or dragging behind.

Puppies' temperaments vary as much as children's do, so some puppies will take to the lead quicker than others. Whatever you do, do not force the issue. Try again tomorrow, and the day after, and again the day after that. Use tidbits or a favourite toy and a happy, confident voice in encouragement. Make sure that any reluctance to walk outside on the lead is not just a fear of crossing the threshold (going out of the front door) into a new environment. If you suspect this to be the case, gently scooping the puppy up under your arm and walking a few steps down the driveway or street before setting him down can often be the answer to initial reluctance. It is advisable not to establish a bad precedent in the puppy's mind. Eventually a Labrador puppy's natural curiosity will get the better of him and he will charge ahead to the nearest interesting sniff, then on to the next.

BEGINNING RING TRAINING
Having trained your youngster to walk nicely by your side in most situations, now is the time to begin ring training in earnest. Right from the outset, establish your routine. When the show gear comes out, it should mean 'showtime' in the dog's mind. No matter how old my show dogs may be, as soon as they see me get the show lead and other paraphernalia together there

is always great excitement and intense interest in the proceedings. Even the oldies momentarily shed a few years and sparkle to attention, up on their toes with wagging tails! This is exactly what you want to achieve, because when a dog shows energy and enthusiasm for what he is doing he is much more eye-catching than the dog who performs as a duty.

To get this message across to the trainee show dog, training must be fun. Only use the show lead when you are showing, and build up an association of ideas to condition your dog to a particular pattern of behaviour. Do not ever allow anyone else to use the show lead to take the dog for a routine walk, or worse still, to lead him to something potentially unpleasant, such as a visit to the vet, to take a bath, or to go to a place of punishment. That show lead means 'showtime', which also has to be fun time.

Your dog will probably get so tuned-in to 'showtime/funtime' that it may go to his head and make him over-boisterous. Providing this exuberance is due to the excitement of the moment, not to poor training of the basics or any lack of discipline, do not worry too much. It is far easier to tone down excitement than to instil it when it is entirely lacking. You can 'knock it out of them' but you cannot 'put it there', which is why you have gone to all that trouble establishing early associations.

A little 'square bashing' is all that is called

for. While the youngster is lunging and bucking with excitement on his show lead, call his name, pat your left leg encouragingly, and walk smartly up and down, in the same line or square, over and over again until the message gets through. Because of all his early learning, he knows you are the boss and will not resent it. After your command and a slight jerk or flick of the lead, do not wait for him, just go! He will have to follow and pay attention to you, and not to that interesting event going on in the other corner, or he will fall over himself. Ignore his inattention, just march. It will work. Take a tip from the obedience people and help get the dog's attention to start with by always taking off with your left foot (the one closest to the dog). You can use words of command to reinforce your wishes, but preferably not the same ones you use if you have trained for obedience or your dog will be confused as to how he should proceed, close to heel or striding out at half an arm's length from you.

Having trained a number of Labradors (and some other breeds) to show, I avoid too much square-bashing at home. You can so easily kill enthusiasm with too much training and repetition, and this is especially so with a sensitive youngster who takes everything very much to heart.

IN THE RING

If you are the first class in the ring, you will not be able to watch previous classes to see what the judge likes exhibitors to do, so listen to instructions. If you are asked to run a triangle, and then move up and down in a straight line, this is what the judge wants. Frequently, a class will run round the circumference of the ring, en masse, before the individual examination of each exhibit. The judge will be 'getting his eye in' as to the quality of the class in general, but will also note any eye-catching movers for particular attention later. Be prepared. Neither crowd the dog in front nor allow the competitor behind you to invade your space. Stand your ground and keep up. Pay attention to your own dog so that he does not interfere with any other exhibit. A quick soft command or flick of the lead should suffice.

There are two schools of thought as to how one should hold the lead. Some people prefer a loose hold, with the noose of the slip down over the dog's shoulders and the handler holding the lead in an underarm fashion with the palm of the hand up. Others like the lead coming from under the dog's chin, held above the dog with very slight tension in the lead between dog and handler, the handler holding the lead with an overarm posture, palm of the hand down.

Your own build, the personality of the dog and the dog's physique will determine which method you use. You will come to your own conclusion on this. For myself, I prefer to use a little tension in the lead when running in a confined space or with a number of other exhibits. It gives me just that little bit of extra control, so I know precisely where the dog's feet are going. This is particularly important when negotiating corners of a triangle or a slight downward slope of a ring. Both these features can show up flaws in a dog's make-up, and a wily judge may be watching. So if your dog is a lovely mover, use these features to your advantage. Do not be penalised for lack of good handling.

Hold any slack of the lead neatly looped in the hand, preferably not dangling untidily. Hold the lead sensitively, as if it were the reins of a horse, to get feedback from the dog. You are a partnership in the show ring, and you need to get all the information possible back from the dog in order to perform well. Your dog will show himself off to better advantage if you hold him at half an arm's length away from you when standing and moving.

Be aware of what your own feet are doing, so that you do not tread on any paws. This sounds pretty obvious too, but practise a spot of square-bashing on your own, without the dog, but still holding the lead. This will help you concentrate on your dog and not worry about your own feet when the time comes. Again, it may seem obvious, but plan your own footwear in advance. Setting the right pace for your dog on the move is something that really does take experience. Each dog moves at his own optimum best pace. No amount of instruction will teach you to judge this for yourself if you have not already learned and understood what is being looked for when you are asked to move your dog. This question is a whole chapter in itself, so suffice it to say here that an experienced judge will be able to glean about 90 per cent of what he wants to know about your dog just from watching him move. It will pay you to spend some time trying to get to grips with the correct pace if you are ever to become serious about showing. However, a tip worth remembering is that your dog will measure his stride to yours, so if you mince along with tiny steps, he will too.

TEACHING TO STAND TO ATTENTION
As I said earlier, good handling looks so easy but it is achieved only with careful attention to detail. If you have been able to follow the basic training, the next step will follow on easily. You already have a good rapport with your pupil who trusts you and watches you.

As with many lessons, I also teach this one in my kitchen. As part of our daily routine, I give each of my dogs a cuddle then tidbits while they are standing in line. They come to look forward to this. I am never quite sure whether the cuddle or the tidbit is looked forward to most, but I suspect it is the latter! If several dogs are all together jostling for position and my attention, there is heightened attentiveness on their part just in case they miss anything.

Hopefully, as part of basic training, your puppy will have learned his name and now is the time to use it. I arm myself with a pocketful of some dried kibble or biscuit meal in a rustly paper or polythene bag and, calling each dog by name, toss a piece to each one in turn. My dogs get very adept at catching, and the older ones seldom miss. Of course, a puppy's reactions and co-ordination will be too slow to catch at this stage, but they stand in line with the rest.

I thus have a semi-circle of dogs standing up on their toes, to attention, often quivering with anticipation and waiting their turn. The new puppy picks up the excitement which is very infectious and, without knowing why at this

stage, will stand, sit or bounce to attention too. Sometimes new puppies incur a grizzle of disapproval from one of the older females if too much pushing and shoving to get to the front goes on. This is also useful in the learning process. At this point, I usually admonish the culprit verbally and tell them all to "Get back", whereupon all the dogs take a step backwards. You must choose your own terminology here, because this command can mean something very different to some of the working fraternity. My dogs know that "Get back" means: "Do not crowd me. Take a step backwards to spread out the semi-circle." Calling the attention of each dog by name, I toss or give a tidbit to each in turn. There are lots of tidbits, so if someone should fail to catch and miss their turn, this serves to get them more on their toes next time. You can be sure the dogs are not only paying attention to my voice, they notice the slightest gesture of my hands and change of facial expression in their enthusiasm to get their share of the loot!

This little training session lasts no more than a few minutes a day, but if repeated regularly, it will set a pattern of behaviour in a dog's mind. Soon, if a puppy is alone with me in the kitchen and I get out the rustly bag with or without the tidbits, there is an instantaneous reaction: puppy standing to attention, eyes fixed on me, smiling face and wagging tail in keen anticipation. The dog has been conditioned to a rustly bag.

To bait, or not to bait? One thing that may have already struck you if you have watched a few Labrador shows, is the different methods of standing your dog for the judge's scrutiny. Broadly speaking, there are three ways to do this:

1) Free standing, with the dog facing in front of you, about an outstretched arm's length away, with a loose lead, well down, flat over the withers and maintaining eye contact. This is the method I prefer, as I think it shows off the dog's natural assets to best advantage. My own train-

'I have a semi-circle of dogs standing up on their toes, to attention, often quivering with anticipation and waiting their turn'

STANDING TO ATTENTION
Demonstrated by Penny Carpanini and Sh. Ch. Covetwood Elouise of Carpenny.
Photos: Clare Maiden.

FREE STANDING

1. A light tap on a front foot will remind your dog to stand perpendicular.

2. 'Elouise' is too stretched out behind. Give a quick tap on the lead, and rock your own balance from the front to the back foot, thus encouraging the dog to shift her back leg forwards.

3. The back foot has moved forward, the lead is relaxed – and the reward is coming!

4. Now Elouise is showing herself off well. The loose lead does not break her neck-line or topline. Her weight is equally balanced on all four legs, and there is a good, clear space framing her profile. Note the handler's hands are held well into the body making full use of a fairly long lead. The level of the hands is crucial, as Elouise's attention is divided between the reward and the handler's eye contact.

BAITING

1. Baiting gets a dog's undivided attention, and it can be an easier option when handling a bored, lack-lustre dog, or even a hyperactive dog. However, it is all too easy to give your dogs faults by over-handling. In this photo, the bait is being held too high. The head has disappeared into the shouders, effectively straightening the front angulation and dipping the topline.

2. Standing away from the dog while baiting improves the topline – but compare this picture with the next.

3. Elouise looks a lot better free standing. If your dog is correctly made, have confidence in its ability to show itself off.

STACKING

4. To teach your dog to stack, first set the front legs and feet perpendicularly when viewed from the front or the side.

5. Then move the back legs, so the back end balances the front, with the legs set squarely under the body.

ing methods are geared to achieving this way of presentation.

2) Baiting, with the dog standing to attention in front of you but in contact with you, as he nibbles on a piece of liver or other tidbit held in your outstretched hand. This method of handling is probably the cause of the most common of all handling faults, namely over-handling. Done well, however, an otherwise mediocre dog can look exceptional, as one can encourage the neck to extend, level off a dippy top line and otherwise improve the outline of the exhibit. Proponents also believe they have better control of their dog through baiting, and when these methods win CCs who can deny their success?

3) Stacking, where the dog stands in front and across the handler, who places each foot down in exactly the right position to show the dog off to good advantage. There is no eye contact. The lead is usually held under the chin and up over the dog's withers, with slight tension maintaining the point of contact with the exhibit. This takes training, patience and repetition to achieve well. It is, by its nature, a static pose and seldom goes with tail-wagging.

There is really very little more to teach the dog apart from this. He will already be quite used to being handled all over from his early training. You could get a friend to run their hands over the dog as a rehearsal if you are unsure before your first show. All the rest of the learning has to be done by you, the handler.

COMMON FAULTS IN HANDLING

OVER-GROOMING

Bad grooming practice before the show is a self-inflicted failing many a novice exhibitor indulges in. The texture of the coat is an important feature of the Labrador. This can be detrimentally altered by bathing too close to show day, or using grooming products more in keeping with long-coated breeds. The Labrador coat texture should be waterproof, feel slightly hard to the touch, with a definite undercoat of softer downy fur. The judge looks for this double coat by turning back the top coat halfway down the dog's flanks.

Over-grooming can remove the precious undercoat. Preserve the undercoat for as long as possible by restricting grooming to a rub-down with a wet leather or sponge cloth and water. Avoid using a harsh comb or brush until it becomes necessary to clear out the dead coat altogether. (At which time you will have to forget showing until the new coat grows in again. This does not usually take too long with a Labrador.) Give the dog a regular grooming, but avoid shampooing him immediately before a show as this often softens the coat for a few days. A good swim in a river is far better for him. However, it is socially unacceptable to present a dirty dog for the judge to look over.

TAIL: A common mistake when trimming the tail twizzle (that little tuft of untidy fur at the tip of the tail) is to cut it square to the line of the tail. The tail should end in a blunt point or be slightly rounded. Otherwise it spoils the overall outline of the dog. The Labrador tail should be otter-shaped, thick at the base and tapering to a point at the tip. At least one judge of my acquaintance makes a point of checking the underside of the tail for signs of further trimming here too!

TOENAILS: Toenails should wear down naturally with a normal-shaped Labrador foot.

However nails, even on good feet, cannot wear down if the dog is constantly exercised on soft ground. You have to remember that once grown beyond a certain point, the nails will not wear down level even if the dog is walking on concrete, because pressure on the nail quicks is painful and the dog will walk down on his pasterns to avoid this, so perpetuating the problem.

The remedy is to check the length of the toenails at least a week before a show and trim them level as necessary. It is best not to leave this task to the last minute, as one crafty judge I encountered over the years used to look for signs of nail trimming as an indication of poor quality feet and would penalise accordingly. Take care with this task too, because if the nails are trimmed unevenly (longer on one side of the foot than the other), it can cause a dog to pin-toe in or out while moving. Worse still, if the quick is cut, it is very painful and can cause lameness.

OVER-BAITING

Speaking as a judge, one of my pet hates is the handler who constantly stuffs the dog with sticky liver tidbits immediately prior to my examination of the head and teeth. I can never understand what the handler hopes to gain from this. Firstly, with a mouth full of food, the dog's expression is certainly not improved. Secondly, the dog will be dancing around looking for more food, rather than standing quietly for a hands-on examination. Thirdly, it is decidedly unpleasant to have to handle a dog who is drooling liberally.

Anticipation of a tidbit reward is far more effective in enhancing your dog's attentiveness to you. Do not keep telling him he is a good dog for no reason, or it will not mean anything and he will cease to listen. Give food after the judgment as a reward for doing well, along with verbal praise.

BADLY POSITIONED HANDS

The way you move your hands is crucial. By holding them too high, the handler loses the dog's neck as it sinks back into the shoulders, spoiling a clean neck line and allowing the top line to dip in the middle. If the exhibit has a tendency to length of loin, this is accentuated and, regardless of the actual length of upper arm, that can be obscured too. The exhibit is often stretched out too far behind, looking long in the couplings, which can give the back end a weak appearance.

The remedy is preferably to stand the dog further away from you. Allow the dog a chance to find his own natural balance for a moment. Stop feeding him, at least until the judge has finished the hands-on examination. Animation really comes into its own at the end, after the hands-on examination, when the judge is making a final walk-round to confirm that no one has been missed. This is the vital make-your-mind-up-moment, when it is still not too late to make that final good impression. This is when you need to use bait to get the very best out of the dog.

Later, at home, watch yourself handling in a full length mirror, baiting and not baiting. Be objective! If you can confirm your handling method by watching yourself on video, so much the better. Try to analyse why you are doing what you do when handling and relate it to your knowledge of the dog's form and structure. Armed with this objective mental picture, measure it against the ideal of the breed. If you perceive failings in your exhibit, try to find ways of minimising their impact by enhancing his best features. Remember this is showtime, and you and your Labrador are putting on a performance.

CRABBING

This generally refers to a dog's movement. Going in a straight line away from the judge, the crabbing dog moves askew, with the front legs moving beside and parallel to the line followed by the back legs, just like a crab.

One solution is to look to your footwear. Boots or clumpy shoes may make a puppy nervous of being trodden on, so he pulls his front end away from danger. A pattern of behaviour quickly builds up and persists long after the offending shoes have been thrown away. Always train a dog when you are wearing comfortable, lightweight, soft-soled shoes.

Also try running the dog on the other side of you, so he finds himself running in towards you and starts to straighten himself out. Chop and change sides when moving him, to break the crabbing habit. Remember, though, if you are handling your dog on the other side of you, and you are asked to run a triangle by the judge, go out to your left, across the ring and back to the judge, not the other way around as you usually do. Otherwise you will place yourself between the judge and the dog he is trying to judge.

PACING

This is when a dog habitually moves using both legs on the same side together, rather like a lizard or a rat. It can look very peculiar and the gait rolls like a seafarer's. It is quite obvious to onlookers that the handler is unaware of his charge if he takes no steps to correct this fault as it occurs. Such movement does not necessarily indicate unsoundness, so it is nothing to be ashamed of. It is unsightly, though, and not typical, and therefore it will be penalised.

Pacing means that a bit more square-bashing is called for. Choose a definite straight line and stick to it as you move up and down. Check the dog is with you when you start. Say your dog's name to get his attention, give the command, flick the lead and start off smartly, left foot first (the side nearest to the dog). Sometimes this alone will start the movement correctly and it will continue, or your exhibit may revert to pacing after a few strides. If this happens, do not stop. Continue to walk smartly up and down, but insert a step-hop-step among the left-right-left strides. This is a surprise for the dog, who is unable to slacken his pace as you keep going. A dog usually matches his stride to yours, so to wrong-foot him occasionally can prove corrective when it comes to pacing.

Most Labradors, having a naturally long stride themselves, can develop a pacing action if they are habitually lead exercised too slowly day after day. I had a dog when my children were small who was a naturally beautiful mover. However, he developed a tendency to pace, habitually walking to heel with my baby in the pram. I did not want to stop taking him with us every time we walked out, so I had to develop a different association of ideas. Through the use of different types of lead and different commands, he learned that pacing was acceptable

HANDLING FAULTS

1. Here the dog is standing quite well, but the handler is not helping by standing too close, with too short a lead – but it is a good to hide a poor front and poor feet!

2. The handler is standing too close to the dog. The dog is standing well, but the lead is badly placed, spoiling a good, clean outline. Remedy: loosen the lead and check it lies it on top of the coat, not under it.

3. A common fault is to forget the dog has a back-end. Just look at what can happen to hind angulation with bad handling. The dog could be getting tired and bored, so move her and start again. If you have taught your dog to catch, now is the time to carefully throw a reward, so she must make a slight jump to catch it. This almost always restores a good, balanced posture.

with the pram, but not in the show ring where we went faster.

Another point that may be helpful to remember is that the faster a dog moves, the closer the legs will come to the mid line. If you know you have a dog who moves rather close behind, do not make the mistake of thinking that the faster you go, the less it will show. Quite the reverse is true!

LEAD LENGTH
Another common handling fault is trying to show a dog using a lead that is too short for you. Most show equipment comes in standard sizes, but if you are tall you will need a longer lead than if you are short. For myself, I like to have the use of at least a metre of lead between my hands and the dog. Add on the length of lead necessary for the noose to lie comfortably down over the dog's shoulders without ruffling his fur the wrong way, and you come up with a good working length of lead. If the lead is too short, not only will you have your dog standing too close, bringing similar difficulties to those described under baiting, but the lead will almost certainly cut the attractive top line by disturbing the fur on the nape of the neck. The judge can see this is the case but, when it is make-your-

mind-up-time, everything counts if the competition is strong.

CHANGE IN TEMPERAMENT
If you have a bitch who loses enthusiasm for showing, it may be that she is just coming up to her first season, and so she may become a slave to her hormones. The problem is transitory and clears spontaneously, but it may reappear with her next season. At this time, some bitches may show other unexpected changes in temperament, such as becoming snappy when another bitch sniffs at the rear end. Put it down to PMT and avoid showing your bitch at these times!

BOREDOM
Over-training or over-showing can dull a dog's enthusiasm for showing. He may stand beautifully, have perfect manners while his teeth are being examined, and keep perfectly to heel on the move. His behaviour may be exemplary, but he has boredom written all over him. Even the most perfect exhibit looks nothing if the sparkle has been knocked out.

This is the most difficult of all problems to correct. It is why I set such store by early good associations, and why I do not rush to the nearest ring training class every week. A lot will depend on the age of the dog and how long the lack-lustre performance has been going on, as far as an ultimate prognosis for this problem is concerned. In most cases the best course of action is to track back and try to undo all the mistakes that your dog has learned since you began.

THE REMEDY: Begin by forgetting showing altogether for three to six months. No practices. No visiting shows with your dog. No baiting for scraps in the kitchen. No getting out the kit bag in front of the dog. Totally disassociate your dog from showing for a fairly long period. In the meantime, teach something quite different. Play hunt the thimble in the sitting room, or have a go at scent discrimination or flyball. Anything, just so long as it is *fun* for you both. You will be starting afresh, planting a new association of ideas in the dog's mind: "Here comes the plastic chop bone. Goody, goody, a game is coming up!" If you are playing hunt the thimble (or hunt the plastic chop bone), when the dog gets too clever at finding it, transfer the game outside to the garden, then to the local park when you are out walking, or even the shopping precinct car park on a quiet day. Ultimately, that plastic chop bone will become the main focus of your Labrador's life – and yours! This will become your new showing aid.

You will also have to change your show equipment, involving a different lead, a different set of show clothes, bag and shoes. Identify all the little clues that associated shows with boredom, and exchange them for newly acquired 'fun' gear. When eventually you go back into that show ring, have the plastic chop bone in your pocket, but take no apparent notice of how the dog stands, how you hold the lead when you move, and so on. Act as you would if you were going for a walk or about to play hunt the thimble or whatever. When the judge goes over your dog you must react as you would when encountering a colleague at work. Do not pay more than casual attention to the dog, keeping everything as natural and unstructured as possible. With a bit of luck your dog will be so focused on his toy in your pocket, and the game you may have with him, that he will only have a

vague memory of what showing was all about previously.

Transferring allegiances or interests is not an easy option, but it can be done, because I have done it. I have an old, much-loved veteran now, who went through a bad patch as a youngster of about a year old. He turned from an enthusiastic show puppy of great promise into a zombie without much will to do anything. I was heart-broken. The remedy came by chance. I had a very realistic-looking rubber frog, bought as a joke for a friend. The dog saw this up on the mantleshelf. He was mesmerised, and could not take his eyes off it. I took it down and he bolted behind a chair, eyes fixed on it. At last I had found something he took more than a passing interest in. He had no appetite either, so all the usual treats were useless as aids to showing.

Every day thereafter, I would let him into the room with the frog, take it down in front of him, handle it, then put it back again. After some time, his fear turned to curiosity, then to interest and, later still, to real enthusiasm to get hold of the frog. I never let him touch it or sniff closely at it. I just let him see it. The upshot was that after a couple of months I had found something my lovely dog was passionate about and would stand to attention for, wagging his tail like crazy. We started showing again, frog in pocket. He knew it was there, but I would save revelation until I really needed him on his toes. A quick flash of a frog leg was often all it took! When the frog was not in my pocket, it lived in the show bag and was never seen except on show days.

I made that dog up to a Champion. He won ten CCs, BOBs, and BIS's as well. Then one day, due to a lapse of attention on my part, the show bag was left open and unattended in my hallway. My Champion got his revenge, found the frog in the bottom of the showbag and 'killed' it! I tried to replace it but could not. We did not really need it any longer anyway, because a new pattern of behaviour had been established. However, the silly dog still looked for his frog for a long time afterwards. Which only goes to show that dogs do not reason, they learn by cause and effect.

12 *ON WITH THE SHOW*

In Britain, the Labrador is judged in the Gundog Group, and it is at Championship shows where the strongest competition is met. Usually an entry of 250-450 can be expected, and Club shows generally draw a bigger entry than all-breed shows.

The initial classes are judged depending on age – Puppies up to 12 months , Juniors up to 18 months – followed by a classification which is dependent on the number of awards a dog has achieved. Finally, the Challenge Certificates are awarded to the Best Dog and the Best Bitch, and the title of Best of Breed is awarded to one of the pair. The Best of Breed winner then goes forward to be judged in the Group ring. The Group winner will compete for Best in Show.

A dog becomes a Show Champion when it has gained three Challenge Certificates under three different judges. The dog cannot gain this title until it is over 12 months of age – and so it must be this age when the third CC is awarded. In order to become a full Champion, a Labrador must also qualify in the field.

INFLUENTIAL BRITISH BLOODLINES
The Labrador, being such a popular breed, nearly always has large entries at shows, thus making competition exceedingly strong. Indeed, it is very difficult to make up a Champion in the UK. Success requires extraordinary dedication, and many of the breeders mentioned in this chapter will always be acclaimed for having the genius to bring together bloodlines which produce top winners. Undoubtedly, they have made an invaluable contribution to succeeding generations of Labradors, which has resulted in the

strength of the breed today.

Of the dogs featured, there are several whose impressive achievements in the show world and accomplishments in producing terms are such that their names will ring proud for many a year.

SANDYLANDS
This kennel is famous the world over and is owned, of course, by Gwen Broadley in partnership with Garner Anthony. Mrs Broadley started in Labradors as a young girl in the 1920s, with a black bitch named Juno of Sandylands. It is interesting to note how her prefix was selected. While she was walking Juno one day, a man stopped to admire the Labrador, and asked for the kennel name. Mrs Broadley looked up, noticed a sign saying Sandylands Promenade, and decided there and then to use it.

The kennel has had enormous success over the years and, at time of writing, 77 Champions have been bred or owned at Sandylands. The vast majority of these title holders have been Labradors, but a few have been in other gundog breeds – English Springers, Cockers, Flatcoats and Pointers. This is a spectacular achievement, and no other British Labrador kennel has come anywhere near equalling such an incredible record.

There have been so many outstanding Sandylands dogs that it would be difficult to mention them all, but the three most dominant have probably been Ch. Sandylands Tandy, Ch. Sandylands Mark and Ch. Sandylands Tweed of Blaircount, the latter bred by Mr and Mrs Grant Cairns and indeed a legend. Ch. Sandylands Mark has had an enormous influence in the breed and has sired 27 Champions – no mean

Sh. Ch. Sandylands Bliss, owned by Gwen Broadley.

Photo: Anne Roslin Williams.

achievement. He died in 1979 at almost 14 years of age.

More recently, Sh. Ch. Sandylands Bliss brought home many CCs – she was a most gorgeous cream bitch, and full of quality. It was a sad loss when she died young in November 1994, following a Caesarian operation. Fortunately, two of her offspring are doing well in the show ring, Sandylands Gadabout (male) and Sandylands Gracia.

Today at Sandylands there are some notable dogs, including Sh. Ch. Sandylands Royal Escort, Ch. Sandylands My Guy and Sh. Ch. Sandylands Gentry, the latter being the latest Champion, gaining his title at the Labrador Club Ch. Show, in June 1995.

Mrs Broadley is greatly admired throughout the world for her wealth of knowledge and her dedication to breeding top class Labradors. Her contribution to the world of Labradors is immeasurable, and there can be very few dogs in the show ring today who do not have 'Sandylands' in their pedigree. As a judge she was highly sought-after, and until the mid-80s (when she retired) was a greatly respected all-rounder judge both in the UK and worldwide.

ARDMARGHA
The Ardmargha kennel is owned by Harold and Margaret Clayton, and was established in 1943 with the purchase of a black Labrador called Finn of Ardmargha, born 14.5.43, whose parents were Irish Ch. Black Prince of Marlu ex Irish Ch. Lady of Ballyholme. The prefix is derived from the Irish name Armagh.

At a later stage, two black bitches (sired by Sh. Ch. Kinley Skipper and out of Ch. Sandylands Truth) were bought from Gwen Broadley, one of whom was Komely, and it was from this bitch that Margaret and Harold have bred their present line. A total of seven British Champions or Sh. Champions have emerged from this kennel, plus nine abroad. The best-known are Ch. Kilree of Ardmargha, Ch. Faith of Ardmargha, Ch. Kimbo of Ardmargha, Sh. Ch. Ardmargha Mad Hatter and Sh. Ch. Ardmargha So Happy.

Faith was an eye-catching yellow bitch, an outstanding show girl and a joy to watch. She was also a Group winner, as was Kimbo who gained his title as a junior. Mad Hatter was awarded many wins including Reserve Best In Show All Breeds at the West of England Ladies Kennel Association Show (WELKS), plus Group wins. He proved to be a great sire and is behind many of today's top winners, including the record CC holder, Sh. Ch. Croftspa Hazelnut of Foxrush, owned by Judith Charlton. Mad Hatter is also the great grand-sire of Sh. Ch. Bradking Hugo. Mention must also be made of

Hope of Ardmargha (Faith's sister), who was never shown but produced four Champions and has obviously been quite an influence in the breeding programme.

Until recent years, Ardmargha dogs were trained to the gun, used for shooting and also ran successfully in trials. However, Harold had to give up shooting because of eyesight problems.

BRADKING

Dogs have always been a passion for Arthur and Peggy Kelley, who initially began with Dalmatians in the 1940s. However, about ten years later their first Labrador appeared on the scene, a chocolate dog puppy purchased from the head gamekeeper on Lord Bradford's estate. To the family he was known as 'Brad, the King of Dogs', and some time later when a prefix was needed, the name Bradking sprang to mind, in memory of their first beloved Labrador.

When seeking a foundation for the kennel, the Sandylands dogs appealed for type and two bitches were purchased by the Kelleys. They were Sandylands Clove and Sandylands Carona, and the latter became the dam of the kennel's first Champion, Sh. Ch. Bradking Bonny My Girl, a very apt name. She was an outstanding brood and, when mated to Ch. Follytower Merrybrook Black Stormer, produced all three colours, one of which was the chocolate dog,

S.A. Ch. Bradking Bonny's Prince of Jeronga. Another was the highly successful bitch, Sh. Ch., Am. Ch., Can. Ch., Bermuda Ch., Mex. Ch. Bradking Black Charm, who won eight CCs before she went to Canada (Shadowvale kennels) where she became one of the top winning bitches in North America.

In Britain, she left her yellow son Sh. Ch. Bradking Cassidy, who sadly died of cancer at eight years of age, and his chocolate litter sister Cassandra (two CCs). Cassandra, when mated to Ch. Fabracken Comedy Star, produced Sh. Ch. B. Bridgette of Davricard, a chocolate bitch owned by David Craig.

Keysun Ruling Star of Bradking (a Cassidy daughter) has undoubtedly left her influence in the kennel. From a mating to Ch. Kupros Master Mariner, three further Champions emerged. Sh. Ch. B. Molly Mo (Crufts CC winner) co-owned by David Craig, Sh. Ch. B. Music Maker of Kingstream and Am. Can. and Mex. Ch. B. Mike.

The kennel's latest title holder is the famous Sh. Ch. Bradking Hugo who is, to date, the male breed record holder with 38 CCs (sired by Bradking Jason out of Quaker Girl of Lyndhurst at Bradking). A magnificent dog, combining quality with substance, his head and expression exude kindness and honesty. His show career has rapidly reached the top, starting by winning Top Labrador Puppy 1993, and Top Labrador '94 and '95. In 1994 he won 21 CCs (more than

Sh. Ch. Bradking Hugo (Bradking Jason – Quaker Girl Lyndhurst at Bradking): The male breed record holder with 38 CCs to date.

Photo courtesy: Mr and Mrs D. Kelley.

the Top Dog All Breeds), putting him into the Top Ten winners All Breeds in the UK. In both 1995 and 1996 he took the CC at Crufts. Hugo has a a highly commendable record, and is a great credit to his breeders, Arthur and Peggy Kelley.

CAMBREMER

The Cambremer kennel is owned by Joyce and Leslie Brabban from Bishop Auckland, Co. Durham, and was established in 1965. Interestingly, Cambremer was chosen as their prefix because a French racehorse of that name won the English St Leger. Later, the Brabbans discovered that Cambremer is also a village in France.

Joyce and Leslie have bred eight UK Sh. Champions, two Am. Champions and other title holders in Europe and Scandinavia. They have also won 80 Challenge Certificates, which is no mean achievement. Their first Champion was a yellow dog namely Glenarem Skyrocket, a very smart and stylish Labrador, who, when mated to Braunspath Simona of Cambremer (one CC), produced Sh. Ch. Cambremer St Clair. She was not only beautiful but a good producer, too. When mated to UK Sh. Ch. and Am. Sh. Ch. Receiver of Cranspire, she produced the brothers Sh. Ch. C. Countdown and Celebrity (three CCs in Sweden). However, St Clair was bred to Ch. Fabracken Comedy Star and from this litter emerged a lovely black bitch, Cambremer Montclair, a winner of two CCs and three Reserve CCs. This bitch, with her great breed

type, has had an enormous influence on the Cambremer kennel. She produced the following progeny – Sh. Ch. C. Madonna, Sh. Ch. C. All That Jazz, Sh. Ch. C. Jazz Singer, Swiss and Int. Ch. C. Du Vallon de Villard, C. Copy Cat (one UK CC, three CCs in Sweden), Norwegian Ch. C. Bianca, C. Classical Jazz (two CCs) and C. Striking Midnight Over Lawnwood, all black apart from the last, who was yellow.

Cambremer were top winning kennel in the UK (Pedigree Chum/Our Dogs Competition) in 1987/88/89/91/92 and current leaders in 1995. C. Montclair was Top Brood Bitch in 89/90/91/92. Sh. Ch. C. Madonna was Top Labrador in the UK, 1992 (Dog World/Pedigree Chum Competition).

There is no doubt that this kennel has made a big impact on the show scene in recent years, and the achievements speak for themselves. However, one of Joyce and Leslie's greatest thrills was at Crufts in 1989, when Sh. Ch. C. Madonna won CC and BOB, and Sh. Ch. C. Jazz Singer won the dog CC. Since then, they took BOB again at Crufts 1995, with Sh. Ch. Cambremer Be Generous (a daughter of Madonna), who went on to gain fourth place in the Gundog Group. It is worth noting that all the aforementioned top winners are black, but Cambremer have also produced some very notable yellows, including C. Oh So Sharp (one CC), Sh. Ch. C. Sharpshooter and also C. Clancy (one CC).

At present, Sh. Ch. C. All that Jazz, a very typy and happy showgirl, is proving to be a

Sh. Ch. Cambremer Madonna (Ch. Charway Blackthorn of Follytower – Cambremer Montyclair): Top Labrador 1992.

Photo courtesy: Joyce and Leslie Brabban.

great brood for the kennel, having produced one UK, two Am. Champions and several CC winners. She is superbly constructed, and every inch a Labrador. Credit goes to Cambremer for consistently producing Labradors out of the top drawer, as their wins in the show ring have proved. .

CARPENNY

Penny Carpanini founded her kennel in 1970 with a Lawnwood's bitch, who produced two very notable Labradors, Carpenny Veuve-Cliquot and Carpenny Camargue. It was Camargue's progeny who really made their mark on the show scene and brought the kennel to the fore. A most invaluable brood, she produced three Champions and five Junior Warrant winners. Her first litter to Sh. Ch. Receiver of Cranspire produced Ch. Carpenny Chevalier and his brother NZ Ch. Carpenny Chateau Cranspire, owned by Ken Hunter before being exported. From her next litter came Sh. Ch. Carpenny Bonhomie, a dog out of the top drawer who has had a highly successful career (by Ch. Trenow Brigadier). Both these dogs have sired many top winners in the UK and overseas.

One of the most beautiful bitches from this kennel was Sh. Ch. Audacity of Carpenny, bought in at seven weeks. An exquisite yellow, and full of quality, she was made up at 16 months of age. This was a remarkable achievement since competition in bitches is particularly strong. She was exported to Mme Laffitte in France, where she continued her winning ways. Her litter brother is Aus. Ch. Authority of Carpenny (owned by Anna Spanswick, New South Wales).

Penny is, at the time of writing, the only UK breeder to import from the USA. Hawksmoor Webster (black dog) and Tabatha's Mirth (bitch), are both by Ch. Dickendall Arnold, a top sire in his own country. Webster is already siring winning stock here.

Sh. Ch. Covetwood Elouise Of Carpenny, a pretty yellow bitch, is the latest Champion to keep the flag flying at Carpenny, gaining her title at the West of England Ladies Kennel Association Show (WELKS) in 1995.

CHARWAY

This kennel is owned by Janice Pritchard, who started showing Labradors as a very young girl. In fact, she bred her first litter in 1965. The prefix comes from part of Janice's maiden name, Charlton, and part of her home address, Northway.

Charway Labradors are primarily black, and since the 1970s the kennel has been based on Ballyduff, Sandylands and Timspring lines. From this combination, Janice has produced some excellent Labradors, including five UK Champions and many overseas. Her first title holder was Sh. Ch. Charway Nightcap, followed by Ch. Charway Little Sian, Sh. Ch. Charway Blackthorn of Follytower (owned by Margot Woolley), Ch. Charway Ballywillwill, and Ch. Charway Ballylinnet.

Undoubtedly, Ch. Charway Ballywillwill has been the most important dog in the kennel, and has also influenced many lines in today's show world. He is the sire of eight UK Champions and others abroad, plus a whole string of excellently-producing bitches. In 1981, he was Top Show Labrador (Dog World), and top sire in 1984, 85 and 87. He hit the high spots in 1981 by winning the Gundog Group at the Welsh Kennel Club Show.

The bitches in the kennel have been great producers, and one must mention Roseacre Hollyberry of Charway, Charway Simona, Charway Sally Brown (chocolate, two Res. CCs) and Wetherlam Black Cherry of Charway.

Charway Labradors abroad have been extremely successful, particularly in the USA where there are currently seven Champions, plus one in Canada, two in Finland, two in Germany, two in Holland and two in South Africa. Others in the kennel at present who have won high awards are Charway Uncle Tom (two Res. CCs), Charway Black Magic (one Res. CC) and Cambremer Tom Cobley of Charway (two Res. CCs). Janice has always been interested in work as well as showing, and some of her dogs are worked during the shooting season.

PRIORISE

Marilyn Prior was given her first Labrador as a wedding present in 1960, but it was Huntergate

Ch. Aditis Becky at Foxrush , a Norwegian import (left) and Sh. Ch. Croftspa Hazelnut of Foxrush.

Photo: Anne Roslin-William, courtesy of Judith Charlton.

in North Yorkshire where Judith was born. There have been few litters bred at Foxrush, due to business commitments, but puppies bought in have proved highly successful, particularly those bred by Mr and Mrs Chapman (Croftspa).

The first to be made up was Sh. Ch. Croftspa Charlotte of Foxrush, a very smart and compact Labrador. However, the bitch who made an enormous impression on the show scene was the world-famous Sh. Ch. Croftspa Hazelnut Of Foxrush, the breed record holder with the stunning total of 45 CCs and 15 Res. CCs. She was born in 1983, sired by Sh. Ch. Ardmargha Mad Hatter out of Foxrush Caprice of Croftspa. Now in her thirteenth year, she will be remembered for her great breed type, lovely flowing movement and for always giving her best. Judith recalls that one of the most memorable wins was when she was awarded the CC, by Gwen Broadley, at the Yellow Labrador Club Ch. Show in 1986.

Ch. Aditis Becky of Foxrush was imported from Norway, and the bitch who is at present keeping the flag flying is Sh. Ch. Foxrush Peach Blossom (12 CCs, three Reserve Groups). Her brother is Swed. Ch. F. Pinoccio.

HEATHERBOURNE
Heather Wiles-Fone is the owner of this well-known kennel, established in 1967 with the pur-

chase of two yellow bitches by Ch. Sandylands Tandy. At that time, Heather lived at Bourne Farm and the combination of her christian name and that of her home produced the prefix Heatherbourne.

From this kennel, 20 Champions have emerged (nine in the UK and 11 abroad). The first title holder was Sh. Ch. Heatherbourne Harefield Silver Penny, a beautiful, strongly-constructed yellow bitch (Gundog Group Winner), who is behind all Heatherbourne Labradors in the kennel at present. When mated to Sandylands Charlie Boy, she produced Sh. Ch. Heatherbourne Silver Czar and, mated to Ch. Sandylands Mark, she produced Heatherbourne Moira (Res. CC).

Ch. Heatherbourne Lawnwoods Laughing Cavalier was the next dog to be made up, a kind, honest dog who also qualified in the field. He sired Sh. Ch. Heatherbourne Top Tune (nine CCs, ten Res. CCs).

Moira was a great brood and had enormous influence in the breeding programme. She produced four Champions, Sh. Ch. H. Statesman, Int. Ch. H. Forget-Me-Not (Canada), Sh. Ch. H. Fisherman and Ch. H. Bandmaster (Norway). Fisherman had a spectacular career, winning his first CC as a puppy of ten months, plus BOB Crufts 1983 and two Gundog Groups.

Sh. Ch. Copperhill Lyric of Heatherbourne (by Silver Czar and bred by Miss J. Startup) was

Sh. Ch. Copperhill Lyric of Heatherbourne: Gundog Group winner.

Photo: R. Willbie, courtesy Heather Wiles-Fone.

a magnificent showgirl, always gave of her best and won two Gundog Groups. She also featured in many TV programmes. She produced the Champion littermates H. Court Jester and Cinderella, plus Int. Ch. H. Brown Sugar (owned by Mr and Mrs A. Banbery in Switzerland). In 1984, Court Jester and Cinderella took the double at Three Ridings Labrador Club Championship Show, with Cinderella going BOB.

The latest Heatherbourne bitch to make her mark on the UK show scene is H. Royal Velvet (Res. CC, Ladies' Kennel Association 1995 and Res. CC Crufts 1996). Heather is well known as a Championship show judge in Britain and abroad, including Australia, the USA, and South Africa. She also judged Labradors at the World Show, Berne, Switzerland, in 1994.

POOLSTEAD

The Poolstead kennel is known the world over, and owned by Bob and Didi Hepworth, from near Macclesfield, Cheshire. They have had enormous success over the years, with 27 UK Champions, 24 of whom were bred by them. To date, the kennel has won 110 CCs.

Didi grew up with Labradors but it was the purchase of the bitch Braeduke Julia from Ann Wynyard that laid the foundation of the Poolstead kennel. The prefix, incidentally, came from the name of the wood surrounding the cottage where Bob and Didi used to live.

Braeduke Julia of Poolstead was to become the most influential Labrador. From five litters (by four different sires) she produced four UK Champions and one American Champion. Virtually every dog in the kennel goes back to her, together with a bitch bought from Fred Wrigley, Poolstead Kinley Willow, who became the kennel's first Champion. Willow also proved to be a wonderful brood bitch, and the kennel is based on the lines of both Julia and Willow.

There have been so many highly successful

Labradors at Poolstead that it is difficult to list them all, but Sh. Ch. Poolstead Problem deserves particular mention. He was a very special dog to Didi (the only survivor of a litter, hence the name) as well as a marvellous character, and an important influence on the kennel.

The Hepworths' showing career has included great moments, particularly taking three CCs over four years at Crufts with Ch. P. Powder Puff, Sh. Ch. P. President and Sh. Ch. P. Pinnacle (all Julia's progeny), and winning the Gundog Group at Paignton Championship Show with Sh. Ch. P. Preferential, a son of Problem.

In 1991, Sh. Ch. P. Pipe Dreamer, a lovely short-coupled black bitch, was BOB at Crufts. She was also Best In Show the same year at the Labrador Club Championship Show, and Best Bitch at the Labrador Club of Scotland Championship Show. It has to be said that the bitches at Poolstead have been tremendous producers. There can be few kennels which have consistently bred Labradors of the same type – they are like peas in a pod.

Dogs gaining their titles in the UK have been: Champions P. Kinley Willow, P. Powder Puff, P. Pinnacle, Sh. Champions P. Porcelain, P. President, P. Popularity, P. Problem, P. Purdey, P. Pictorial, Mansergh Sailors Beware, P. Postal Vote, P. Preface, P. Preferential, P. Past Master, P. Matchmaker, P. Pegg, P. Pearl Necklace, P. Pocket Picker, P. Pocket Money, P. Pipe Dreamer, P. Pipe Smoker, P. Publican, P. Pumpkin.

In other kennels there have been: Ch. P. Personality of Lawnwood, Ch. P. Pin-up of Fabracken, Ch. Follytower P. Pinafore and Sh. Ch. Pure Silk of Martinside. There have also been numerous Poolstead Champions in many parts of the world.

ROCHEBY

Marion and David Hopkinson, from Yorkshire, are the owners of this highly successful kennel, established in 1966 with foundation bitches from the well-known Kinley kennel. The prefix Rocheby was taken from the local Roche Abbey.

Success has undoubtedly been due to the excellent brood bitches in the kennel, and the early winners who spring to mind were R. Spring Song (three Res. CCs), Sweet Talk of Rocheby and R. Fairy Tale. The latter was one of Marion's favourites to show, always steady and reliable.

Rocheby have certainly made their mark in the show world and have produced five UK Champions, plus many more abroad. The first title holder was Sh. Ch. Rocheby Acorn, a lovely type yellow of excellent conformation, followed by Sh. Ch. R. Royal Oak, Sh. Ch. R. Popcorn, Sh. Ch. R. Country Maid (owned by Mr and Mrs L. Hepworth) and Sh. Ch. R. Polkadot.

Not only is Acorn a super Labrador, but she is also a marvellous producer, particularly when bred to Poolstead Pretentious at Rocheby, a dog purchased by David in 1986 from Bob and Didi Hepworth. Her first litter produced outstandingly successful Labradors: Sh. Ch. Rocheby Popcorn (15 CCs and BOB, Crufts 1992), Sh. Ch. R. Royal Oak, R. Cornflake (three CCs, Sweden), and American Ch. R. Rippling Corn. A repeat mating produced R. Whisky Mac (one CC and Res. CC, Crufts 1995), Sh. Ch. R. Polkadot, and R. Prim 'N Proper. This is no mean achievement, and Acorn was deservedly awarded Top Brood Bitch 1995. Crufts 1996 proved a great thrill for the Hopkinsons when Sh. Ch. Rocheby Polkadot went Best of Breed and Reserve in the Gundog Group.

Poolstead Pretentious at Rocheby has been most influential in the breeding programme, and, although never shown, he earned the title of Top Stud Dog 1990-95. He sired a CC winner or Res. CC winner at Crufts from 1992-95, a remarkable record. Furthermore, he has produced top-class stock from a wide range of bloodlines, including Sh. Ch. Follytower Pandora at Rocheby, and Foxrush Pedlar (Res.

'Rocheby have certainly made their mark in the show world and have produced five UK Champions, plus many more abroad'

196

CC, Crufts 1993). His famous son, Sh. Ch. R. Royal Oak, has been equally dominant in producing countless winners. Both CC winners at the World Show 1995 were sired by him, as was the bitch CC winner in 1994.

Rocheby have made a big impact on the Labrador show scene today, undoubtedly due to Marion and David's hard work and dedication to the breed. Marion says: "We never could have envisaged the wonderful times we have had, the friends we have made and places we have seen, all due to our friend – the dog."

SIMANDEM

Simandem Labradors are owned by Tom and Margaret Grant from Leicestershire. Tom was breeding Labradors over 20 years ago and, having bred all three colours, decided it was time to look for a challenge – chocolates.

This decision led the couple, in 1984, to purchase their first show dog, chocolate Simandem Ocean Swell, from Peggy Stevens in Devon. At the same time, Mrs Stevens was thinking of giving up showing and breeding, and asked whether the Grants wanted to take on the prefix. It originates from two dogs, Simon (Charway Blackthorn of Follytower) and Dem (Balrion Miss Demeanor), the latter being the kennel's foundation bitch.

Simandem Ocean Calm has been a major influence in the kennel and is the dam of Sh. Ch. Simandem Kings Neptune, born 28.6.88 (sired by Sh. Ch. Balrion Kings Ransom). Kings Neptune is undoubtedly the star of the kennel, a superbly-balanced black dog and so typical of the breed, always shown in immaculate condition and still winning CCs at seven and a half years of age. His career took off in 1990 when he won BOB at Crufts from the junior class, and was Top Dog in the same year. To date he has been awarded 29 CCs.

Wins in 1995 include eight CCs (six BOB), Top Gundog, Leicester Gundog Super Match, Gundog Group 4, South Wales Kennel Ch. Show, Gundog Group Winner, Belfast Championship Show, and Reserve Best In Show Gundog Breeds of Scotland.

Furthermore, Neptune has left his stamp on his progeny and has sired five UK Sh. Champions and three American Sh. Champions – this includes the BOB winner at Crufts 1995, Sh. Ch. Cambremer Be Generous. In 1994 Neptune was awarded the accolade of Top Stud Dog. Other Labradors from this kennel to gain high awards are Sh. Ch. Beltarn Princess Malinka at Simandem, Simandem Sultan (chocolate, two CCs), Simandem Debutante of Ballyhenry (chocolate, Res. CC). Many winners overseas have included Italian Champion Simandem King Solomon (Neptune's brother) and Danish Ch. Simandem Woodchuck.

STAJANTOR

Vic and Janet Cole live in Cambridgeshire and their interest in showing Labradors started in 1962 with the purchase of a yellow bitch puppy from Mrs Townsend (Jaysgreen), followed by another two years later. Subsequently a two-year-old bitch joined the kennel (Lochranza/Sandylands breeding), and these were the foundation stock who are in their lines today.

One of the early highlights of their showing career was at Crufts 1972, when Stajantor Matchmaker was awarded Res. CC. However, at Crufts 1980 they attained even greater heights with Sh. Ch. Stajantors Honest John winning BOB and reaching the final six of the Gundog Group. Two years later he took Res. CC at Crufts. Honest John was the first title holder from the kennel, always an enthusiastic shower and lovely free mover.

Sh. Ch. Stajantor Dam Buster became a Champion in 1984, and in 1987 Sh. Ch. Astrelettia Next Edition of Stajantor gained his title. In 1992 Sh. Ch. Ballyduff Dawn of Bannerbridge was made up, having come to live with Vic and Janet when she was two years old. This beautiful black was very typical and bred by Mrs Cuthbert (out of Stajantor Amy of Ballyduff). She gained five CCs, five Reserve CCs, and was five times BIS Labrador Club Open Shows and BIS All Breeds Open Show.

Stajantors Dozer and Stajantors Alice (litter brother and sister), born October 1992, have been hitting the high spots. At the Gundog

Trenow's first Champion, Astonbrook Crusader (centre) aged fifteeen, with grandchildren Sh. Ch. Trenow Briar Rose, a multiple CC and Group winner, and Ch. Trenow Brigadier, the quickest bench Champion and equal youngest Full Champion in the breed.

Photo courtesy: Mr and Mrs R.A. Floyd.

Society of Wales 1995 Championship Show they gave Janet an enormous thrill when they did the double, both being awarded the CC! To date Dozer has one CC, two Res. CCs, while Alice has one CC and both have numerous Best of Breed wins at Open Show level. Both Janet and Vic judge the breed in the UK and internationally.

TRENOW

The kennel of Maureen and Tony Floyd originated in ealy 1970s, the Cornish affix being the name of the cottage in which Tony was born near Penzance.

Their first Champion was a son of Ch. Ballyduff Marketeer named Sh. Ch. Astonbrook Crusader (pure Nokeener breeding), and his lovely temperament has shown through the gen-

erations of Trenow Labradors. His last-born son, Joline Inkling of Follytower, purchased from Margot Woolley at 15 months, was mated to Trenow Minuet, the daughter of Trenow's foundation bitch, Roseacre Madonna of Trenow (a Sh. Ch. Ardmargha Mad Hatter daughter). The Trenow bitch line is descended directly from Madonna through Minuet. Minuet was a Secret Song of Lawnwood daughter, and her brother was the Ch. Trenow Musicman who was shot over most of his life, and won the Open class at Crufts 1988, a week after completing a full season's work. He died in 1994, but has recently sired two champions in Australia via artificial insemination.

Minuet herself (15 years old in 1996) has been an invaluable brood bitch, producing champions and CC winners in the UK and over-

Ch. Warringah's Waltzing Matilda (left) and her mother, Ch. Warringah's Fair Dinkum.

Photo: Theo Bergstrom, published by kind permission of Pedigree Petfoods.

seas. One third of her entire progeny is in the Stud Book. When mated to Inkling, she produced Ch. T. Brigadier who became the quickest Sh. Ch. in the breed, gaining the title from five consecutive shows. He went on to qualify at an Open Stake FT, making him the equal-youngest full Champion in the breed. Among his winning progeny are the well-known Ch. Carpenny Bonhomie, Sh. Ch. Sandylands Bliss and the Int. Ch. Blondella Bonnie Lad.

Brigadier's litter sister, Sh. Ch. T. Briar Rose, was a top winning bitch, gaining her first CC at Crufts under the late Joan Macan, and going on to be a Group winner with multiple CCs. A repeat mating produced Aust. Ch. T. Secret Agent. Sh. Ch. T. Briar Rose has produced two

Champions in Australia, Ch. T. Prelude and Ch. T. Megan, T. Morag in Norway, and, in the UK, T. M'Lady (one CC) and her latest daughter, T. Cider with Rosie (two Res. CCs by the age of 14 months and one CC at Midland Counties Labrador Club 1996). All Trenow dogs receive basic gundog training and have the opportunity to work on local shoots, as well as shooting with Tony.

WARRINGAH
Carole and David Coode, from Surrey, are the owners of this successful kennel. Their first Labrador entered the household in the form of a first wedding anniversary present from David to his wife in 1967. At that time, they were living

in Warringahshire, on the North Shore of Sydney, New South Wales, Australia, hence the prefix.

On returning to England in 1974, they established the kennel with the purchase of two bitches from Marjorie Satterthwaite – Brentville Marcella of Lawnwood and a year later Lawnwoods Hot Pants of Warringah. The latter was mated to Secret Song of Lawnwood and produced two Champion daughters, Sh. Ch. W. Hot Favourite and Sh. Ch. W. Hot Property, who in turn both produced Champion sons, Ch. W. Foresquare, and Ch. W. Harlech. Ch. W. Fair and Square also deserves a mention as a well-boned yellow male of excellent conformation. He sired five Champions and many top winners and, importantly, passed on his kind temperament.

To date the kennel has produced 12 Champions in the UK (nine full Champions), plus nine abroad. Crufts 1986 stands out in Carole and David's memory, when their black, Ch. W. Harlech, went BOB and Reserve in the Gundog Group. Furthermore, there were three Champion Warringah dogs in the line-up of the Open dog class – a spectacular achievement at such a prestigious show.

Ch. W. Fair Dinkum has had an accomplished career as a brood. In only three litters she has produced eight Champions, two of the best-known being Waltzing Matilda and Flinders. The kennel's latest title holder is Ch. W. Whortleberry, a very typy black bitch who, during 1995, made her presence felt in the show ring by winning four CCs, certainly living up to the Warringah name.

OTHER TOP KENNELS

Due to limited space it has been impossible to feature all the top kennels, but the following deserve a mention. Cornlands (Peggy Rae) and Lawnwoods (Marjorie Satterthwaite) are both long-established and have consistently produced top-quality stock. Kupros (Mr and Mrs Peter Hart) are breeders of the well-known Ch. Kupros Master Mariner, an influential sire within the breed. Fabracken (Anne Taylor) until February 1996 held the record as breeder/owner of the top winning CC male – Ch. Fabracken Comedy Star (35 CCs); Balrion (Mr and Mrs J Crook) produced the famous Sh. Ch. Balrion King Frost (28 CCs and BIS All Breeds); Blondella (Mr and Mrs K. Burton) produce super breed type, particularly Sh. Ch. B. Balance, BIS Labrador Club Show 1990; Lejie (Mr and Mrs Timms) and Carromer (Mr and Mrs Reynolds) have both made their mark on the show scene in recent years.

Other famous kennels of note include:
Blaircourt: Mrs Margie Cairns
Ballyduff: Mrs Sheelin Cuthbert
Mardas: Mr and Mrs David Hepper
Lindall: Mr and Mrs Alan Porter
Newinn: Mrs Rosemary Hewitt
Gallybob: Mrs Sheila Walton
Trewinnard: Mr Tony Pascoe
Kimvalley: Mr and Mrs Don Beckett
Novacroft: Mrs Dot Gardner
Jayncourt: Mr and Mrs Peter Palmer
Veyatie: Mr and Mrs Jim Nolan (Scotland)
Rossbank: Mr and Mrs John Steven (Scotland)
Lasgarn: Mr Richard Edwards (Wales).

'In only three litters Ch. Warringah Fair Dinkum has produced eight Champions'

13 THE LABRADOR IN NORTH AMERICA

Championship titles (Ch.) require the acquisition of 15 points in conformation competition. A dog or bitch must be awarded the Winners ribbon to be eligible for points. A Winners Dog (WD) and a Winners Bitch (WB) are selected at each show. A minimum of six of those points must come from two 'major' wins. Major wins consist of three to five points. The number of points awarded to the Winners Dog and Bitch are determined by the number of dogs entered in the breed, and the number of dogs that must be defeated for that breed in a specific Division. Dogs competing for

Championship titles do not have to defeat existing Champions. Classes are divided according to age and experience and range from 6-9 months Puppy to Open and Best of Breed (BOB) competition. Dogs that have already completed a Championship are exhibited in the Best of Breed Class.

In addition to the 1,220 All-breed shows that offer Championship points, there are 24 Specialty shows for Labrador Retrievers. Specialty shows sponsored by regional clubs are very popular as they are sure to have a large number of dogs and an opportunity for major

Am. Can. Ch. ShaRays Emmanuel CD, JH, CGC (Am. Can. Ch. Jolly Captain Gibson Am. Can. CD, JH – Am. Can. Ch. Wyntercreek Royal Velvet Am. Can. CDX, JH, CGC): Best in Sweepstakes at the 1990 LRC, Inc. Specialty Show. Bred by Ray and Sharon Edwards, Sharay Labradors, Washington.

Photo by Callea, courtesy Sharon Edwards, ShaRay

points. The AKC does not require any sporting dog to pass breed specific performance tests before awarding a Championship title. However, the US parent club, The Labrador Retriever Club, Inc. requires members' dogs with a conformation Championship, to obtain a Working Certificate (WC) before using the title of Champion.

To own or breed a Labrador that achieves the title of Dual Champion has been the goal of many Labrador owners. To earn the coveted title a retriever must have a Field Championship and a conformation championship. Only thirty-six Labradors have achieved this distinction. Amateur titles do not add a dog to the elite list.

Michael of Glenmere, a black male whelped in 1935, became the breed's first Dual Champion in 1941. The last two Labradors to achieve this status were Dual Ch./AFC Warpath Macho in 1981 and Dual Champion/AFC Hiwood Shadow in 1983, both black males. At the present time, there are no living Dual Champions. As owner interests and breeding remain specialized there seems to be less and less opportunity for additions to this special list.

To become a Triple Champion a Labrador must have a conformation title and a Field Champion title (Amateur titles do not count), and either an Obedience Championship or Tracking Championship. There are no Triple Champions in the US and there appears to be little opportunity for a dog to achieve that goal soon.

A SAMPLING OF SHOW BREEDERS IN THE USA

English kennels have contributed consistently to many show winning lines in the USA, and imports continue to be used regularly. Kennel names like Ballyduff, Blaircourt, Bradking, Kinley, Kupros, Lawnwood, Poolstead, Sandylands, and more recently, Lindall, Cranspire, Rocheby and Cambremer, appear in contemporary pedigrees. New books published about the breed in the USA have devoted many pages to American breeders, so any attempt to review show breeders within the confines of this chapter is only a superficial examination. The brief kennel résumés included here are a sampling of breeders whose stock has been represented consistently at specialty shows; those whose breeding programs have achieved conformation, obedience and hunting retriever test titles; and those breeders with four or more generations. In addition, a diversified view of show breeders across the country is represented in the captions and photographs accompanying this chapter.

AYR

Nancy Martin, Pennsylvania. Breeder/judge. Acquired first Labrador in the 1950s. Owned and showed littermate to Ch. Spenrock Banner, Ch. Great Scot of Ayr. Actively runs dogs in hunt tests and has put obedience and tracking titles on her dogs. Breeding lines based on Sandylands and Ballyduff. Imported Ch. Sandylands Morningcloud and Ballyduff Sparkler. Has judged multiple National Specialty shows in the USA and Specialty shows abroad. Her lovely chocolate, Ch. Meadowrock Fudge of Ayr CD, TD, was a favourite, as was Ch. Ayr's Sea Mark WC, grandsire of her present co-owned Champion, Ch. Ayr's Real McCoy CDX, JH. Authored two books on the breed.

BARBAREE

Linda Oldham, New York. Breeder/judge. Shows her Labradors to advanced degrees in obedience. Has judged a National Specialty and regional Specialties. Her black male, Ch. Barbaree's Dark Command UD, WC, is a good example of a Champion with an advanced obedience degree.

BEECHCROFT

Mary Weist, Maryland. Breeder/judge. Acquired first Labrador in 1970. Concentrated on Ballyduff lines and favours line breeding. Outstanding producer, imported Ch. Ballyduff Lark. Has judged a number of Specialty shows in the USA and abroad.

BORADOR

Sally Bell, Ohio. Has owned Labradors for more than 25 years and incorporated a variety of lines. Feels Ch. Boradors The Captain's Brat,

ABOVE LEFT: Ayr's Real Humdinger JH (left) bred, owned and trained by Nancy Martin, Ayr, Pennsylvania, and (right) littermate, Ch. Ayr's Real McCoy CDX, JH (Ch. Dickendall's Ruffy SH – Ayr's Mollywog of the Sea) bred by Nancy Martin and co-owned with Joanne Summers.   *Photo courtesy: Nancy Martin.*

TOP RIGHT: Ch. Beechcroft Wren of Shadow Glen UD, JH (Ch. Strinedale Black Rod – Ch. Ballyduff Lark) is a multiple Best of Breed winner and OTCH. pointed. She finished her three Obedience titles at two years, winning three Dog World Awards for her scores – something no other Labrador has done. 'Wren' was bred by Mary Weist, Beechcroft, and Christine Kofron DVM, Valleywood, and she is owned and trained by Margaret S. Wilson.   *Photo courtesy of Margaret S. Wilson, Shadow Glen, Maryland.*

BOTTOM: Ch. Braemar Fiscal Folly JH (Ch. Raintree Braemar Bailiff CDX, WC – Ch. Braemar Bonny Bairn CDX, JH): Bred, owned and trained by Jane Borders, Braemar.   *Photo courtesy: Jane Borders.*

National Specialty winner, her best bitch. Her dam, Ch. Mansergh Grande Dame, was imported from Mary Roslin-Williams. Ch. Boradors Ridgeway Reflection was a good show dog and producer.

BRAEMAR
Jane Borders, California. Breeder/judge. Also judges hunting tests for retrievers. Competed in obedience with a Labrador in the late 1960s. Acquired the lovely yellow bitch, Ch. Braemar Heather CDX (Ch. Barnaby O'Brian CD, WC x Hera D'Or CDX, WC), as a puppy in 1971.

Concentrated her bitch lines with judicious crosses back to Ch. Lockerbie Brian Boru. Stud dogs of note include Ch. Braemar Prime Minister, Ch. Braemar Anchor Bay WC, and Ch. Braemar Oakmead Magnum Force. UK Ch. Kupros Master Mariner behind present import.

BROAD REACH
Martha Lee Voshell, Virginia. Acquired first Labrador, a yellow bitch, in 1966 and entered first obedience test in 1968, eventually completing UD. Strong interest in field work and obedience, as well as conformation shows. Owned

Pictured left to right: Ch. Zipper's Hustlin' Wahoo UDT, WC (FC Zipper Dee Do – Ch. Baroke Honey B. of Willowhaven); Ch. Broad Reach's English Muffin UDT, WC; and Ch. Yarrow's Broad Reach Sapphire UDT, WC (Ch. Poolstead Peer – Yarrow's Astarte of Windfall). Photo courtesy: Martha Lee Voshell, Broad Reach, Virginia.

and trained first Champion/UDT in US breed history, Ch. Broad Reach English Muffin UDT. Owned and trained the only bitch to have a Master Hunter title and an Obedience Ch. title, OT Ch. Broad Reach Porter's Creek Kis MH. Bred, owns and trains the black bitch, Ch. Broad Reach Gripper MH. Judges hunting tests for retrievers. Runs field trials.

CAMPBELLCROFT, REG.
Don and Virginia Campbell, California. Foundation bitch traces lines to Ch. Spenrock Banner through Ch. Agber Daisy of Campbellcroft CD, WC. Concentrated on judicious crosses to Ch. Lockerbie Brian Boru. Owned and bred Am./Can. Ch. Campbellcroft's Angus CD, WC, and his daughter Ch. Breton Gate Carnigorm CD, JH, both National Specialty winners.

CHUCKLEBROOK, REG.
Diane Pilbin, New Hampshire. Started in Goldens. First Labrador was a yellow daughter of Ch. Spenrock Banner, Ch. Spenrock's Bohemia Champagne. Proved to be a terrific producer with Champions from each of her litters and Diane's conversion to Labradors. 'Chamey's' chocolate grand-daughter, Ch. Chucklebrook Fanny Farmer, is a present favourite and producing in the same manner as her grand-dam.

DICKENDALL
Kendall Herr, Dickendall. Breeder/judge. Acquired first Labrador in 1963. First champion, a black male, Dickendall's Flip Flop CDX, WC. Formed a breeding partnership with June Sasaki (Davaron), Honolulu, Hawaii. Has judged a National Specialty and at Specialty shows abroad. Breeding programme includes recent crosses to Finnish champion. Present stud dogs are outstanding producers, Ch. Dickendall's Ruffy SH and his son, Ch. Dickendall Arnold JH.

FRANKLIN
Dr and Mrs Bernard Ziessow, Michigan. Breeders/judges. Established in 1951. Both judged, but Mrs Ziessow has retired. Dr Ziessow also judges hunt tests for retrievers.

Foundation bitch, Am./Can. Ch. Pitch of Franklin, a daughter of Ch. Pickpocket for Deer Creek x Warwyn Warbler. Ch. Franklin's Tally of Burywood produced 16 Champions. This kennel has produced two field Champions, National and BIS winners, Master Hunters and many obedience-titled dogs.

HENNINGS MILL
John and Dorothy Galvin, Ohio. Original line goes back to Lockerbie, Briary, Broyhill, and Gairloch. All figure prominently in early breedings. Present breedings are strongly influenced by imports.

INSELHEIM
Barbara Reisig-Beer, Michigan. Family had a Labrador when she was a child in 1966. First purchase was a black male, a Shamrock Acres-bred dog. Loved the yellow coat colour and in 1978 acquired Ch. Springfield's Dinorah CD, WC (Ch. Mardas Brandlesholme Sam's Song x Ch. Springfield's Musette) from Mrs Clark's Springfield kennel in Virginia. Dinorah produced several Champions and was Best of Opposite Sex at the 1983 Labrador Retriever Club Specialty Show.

JOLLYMUFF
Diane Jones, New Jersey. Breeder/judge. Acquired first Labrador in 1967 and her first show dog from Ted Squires, Tudor. Trained and showed early dogs in obedience. Co-owned Ch. Sandylands Markwell of Lockerbie with Helen Warwick. Considers him an outstanding producer. Ch. Jollymuff Sugar Hill bred to Am./Can./UK Sh. Ch. Receiver of Cranspire her best litter – four finished.

JUSTES B
Juxi Burr, New Mexico. Began with Standard Poodles and graduated to Labradors in the mid-1960s. Initiated her breeding programme with a bitch called Ironwood Two Bits, a NFC Deltone Colvin daughter. Has included Shamrock Acres, Winroc, Campbellcroft and some imports in her breeding programme. Regularly trains for obedience and hunting tests. Judges hunt tests. Considers Ch. Shamrock Acres Schwechater G

her most successful show dog, and his daughter, Ch. Justes B Happiness Is, one of her best-producing bitches.

KILLINGWORTH
Lorraine Robbenhaar-Taylor, Maine. Breeder/judge. A small hobby kennel established in 1960 and never keeping more than five to ten dogs. After many years of making its home in Connecticut, this kennel has recently moved to Maine. Bred and owned Ch. Killingworth's Thunderson, sire of 25 Champions and many Specialty winners. Mrs Taylor is on the judging slate for the 1996 LRC, Inc. National Specialty. Her West Lake Beginner's Luck (Ch. Welly Bobs Black Tuxedo x Killingworth's Rosey) was Winners Bitch at the 1994 Labrador Retriever Club of Central Connecticut Specialty.

LOBUFF
Jerry Weiss and Lisa Agresta, New York. Both father and daughter judge. Purchased their first Labrador in the 1960s. Owned a black daughter of Ch. Spenrock Banner, Ch. Spenrock's Cognac. Consider Ch. Lobuff's Seafaring Banner one of their most outstanding dogs (his head-study appears on the cover of *The Book of the Labrador Retriever* by Anna Katherine Nicholas).

RAINELL
Lorraine Getter, New Jersey. First Labrador was a black bitch that became Am./Bda. Ch. Ruslyn's Tugboat Annie CD. Early breedings to Ch. Lockerbie Sandylands Tarquin and then purchased a Ch. Lockerbie Brian Boru son, Ch. Briary Brendan of Rainell. Brendan's son, Ch. Rainell's Dynasty won Winners Dog at the Labrador Retriever Club of the Potomac Specialty Show.

SHAMROCK ACRES
Sally McCarthy-Munson, Wisconsin. Began breeding Labradors in the late 1950s. Trained and showed in obedience and ran field trials with her first Labradors. Acquired two puppies from Whygin in 1959 to expand the kennel. Has owned and bred multiple top producers based on

these lines, among them Am./Can. Ch. Shamrock Acres Sonic Boom, 12 times Best in Show, Am./Can. Ch. Shamrock Acres Light Brigade and Ch. Shamrock Acres Yellow Ribbon, a Group winner and dam of 11 Champions. To date, Shamrock Acres has produced 512 Champions, two Dual Champions, 25 Field Champions, 37 Amateur Field Champions, two Obedience Trial Champions, 54 Labradors with hunting test titles and 579 with obedience titles.

SUNNYBROOK ACRES
Fran Ippensen, Missouri. Judge. Acquired first Labrador in the late 60s. Am./Can. Bah. Ch. Sunnybrook Acres Ace O'Spade Am./Bah./Bdr. CD, Am./Bah. CDX, TD, WC (BIS Am./Can. Ch. Shamrock Acres Ebonylane Ace CDX x Ch. Sunnybrook Acres Ray's Honey UD, WC, was a favourite foundation bitch from Shamrock Acres lines.

TABATHA
Carol Heidl, Ohio. Started in early 1970s. First champion, a yellow, Ch. Tabatha's Dodena of Franklin CD, TD, WCX (Ch. Shamrock Acres Light Brigade x Ch. Franklin's Spring Dawn). Her Tabatha's Dazzle won the 1993 National Specialty Show.

WINDSONG
Betty Dunlap, Michigan. Owned Labradors more than 30 years. First Champion purchased from Dr Gary Nash, Ch. Windsong's LZY Tauni Mara. Purchased foundation bitch, Briary Maeve, from Marjorie Brainard, as well as BIS winner, National and Specialty winner, Ch. Briary Bell Buoy of Windsong. Judges Sweepstakes, and judges and runs dogs in hunting tests for retrievers.

WINGMASTER
Winnie Limbourne, California. Breeder/judge. Early dogs from field trial lines. Acquired the good winning chocolate dog, Ch. Gunfield's Super Charger, and bitches from Shamrock Acres, Briary and Braemar. Has kept a number of stud dogs.
WINROC, REG.

Mr and Mrs A.L. Foote, California. Hobby kennel started in 1959. Eight generations of present bitch line trace back to the import, Ch. Sandylands Tanna. Has produced NAFC and National Specialty Show winners, as well as High in Trial dogs and Master Hunter title holders. Judges Sweepstakes classes and hunting tests for retrievers.

WYNDCALL
Mary Feazell, Texas. Hobby kennel. Traces foundation stock back to Shamrock Acres through Ch. Shamrock Acres Wild Honey. Has run dogs in field trials, and early breeding included crosses to FC Air Express. Tries to maintain strong retrieving desire.

CANADA
The Canadian Kennel Club (CKC) bases its conformation championship, field championship, and obedience titles on a point system similar to the US method. However, slight differences do exist – conformation titles require only 10 points; only one tracking title is offered; and to achieve the title of Obedience Trial Champion, a dog need only complete all three obedience titles for the award (no further competition is required).

Dog show classes, Obedience Trial classes and Field Trial stakes are also similar to the American Kennel Club divisions. Canadian Field Trials have slight differences in their rule book, but basic qualifications are the same as in the US Field Championship titles have the same requirements and are identified as: Canadian Field Champion (CFC) and Canadian Amateur Field Champion (CAFC). In Canada no live game is used, but pheasants and ducks are the birds of choice for major stakes.

Unlike the American Kennel Club, the Canadian Kennel Club officially recognises the working certificate as a suffix to a retriever's name. The CKC has guidelines for three test levels for all retrievers, Irish Water Spaniels and Standard Poodles – the Working Certificate (WC), the Working Certificate Intermediate (WCI) and the Working Certificate Excellent (WCX).

Dual and Triple Champions

Dual Champions are not easy to achieve in any country, however Canada does have a very good list. The first Dual champion earned his title in 1943, Can. Dual Ch. Li'l Larry.

Kerry and Lori Curran's Whistlnwings Labradors in Alberta is home to two Triple Champion Labrador Retrievers—Can. Triple Ch. Kenosee Jim Dandy, WCX (FC/Can. FC Pelican Lake Andy x Kenosee Jo) and her daughter, Can. Triple Ch. Whistlnwings Kitty Magee WCX (Am./Can. Ch. Monarch's Black Arrogance CD x Can. Triple Ch. Kenosee Jim Dandy, WCX).

A SAMPLING OF SHOW BREEDERS IN CANADA

AMARANTH

Joan Calder, Ontario. Established in 1978. Foundation stud a son of a South African field trial champion from Zelstone and Sandylands lines. Can. Ch. Amaranth's Talisman CD, WC was the number one show Labrador in Canada in 1987. His daughter was the number one obedience dog the same year.

BEAUTAWN

William Gugins, Alberta. Began with Labradors in 1966 by purchasing a dog for hunting. Second dog was a daughter of Am. Ch. Lockerbie Brian Boru and provided this kennel's first homebred brood bitch, Beautawn's Brandy on the Rocks CDX, WC, a Specialty show progeny class winner. Brandy's offspring have proved to be outstanding show dogs with Best in Specialty and BOS wins. Ch. Beautawn's Country Taffy had multiple-group placements, was a BPSI winner and Number Two female Labrador in Canada before she was ten months old.

CHABLAIS

Jean-Louis Blais and Madeleine Charest, Quebec. Although a relatively young kennel it has produced some outstanding winners. The lovely yellow bitch, Am./Can. Ch. Chablais Myrtille won Specialty Sweeps in the USA and Canada, and at maturity has continued her success with Best of Breed wins in both countries.

Her daughter, sired by Ch. Sandylands Marshal, JH, Chablais Mia, was Winners Bitch at the LRC of Potomac show in April 1995.

EBONYLANE

Pat and Mike Lanctot, Nova Scotia. Established in 1974 on Shamrock Acres lines with the Best in Show winner Am./Can. Ch. Shamrock Acres Ebonylane Ace CDX, WC. Ch. Ebonylane's Shadow was bred to Australian import, Can. Ch. Astroloma Joshua and produced Ch. Ebonylane's Aslan, who became Canada's top producing sire of all time with over 100 Champions.

SHWARTZENBERG, REG.

Ursela and Dieter Dohmen, British Columbia. Kennel has been registered since 1975 and has only one litter each year. Ursela and Dieter both teach obedience and field trial classes and have run dogs of their own breeding in field trials. They bred the Can. Dual Ch. Duke Von Shwarzenberg CD.

WINDANNA KENNELS (PERM.) REG.

Charlie and Judy Hunt, Alberta. The Hunts purchased their first Labrador in 1975, a fox-red puppy bitch. They have produced over 55 homebred champions, 36 CD titled dogs, 12 CDX titled Labradors, two obedience trial Champions, and some 26 field titled dogs. The Windanna bitch line goes back to BPIS Ch. Windanna's Snow Queen CD, who produced seven Champion offspring in two litters. This kennel received the Canadian Kennel Club's Top Labrador Breeder Award in 1991. Charlie and Judy both judge conformation and both are NAHRA (North American Hunting Retriever Association) judges.

WHISTLNGWINGS

Kerry and Lori Curran, Alberta. This kennel is the home of Canada's only Triple Champion Labrador Retrievers, Can. Triple Ch. Kenosee Jim Dandy WCX and Can. Triple Ch. Whistlnwings Kitty Magee WCX. Both achieved their triple titles before they were five years old. Kerry and Lori have been running field trials for more than 25 years, and Kerry is

ABOVE: Two Canadian Triple Champions, Whistlnwings Kitty Magee (left) and her dam, Kenosee Jim Dandy WCX. Owned and trained by Lori Curran, Whistlnwings, Alberta, Canada. *Photo courtesy: Lori Curran.*

BELOW (LEFT): Can. Ch. Makaila's TKO of Whistlnwings CDX, WC (Am. Ch. Sailin' Cajun's Casanova CD, WC – Can. Ch. Whistlnwings Autumn Thunder CD, WC). 'Taco' is the Curran's first yellow. His dam is a litter sister to Canadian Triple Champion Whistlnwings Kitty Magee WCX. *Photo courtesy: Lori Curran.*

BELOW (RIGHT): Can. Ch. Windanna's Prairie Blizzard CDX, WC (Can. Ch. Windanna's National Dream – Ch. Windanna's Scarlet Paintbrush) *Photo courtesy: Charles and Judy Hunt.*

a popular field trial judge. In 1991 their Ch. Whistlnwings Autumn Thunder WC went Best of Opposite Sex. Her yellow son, Can. Ch. Makaila's TKO of Whistlnwings CDX, is now being trained.

A SAMPLING OF AMERICAN-BRED PRODUCERS

It has been said that "a dog is not a producer until its offspring produce."

The following dogs and bitches, all bred in the USA, fit these criteria. Their pedigrees represent a cross-section of conformation and performance lines.

Ch. Lockerbie Brian Boru WC
Whelped: 1st September 1967
 Lockerbie Panda
Sire: Ch. Lockerbie Kismet
 Lockerbie Sandylands Tidy
 Ch. Lockerbie Sandylands Tarquin WC
Dam: Lockerbie Tackety Boots
 Ch. Lockerbie Pebblestreet Dinah
Colour: Black (y)
Breeder: Lockerbie Kennels
Owners: Ceylon and Marjorie Brainard

Brian was not a particularly large male, but he had great masculine character and all the correct breed characteristics for type – good head and coat, plus topline. All were passed to his progeny. He was described by his owner in a magazine interview as "a very neat little dog who certainly had quality he could pass on."

Brian was only shown enough to complete his Championship, and then he qualified for his LRC, Inc. Working Certificate. As a six-month-old puppy, he tore a ligament in his hock, which left him with a lifelong problem that inhibited further showing.

Brian's first breeding was to a daughter of the Brainards' first Champion and he produced the lovely yellow dog, Ch. Barnaby O'Brian CD, who became a big winner, and thus began Brian's career at stud. He was bred to his kennelmate, Ch. Lockerbie Shillelagh, several times, producing multiple Champions, among them two that stand out – the black dog, Ch.

Briary Brendan of Rainell and the black bitch, Ch. Briary Bonnie Briana.

Bonnie was a very good show girl and drew attention to herself on all occasions, winning at a number of Specialties. She became the dam of Briary Marzipan, the dam of the Specialty winner and good producer, Am./Can. Ch. Davoeg Silky Beau. Beau goes back to Brian on his sire's bitch line, as well.

Am./Can. Ch. Campbellcroft's Angus CD, WC, is a Specialty winning son from one of Brian's last litters. The line continues with multiple Specialty BOBs through Angus' daughter, Am./Can. Ch. Breton Gate Cairngorm CD, JH. Brian sired 61 AKC Champions and can be found in many conformation pedigrees.

Am./Can. Ch. Shamrock Acres Light Brigade
Whelped: 6th July 1964
 Ch. Whygin Gold Bullion
Sire: Ch. Shamrock Acres Casey Jones CD
 Ch. Whygin Gentle Julia of Avec
 Ch. Whygin Poppett
Dam: Ch. Whygin Busy Belinda
 Bengali Sari
Colour: Yellow
Breeder: Mrs James McCarthy
Owners: Mrs James R. Getz and Mrs Sally McCarthy

'Briggs' was an outstanding show dog and sire. He produced 93 AKC Champions and won 12 Best in Show awards and 75 Sporting Group placements. In 1968 he received the Ken-L-Ration Sporting Group Award for the top Sporting Dog in the United States.

Briggs is described by his owner and breeder as "an elegant dog with a beautiful head and expression which he passed on to his offspring. He was well-balanced and sound-moving, with a good tail and tail carriage, and an excellent coat. He was easy to live with and very willing to please. He also had an engaging grin."

Two of Briggs' outstanding sons are Ch. Royal Oaks VIP O'Shamrock Acres CD, WC, sire of 34 champions and Mex./Am./Can. Ch. Franklin's Golden Mandigo CD who produced 30 Champions.

Am./Can./Bdr. Ch. Spenrock's Banner, WC
Whelped: 30th June 1964
 UK Ch. Sandylands Tweed of Blaircourt
Sire: Ch. Lockerbie Sandylands Tarquin, WC
 Sandylands Shadow
 UK Ch. Sandylands Sam
Dam: Ch. Sandylands Spungold
 Pentowen Sandylands Tiptoes
Colour: Black (y)
Breeder: Mrs Dorothy Franke
Owner: Janet I. Churchill (Spenrock)

Banner's sire, Ch. Lockerbie Sandylands Tarquin WC, was imported from England as was her dam, Ch. Sandylands Spungold. Two of her littermates were Champions, Ch. Lewisfield Spenrock Ballot and Ch. Great Scot of Ayr.

Banner had a notable show record with American, Canadian and Bermuda Championships, 85 Best of Breeds in America and 13 Group placements, as well as many BOBs in Canada. Banner loved to show, and did so with style, grace and enthusiasm. She was an outstanding trained gundog and used by her owner on ducks, geese, quail and pheasants. Banner was also a superb sled dog either as a team leader or solo. Banner was well-proportioned with a lovely head and expression, as well as correct coat and otter tail. She was very sound and moved with a delightful spring to her step. Soundness and correct Labrador type were passed along to her offspring.

Banner was the dam of 13 AKC champions, one UD, one CDX and one CD title holder. She whelped six litters and had her first litter at the age of four, bred to Ch. Sandylands Midas. A bitch from this litter, Ch. Spenrock Sans Souci, won the Labrador Retriever Club National Specialty Show in 1970. Sans Souci was never bred, as her owner considered her too valuable as a gundog. This litter also produced Spenrock Spun Candy, Ch. Spenrock Phantomshire Amber and Spenrock Statesman, a dog who won a five point major just before his untimely death.

Banner's second litter was sired by Ch. Lockerbie Goldentone Jensen. This litter produced some very well-known Labradors: Ch. Spenrock Cardigan Bay (placed in Groups, sire of Ch. Agber's Daisy of Campbellcroft and Ch. Agber's Daniel Aloysius), an outstanding gun-dog; Ch. Spenrock Bohemia Champagne (foundation bitch for Chucklebrook Kennels); Spenrock Delta Minnow (foundation bitch for Robert Montgomery); Ch. Spenrock Cognac (foundation bitch for Lobuff Kennels); Ch. Spenrock Cajun; Spenrock Egyptian Candor; Spenrock Defender; Spenrock Candor UD; and Spenrock Kim Huntley.

Banner's third litter was small and also sired by Ch. Lockerbie Goldentone Jensen. Ch. Spenrock Topaz became the foundation bitch for George and Louise White. Ch. Spenrock Topgallant was a good winner in the USA and Canada. For her fourth litter, Banner was bred again to Ch. Sandylands Midas. This litter produced Ch. Spenrock Hello Dolly (foundation bitch for Rosalind Paul), Spenrock Dynamo (foundation bitch for Jane Babbitt), Spenrock Domino (stud dog for Mr A.B. Hancock at Claibourne Farm in Kentucky), Spenrock Defender and Spenrock Dragon, a field trial dog. Ch. Rivermist Tweed of Spenrock sired Banner's next litter which included Ch. Spenrock Boomerang, Spenrock Brandy Snifter CD and Spenrock Bucephalus.

Banner's last litter was sired by Ch. Lockerbie Stanwood Granada. This litter produced Ch. Spenrock Anthony Adverse, who as a puppy placed Best in Match under Gwen Broadley. Unfortunately this dog sired only a few litters, but he had a lasting influence through his daughters, especially Ch. Briary Abbey Road, Briary Allegra and Ch. Briary Bustle (foundation bitch for Finchingfield Kennels) and Spenrock Amanda. Other excellent males from this litter were Ch. Spenrock Ambassador and Spenrock Argonaut.

Banner was one of the most influential American-bred Labradors. She could show and work in the field, as could her offspring. She passed on correct breed type, and through her offspring, was responsible for many foundation bitches or stud dogs all over America. Best of all, she was a great companion – there has never been another like her.

JANET CHURCHILL
Spenrock Farms, Maryland

Ch. Dickendall's Ruffy SH
Whelped: 20th May 1987
 Dutch Ch. Cranspire Skytrain
Sire: Am./UK Sh. Ch. Receiver of Cranspire
 Polly's Pride of Genisval
 Ch. Eireannach Black Coachman
Dam: Ch. Moorwood Jewell
 Ch. Beaver's Lavinia of Moorwood WC
Colour: Black (y)
Breeder: Rosalind Moore
Owner: Kendall Herr and June Sasaki
(Dickendall-Davaron)

A masculine headed, well-coated dog with good
angles and topline, 'Ruffy' began his show
career with a Best Puppy and BOS in Sweeps
wins at the LRC of the Potomac Specialty in
1987, and Winners Dog, Best of Winners and
Best Puppy at the Miami Valley LRC the same
year. After completing his conformation title, he
was trained and run for his Junior title by
Joanne Sommers and his Senior title by Bobby

Ch. Dickendall's Ruffy SH with sons, Ch.
Dickendall Arnold JH, Ch. Ayr's Real McCoy
CDX, JH, and grandson, Ayr's Maximum Zest
CD, JH.

    Photo courtesy: Nancy Martin
      and Faith Hyndman.

George. He stamps his get with many of his
own physical characteristics, as well as strong
retrieving instincts. His son, Ch. Topform's
Edward MH, a Qualified All-Age field trial
competitor, is the only dog in the USA to hold
that distinction. A daughter, Cumberland Ida
Klaus MH has qualified 32 times at the Master
level in Hunting Tests. Two offspring have been
outstanding winners: Ch. Lobuff's Bear
Necessities was the Number One winning
Labrador in the USA for two years in a row, and
Ch. Broadreach Bocepious was Number One for
one year. His owners describe Ruffy as "...pleas-
ing in appearance, with a classic Labrador temperament – easy to live with, easily trained,
eager to please – a real people dog!" Ruffy is
the sire of several producing sons: Ch.
Dickendall's Arnold JH; Ch. Ayr's Real McCoy
CDX, JH; and Ch. Tabatha's Drifter at
Dickendall JH.

FC/AFC Candlewood's Nellie Be Good
Whelped: 18th June 1973
 FC/AFC Paha Sapa Chief II
Sire: '68 NFC/'67 and '68 NAFC Super Chief
 Ironwood Cherokee Chica
 FC/AFC My Rebel
Dam: Gahonk's Rebel Queen
 Canvasback Dee
Colour: Black (y)
Breeder: Bower Playfair
Owner: Mary C. Howley (Candlewood)

As the dam of five field Champions, 'Nellie'
figures prominently in many contemporary field
trial pedigrees. She is the backbone of
Candlewood Kennels. Nellie finished her FC
with Mary handling, and qualified for two
National Amateurs and one National
Championship Stake. Bred to NAFC/CNF River
Oaks Corky, Nellie whelped three outstanding
producers. Her two daughters, FC/AFC Black
Gold's Candlewood Kate and Candlewood's
Delta Dash, are both following their dam with
five field trial titled progeny. Delta Dash is the
dam of the '92 NFC/'91 NAFC Candlewoods
Super Tanker. Nellie's yellow son,
Candlewood's Nifty Nick, has become a produc-
er in his own right. The yellow '93 NAFC/FC

MD's Cotton Pick'N Cropper is a direct descendant of Nellie through his sire, FC/AFC Candlewood's MD Houston.

FC/'74 NAFC Ray's Rascal
Whelped: 2nd October 1967
 CFTC Bandit of Carnmoney
Sire: Carnmoney Spud (Canadian import)
 Carnmoney Boots
 AFC Black Mike of Lakewood
Dam: Miss Fiddlesticks
 Kemper's Sassy Sue
Colour: Black (Bb)
Breeder: Mr and Mrs A.L. Foote (Winroc, reg.)
Owners: Raymond and Dorothea Goodrich

Rascal's conformation characteristics were typical for the breed, but lacking in any remarkable features. He was a medium-sized, medium-coated dog with good depth of body and balance, and a great desire to please. Always owner-handled and trained, and a house dog all his life, Rascal left a strong legacy in his offspring. He was a brilliant marker and that skill took him to the top of the Derby list in 1969. Rascal completed his first National Amateur at two years and eight months, and earned his Field Trial Championship on his third birthday. Six weeks later he finished his first National Open at St. Louis, Missouri. Rascal qualified and ran in each of the Nationals after that until his untimely death at eight and a half years. In 1974 he won the National Amateur Stake. Rascal also won five double headers and was denied five more by his housemate and companion, FC/AFC Carnmoney Brigadier, by placing second to him in the Open and Amateur at five trials.

  Rascal was pheasant hunted every year of his life and had a penchant for breaking on natural birds that, thankfully, did not carry over to field trial competition. As Rascal was a very biddable dog, owner Ray recalled that verbal corrections were frequently all that were required to fix a problem. Ray also described Rascal as affectionate to the family, but somewhat aloof to outsiders. Rascal passed on his marking brilliance, training biddability and soundness to his offspring regularly. He produced more than 40

progeny with Open or Amateur placements. His son, Rascal's First Edition, became National Derby Champion in 1972. Two other sons – FC/AFC Paladin VII and '79 NFC/AFC McGuffy – both exhibited his excellent marking and line running ability. Rascal was awarded the Thomas W. Merritt Memorial Trophy as an Outstanding Sire of Field Trial Retrievers in 1978. He can be found in pedigrees of many outstanding field trial competitors today, including three-time National Champion, NFC/AFC Candlewood's Tanks A Lot.

'76 NFC/AFC San Joaquin Honcho
Whelped: 23rd January 1973
 NFC Whygin Cork's Coot
Sire: FC/AFC Trumarc's Raider
 Luka of Casey's Rocket
 Carr-Lab Penrod
Dam: Doxie Gypsy Taurus
 Bain Gypsy Jet
Colour: Black
Breeder: James Vander Sanden
Owner: Ms Judith S. Aycock

'Honcho' was a medium-sized male, weighing about 75 lbs in working weight. Judy purchased Honcho when he was 20 months old from John Folsom, a professional trainer. He was trained by Judy with Rex Carr's help for a brief but distinguished field trial career. He did not run in the Derby, but accumulated a career total of 74 Open points, 64 Amateur points, won a double-header (an Open and an Amateur at the same trial), became a National finalist three times and won the National Championship handled by Judy in 1976. He retired from field trial competition in 1979 after a near-fatal bout of pulmonary blastomycosis. His weight dropped from 75 to 50lbs, and only his constitution, Judy's dogged determination, and an experimental drug were responsible for his survival. In his retirement, Honcho became a pre-eminent sire of field trial dogs, and a hunting dog and devoted friend. He was the leading sire of All-Age point earners in 1982-1990; the sire of one National Champion, three National Amateur Champions, one Canadian National Champion, and one National Derby Champion. Among his

1976 NFC San Joaquin Honcho: A producer of one National Champion, three National Amateur Champions, one Canadian National Champion, one Derby Champion and 75 more offspring with Field and/or Amateur Field Champion titles.

> *Photo courtesy: Ed and Judy Aycock.*

offspring are 75 Labradors with the titles of Field Champion and/or Amateur Field Champion.

Honcho had so many human qualities that we communicated with him verbally as we would any member of our household. He was a house dog and frequently spent all or part of the night on the bed with us. He was a gentleman with impeccable manners, a superb athlete with an intense desire to please, a very intelligent and forgiving companion, and the most prepotent sire of all time.

> *JUDY AND ED AYCOCK*
> *Sanger, Texas*

Am./Can. Ch. Chocorua's Seabreeze
Whelped: 19th December 1983
 UK Sh. Ch. Balrion King Frost
Sire: Am./Can. Bda. Ch. Shadowvale's Frosty Knight

Int. Mex./Am./Can./Bda./UK Sh. Ch. Bradking Black Charm CD, WC
 Ch. Jayncourt Follow Mee
Dam: Am./Can. Ch. McDerry's Midwatch Starkist Am./Can. CDX
 Ch. McDerry's Midwatch Star Gazer CD
Colour: Yellow
Breeder: Marion Lyons (Chocorua)
Owner: Marion Lyons

"My lasting impressions are concentrated on the fact that I believe that in my Best of Breed, I had the honour to judge one of the most beautiful Labrador bitches that I have been fortunate enough to see."
Richard Wiles (Heatherbourne)
Judge's Critique,
 LRC of Central Connecticut 1986

At the time of this critique, 'Ivy', handled by Norman Grenier, was on her way to becoming the top winning bitch in the history of the breed in the USA. Her show career included two All-Breed Best in Show, 16 Group I, 12 Group II, ten Group III, eight Group IV, and 122 Best of Breed. Her Breed wins included: Best of Breed and Group IV at Westminster; Winners Bitch and Best of Opposite Sex at Westminster; four Best of Breed at Specialty shows; a Best of Breed at the LRC, Inc. National Specialty at nine years of age from the Veteran Class; and Best of Opposite Sex at the National Specialty before two years of age. Ivy was Number One Labrador Retriever Bitch in the USA for three years and ranked in the Top Ten Labradors for four years.

Ivy stood 22ins at the shoulder and weighed 74lbs when fully mature. She was well-proportioned, with correct topline and underline, lovely reach of neck, and wonderful head with melting expression. She was moderately angulated which gave her movement equal reach and drive – totally in balance. She was very strong in body with excellent feet and legs. Because of her moderate angles, her offspring never seemed to get quite the angulation or turn of stifle which has become popular. However, her lovely head and body type has been passed on through four generations, and we still see her black pigment

Am. Can. Ch. Chocorua's Seabreeze at nine years. 'Ivy' was owned and bred by Marion Lyons, Chocorua Labradors.   *Photo courtesy: Marion Lyons.*

and dark eye in the yellows. Ivy's adoring temperament and willingness to please is quite evident in her grand and great-grandchildren. All offspring possess a great desire to hunt, swim and retrieve, like Ivy's dam passed on to Ivy herself.

Ivy's dam, Am./Can. Ch. McDerry's Midwatch Starkist Am./Can. CDX, acquired her Championship, but it was not an easy task. Her tail, which was sickle-like, held her back considerably. However, with careful breeding there is only an occasional 'high tail' in the family, and close attention must always be paid to this point. 'Derry' was an outstanding obedience competitor with 12 High in Trials and many First Place ribbons. She was even more talented in her field work and has thankfully passed this on, through Ivy, to four generations.

MARION LYONS,
Chocorua, New Hampshire

Am./Can. Ch. Whygin Campaign Promise
Whelped: 22nd November 1959
 Ch. Hugger Mugger
Sire: Ch. Wildfield Mickey Finn
 Ch. Woodcroft Daisy
 Ch. Whygin John Duck
Dam: Ch. Whygin The Bedford Brat
 Whygin Dark Magic
Colour: Black
Breeder: Helen W. Ginnel (Whygin)
Owner: Mr and Mrs James B. McCarthy
(Shamrock Acres)

'Missy' is described by her owner as "well-balanced with a beautiful head and expression. She was a sound mover. Missy was very easy going and versatile, a fun dog to be around." She was used as a gundog regularly, and was excellent with children. In 1961 she won Best of Breed at the Labrador Retriever Club, Inc. Specialty Show, Best of Opposite Sex at Westminster and Best of Opposite Sex at the International Show in Chicago, Illinois. She was Best of Opposite Sex at the Labrador Club Specialty show in Ontario, Canada in 1963.

Missy was the dam of 17 Champions, among them Ch. Shamrock Acres Royal Oaks Wag CD, the dam of Ch. Royal Oaks VIP O'Shamrock Acres CD, WC, a sire of 34 Champions.

14 THE LABRADOR WORLDWIDE

GERMANY

After the Second World War Labradors were a rare breed in Germany and, even today, they are not widely known to the general public. German hunters preferred the German hunting, pointing, and retrieving breeds with their wide variety of size, colour, and coat structure. Specialised British breeds like Pointers or Retrievers were a rarity in the hunting field and mainly owned by aristocrats who had relations in England, or military staff who brought their pets with them when on duty in Germany.

Until the 1970s, Labradors were shown very rarely. Breeding was done occasionally, but often without registration of the resulting litters. The first Labrador mentioned in the field trial register (Jagdgebrauchshunde-Stammbuch) of the German hunting breeds was Abraham v.d. Gaesdonck, a black dog who won first prize in a trial (Jagdgebrauchsprufung) in October 1965, competing against five Golden Retrievers.

In subsequent years, an increasing number of Labradors competed in the annual autumn trial organised by the German Retriever Club or DRC. These trials were, and are, in no way comparable with traditional field trials in England. German retriever trials adhere closely to rules and regulations laid down for the HPR breeds, based on the demands of hunting in Germany.

HUNTING

In Germany, the legal right to hunt is fixed to the ownership of land (mainly farm and woodland). Owners of small areas of land are bound by law to unite their properties and thus form major hunting grounds with a minimum area of 75 hectares, the average hunting ground covering 300-500 hectares. The right to hunt these units is leased to an individual hunter, or a group, usually for nine years. On such fairly small hunting districts, with a restricted amount of game, the hunter usually prefers a single dog from a HPR breed to tackle all types of hunting, except for working foxes and badgers. Early Labrador fanciers in Germany trained their dogs for the same non-specialised jobs, and the breed did a remarkably good job under these conditions, and still does, though it came as quite a surprise to some purists in England.

EARLY RETRIEVER COMPETITIONS

With little knowledge of the British tradition of field trials, German Labrador owners started basic training with obedience and retrieving of wounded game. The same importance was given to tracking exercises with dead pheasants or rabbits, to prepare the dog for work on running game, as well as blood tracking of wounded deer or boar. Retrieving a heavy fox over a fence or ditch is essential, as is flushing ducks from the reeds. The Labrador's willingness to please meant that lessons were learned well, and performance was of high quality compared with local HPR dogs, whose highly-strung temperament and lack of steadiness occasionally tend to ruin good shooting opportunities. Whenever Labradors appeared in all-breed hunting competitions, they were complimented on their performance, and the breed's popularity rose steadily. Demand for puppies created plans for a breeding programme.

FOUNDATION OF THE GERMAN RETRIEVER CLUB

Increasing numbers of retrievers were imported, mainly from England, Holland and Denmark, until in 1963 a dozen enthusisasts founded the DRC (Deutscher Retriever Club). This was a breed club for all the retriever breeds and was soon acknowledged by the VDH, or German Kennel Club. In the early days, Golden Retrievers formed the majority of registered dogs. The DRC's charter was to support the breeding of a healthy working gundog complying to the original British standard. In addition to hunting competitions, the first exhibitions and local shows were arranged, after lengthy and controversial discussion of rules and regulations.

In 1966, the first Labrador litter was registered by the DRC, sired by Irl. FT Ch. Strokestown Flash out of Jill of Quoile; six yellow puppies were registered. In those days, the VDH would only allow the registration of six puppies per litter, which meant surplus puppies had to be culled or were sold without registration. These rules were only abandoned under legal pressure in the late1960s.

The oldest German Labrador kennel still active is Eberhard Keimer's vom Sennewald. Founded by his father Hubert in 1968 with a mating of two English imports (Philip of Hooke x Tessa of Keith), the kennel produces popular stock for local hunters.

BREEDING IN THE SEVENTIES

Another early kennel with substantial success was von Wolfberghusen, owned by Anni Fraas in Wolfratshausen in Bavaria. Breeding the English import Strattonley Kite to the German-bred Alice of Astrope Folly, Mrs Fraas produced her first litter in 1971. She kept two black bitches both of whom she later mated to Cliff, a black import (FT Ch. Greatford Park x Maindyke Jane) with a good trial record in Germany. During the following years, Mrs Fraas regularly bred successfully for good temperament and looks, mating her stock to German and carefully-selected imported stud dogs (e.g. Poolstead Purser), and stimulating the small group of German Labrador breeders to follow her example. She stopped breeding only a few years ago.

A highly-recognized kennel was founded in the spring of 1972 when Leni Niehof (now Dr Niehof-Oellers) bred her first litter under the kennel name vom Keien Fenn. Her ambitious goal was to breed dual-purpose Labradors. Her foundation bitch, Owlcroft Helena (Cookridge Khan of Owlcroft x Owlcroft Jacarine Star), was imported from England. This beautiful black bitch won consistently in the show ring, acquiring the German Retriever Club Champion title in 1973, 74 and 75. She became an International, VDH, and Czechoslovakian champion. Owlcroft Helena was also very successful in German all-rounder hunting competitions for retrievers (mult. Sp. JGP and JGPR).

Int. and Germ. Ch. Grog vom Keien Fenn (front) and Chocolate Jenny.

Photo: Dr Kraft.

Her first mating to Poolstead Purser (who also qualified in Germany in hunting trials) produced Aska vom Keien Fenn, a bitch well on the way to reach the same dual-purpose qualifications as her mother, before her untimely death due to accidental poisoning. The successful bitch line continued over the years via Aska and Cita (whose brother Capone was made up to Int. Ch.) to Inka who became the mother of Leicester vom Keien Fenn, an excellent yellow hunting stud dog with typical, sound progeny. Batjana vom Keien Fenn, mated to the Swedish dog Nattens Akilles, produced Grog, a yellow dog sold as a puppy to Drs Fritz and Isabella Kraft, who made him up to an outstanding International and German Champion. Grog won the Retriever Club Show in 1979 and qualified with excellent results in all German hunting competitions (JEP, BLP, JGPR, SP JGP, SWII/III, Btr). The bitch line was continued with Juma, Ojoea, Pira, Quesca and Riesling, all following Leni Niehof-Oellers' four objectives: typical character, good health, working ability and beauty. In recent years, Leni has turned her interest to field trial blood and imported N'debele Zibet and FT Ch. Tibea Tosh.

During the seventies several dogs were brought into Germany from Britain. Some of them, including the following, made an impact on German Labrador breeding in the following generations:

1972 – Poolstead Purser, Owlcroft Helena, Dorrfield
       Black Rumple, Timspring Stargazer, Powhatan
       Wanda, Palgrave Sandringham Claret.
1973 – Onteora Lady of Powhatan.
1976 – Ben of Coryton Chruston.
1977 – Damsel of Ballyduff, Curnafane Mark.
1978 – Blondella Maggie May, Corniman Black Molly.

From Sweden came:
1975 – Tidernas Aztek.

And from Denmark:
1977 – Dunsinane Froh.

There were quite a few other imports who were not used for breeding because they did not come up to DRC standards for stud dogs and brood bitches. Several imports failed in hips or were discarded due to missing teeth, which led to the ridiculous situation of a beautiful British bitch with only one missing tooth not being given a breeding permit in Germany. She was then sold to a breeder in Holland who not only bred from her (all puppies had complete dentition), but also made her up to a Dutch Champion!

GROWING INTEREST IN LABRADORS
Within the first twenty years of breeding under the rules of the DRC, a steady development in the registration numbers of Labradors can be traced. Only fourteen Labradors were registered by the German Retriever Club by 1968, 67 by 1973, 303 by 1978, and 1554 by the end of 1983.

It is interesting to read what the club secretary wrote on the occasion of the club's twentieth anniversary: "It is noticeable that over the last twenty years the quality in the breed is improving slowly. Compared to other countries, I must confess we still have a lot to do. Our more and more stringent regulations unfortunately are necessary as not everybody is taking the selection of sire and dam seriously enough ... It is a mistake to believe that a good stud dog will compensate for any obvious weakness in the bitch line ... We must more carefully look into the gene pool rather than at the exterior only. X-raying of the hips is a rare exception..." This all sounds very basic to us today.

BREEDING IN THE EARLY EIGHTIES
With the mating of Curnafane Mark to Gusta von Wolfbergshusen, Karl Lutz started his kennel vom Hohen Stein, and the mating of Poolstead Purser to Brookvale Lisa created Hans-Georg Keimer's kennel vom Schnelter Bruch. Both kennels exist today and have produced good-looking working stock over the years. Monika von Klinggraff started her vom Klingerhuf kennel based on her foundation bitch Alexa vom Keien Fenn. This is still a highly-regarded kennel, concentrating on producing

shooting dogs with a typical outlook. Although few of them actually qualify in trials, they gain great merit in real and sometimes arduous hunting conditions.

In 1979, Timspring Greylag was imported by Mrs Buttner and was soon successful at shows, winning the titles of Int., German, and VDH Champions. He also achieved a hunting qualification as he was placed in the Bringleistungsprufung (BLP), a retrieving and obedience test with cold game. He was used as a popular stud dog for some years. At the same time Ursula Bommer established the of Rembo kennel based on her foundation bitch, Dweerbeekhof Alice (Ch. Sandylands Strinesdale O'Malley x Tina Gwyneth). She also imported Blondella Morning Glory, who became a German Champion and qualified in the field. Mrs Bommer first mated her bitches to Timspring dogs (Ch. Timspring Greylag and Timspring Touch on Wood) several times, before she turned her breeding programme to Poolstead stock.

Her husband's Poolstead Pure Fluke became Int., German and VDH Champion, won the Club Show in three consecutive years, starting in 1985, and also qualified in the field (BLP). Pure Fluke and his brother Pure Luck were used at stud regularly in Germany. With her later imports, mainly Poolsteads, Mrs Bommer concentrated on breeding mostly yellow, typical-looking dogs, a little heavier and stronger in bone than most contemporary German Labradors.

Well known and very active in the Retriever Club were Heinz and Ulla Fleermann with their kennel von Ballycorner. They started breeding in 1978 with a black British bitch, Damsel of Ballyduff, who won well at shows for several years. The Fleermanns concentrated on using stud dogs with Ballyduff background, mainly their own black imports Curnafane Sam of Ballyduff, Curnafane Mark and the yellow Elterwater Mi'Lord. They also imported some bitches; besides Damsel, dams important to their breeding were the blacks Elterwater Sagacity (imported in whelp to Ch. Follytower Merrybrook Black Stormer) and Balrion Lady Be Good. The Ballycorners had some good successes at shows, but were rarely seen in the field.

THE FOUNDATION OF THE LABRADOR CLUB OF GERMANY (LCD)

The Fleermanns were also instrumental in the formation of the specialist Labrador Club Deutschland (LCD) and the separation of Labrador breeders from the original DRC, the Deutscher Retriever Club. There had been increasingly divergent discussions among the representatives of the different breeds inside the DRC about breeding regulations and competition rules, a situation which finally brought together a group of dedicated Labrador breeders in 1984. They left the DRC and formed the LCD. As this action was not approved by the representatives of the DRC, it took quite a long time and much legal action before the LCD was fully acknowledged by the VDH. Sadly, Heinz Fleerman died quite young and before he could see the ever-increasing popularity of Labradors and the Labrador Club. His wife Ulla was president of the LCD for several years.

The concentration on the special needs of Labradors has led to a major improvement in the quality of the breed in recent years. Guidelines for breeding were based on the Standard for the breed only, and the majority of the founder members can be described as belonging to the show side of the breed, thus the breeding of shooting dogs and the organisation of trials was originally undertaken by a small minority of early LCD members. Today the LCD is strong in all spheres of Labrador activity.

RULES AND REGULATIONS FOR BREEDING IN GERMANY

In contrast to the registration procedure in most neighbouring countries where pedigrees are issued by a central kennel club, in Germany the authority for the control of breeding and for issuing pedigrees lies with the breed clubs. The VDH originally accepted only one club per breed, but in the late 1970s was ordered by the verdict of a high court to accept a second or even a third club per breed, provided these new clubs complied with basic rules set by the VDH.

This led to the current situation involving two different breed clubs, with two different sets of rules, for breeding Labradors in Germany. The aspiring breeder has to make a decision as to which club's rules he will follow. He may change to the other club for breeding purposes only if he decides that the second club suits his needs better. Today, many more Labrador puppies are bred under the rules of the Labrador Club (LCD) than within the DRC, so we shall outline the rules of the LCD as they stand in April, 1996.

1. The dog must have a pedigree issued by a club controlled by the FCI or an associated club (KC, AKC), and must have a permanent identification (tattoo in the right ear).

2. At the age of 12 months or older the dog must pass a temperament test following a Swiss system which was established to identify and eliminate dogs with untypical behaviour like aggressiveness, undue shyness, or gunshyness. A dog who fails the test may repeat it.

3. At the age of 15 months or older the dog's conformation is assessed individually by a championship show judge; this is done at a special event without any competition or placing of the dogs, sometimes after the end of a show, and a very detailed critique is written. The judging adheres to the FCI Standard, which is identical to the British Standard, and the dog must obtain a grading of 'very good' or 'excellent' for his breeding permit. As a concession to the dogs of field trial type who have high merits in hunting trials, these dogs may be used for breeding if they obtain the grading 'good' and a certain high number of points in advanced hunting competition. Currently, the VDH presses the breed clubs hard, insisting on full dentition in breeding stock, but at the time of writing one or two missing teeth are widely tolerated.

4. The dog must have an official hip score certificate. Hips are scored following the FCI system. There are five grades: A (free of HD), B (transitional or borderline), C (mild), D (moderate) and E (serious). Grades D and E never get a breeding permit. Labradors with grade C may be mated, but only to a partner with grade A. Dogs with grade C are used as stud dogs only very occasionally, and brood bitches with C are quite rare too.

5. Since 1992, a clear eye certificate must be produced to the club authorities before any mating. A list of specialised veterinarians for eye tests is available, and the certificate must be renewed every twelve months. Labradors affected by GPRA or HC are excluded from breeding. Parents and children of a dog affected by GPRA are classified as proven carriers and are excluded from breeding too.

6. The evaluation of elbow status is highly recommended, to eliminate dogs with OCD and LPC, but not yet mandatory for members of the LCD.

This list shows several obstacles and pitfalls that restrict the German breeder's liberty over the choice of stud dog and brood bitch. This fact is increasingly under discussion today, as it can reduce the gene pool in the breed, and may lead to a devastating outcome if a frequently-used stud dog is identified later in his life as a carrier of unfavourable genes.

SUCCESSFUL BREEDERS OF THE EIGHTIES
The kennel of Fritz and Isabella Kraft, aus Luhlsbusch, was founded in the early 1980s. Their very successful yellow dog, Grog vom Keien Fenn, has been mentioned earlier, but the couple looked to England for their idea of a Labrador with specific emphasis on health and dual-purpose quality. Their first bitch, Chocolate Jenny, was successfully qualified in German hunting trials and was first mated to Wetherlam Sultan who lived in the Netherlands. A second litter, by Dual Dk. Ch. Timspring Sultan, produced only Betsy, qualified in the field but retired from breeding after a very difficult whelping, followed by many years as a guide dog for the blind.
    The Krafts were the first breeders to use frozen semen (from Am. Ch. Clemmsen of Killingworth) to produce a Labrador litter in

Germany. The second bitch they imported was Lawnwoods Camilot, out of one of the first litters by Ch. Lindall Mastercraft. She became the mother of the first all-chocolate litter in Germany, sired by the German-bred Hardway Chocolate Clay. Camilot's daughter Donna from this litter, owned by Dr Ditschuneit, had a great trial career and passed through all available hunting competitions with superior scores, among them some very difficult all-round and blood-tracking competitions open to all gundog breeds at international level (VSwP Pfalzer Wald and PnS in Strass).

With the import of the blacks, Lawnwoods Wish Me Luck and Floral Dance at Lawnwood, the aus Luhlsbusch kennel achieved real recognition. Whether in the show ring, where these outstanding showy dogs qualified for Int., German and VDH Ch. titles, or in the field, with remarkable work in hunting competitions, they were obviously a major improvement on the German Labrador scene. Lucky, especially, was and still is used all over Europe as a significant stud dog.

Remarkable offspring were Freya, Gina, Kerry Boy, Julia, Hella and Humphrey. Frizt Kraft wished to improve their kennel further, and acquired three more blacks to join the team; Charway Sea Beaver, Charway Blackjack and Lawnwoods Towntalk, all trained and successfully handled in the show ring to various Champion titles, and in field trials. Dr Kraft's champion dogs were used many times with their own and other breeders' bitches and produced healthy, typical Labradors, full of character, hunting passion and the will to please.

Black, yellow and chocolate offspring of those

imports are widespread over Europe. Ronja, Rosine and Sally achieved the highest recognition in the hunters' club competition. Isabella Kraft's comprehensive knowledge about Labradors in many countries helps her not only to continue successful breeding, but also to publish some extremely helpful information for breeders. These include her famous booklets on GPRA pedigrees and, in conjunction with Gary Johnson, The Workers, a pedigree book about British field trial champions. The Krafts are also interested in working Smooth Fox Terriers. Fritz has bred, trained and owns the top working bitch (1995) of this breed in Germany.

The Labrador population expanded enormously during the 1980s and the number of kennels followed suit. The offspring of some still influence the modern Labrador scene. A personal selection of breeders and kennels from those years includes:

Gerd Gobl (of Blackwood Castle) whose imported Wesko Trudi of Elterwater not only became a Champion herself, but started a very successful line of typical show and working bitches for him, including among others the top winning Ch. Quick Big Lady of Blackwood Castle.
Elfriede Schultes (vom Fresenbrink).
Karin Brandt (vom Masurenweg).
Carola Kreutzfeld (of Hunter's Heide).
Monika Gunder (vom Lauterbachtal).
Maria von Hobe (von Ohrfeld) who concentrates on producing typical shooting dogs. She also bred Int. Ch., D. Ch., VDH Ch. Justus von Ohrfeld (owner, Dr Kamlah), a superb dog who, besides his show wins, excelled at trials for

*Pictured left to right:
Ch. Charway
Blackjack, Ch.
Charway Sea Beaver,
Ch. Lawnwoods Wish
Me Luck.*

Photo: Dr Kraft.

retrievers and in competitions for all gundog breeds.

Annika Schaffer (Scandica), based on chocolate stock from Brulin's Swedish Puhs kennel. Her Ch. Puh's Brown Autumn was a successful addition to the chocolate Labrador population in Germany.

With the ever-growing popularity of the breed, it became more and more difficult to see improvements in the average appearance of the dogs. High prices for puppies inevitably encouraged breeders who had short-term profit as their major objective. Therefore the comments of foreign judges on the majority of the dogs at shows in Germany were polite but nevertheless unambiguous – there was no, or at best, slow improvement at the end of the 1980s. The dogs winning or placed at shows were mainly imports or owned by foreign exhibitors. Only very few Labradors bred in Germany could compete successfully in other European countries. This caused the Labrador Club of Germany (LCD) in particular to gather together ambitious people aiming for show quality instead of quantity.

Heinz Meller, later to become president of the LCD, imported Ch. Sunny Loch's My Mystery Man (Sh. Ch. Heatherbourne Court Jester x Sunny Loch's Kinlochgowrae), a yellow dog bred in the Netherlands by Tuus van Adrichem Boogaert-Kwint. Over the years he accumulated 28 CACs, eight CACIBs, 16 BOBs, and four BIS. 'Mister' significantly improved the breed in Germany and some other European countries. Several of his daughters became foundation bitches for newer kennels, and it is obvious that Mister has put his stamp on them, providing not

only good quality but also health and typical temperament. Heinz Meller used him and his offspring successfully to slowly build up his own kennel Mystery Mistral.

Another kennel with remarkable success is Christina Gabriel's Fameflair. She started in the breed with Ch. Dee-Fair Amazing Fame and Ch. Dee-Fair Sweet Sensation Queen, both Danish imports and qualified as Show Champions with working qualification. With their offspring and some carefully selected imports from England (e.g. Donacre High Promises and Ruselton Dion Dublin), the kennel is well-established in the show ring, winning first prizes among the best stock in Europe today.

More dual-purpose ambitions are to be found at Romney's, the kennel of Beate and Gereon Ting, which is based on the two very nice Dutch dual-purpose bitches, Cookie van de Zeeschelp and Fairywood's Fauve. Fauve's daughter Ch. Romney's Crazy Diamond (by Ch. Charway Blackjack) is winning in the show ring (four CACs, one CACIB, one RCACIB, one BOB, and one BOS) and in the field (BLP, FT, Markproeve). Blondella Balletina was imported in 1993 to further improve the kennel.

Two younger kennels which favour the chocolate are Cadonau's owned by Monika Cadonau and based on the two Belgian imports, Ch. Musicman of Fisherman's Mascot and Ch. Olivia of Fisherman's Mascot, and Eva Ebeling's Franconian, based on the two Swedish imports, Utnas Famous Faxe and Tjotte's Showstealer.

Tamara Buttner, who imported Timspring Greylag in 1979, is now back in the ring. Her yellow US bitch Heroncourt Ginostra's Lollo,

Yenny aus Luhlsbusch.

Photo: Dr Kraft.

who has one CACIB (Ginostra's Dandylion x Heroncourt Zoey) produced some promising offspring for the kennel Ginostra's.

The LCD breeders' list named 105 breeders in 1995. The list includes quite a number of highly-motivated people who have fallen in love with the Labrador only recently, and are now hoping to experience the joy and delight of having puppies that hopefully develop into healthy, typical and good-looking Labradors.

We will finish with some statistics. In 1995, there was the opportunity to attend 15 shows in Germany where CACs and/or CACIBs were on offer. Out of the 60 major awards (best dog and best bitch, best young dog and best young bitch and so on), thirteen were scooped by dogs bred in Germany. They are as follows:

JCAC Fameflair Clinton So Far (H. Moller) x2
JCAC Ashauser Beethoven (B. Morack)
JCAC Mystery Mistral's Advantage (H. Meller) x4
JCAC Cindy Love vom Juratal (S. Seitz)
JCAC Scandica Oh Sofin (K. Schaffer)
JCAC Heidi von Guam-Breitenberg (J. Nusser)
JCAC Inja Nightmare of Fire (P. Meller)
CACIB Buddy vom Grafenrain (D. Schulmayer)
CACIB Mystery of Melody vom Lauterbachtal (H. Meller)
CAC Gina of Hunters Heide (C. Kreutzfeld)
CAC Graf Scotty a. d. Burghaus (I. Patzel)
CAC Tracy of Blackwood Castle (E. Paulus-Gobl)

CACIB Fameflair Amazing Mister (H.Moller)
All the other winners are imports or owned by foreign exhibitors.

THE LABRADOR TODAY
In the (nearly completely) open European community, a frequent exchange of knowhow and stock has resulted in a remarkable rise in quality. In common with other countries, bitches are currently regarded as slightly better than dogs. British judge Mrs Cairns (Blaircourt) commented at the recent Nurnberg CACIB show that: "such excellent yellow winners I had not placed for a while."

On the other hand, it is debatable whether the health status of German Labradors is better than in other European countries as a result of our stringent breeding rules. Only time will tell!

THE NETHERLANDS
Anja Verbeek de Neef
HISTORY
Labradors are a much-loved family dog in Holland and numbers have steadily risen over the years. In the beginning the breed was known only to fans. These were usually people who used the Labrador for hunting. The Nederlandse Retriever Club (NRC) was founded in 1933, and was, for a long time, the club which promoted the use of all breeds of retriever in the field. After the Second World War, the Labrador Retriever almost disappeared in Holland. Only a

few Labradors were registered with the Dutch Kennel Club during the 1950s. In the 1960s, more Labradors from the UK came to the Netherlands, and breeding was started by the Sabo kennel.

In the 1970s, Mrs de Haas with her Canis Frisiae kennel, was an important contributor to Labrador development, with six Champions so far. The Dutch Labrador became known and loved by everyone. The big boom in popularity started in the second half of the 1970s. In the early 1980s, Mrs Bloemendaal from the Ladylands kennel had a lot of success and exerted much influence in breeding circles at the time. Chocolates were unknown until the late 70s. Some breeders changed this, and chocolates are now very popular in Holland.

Some of today's well-known breeders started their kennels in the early 80s with imports from famous English lines, and they became successful over the years. They include Fogel Hlara, Silronray's, Withara, Farbourne, Fairywood and Toplicht.

THE DUTCH LABRADOR CLUB

The Dutch Labrador Club, founded in 1964, has grown enormously in recent years. The first Club show in 1965 had an entry of 51 Labradors. In 1995, however, there were more than 800 entries. The first Champion club show was organised in 1971. Several committees give expert advice about breeding and hunting, plus up-to-date information about the care of the Labrador. The club does this by publishing a magazine every two months and organising a show every year. It promotes showing and working tests. It mediates in the selling of puppies, provided that parents of pups sold through the club comply with certain standards. Conditions are applied (among other things) to exterior, working ability, health (HD and genetic eye deviations such as PRA and Cataract), the number of litters produced by, and the age of, the dam. Since April 1st 1994, it is obligatory for stud dogs to be screened for OCD/LPCM and the results published in The Labrador Post.

It is noticeable that prospective puppy buyers are becoming more knowledgeable, and asking for more information from breeders before deciding on the acquisition of a pup. Breeders whose dogs are shown to be free from OCD/LPCM have a distinct advantage. Since the introduction of the New Civil Code for The Netherlands, puppy buyers can claim redress under certain clauses, so it is common sense for breeders to breed only sound dogs and give prospective buyers all the information possible. A breeder who fails to meet these standards will be placed on the so-called 'black list' and have membership of the club withdrawn. The Dutch Labrador Club presently has approximately 5,500 members. The number of Labradors has increased enormously, and in 1995 there are approximately 30,000 Labradors in our country. The annual number of puppies born is over 3,800 (1995 figures).

THE SHOW SYSTEM

At the present time, it is not easy to become a Dutch Champion. The quality is very good, thanks to breeders who have imported stock, and competition is fierce. Every month sees a show somewhere in Holland, and so each month there is one chance to earn a ticket. The Winnershow in Amsterdam is the most important show, attracting more than 4,000 dogs of all breeds.

The Dutch Retriever Club (for all retrievers) organises approximately eight field trials every year (entry of only ten dogs). It is very difficult to become a member of this club, because of severe balloting. As one can imagine, it is very hard to train a full-size Labrador with so little opportunity to take part in field trials. The Dutch Labrador Club organises many working tests, mainly with dummies and/or cold game. To become a Dutch Champion it is not obligatory to get a field trial qualification, as it is for the international title.

Four CACs, under at least three different judges, of which at least one must be after 27 months of age, are necessary for a final Championship. Winning the Winnershow at Amsterdam or the Labrador Clubmatch provides two points. The winner title at the Winnershow is a special qualification that can be added to the dog's name: 'Winner 95'. The Netherlands has always been a very 'open' country. That means, for example, that at Dutch shows many entries from abroad can usually be seen. Labradors from Belgium, France, Germany and some Scandinavian countries are quite normal in Holland. For us it is also quite easy to go to those countries to show our dogs. The Dutch breed-shows, which normally have English judges, are especially popular with breeders from abroad. If your bitch is in season, you lose your chance, as in-season bitches cannot participate. If your dog is 'out of coat', you can still enter. That is why foreign judges regularly see dogs who are out of coat.

LEADING KENNELS

SILRONRAY: S.G. Liebrechts van Peursem.
In 1972 the first Labrador, a dark yellow male called Buster was acquired. He was bred out of pure English field trial lines. This was the start of a growing interest in the breed. To begin with only males were kept, then in 1982 the first litter was whelped out of a Sandylands Strinesdale grand-daughter. Since then, many dog have been shown – the following have been most influential. Ch. Sandylands Kingfisher, a nice once-in-a-lifetime dog, fulfilled all expectations and promises by winning many CCs and BOBs at breed club shows in Germany, Belgium, Switzerland and Denmark. He was joined by his half-sister Ch. Sandylands Claire, and later by Sandylands Scilla who is now six years old.

Rodarbal Raincloud was also very special, coming to the kennel at the age of four, after winning classes and Res. CC in England. She won Res. CC at NLV Clubshow in 1984, and, mated to Kingfisher, produced BS-Europech. Silronray's Miss Mansell and CC winner S. Lafitte. The next step was to import Bradking Solo and the chocolate Cambremer Bravo of S. to be used for Kingfisher's progeny – all going back to a great favourite, Bradking Cassidy. They continued to produce the Labrador of the type that was wanted – strong boned, balanced, stylish and with impeccable temperament.

The chocolates in the kennel all go back to Simandem Sam Brown of Balrion, who did not receive the attention he deserved in his lifetime. All his progeny have a deep, rich chocolate colour. Sandylands, Bradking and Balrion were thus the foundation of the kennel. At the moment, a yellow bitch, Ramah Victoria, bred by Mrs Waring (all-Sandylands lines again) is being campaigned, and there are high hopes for a dark yellow (fox red) puppy bitch, Silronray's Fox-glove.

FOGEL HLARA: Pieta van Dee-Vogelaar.
The kennel started in 1976, but the first litter was not bred until 1980. The black bitch Strega from Sweden arrived in Holland pregnant. She produced an all-black litter of twelve. Out of this litter came our first Champion, Fogel Hlara Gulliver, who proved to be a great influence on the kennel, also producing chocolate progeny. In 1984, the chocolate male Wetherlam Nutcracker came to the kennel. He turned out to be a great sire, producing a nice type of Labrador with really good hips. Through his influence, the type of the chocolate Labrador greatly improved in the Netherlands.

In 1987, the chocolate bitch, Canette von Thornhem, became the first chocolate Dutch Champion. Wetherlam Nutcracker sired five champions. In 1988 Balnova Sultana, a black male carrying chocolate, was imported from England. He became a Dutch Champion and greatly influenced the growing Labrador population in Holland. To date, he is the sire of five Champions, the latest being the black bitch Fogel Hlara Guinevere.

She is the great grand-daughter of Wetherlam Nutcracker, and the kennel's first Champion Fogel Hlara Gulliver also shows up in her pedigree. Donalbain Shadow, born in 1991, was the third male imported from England to be used on the Wetherlam Nutcracker and Balnova Sultan progeny. His daughter, Unique van de Otterhof, is a black bitch with clear eyes, perfect hips and elbows, nice looks and a perfect character. Current hopes are placed in two promising youngsters, Tabatha's Lieutenant and Rosanen Sealord.

WITHARA: Marie Louise van Haersma de With.
Powhatan Black Moyola was purchased and mated her to Ladylands Black Arrow. This combination produced Withara's Bonnie Jean and

Withara's Regal's One to Behold.
Photo courtesy: A. Verbeek-de Neef.

Paprika Dream at Silronray's.

Nl Ch. Fogel Hlara Guinevere.
Photo courtesy: A. Verbeek-de Neef.

Withara's Charming Black Gypsy. They both did well at shows. Jean went BOB at the Dutch National Show at Apeldoorn and was also a very good gundog. She produced Withara's Fair Black Magic who became a German Champion. Gypsy produced several championship winners in Holland and abroad. Some of her progeny have also done very well in the field. Her daughter, Withara's Key To Happiness (German Clubsieger 1995), produced Withara's Classiques One To Remember with the English import Copsehill Moonlight Classique. She also produced Withara's Regal's One To Behold with Am. Can. Dutch Ch. Beechcroft's Regal Air, who has at nine months already done very well at shows and will hopefully, together with the rest of her family, keep the line going well in the future.

TOPLICHT: Elza Gravestein.
A yellow Labrador purchased in Holland was the start of an involvement with the breed which encompassed obedience training, showing and gundog training. The next acquisition was a light yellow dog puppy, Ballyduff Sailor Boy (Thor's Lightning Boy – Ballyduff Ballad) who became a Dutch, Luxembourg and German Sh. Ch).

In 1980 Squire of Ballyduff was mated to Balrion Royale Mischief of Rodarbal and the resulting Sh. Ch. Rodarbal Rainbow became the foundation bitch of the kennel. She produced four Champions: Toplicht Sailor's Beau Sun, Toplicht Sailor's Silver Star and Black Star, and my dog, Toplicht Tintagel's Tagel Moon. Two puppies were exported to Beverly Lubbert (Tormentil) in Canada, and they became Can.

Chs. Toplicht Sultan's Honey Moonraker and Toplicht Fleur's Charlee My Girl.

FAIRYWOOD: Toos van Elewoud
The first important Labrador for this kennel was the chocolate bitch Sacha, a combination of Coffee Cream of Kenstaff – Cadree Bruce. Sacha was a great bitch with a great character who produced beautiful chocolate, black and even some yellow Labradors. Finally, it decided to breed only chocolate and black Labradors, going for chocolate with a capital C. Sacha produced a great chocolate Champion bitch named Fairywoods Acer (Dutch Ch. Lux. Ch. 2 – Winster 2 – Bundessieger, VDH Champion, Europasieger, and BOB at the Dutch Labrador show). Her brother, Fairywoods Almighty Blitz, was also quite successful, becoming a Dutch Champion and Int. Champion. Out of Fairywoods Acer, the following Champions were born: Fairywoods Glendalough Eger (black dog), Fairywoods Lu-Lu (chocolate bitch, Dutch Ch., Lux. Ch., Bundessieger, Winster).

Fairywoods Lu-Lu produced the great-looking bitch Fairywoods Valentine and the very promising bitches Fairywoods Tribute to Sacha and Fairywoods Blue Bell, both now 18 months old.

FARBOURNE: Anja Verbeek de Neef.
Roseacre Seashell was Anja's first show dog. She was imported from the Roseacre kennel in England, and won many prizes at home and abroad. In 1986, Miss Poppins Of Cranspire was acquired and Int. Ch. Farbourne's Cover Girl was later produced.

With some ups and lots of downs – HD, PRA,

Fairywood Acer.
Photo courtesy: A. Verbeek-de Neef.

Farbourne's No Problem.
Photo courtesy: A. Verbeek-de Neef.

and wrong combinations – the kennel was slowly built up. The turning point was importing the black bitch Rocheby Oakapple via Marion Hopkinson. Rocheby Oakapple was of the greatest influences on the kennel. She gave beautiful offspring, and produced Farbourne's Endless Love. The litter from the combination of Endless Love with Trendlewood Distinction At Trewinnard gave Farbourne's Out Of The Blue.

Out Of The Blue was, in February 1996, group winner in Eindhoven and fifth BIS. As a result he was invited by the Dutch Kennel Club to join the Topdog of the Year event in February 1997 – the first Labrador Retriever to do so. Her brother, Farbourne's Right On Time, won the Junior title at the 1994 World Show in Switzerland. Farbourne's Queen Of Diamonds (Tibblestone Rising Flood – Bradking Solo) won the title Europasieger in Dortmund, and is still doing a lot of winning.

Anja has bred with well-known English lines only, such as Rocheby, Poolstead, Bradking, Cranspire and Carromer. The four dogs currently flying the flag are: Rocheby Royal Marine, Farbourne's Prime Time, Farbourne's Touchdown and Stormley Macintosh.

FINLAND
Eeva Rautala and Maria Swanljung

BACKGROUND
The history of Labrador breeding in Finland is relatively short, starting in the 1950s. The Finnish Kennel Club was founded in May 1889, and is thus the oldest in Scandinavia, while The Retriever Club began in 1963, for all retriever breeds jointly. The Labrador Retriever Club was founded in 1980. One of the main objects of the Labrador Club is to encourage breeders to keep the Labrador as a dual-purpose breed. To emphasise this, since 1982 the club has awarded a trophy and the title of Labrador of the Year to the best dual-purpose Labrador with awards from both field trials and shows. Likewise, the Show Labrador of the Year and the Field Trial Labrador of the Year have been awarded to give credit to the top winners in these fields.

For several decades the Labrador population was rather small in Finland. Before 1988, when the Finnish borders were closed to foreign dogs from rabies countries, the main imports were from Britain and Sweden. In the 1970s Labrador breeders often used Swedish-owned stud dogs for their bitches. These were often British imports of mainly Sandylands and Ballyduff breeding. Finnish breeding was thus rather dependent on imported or foreign stud dogs, and breeding material and many of the top winning dogs in the 1970s and 1980s were imported.

NEW POPULARITY
In the 1980s the Labrador population started to grow. It has become the fourth most popular breed in the country, with around 2,000 registrations in the 1990s. In a country of only five million inhabitants, that makes the Labrador almost as popular in Finland as in Britain or the USA. The opening of borders in 1988 made it possible for Finnish breeders and exhibitors to expand international co-operation in a compeletely different way than before. With no more quarantine, it became possible to attend shows abroad, send bitches to be mated abroad and so on. Nowadays, Finnish-bred Labradors can hold their own in many ways, and also on an international level (World Winners 1991, '92 and '94

were all Finnish-bred dogs) and imports have declined. In 1995, the Finnish Kennel Club registered 27 imported Labradors, still mainly from Britain and Sweden. As the general quality of the breed has improved, quite a few exports have been made instead to most countries in Europe and also overseas, including the USA and Canada.

The breeding and training of guide dogs for the blind has been an active programme since the 1950s. A majority of these dogs are Labradors and bred under the affix Opas. Labradors have also been used as narcotics dogs for about 25 years and are bred under the affix Tullin.

BREEDING CONCERNS
Finnish Labrador breeders are conscientious concerning health problems in the breed. Hips have been X-rayed from the start of breeding and eye examinations started in 1970s. Elbows are still X-rayed on voluntary basis, but more and more breeders consider this almost compulsory nowadays, at least for males used at stud. The health situation has therefore been very good. A requirement of the Kennel Club for registration of puppies is that the parents must have been examined for hips (A-D hips) and eyes.

A phenomenon that appeared about the mid-1980s was the division of the breed into so-called show versus working lines. This is a great pity and has made the breeding of dual-purpose Labradors more difficult, as in so many other countries. It is to be remembered that to become a Finnish Champion the dog must also have been qualified in field which is a sort of working test. We shall here give a brief presentation of the current situation and introduce some of the most successful kennels, starting with more show-oriented kennels and ending with the pure working dog breeders.

LEADING KENNELS
FOLLIES
Helena Kaitila started Follies kennel with Fin. Ch. Susanset Inez in the 1970s. She was bred by Oili Aspegren (Susanset kennels), one of the top winning kennels in the 1970s with quite a few Champions and some excellent chocolates on her merit list. The present stock at Follies is mainly based on the British imported bitches Heatherbourne Partypiece (one CC), Fin. Ch. Balrion Witching Hour and Balnova Blushing Bride. Very successful litter sisters were Fin. Ch. Follies Uriah Heep, Fin. Ch. Follies Ursula Andress and Follies Up to Date with three CCs (Pastime's Time Bomb x Follies Milk and Honey). One of the absolutely top winning males in the 1990s is Int. Fin. Ch. Follies Cutty Sark (Wetherlam Mace x Follies Viscountess), owned by Juha-Pertti Leino (Brookhill's kennel) and a great-grandson of Witching Hour. He has several BIS and BOS wins at the biggest breed speciality shows under famous specialist judges. Several Champions have been bred by this kennel in which Helena's daughter, Anna-Liisa Kaitila, is now also active.

MELLOWS
Another established breeder is Birgitta Johansson of Mellows kennels. She started out in the mid 1970s with Swedish import bitches. Later, she imported two beautiful yellow bitches from England, Fin. and Nor. Ch. Roseacre Madcap and Roseacre Silver Gilt (two CCs). Both have left some very successful offspring such as the yellow male Fin. Ch. Mellows Xanthos, Mellows Fieldmaster (two CCs), Fin. Ch. Mellows Fair Fantasy and Fin. Ch. Mellows Blonde Magic. Some imported stud dogs at this kennel are Wetherlam Mace (two CCs) and Heavy Loaders And The Band Played (one CC). Birgitta also trains her dogs and competes at field trials.

HIRSIPIRTIN
The well-known Hirsipirtin kennels of Ritva Tervo began in the late 1970s with Mellows Katanja and another foundation bitch Fin. Ch. Follytower Hedda from Britain. Hedda's son Fin. Ch. Hirsipirtin Gummiseta was a winner at shows and a good producer. Another famous stud dog is Hirsipirtin Q-makoira, who has been a very prominent sire of numerous show winners in recent years. He is by the Norwegian stud dog, well-known all over Scandinavia for his winning progeny, Int. Nord. Ch. Licithas Blizzard out of Fin. Ch. Hirsipirtin Emma, an

excellent brood bitch with many winning off-spring. Ritva has imported several dogs over the years, one of the latest being Fin. Ch. Narjanas Lamborghini from Norway. Hirsipirtin kennels has been successfully breeding winning show dogs as well as breeding stock for other kennels.

TWEEDLEDUM

Kirsi Luomanen's kennel, Tweedledum, has bred and owned many successful show dogs, the original foundation bitch being Swedish-bred Nattens Drottning in 1978. Kirsi has been involved in many imports through the years, such as the British-bred males Kupros Kassidy, Roseacre Madigan and Cambremer Star Trekker. Present-day stock is mainly based on the Swedish import Winnie's Kajal and British import Jayncourt Jingle Jangle. Kajal's beautiful young black daughter, Tweedledum Mascara (two CCs) has had a very good start in her show career. Jingle Jangle's offspring include the stud dogs Am. Ch. Tweedledum Pop My Cork and Tweedledum Steamy Windows (one CC), and the bitches Tweedledum Puddle Jumper, Tweedledum Which Witch, and Fin. Ch. Tweedledum Sweet and Rosy (owned by Rauni Aslamo, Rosanan kennel). N. Ch. Tweedledum Murphys Law has been a popular stud dog in Sweden in the 1990s.

ROSANAN

FT Ch. and Ob. Ch. Susanset Illusia (a litter sister of Fin. Ch. Susanset Inez) was the foundation bitch of Rauni Aslamo's Rosanan kennel. During her career, Rauni has imported and bred some top winning Labradors: Fin. Ch. and Ob. Ch. Proud Sinfonia (from Sweden) who was the breed's Top Winner in 1979, 80 and 81; Fin. Ch. Poolstead Pipit, Top Winner in 1983; Illusia's son, Int. and Fin. Ch. Rosanan Dandelion did very well in shows and appears in some of today's winning pedigrees and her grand-daughter, Fin. Ch. Rosanan Taste of Honey is behind the many Champions of the Mailiksen kennels.

In the 1990s, Rauni has imported Fin. Ch. Narjana's Ian from Norway and Fin. Ch. Gallybob Quiggley from Britain. The latter is the sire of a young black dog Rosanan Emperor (ex Caveris Kan-Tippa), who has had great success in the show ring lately. Fin. Ch. Rosanan Mardi Gras (Fin. Ch. Aprilmist Grasshopper x Caveris Kan-Tippa), a beautiful black dog, has also had a great show career these last years. Another beautiful Labrador bred from this kennel is a yellow bitch, Fin. Ch. Rosanan Pink Rose (Fin. Ch. Caveris Mirage x Rosanan Primrose), one of our country's top Labradors with many great wins in shows. Up-and-coming from this kennel are the yellow bitches Rosanan Golden Rosebud (two CCs) and her litter sister Rosanan Garden Rose, with two CCs (Ch. Lejie Royal Mail x Fin. Ch. Rosanan Summer Rose), and a young yellow male Rosanan Royal Prince with one CC, (Fin. Ch. Gallybob Quiggley x

Tweedledum Mascara, bred and owned by Kirsi Luomanen.

Photo courtesy: Maria Swanljung.

Fin. Ch. Rosanan Pink Rose, bred and owned by Rauni Aslamo.

Photo courtesy: Maria Swanljung.

Fin. Ch. Caveris Kanske). The latter two are co-owned with Riitta Lipponen of Tsarodej kennels.

TSARODEJ

The foundation bitch, Mallards Partridge Purple, was imported in 1978 from Sweden by Riitta Lipponen. She is behind Fin. Ch. Tsarodej April Flower who is the foundation bitch of Mirja Ikonen's Aprilmist kennels. Recent winners from Tsarodej include the Champion bitches Int. Fin. Est. Ch Tsarodej Sad As Salina, Fin. Ch. Tsarodej Ups And Downs, Fin. Ch. Tsarodej Mandy, and the chocolate bitch Fin. Ch. Tsarodej Tanita Tikaram. The black male Int. Fin. Est. Ch. Bubbling Churchill, owned by Tsarodej, has produced some nice offspring and been winning at top level in shows.

WETTEN

The foundation bitch of Eeva Rautala's Wetten Kennels was Fin. Ch. Chara Star, a daughter of Roseacre Senta, imported from Britain in 1979 by Andrea Standertskjold (Horsemans kennels) and there mated to UK Ch. Timspring Sirius. Chara Star was a true dual-purpose bitch with top awards at both shows and field trials. She has Champions and show winners in her progeny, including her grandson Wetten Osteri (three CCs), a black male born in 1991 who has been a consistent winner and one of the top males of recent years. Another bitch line was started 1991 with Hirsipirtin Bonbon (one CC), who is by Multi. Ch. Blondella Bonny Lad.

PALABRAS

Hannele Jokisilta of Palabras Kennels started out in 1984 with Fin. Ch. Reflect Remezelda. Her great grand-daughter, Int. Fin. Est. Ch. Palabras Look Out for X, is one of the top winning bitches lately, but several other Champions have also been bred by this kennel. From the same lines are the males Fin. Ch. Palabras Spacecraft and Fin. Ch. Palabras UBFourthy, who have both done well at shows and produced winning offspring. Up-and-coming are the young yellow male Palabras Blue Bayo and Palabras Blues Brother.

MAILIKSEN

Maissi Lappetelainen of Mailiksen kennels bought Fin. Ch. T Ch. Rosanan Taste of Honey in 1982. This bitch was an excellent brood bitch and has produced many Champions and show winners over the years. Her daughter, born in 1989, Fin. Ch. Mailiksen Milk and Honey was the most successful one in recent years, earning numerous BOBs, Group and BIS placings. Mailiksen has been the leading Labrador breeder in the north of Finland for many years.

CAVERIS

Carita Hallgren of Caveris kennel started breeding in 1985 with Fin. Ch. Mellows Honeysuckle. The beautiful bitch Int. Fin. Est. VDH. Ch. WW-91 Caveris Ellen (born 1986 by Hirsipirtin Q-makoira x Mellows Pop Primavera) has been extremely successful in Finland as well as in other countries. Not only has she been the Top Winning Show Labrador four years in a row (1988-91), but also Top Winning Gundog in 1988-89. One of her most memorable wins was BIS at the Dutch Labrador Club Ch. Show 1990, which had over 500 entries. The imports made by this kennel include Fin. Ch. Charway Sea Badger and Int. Fin. Ch. Charway Huckleberry, both popular stud dogs with excellent show careers. Carita has bred many Champions and show winners, including these International Champions: Int. Fin. Est. Ch. Caveris Mimosa, Int. Fin. Ch. Caveris Saimens Saga and Int. Fin. Ch. Caveris Kan-nibal, another popular stud dog with CCs from five countries and some wins in the USA.

MALLORN'S
In the early 1980s, Anu Saurama's Mallorn's kennel started with a chocolate bitch, Fin. Ch. Sandy. Her two chocolate daughters Mallorn's Aprilfool and Mallorn's Applesauce (by Roseacre Madigan) have done well in shows but also proven to be good brood bitches. Mallorn's Aprilfool mated to Cambremer Star Trekker produced Fin. Ch. Mallorn's Jersey Sour, a chocolate bitch who has done very well in shows and is owned by Loresho Kennels, as is Mallorn's Applesauce. When mated to Am. Ch. Dickendalls Arnold she produced Mallorn's Missionary Man (one CC) who has been a popular stud dog. Another bitch line in 1987 came from the black bitch Fin. Ch. Craneridge Andwella who has left some nice offspring in the black bitches Mallorn's Koh-I-Noor and Mallorn's Kiss Me Kate, by Am. and Can. Ch. Beechcrofts Danish Skydiver. Koh-I Noor, mated to Am. Ch. Dickendalls Arnold, produced the black male Fin. Ch. Mallorn's Onassis who has been the breed's Top Show Winner in 1994. He is owned by Marina Saarentaus (Grumbling Kennel). Kiss Me Kate, mated to Fin. Ch. M'Ladys Snow-Ball, produced a lovely black bitch Mallorn's Poison (two CCs).

LORESHO
Loresho, the affix of Annaliisa Harjukari's kennel, started out with the chocolate bitch, Mallorn's Applesauce in the mid 1980s. She has produced very successful offspring, one of them being Fin. Ch. Loresho Oystercatcher with the Bubbling kennel. A beautiful black granddaughter to Applesauce, Fin. Ch. Loresho Fine Black Lace (Int. Fin. Ch. Charway Huckleberry x Loresho Ringed Plover) has had many great wins in shows, as well as her daughter Loresho Jell-O with two CCs (by Mardas Maroon). Both belong to the absolute top rank of bitches. The successful chocolate bitch Fin. Ch. Mallorn's Jersey Sour has also produced very nice offspring in this kennel, the black males Loresho Love Mission (two CCs) by Mallorn's Missionary Man and the young Loresho Ozzie (two CCs) by Int. Fin. Est. Ch. Bubbling Churchill.

BUBBLING
Maria Swanljung started her Bubbling kennel in 1988, based on a chocolate bitch, Fin. Ch. Loresho Oystercatcher (by Fin. Ch. Charway Sea Badger). This bitch has proven to be a good show and brood bitch. Mated to Int. Fin. Ch. Exhibition Man de St Urbain she had a whole chocolate litter, from which the most well-known is the very successful chocolate male Int. Fin. Est. Ch. WW-94 Bubbling Bedouine (owner L. Bergh). A repeat mating produced Bubbling Excalibur who has started out well in France. Another litter with Nl. Lux. D. Ch. Lejie Royal Mail produced the black male Int. Fin. Est. Ch. Bubbling Churchill, who is with the Tsarodej kennel. Many quality chocolates have been bred by this kennel. Worth mentioning are the upcoming chocolate bitches Bubbling Gnocchi (two CCs) and the lovely Bubbling Indira who was BIS in the yearly Labrador Puppy Show 1995.

APRILMIST
The breed's Top Show Winner for three years was the beautiful yellow bitch Int. Fin. Dk. Esp. Ch. WW-92 Aprilmist Apricot Flower, bred in 1986 by Mirja Ikonen of Aprilmist kennel. Her sire is Int. Nord. Ch. Mallards Clay Basker and dam is Fin. Ch. Tsarodej April Flower. This bitch has had a tremendous show career at home as well as abroad, and was again as a veteran Top Show Winner in the breed in 1995. Fin. Ch. Tsarodej April Flower has also produced other show-winners and the top winning obedience

Fin. Ch. Loresho Oystercatcher, bred by Annaliisa Harjukari, owned by Maria Swanljung.

dog, Ob. Ch. Aprilmist Greedy Speedy. Another bitch line was founded with Fin. Ch. Hirsipirtin Boheemi by Multi Ch. Blondella Bonny Lad.

STRONGLINES

Tiina Rantanen's foundation bitch Fin. Ch. and T Ch. Applehill's Mayday, by Int. Nord. Ch. Licithas Blizzard, was born in 1985 and has been an excellent brood bitch with many Champions in her progeny. These include International Champions such as the yellow male Int. Fin. Ch. Stronglines Shuttlecock and the yellow bitches Int. Fin. Ch. Fin and T Ch. Stronglines Incandescent and Int. Fin. Ch. Stronglines Immaculate. A beautiful grand-daughter of Mayday by Ch. Gladlab Chase Me Charly was Fin. Ch. and T Ch. Eu. JW-91 Stronglines My Point of View. Her litter sister Fin. Ch. Stronglines Merry Mermaid has also had a great show career. Not only are her dogs very successful at shows but Tiina Rantanen also trains them for tracking and field trials.

M'LADYS

The foundation bitch of Marika Nahkuri's M'Ladys kennel is the yellow Pastime's Side-Kick (one CC). The first litter was born in 1990 and immediately produced a great show winner and stud dog, Fin. Ch. M'Ladys Snowball by Fin. Ch. Palabras Spacecraft. He was Top Show Winning Labrador in 1992 and 1993. His sister, Fin. Ch M'Ladys Snow Star and brother Fin. Ch. M'Ladys Snow-Line have also done well in shows. Another litter with Multi Ch. Blondella Bonny Lad produced Fin. Est. Ch. M'Ladys Chance of Wind and M'Ladys Before the Wind (two CCs). Another Champion son is the black Fin. Ch. M'Ladys Rainbow.

HALOLAN

This new kennel owned by Tiina Tikkanen, in the north east of Finland, has bred and owned several Champions and show winners. The best-known is the yellow bitch Fin. Ch. and T Ch. Halolan Leidi Lollipop, born 1990, and the stud dog Fin. Ch. and T Ch. Carrier Ruutiukko. This kennel has imported the yellow male Fin. Ch. Imperial de St Urbain.

HORSEMANS

One of the early Labrador breeders is Andrea Standertskjold of the Horseman kennel. She originally started breeding from Fin. Ch. Tekla i Vassen, born in 1968. In 1979 she imported from Britain a black bitch, Roseacre Senta (one CC), by UK Ch. Follytower Merrybrook Black Stormer ex UK Ch. Roseacre Siani, on whom her present lines are based. In 1980 she imported from Norway Nord. FT Ch. Fin. Ch. Kevin Keegan av Sverresborg, by Int. Nord. Ch. Minvans Junior ex N. Ch. Ballyduff Kerry. He was one of the most successful field trial dogs, also doing very well in shows, and thus a true dual-purpose Labrador. Five years in a row he won the Field Trial Championship for Labradors. He was also a very good stud dog, producing dual-purpose offspring. Horsemans kennel is nowadays one of the leading breeders of field trial Labradors and the home of Horsemans Morten and Horsemans Ofelia who have been winning in field trials.

ETHUSAN

The foundation bitch of Raija Matikainen's Ethusan Kennels was Fin. Ch. Kamrats Barbara born in 1976 (UK Ch. Powhatan Solo ex Badgerland Jess of Powhatan). Mated to Nord.

FT Ch. Fin. Ch. Kevin Keegan av Sverresborg she produced Fin. N. FT Ch. Fin. Ch. Ethusan Yliveto, who followed in his father's footsteps as a great dual-purpose Labrador. He won the title of Labrador of the Year an incredible five times, in 1986, 87, 90, 91 and 92, and was Field Trial Labrador of the Year in 1989 and 1992. He has numerous field trial wins to his credit. In 1986 Raija imported the Fin. FT Ch. Falcon of Drakeshead (by UK FT Ch. Haretor Mark of Drakeshead). He has 23 open class first prizes in field trials and was FT Labrador of the Year in 1993. He has produced field trial Champions and other field trial winners. Ethusan is the most successful field trial kennel in Finland.

SIRMAKAN

Taisto Virtanen's Sirmakan kennel's foundation bitch is Iliadens Kaly'pso (by Manymills Electron), a black bitch imported from Sweden in 1984. Mated to FT-bred dogs by Taisto and his wife, Pirjo, she has produced many FT winners including Fin. FT Ch. Sirmakan Vismutti and Sirmakan Dominantti, who was winner of the Field Trial Championship for Labradors in 1995. In 1989 they imported from Sweden a black male Flaxdale Jarvey (by Sandringham Bluff ex Drakeshead Faith), the sire of Dominantti and many other FT winners. Sirmakan kennel was awarded the title of Field Trial Breeder of the Year in 1995.

Other notable FT breeders are Mr and Mrs Riitta Ossi Kahara's Baldioran kennel who also breed show dogs from a different line, and Arto Suuronen's Tupla-Pummin kennel which has also bred and owned FT Champions.

SWEDEN
Jan-Erik Ek.

EARLY DAYS
The first Labrador to make a public appearance in Sweden was a black male called Major who was exhibited at the Swedish Kennel Club Show in Gothenburg in 1899. From then on, a few Labradors were imported, but it was not until Irma Brusewitz-Olson (Kennel av Oppensten) took the breed under her wing that anything real of value happened.

Her first appearance in the Labrador ring took place in 1936 with the British import, Ch. Betty of Tibshelf. Mrs Brusewitz-Olson was devoted to Labradors and imported several dogs who proved their worth in breeding. It is interesting to note that there are still breeders around who have stock going back to hers.

SHOW SUCCESSES
During the late 1950s and 60s, affixes such as Kamrats (Inge E-son Thoor and Ing-Marie Hagelin), Puhs (Brit-Marie Brulin), Aroscas (Gunilla Andersson), Vagants (Karin Wallin), Nattens (Sigyn Littorin), Jidjis (Marianne Furst Danielsson and Mona Iletorp, though Mona eventually started to breed Labradors under another affix, Ingmos), and Alvgardens (Majvor Nasman) started to present impressive results in shows as well as at field trials. All these kennels bred Dual Champions and, although it is now increasingly difficult to abide by this goal, most breeders still seem to aim to breed dual-purpose dogs.

During the 70s and 80s successful affixes were added to those mentioned above. Among them were: Minvans (Ulla Persson), Winnies (Pia Razera-Brulin), Attikonak (Gunnilla Ek), Mallards (Brit and Arnfinn Havaker), Cindys (Inger Lindgren), Minnows (Charlotte Lindell), Willows (Lili Lagerqvist), Smart Fellows (Yvonne Westerlund), Guidelines (Eva Gustafsson), LikeIms (Virge Johansson), Proud (Eva and Sven-Eric Deler), Country Songs (Mona Holmqvist), and Applejacks (J.C. Ericson and M.L. Akesson), and Imps (Inger Olofsen).

CHOCOLATES
In 1961, the first chocolate Labrador arrived in Sweden. This was Cookridge Cola, bred by Yvonne Pauling and owned by Kamrats Kennel. Cola played an important part in chocolate Labrador history in Sweden. She was herself a Champion and group winner, and her daughter Dual Ch. Kamrats Careena (owned by Puhs Kennel) was the first chocolate Labrador in the world to become a Dual Champion. Puhs soon developed a reputation for breeding superb chocolate Labradors and title holders carrying

this affix can be found in many countries, not least America, where five Puhs Labradors have gained their titles over the years. The best known is, no doubt, Swed. Nor. Am. Ch. Puhs Superman, who won BIS at their National Speciality at the beginning of the 80s. Not only did he beat American title holders along the way, but also several British ones who had been exported over the pond after gaining their title in Britain.

TOP WINNERS AND PRODUCERS

There have been many excellent representatives of the breed in this country over the years. It is not possible to mention them all, so I will settle for just a few who stood out during their life-time. They all produced Champions in their turn, and so left their mark on the breed. They are: Karin Wallin's Ch. Braeduke Silsdale Music Man; Brit-Marie Brulin's Ch. Cookridge Raamah and Ch. Puhs Chocolate Lady; Majvor Nasman's Ch. Jidjis Buttercake and Ch. Black Eagle of Mansergh; Gunilla Andersson's Ch. Aroscas Fight; Inge E-son Thoor's and Ing-Marie Hagelin's Ch. Powhatan Sentry (Dog of the Year All Breeds 1971); Inger Lindgren's Ch. Baronor Phoenix; Anne and Harald Liland's and Moa Persson's Ch. Licithas Blizzard; and Roland and Margareta Zetterholm's Ch. Deras Dovregutten.

Several of those were Dual Champions. Gunilla Andersson exported Sandylands Aroscas Welshman's Son to Mrs Gwen Broadley of Sandylands Kennel. Unfortunately, he became sterile and eventually returned to Sweden, but during his time in Britain he had a successful career, winning two CCs and several Res. CCs.

Over the years, many Swedish breeders have imported stock from Britain which have had an important influence on the breed. Bloodlines that have made great contributions include Sandylands, Cookridge, Ballyduff, Mansergh, Poolstead, Lawnwoods, Follytower, Powhatan, Novacroft, Wishwood and, obviously, many more.

HEALTH AND BREEDING

Approximately 2,000 Labradors are registered annually with the Swedish Kennel Club. There

RIGHT: *Roseacre Sedge of Follytower.*
Photo courtesy: Jan-Erik Ek.

BELOW (RIGHT): *Applejacks Marco Polo.*
Photo courtesy: Jan-Erik Ek.

BELOW (LEFT): *Appeljacks Sweet Kokomo.*
Photo courtesy: Jan-Erik Ek.

is a health scheme which says that any Labrador to be used in breeding must have an eye certificate and must be X-rayed. Dogs affected with PRA and RD are not allowed to be bred from, nor is a proven carrier of these diseases.

For the last six years, most breeders have X-rayed elbows on their breeding stock for OCD. The Swedish KC does not require this, so it is up to the breeder's discretion whether he or she chooses to do so. However, The Swedish Labrador Club requires eye, hip and elbow passes in order to recommend puppies to members of the public who enquire about finding a suitable Labrador puppy. Throughout the country, there are a few Puppy Advisers (associated with the Labrador Club). Anyone can phone them, ask for advice on how to find a puppy up to their standards (this means hip, elbow, and eye certificates, and also that both parents must have a first grade at a Championship show or at a Ch. field trial). Any bitch owner in doubt about which stud dog to use can turn to the Labrador Club's stud advisers, who will help to find a suitable dog.

The Swedish Labrador Club started in 1977 and publishes four issues of the magazine Labradoren annually. In it, there are FT results, show results, photos of winners, pedigrees of GPRA-affected dogs (if any) and other useful information. The club held its first Championship show in 1994, and Best In Show went to Musicals Singin' in The Rain. Trewinnard My Song was best male.

Labradors are employed in many different ways in Sweden. Apart from picking-up, they are also used by the police searching for drugs, and, of course, as guide dogs for the blind. Labradors are also trained for rescue work, and some even search for mould in houses – important information for people to have if they are going to buy a house for a £100,000 or more!

SOUTH AFRICA
Carmen Copestake

Are Labradors popular in South Africa? You bet they are! One has only to glance at registration statistics to confirm this. Labradors have consis-

tently been in the canine top ten over the past 15 years. And for all the right reasons. As everywhere else in the world, Labradors here are intelligent, eager-to-please, and must surely rate as the most companionable of all dogs. The demand for the services of a well-bred Labrador is ever-increasing, be it for companion dog, working dog, retriever or guide dog.

GUIDE DOGS
Interestingly, guide dogs have not always been available in South Africa. In 1953, at the age of 30, Gladys Evans became blind. She tells this story: "My mother, who was an American, knew about 'seeing eye dogs' and sent me to England to train with one. There were no facilities in South Africa then. My first dog Sheena came back with me on the liner Carnarvon Castle. She was the first working guide dog in South Africa.

"I was determined to start a Guide Dogs scheme in South Africa. But it was not easy. We had to educate the sighted public to believe that one could trust one's life to dogs. I met with a lot of resistance at first. It took four months to get permission to allow Sheena on a bus! At last, I was allowed to take a ride on a special bus on July 4th 1953. That was my Day of Independence."

The dedicated Gladys Evans devoted her life to the South African Guide Dogs Association. In 1995 she was awarded the R.W. Bowen Gold Medal. This is the highest award for efforts on behalf of welfare for the blind. To date, more than 820 dogs have been successfully trained to be seeing eyes, which has helped to give the blind an independent life.

HISTORY
Good guide dogs, working dogs, sniffer dogs, police dogs, and companion dogs do not just happen by chance. Sound, judicious breeding sustained over many years lies behind the success of Labradors in South Africa.

Records from the Kennel Union of South Africa show that retrievers have been in South Africa since 1883. Unfortunately, these records do not tell us what kind of retrievers they were. But in 1926 the first entry appears which mentions a Labrador Retriever called Roseneath

Bingold, who belonged to a Mr H. Jeppe. It is presumed that H. Jeppe was Harold Jeppe, son of Julius, the Rand Lord and financier. Harold was a very elegant man who also owned Afghans, and was a keen sportsman, art collector, polo player and Olympic hurdler.

After such an illustrious connection in the beginning, very little happened on the Labrador scene until 1951 when Overweather Rip became the first Labrador to win the title of Champion. It was not until 1957 that a group of enthusiasts gathered in Johannesburg to form the Labrador Retriever Kennel Club of South Africa, which, to this day, has the specific purpose of promoting the breed in this country.

So who were these dedicated people who improved and popularised the breed so well that Labradors have been Best in Show winners at all-breed shows no less than 22 times since the club's inception?

INFLUENTIAL BREEDERS
Oscar Wilde, a flamboyant character was an influential breeder and judge in the 1950s and

1960s, as was his wife Pat. Many fine Sandylands, Zelstone, and Follytower dogs, among others, were imported to their well-known 'Brigade' kennels in Johannesburg, which enriched the South Africa gene pool considerably. But the most famous of the Brigade dogs was the popular winner Zelstone Raven of The Brigade who had a big influence on show and field progeny. Other leading breeders of the same era were Peter and Jane Horley (Hussars). Winston of the Hussars (Sandylands Trade Wind x Charmaine of Cannobie Lee) was campaigned very successfully and, at the age of nine, went BIS at the Gundog Club Show in 1974.

In Cape Town is one of South Africa's oldest-established kennels, Rose Marie Cabion's Sleepy Hollow (1960). Sleepy Hollow Follytower Old Oak went BIS no less than nine times. Also in Cape Town is Pam Richardson's Brightwood kennel, the home of many outstanding dogs.

In Johannesburg are Rod and Carmen Copestake (Breckondale) who have made a significant contribution to the breed. Their first

Derek Brown's FT Ch. Breckondale's King Shilling (Ch. Balrion King of the Hill of Breckondale – Breckondale Bad Penny): Winner of the 1994 KUSA Invitational Champion Stake.

Ch. Watercrest Rawhide Reagan, bred by John Steyn.   Photo: John Steyn.

imported sire, Ch. Sandylands Masterpiece of Breckondale (son of Mark), when bred to Ch. Breckondale Caprice, started a dynasty of bitches who are Best In Show winners to this day. The Breckondale bloodlines were further enriched by the importation of many fine Balrion dogs. Both Ch. Balrion Lord of the Manor of Breckondale and Ch. Balrion Bowled a Bouncer to Breckondale were prepotent sires and stamped their likeness on the breed.

Joan van Niekerk of Jeronga fame popularised chocolates. Who can ever forget her beautiful bitch, Ch. Jeronga's Glowing Flame (Sketchley Marcus of Jeronga), who won many awards?

No list could be considered complete without mentioning Stella Crawford Bekker's striking black dog Ch. Mallardhurn Black Earl of Wester Ross, who in turn sired Mike Gie's Field Ch., Ob. Ch., Sh. Ch. Brigade Highway Man. This dog is one of the few triple Champions in the world. Equally worthy of note is Mr M.H. Gie's Brigade Highwayman – the first South African dog of any breed to become a Triple Champion (Breed, Obedience and Field Trial).

FIELD TRIALS

In England, Labradors were initially used as shooting dogs. They have not lost their natural instinct here in South Africa, and breeders constantly receive requests for dogs for shooting. Field trialling is a popular sport in SA, and Labradors are consistent winners.

When one thinks of Field Trials, the name Bill Tait springs to mind. His contribution to field trialling has been enormous. Thanks to his organisational skills, his foresight and, often, his bullying, many innovations were introduced in SA's field trialling. Bill is also a master handler and has made up many field champions, among others, FT Ch. Ballyhue's Black Pipit of Donside. Many of his dogs were imported from the UK and laid the foundation of good local working stock.

When the first Field Trial was held in South Africa, it was a natural shoot type of trial, based firmly on the British model. Bill Tait recalls:

"There was a fairly large dam on this farm with an island in the middle. The guns (about six) surrounded the dam. Then all hell broke loose. There were hundreds of ducks, and every now and then you would see the occasional duck fall out of the sky."

As the sport became increasingly popular and more and more dogs were entered, natural shoots became impractical. Nowadays, live birds are released under more controlled circumstances, which gives the dogs a more even chance. Over the years, field trials in SA have become so unrelated to hunting conditions, and so difficult, that only very experienced trainers get anywhere in the placings. The result is that worthy dogs who never attain placings are less frequently considered for breeding, to the possible detriment of the breed.

To overcome this, in 1994, the Field Trial Liaison Council of the Kennel Union of South Africa introduced the concept of 'hunting retrievers', similar to the NAHRA system in the USA. Here, the novice handler is able to enter the dog in tests and trails. However, there are no placings in the trails. The dog either passes or fails set standards. Points are awarded and records kept, and when a dog accumulates enough points, it qualifies as a 'Working Hunting Retriever', by which time it should be proficient in the field. These SAHRA trials are integrated with the existing retriever stakes in the hope that they will enlarge the small breeding pool. The system has already attracted many new handlers and is proving to be very popular.

For many years there has been a great divide between show and field Labradors. But recently there have been indications that 'show' and 'fielders' are coming together again. It is unlikely that we shall see again the achievement of Bernadette and Mike Gie's triple Champion Brigade Highwayman, but several young dogs and bitches are now winning in both the field and the ring. Let us hope that some dual champions within our beloved breed will perpetuate the qualities for which it is famous.

16 HEALTH CARE OF THE LABRADOR

This chapter is intended to give information on the need to maintain your dog in good health. The veterinary surgeon will want to co-operate with you, as the owner of a Labrador, in keeping the animal well for as long a natural life as possible.

Improved diet and preventive vaccinations are contributing to a much longer life for all domestic animals nowadays. Co-operate with your veterinary surgeon by attending for annual booster vaccines, and remember that it is beneficial to allow the dog to be inspected for early signs of disease.

Between visits, you should inspect your dog for any changes in coat condition, breath odour or for any unusual lumps or swellings. The dog's weight should be observed, and it will be helpful to weigh the animal at three-monthly intervals if suitable scales can be found. A grooming routine, followed on a daily basis, will allow the dog to get used to close handling and will also provide the opportunity for the owner to make the sort of regular inspection the veterinary surgeon recommends, to spot the earliest signs of illness.

SELECTING VETERINARY CARE
The choice of a veterinary surgeon may be based on accessibility, but some people like to make enquiries among other Labrador owners they meet, before deciding which veterinary practice will have the greatest sympathy to their dog and their needs. Treatment prices will vary, and it is fairly easy to phone around to enquire about the cost of a booster vaccine or the fee for neutering. Facilities in practices are not all the same, and one with 24-hour nursing staff residing on the premises and equipment for emergency surgery will have to charge more than another surgery, which adequately provides for vaccination and other injections, but requires you to go elsewhere for more complicated procedures.

Pet insurance has proved a great incentive for veterinarians to provide additional equipment and persons with specialist knowledge, because the veterinary surgeon is confident that payment will be made for all treatments given to the insured dog. Just as the vet should be chosen to provide the type of health attention needed, the insurance companies' provisions should be compared to find the one with an annual premium that will deliver the most help in times of difficulty. Remember that, in the UK, booster vaccines, routine neutering and some chronic or inherited disorders are not covered by insurance. Many companies do not pay for visits to a dog in your home, nor pay in full for prescription diets that could be part of your dog's treatment.

GENERAL GROOMING AND HYGIENE
Labrador Retrievers have relatively easy coats to maintain, but they do require daily grooming, especially when they are moulting. Grooming your dog is an ideal time to inspect the body closely, to look for any unexpected abnormalities and at the general condition. The sooner a health problem is noticed, the quicker the veterinary adviser can be asked for an opinion, and the better the chance of a full recovery in the case of a progressive disease or a tumour.

Your Labrador puppy should be groomed from the earliest age, so that the puppy will associate such handling with a pleasurable experience. Procedures will be easier to carry out if this is started early in life. If a dog is used to being handled in this way, it will be far easier for a veterinary surgeon to make an examination, and a visit to the surgery becomes less stressful for the owner as well as the dog. Before you start to groom your Labrador, carry out a thorough physical examination to check for any abnormalities. Always start at the head, as your hands will be cleaner when touching the orifices on the head than after handling the dog's feet and anal region.

EYES: Inspect the eyes first for matter or discharges in the corner. There should be no excessive watering, and the white of the eye should be briefly checked to see that it is not red or discoloured. The surface of the eye should be clear and bright, and the expression one of alertness. There are specific diseases that affect the eyes, so any abnormal signs should be noted and reported to the veterinary surgeon.

EARS: A painful ear can be a very irritating complaint for your dog, so preventing ear problems is important. If there is a noticeable build-up of wax in the ear canal, this can be easily removed by first softening the wax with an ear-cleaning fluid and then wiping gently with cotton wool. The use of cotton wool buds in the ear is discouraged, and all cleaning should be the most gentle possible. There is a range of ear-cleaners suitable for the Labrador, and your veterinary surgeon will advise on the one most appropriate for routine use.

If there is an excessive amount of wax in the ear canal, or if the ear is hot, reddened or swollen, this is an indication of infection or inflammation, and veterinary attention should be sought quickly. Should an infection be left untreated, the dog will scratch the affected ear repeatedly, and often introduce other infections carried on soiled hind toenails. Oozing and multiplying bacteria in the moist discharges will make the ear much worse, and treatment becomes more difficult.

MOUTH: Check your dog's gums each day for redness or inflammation. This can develop as

tartar builds up on the teeth, and food particles get caught at the gum margin. The decaying food will produce breath odour if not removed, and mouth bacteria can result in even worse halitosis. The teeth and gum margins have pain receptors, so any tartar build-up can lead to a disease which puts the dog off food and even causes bad temper.

Canine toothpastes are now available, which can be used to help prevent a build-up of tartar. If the dog's teeth are cleaned regularly, you will avoid a state of dental neglect so advanced that your Labrador needs a general anaesthetic for a scale and polish at the veterinary practice. Start brushing your dog's teeth at about four months of age, but avoid areas where permanent teeth are about to erupt. At first the puppy will want to play, but, little by little, will become used to having all the teeth cleaned. There may be some resistance at first, but it is far easier to get a puppy used to having teeth cleaned while young and small, rather than waiting until you have a fully-grown dog who objects to the procedure.

Puppies lose their milk teeth between four and six months, and sore gums should be noted at that age. Massaging the skin just below the eye will help when molar teeth are about to erupt. While grooming the older dog, look for signs of abnormality such as mouth warts, excess saliva or white froth at the back of the mouth.

NOSE: Again, remove any discharges, and look for cracking or fissuring. There is little point in worrying about the traditional 'cold wet nose' as a health indicator.

SKIN AND COAT: Examine the whole of your dog's body when grooming. Tell-tale black dirt or white scurf may indicate a parasite infection. Patches of hair loss, redness of skin and abnormal lumps may first be found during grooming. Your Labrador's coat will normally have a slight shine, and oil from the sebaceous glands will provide a waterproofing grease that gives a smooth feel as you run your hand over the hair.

NAILS AND FEET: Nails should be kept short, as over-long nails may splinter painfully, especially in cold weather when the nail is brittle. If the dog is regularly walked on hard surfaces such as concrete, paving stones or rocks, the nails will wear down naturally. Tarmac and grass do little to wear nails down at exercise times. Also, once nails grow too long, they become difficult for the dog to wear down, whatever the surface. As a result, the heel takes more of the weight of the leg and the nails may split, with painful consequences.

Clipping nails is a delicate task. If you cut too short, into the quick, blood will flow and the dog will find it painful. Filing may be safer for the beginner than cutting across the nail with new sharp clippers.

Make a habit of feeling the area between the toes, where tufts of hair attract sticky substances, clay soils form hard little balls between the toes, and tar or chewing gum can be picked up on a walk. You will notice any cuts or pad injuries while handling your Labrador's feet for grooming.

PERINEUM AND GENITAL AREA: Check for swollen anal sacs or unexpected discharges. Segments of tapeworms might be seen near the rectum. A bitch's vulva should not discharge, except when signs of heat are present. The prepuce of a male dog should have no discharge, and the penis should not protrude except if the dog is inadvertently excited during grooming or handling.

GROOMING: Once the first physical examination has been carried out, a grooming routine for your Labrador should be followed. Here is one I recommend:

1. Using your fingertips, massage the coat against the normal backward lay of the hairs. This will loosen dead hairs and encourage the skin to secrete the sebum oil that gives the healthy shine.
2. Use a bristle brush to pick up the hair you have loosened, again working against the lay of the coat.
3. Using a metal-toothed comb, you can now work your way in a methodical manner over the dog's body.
4. Finally, to finish and to bring a shine to the coat, use a bristle brush down the back and limbs. Brush the neck and head, praising the dog or offering a small food reward.

PREVENTIVE CARE – VACCINATION
The use of vaccines to prevent disease is well-established for human as well as animal health. The longer life of the animal, and the comparative rarity of puppy disease and early death are things that have been taken for granted in the last 40 years. Yet many older people remember ill puppies dying of distemper fits, or left twitching with chorea for the rest of their lives. The appearance of Parvovirus in 1979 was an unpleasant shock to those who thought that veterinary treatment could deal with all puppy diarrhoeas. There were many deaths in puppies under twelve months old until they developed immunity either through their mother's milk or when the puppy's own body defences became mature enough to respond to a vaccine injected.

Your veterinarian is the best person to advise on the type of vaccines to use and at what ages to give them, since he or she will have a unique knowledge of the type of infection prevalent in a locality and when infection is likely to strike.

An example of this is in the Guide Dogs for the Blind Association's breeding programme where, for many years, early vaccination was given to the six-week-old puppy. No isolation after this early vaccination was needed. This was contrary to general advice given in the 60s and 70s when figures for puppy disease were acceptably low. Later, when Parvovirus infection was widespread in the early 80s, the mortality rate of GDBA puppies was much lower than among breeders who retained puppies in kennels until 12 weeks or older. The temperament of some breeds was suspect due to a longer enforced isolation after vaccination, and proper socialisation did not take place as the new owners of puppies were advised not to take them out until four months of age, after a final Parvovirus booster had been given. This meant that there were no opportunities to mix with people and other dogs until an age when the older puppy had already developed a fear of being handled by strangers, or was suspicious of other dogs met outside the home.

DISTEMPER: This is the classic virus disease which has become very rare where vaccine is used on a regular basis. From time to time, it is seen in larger UK cities where there is a stray or roaming dog population. This may subsequently lead to infection of show or other kennel dogs who do not have a high level of immunity.

The virus has an incubation period of seven to 21 days, and is followed by a rise in temperature, loss of appetite, a cough and, often, diarrhoea. Discharges from the eyes and nose may be watery at first, but often turn into thick mucoid with a green or creamy colour, due to secondary infections. The teeth are affected when a puppy under six months of age is infected by the virus, and enamel defects show as brown marks – they last for life and are known as 'distemper teeth'.

The 'hard pad' strain seen in the 60s is now considered to be nothing more than hyperkeratosis of the nose and footpads that occurs after all distemper infections, although the name is still in use when dog illness is written or talked about. In over half of all dogs affected with Distemper, damage to the nervous system will manifest itself as fits, chorea (twitching of muscles) or posterior paralysis. Old dogs may develop Encephalitis (ODE), due to latent Distemper virus in the nervous tissue. The vaccines in use today are all modified live vaccines, and highly effective in preventing disease. The age for a first injection will partly depend on the maker's instruction sheet, and partly on a knowledge of the amount of protection passed from the mother to the young puppies. Maternally derived immunity (MDI) might block the vaccine in a young puppy, but blood sampling of bitches during their pregnancy is now used as a method of estimating how soon the puppy will respond to vaccine. The use of a first vaccine at six weeks is becoming more widespread, and this allows for the all-important early socialisation period in the puppy's development.

PARVOVIRUS: This is probably the second most important canine virus disease in Europe and, like Distemper, is largely preventable by the correct use of vaccination. The speed with which an infection could spread from kennel to kennel surprised many, but the disease is caused by a very tough virus that can be carried on footwear which has walked though virus-infected faeces. It may then persist for up to a year, untouched by many commonly-used kennel disinfectants. The sudden death of puppies, caused by damage to the heart muscle, often just after purchase, is no longer seen, but the gastro-enteritis form of Parvovirus still occurs.

This sudden illness takes the form of repeated vomiting in the first 24 hours, followed by profuse watery diarrhoea, often with a characteristic sour smell and a red-brown colour. The cause of death was often from severe dehydration that accompanied this loss of fluid and, once it was understood that puppies could be treated with intravenous fluids similar to those used in the treatment of human cholera victims, the death rate fell. Fluids by mouth are sufficient in less severe cases, provided they contain the electrolytes that need to be replaced. The traditional mixture of a level teaspoonful of salt and a dessertspoonful of glucose in two pints of water has saved many dogs' lives. Vaccination of the young puppy is recommended, though the MDI may partially block the effectiveness of the vaccine, as seen with Distemper. A live vaccine at six weeks, followed by a further dose at 12 weeks will protect most puppies. The four-month booster is no longer in common use, but it is now more usual to see Parvovirus in the recently-weaned puppy or the five-month-old puppy, where immunity no longer protects that individual against infection.

HEPATITIS: This disease, produced by an *adenovirus,* is now quite rare, but one form (CAV-2) is often associated with Kennel Cough infection in dogs. After infection, the virus multiplies in the lymphatic system and then sets out to damage the lining of the blood vessels. It was for this reason that the cause of death was liver failure. The name Hepatitis was given because, on post mortem, the dog's liver was seen to be very swollen and engorged with blood. Other organs are also damaged, and about 70 per cent of recovered dogs are found to have kidney damage. The eye damage known as 'blue eye' seen on recovery is not recognised in the Labrador, but was quite common in certain other breeds. Vaccination at six and 12 weeks, using a reliable vaccine that contains the CAV-2 virus, is very effective as a preventive measure against Hepatitis.

LEPTOSPIROSIS: This disease is caused by bacteria, unlike the previous group of viral infections. Protection has to be provided by at least two doses of a killed vaccine, and a 12-monthly repeat dose of this vaccine is essential if the protection is to be maintained. The type of Leptospirosis spread by rats is the most devastating to the dog and frequently results in jaundice then death from kidney and liver failure unless early treatment with antibiotics is available. The other serotype of leptospira that damages the dog's kidney is seen less often since vaccination and annual boosters have been regularly used. Gundogs and pet Labradors who walk in the country where rats may have contaminated water courses are especially at risk, although sometimes dogs kept entirely in kennels may be affected if rats cross the exercise yards and leave infected urine for the dog to sniff at or lick up.

KENNEL COUGH: As a troublesome infection that causes harsh coughing in dogs, originating from the trachea and bronchial tubes, Kennel Cough is one of the best known canine diseases. Labradors may become infected in boarding kennels, or perhaps after coming within droplet infection distance of dogs coughing at shows, or in public exercise areas. There are five known viral and bacterial agents that may all, or perhaps two of them at a time, cause Kennel Cough. Vaccination by nose drops of a *Bordetella* vaccine can be offered to provide protection, and is often given just a week before a dog goes into kennels. The normal booster vaccine contains protection against three of the other known causes.

The disease develops within four to seven days of infection, so it may not be evident until after a dog has left the kennels. The deep harsh cough is often described "as if a bone or something was stuck in the throat." The dog coughs repeatedly. Even with treatment, coughs last for 14 days, but in some dogs the cough carries on as long as six weeks. Infection may then persist in the trachea, and the dog, if a 'carrier', may get subsequent attacks when stressed. This explains why some non-coughing dogs put into board may cause an outbreak of kennel cough. Once a summertime disease, Kennel Cough outbreaks now occur at any time of the year, often after a holiday period when more dogs than usual are boarded.

RABIES: This virus disease is almost unknown to most UK veterinarians, due to a successful quarantine policy that has kept the island free of rabies in dogs and in wildlife such as foxes. There is some debate as to how much longer this quarantine policy can be maintained, and a proposal to switch to a compulsory vaccination and identification policy for all dogs remains controversial, with arguments in favour of either course. It has been estimated that 75 per cent of a dog population must be vaccinated at any one time to delay the spread of this disease. The virus disease must always be rigorously controlled in animals because of the devastating effect of one human becoming infected with rabies. Inactivated rabies vaccine is available for use in the UK in dogs intended for export. Elsewhere in the world, both live attenuated vaccines and inactivated vaccines are used on an annual basis.

BOOSTERS: Thanks to the development of effective canine vaccines by the pharmaceutical industry, most of the diseases described above are now uncommon in Europe and North America. The need for an annual booster is essential to keep up a high level of immunity where killed vaccines are used, and with live virus vaccines it probably does no harm to inject repeat doses every year. It is easy to become

'It has been estimated that 75 per cent of a dog population must be vaccinated at any one time to delay the spread of Rabies'

complacent about the absence of infectious disease in Labradors, and it is false economy to overlook the need for re-vaccination.

PARASITES
INTERNAL PARASITES
ROUNDWORMS: The most common worms in puppies and dogs up to one year of age are *Toxocara* and *Toxascaris*. Puppies with roundworms start to pass worm eggs as early as three weeks, and most when about seven weeks of age. This is the most dangerous time for the environment to be contaminated with eggs, especially for young children who play with the puppies first, then lick their fingers, thus catching Zoonotic Toxocariasis.

Adult dogs also pass roundworms, which can be seen emerging from the rectum of a nursing bitch who develops diarrhoea. Worms may also appear in the vomit if the worm moves forward from the intestine into the stomach by accident.

Control of worms depends on frequent dosing of young puppies from as early as two weeks of age, repeated every two to three weeks until three months old. To prevent puppies from carrying worms, the pregnant bitch can be wormed from the 42nd day of pregnancy with a safe, licensed wormer, such as fenbendazole. The worming treatment can be given daily to the bitch until the second day after all the puppies are born. Routine worming of adults twice a year with a combined tablet for roundworms and tapeworms is a good preventive measure. With young children in the household, even more frequent worm dosing may be advisable to reduce the risk of migrating roundworm larvae in the child, and possible eye damage.

TAPEWORMS: These are not known to kill dogs, but the appearance of a wriggling segment coming through the rectum, or moving on the tail hair, is enough to deter all but the most unsqueamish dog lover. The biggest threat is from the *Echinococcus* worm that a dog ingests if feeding from raw sheep offal.The worm is only six millimetres long, but several thousand can live in one dog. If a human should swallow a segment of this worm, it may move to the person's liver or lungs, in the same way as it would in the sheep. A major illness would be the unfortunate result, another example of a zoonotic infection.The most frequently-found tapeworm is *Dipylidium caninum*. It is not a long tapeworm compared with the old-fashioned *Taenia* worms, but when segments break off they may be recognised, as they resemble grains of rice attached to the hairs of the tail. The tapeworm has become more common in dogs and cats since the number of fleas has increased, as the intermediate host of this worm is the flea or the louse. When dogs groom themselves, they attempt to swallow any crawling insect on the skin surface and in this way may become infested with tapeworms even though worming is carried out twice a year. Flea control is just as important as worming in preventing tapeworm infection. Three-monthly dosing with tablets is a good idea, less frequently if the dog is known to be away from sources of re-infection.

The other tapeworms of the *Taenia* species come from dogs eating raw rabbits (*T serialis* or *pisiformis*) or from sheep, cattle or pig offal (*T ovis, hydatigena* or *multiceps*).

HOOKWORMS: Hookworms and others are less frequently a cause of trouble in the UK. The hookworm damages the dog's intestine by using its teeth on the lining. *Uncinaria* may be the cause of poor condition and thinness, and *Ancylostoma* can be the reason for anaemia and weakness.

HEARTWORMS AND OTHERS
Heartworms are almost unknown in most of the UK, but are a great problem in other countries and states. Bladder worms are only detected when urine samples are examined. They are similar to the whipworms found in the large intestine and identified when samples are examined after mucoid dysentry affects a dog.

Giardia is a parasite that occurs in dogs in kennels. It should be investigated in dogs with diarrhoea who have come through quarantine. It is a protozoal organism that likes to live in stagnant surface water, and is of especial interest because a similar strain is a cause of dysentry in humans, especially where water-borne infection is blamed for the illness.

ECTOPARASITES

External parasites may cause intense irritation and skin diseases from scratching and rubbing. In recent years, the cat flea has become by far the most common ectoparasite of the Labrador, but more traditional sarcoptic mange, lice and ringworm skin infections do appear from time to time.

FLEAS: The flea that hops may never be seen in the Labrador's coat, but its presence may be detected by the flea dirt or excreta containing dried blood. Grooming your dog over white paper or a light table top may reveal black bits that have dark red blood stains when moistened. Once the flea dirt is found, a closer inspection of the dog may show fleas running though the coat at skin level. At one time they were more likely to live in the hair down the spine towards the tail head, but now they are found in the shorter hairs of the abdomen or neck. This may be due to the fact that cat fleas are the most commonly found variety in UK dogs. Such fleas prefer a softer hair structure for their 'living space'. All fleas are temporary visitors, who like to feed from the dog by biting to suck blood, but in their development and egg-laying stages they may live freely off the dog thereby escaping some of the anti-parasitic dressing put on their host's coat. Re-infestation then becomes possible, and many flea treatments appear to be ineffective unless the flea in the environment is eliminated at the same time.

There is a wide range of anti-parasitic sprays, washes and baths available, and the Labrador owner may well be confused as to how and when to apply these. There is the further problem that some dogs seem able to carry a few fleas on them with very little discomfort, while others exhibit intense irritation and will bite pieces out of themselves in an attempt to catch a single flea. A cat in the household or crossing the garden may drop flea eggs, and in a warm place they can hatch out and develop into more fleas waiting to jump on to the dog.

Flea eggs and immature larvae may lie dormant for months, waiting to complete their development and become ready to bite. Adult fleas too can live for months off an animal, until they become able to find a host to feed from, so treating the dog is only tackling part of the problem. The kennels or the house must be treated as well. Vacuum-cleaning and easy-to-clean sleeping quarters for the dog help enormously in dealing with a flea infestation, once an environmental spray has been applied. The choice of aerosol spray, medicated bath, tablet by mouth or agent that stops larval development is a wide one, and experience will show which method is most suitable when your particular dog is affected.

LICE: These may be found in the dog's coat occasionally, especially on a Labrador leading more of an outdoor life than the average pet dog. Lice spend their whole life on the dog, and fairly close contact between dogs is necessary to spead these parasites. Large numbers of lice cause intense irritation with hair loss. Biting lice can produce anaemia when they are present in large enough numbers to remove blood continuously, at a rate similar to a bleeding ulcer. Liquid treatments applied as a total bath soak are best. Lice eggs can be transmitted from dog to dog on grooming brushes. The lice and their eggs are visible to the naked eye, and should be spotted during your normal grooming routine.

MANGE MITES: These mites cannot be seen during grooming. If they are suspected, scrapings from the skin surface are sent for examination under the microscope. The two forms of mange, *Sarcoptes* and *Demodex*, can be distinguished in this way, but bare skin patches of low grade mange infection may at first seem similar when a dog is examined. There are a number of differences in the two forms of mange that I will not enumerate here, but a simple distinction is that sarcoptic mange is very itchy and spreads, while demodectic mange in the older dog usually remains as a scaly, hairless patch and, although an obvious blemish, does not cause a lot of itching. Anti-parasitic baths with pyrethroids or amitraz, and topical applications of organophosphorous washes will have to be repeated, but are usually effective.

TICKS: Ticks are large enough not to be

missed, and can be expected on gundogs who work where sheep, hedgehogs etc. leave tick eggs about. Applications of pyrethroid or other 'spot' liquids on the neck and rump will keep ticks off a dog for a month. Baths are also effective. Ticks may be removed by first soaking them in vegetable oil, then gently coaxing and lifting the tick's head away from the dog's skin.

CHEYLETIELLA: These cause surface irritation of dogs and intense itching in humans who happen to get bitten. The so-called 'moving dandruff' show up as white flecks on a black Labrador's skin, but may be more difficult to see on a light-coloured dog. Anti-parasitic shampoos will kill the surface feeder, but carrier dogs in kennels may show very few symptoms at all.

MALASEZZIA: This is a yeast-like surface organsim that appears in dogs with low resistance to infection. A patchy coat and dull hair appearance should make a Labrador owner suspect the presence of yeasts in unusually large numbers. Once identified, baths and general hygiene, with improved nutrition, will help your dog to overcome this problem. The yeast will also be found in the ear canal and, if shown to be present on a stained smear in large numbers, the ear should be treated with Miconazole, Nystatin or Thiabendazole.

RINGWORM: Ringworm is found in dogs as a fungal infection of the hairs. The signs of a 'ring' are not always present, and some dogs show quite a violent skin response once infected. Cattle ringworm can be transmitted to country dogs. Ringworm spores can remain in the environment and in old woodwork for a long time. Diagnosis by skin tests is slow but reliable, as the 'Woods' lamp, which uses ultra-violet light, does not identify all types of ringworm. Treatment with anti-fungal washes, or the antibiotic griseofulvin, may be used to eliminate the mycotic infection.

ACCIDENTS AND FIRST AID

The few simple procedures described here do not suggest that there are no other things that can be done as 'first aid', but in most cases the sooner the patient is taken to the veterinary surgery, the better the chance of a full recovery may be. For this reason, splinting broken bones is now out of favour, and more pain may be caused than if the dog is quickly transported to a place where any shock and pain can be treated professionally. X-rays will better show the nature of a fracture, and what is the best method of treatment.

TRAFFIC ACCIDENTS: Labradors, being solid dogs, seldom go underneath vehicles, but they tend to suffer severe chest injuries if hit in front, or pelvic and limb injuries if struck on the side. A dog hit by a car will be distressed and through fright and pain will tend to bite, even when its familiar owners attempt to help. First, assess the injuries, noting any gaping holes and where blood is being lost. Do this before touching the dog's head. Some frightened dogs may try to run away at that point, so a lead or scarf round the neck will help to steady the dog, and a tape muzzle may have to be used before a dog is lifted into a vehicle for transport to the surgery.

A pressure bandage applied to a bleeding area is the best way of staunching blood flow, but improvisation with whatever cloth is to hand is acceptable in a life-saving situation. The dog may be breathing rapidly or gasping with 'air hunger' signs. In this case, the mouth and nostrils should be wiped free of dried blood or saliva to help unblock the airway. If you suspect a spinal injury, slide a board under the dog before picking it up. Otherwise, a blanket is the best way of allowing two or more persons to pick up an injured dog without aggravating the injuries.

CHOKING AND VOMITING: Try to find out the cause of any sudden attack. Grass awns may enter the throat and airways in the summer months, and, at any time of year, a dog playing

'A dog hit by a car will be distressed and through fright and pain will tend to bite, even when its familiar owners attempt to help'

ball or stick retrieval games may get an obstruction at the back of the throat. Even a fine bamboo cane may become wedged across the upper molar teeth. In the case of one Labrador, who had been out shooting all day, a length of cane was retrieved from the upper part of the oesophagus the same evening. Poisonous substances cause retching and vomiting in dogs, and thirsty animals have been known to drink from toilet bowls or lap up bleach and other cleaning substances.

Having initially looked for a foreign body, your first aid measures should be aimed at providing as good an air supply as possible. If there is any blistering or soreness of the lips or tongue, use honey or salad oil to coat the inflamed surfaces. A vomiting dog should be prevented from drinking water and regurgitating it as fast as it is swallowed. Ice cubes left to melt in a dish may be a way of helping the dog, as it will drink the iced water slowly.

COLLAPSE AND UNCONSCIOUSNESS: As in the road accident, assess the dog before touching to determine the cause of the incident, so that appropriate first aid can be given. A dog running in a field on a warm day may have had a circulatory collapse; another dog convulsing may be throwing an epileptic fit; an elderly dog found semi-conscious in the morning after voiding urine and faeces may have had a stroke or vestibular disease. Each condition will need different treatment, but, as a general rule, pull the tongue forward to ensure there is an airway to the lungs, keep the animal cool, and avoid unnecessary noise and commotion. Look for any drugs or poisons the dog may have swallowed, gently feel the left side for gas distending the abdomen, and check the pupils of the eyes and their response to a bright light. The veterinary surgeon will be better able to deal with the situation if a timetable of events, and any contributing factors, can be given in a concise manner.

WASP STINGS: Stings occur more often in late summer. Usually the foot swells rapidly or, if the dog has caught a wasp in its mouth, the side of the face swells up and the eye may become partly shut. Vinegar is a traditional remedy to

apply to the sting area. If an antihistamine tablet is available, this can be given to the dog immediately to stop further swelling.

Biting flies cause swellings on the body, and may be the cause of the 'hot spots' or acute moist eczemas that Labradors can suffer from. Calamine lotions cool the skin but, if licked, calamine causes vomiting.

SHOCK: This occurs to a greater or lesser extent with nearly all accidents. Keep the patient warm, wrapping a blanket, coat or wool garment around the body of the dog. Unless you have reason to think an anaesthetic will be given, or other contraindications exist, offer fluids by mouth in small quantities. Oral rehydration solutions can be obtained from your veterinary surgeon, and a packet should be kept in every emergency first-aid kit. As an alternative, a solution of half a teaspoon of salt and half a teaspoon of bicarbonate of soda dissolved in a litre of water may be given a few dessertspoonfuls at a time.

SKIN DISEASES
PARASITIC SKIN DISEASES: Such diseases are probably still the most common problem in Labradors, and next is atopic dermatitis. (See Chapter Sixteen: Breed Associated Diseases.)

Flea bites may not be obvious, especially in a dense-coated breed. Once a dog becomes sensitised to the proteins injected by the flea when it first bites, any subsequent contact with flea saliva may bring on an itchy rash, even though no live fleas are found on the dog. The various other causes of parasitic skin disease have already been outlined in the section on external parasites.

OTHER PRURITIC SKIN CONDITIONS: Anal sac irritation will cause a dog to nibble at the hair around the tail base, or it may be responsible for a dog licking and nibbling anywhere around the hindquarters. The glands may be so impacted that they cannot be emptied out during the straining necessary to pass faeces. An infected lining of one or both sacs may also be the cause of irritation, and this can often be detected by a fruity odour to the sac's contents, or, at its worst, a smell like rotten meat.

Bacterial dermatoses result from multiplication of skin bacteria such as *Staph. intermedius.* Red blotches and ring-like marks around a central pustule are most clearly seen when the hairless areas of the abdomen are inspected. Skin swabs may be used to identify the bacteria present, and this information can then be used to choose the most appropriate antibiotic for the infection causing the irritation.

HAIR LOSS AND ALOPECIA: A Labrador's coat is normally shed twice a year, but sometimes the growth of new hair is delayed and the coat appears thin, lifeless and, if groomed excessively, bare patches can develop. Investigations into the possibility of thyroid disease may be needed when there is a failure of hair to grow. Other hormonal skin disease may cause symmetrical hair loss on the flanks of a bitch, or bare tail head areas (stud tail) in some dogs. Veterinary advice should be sought.

DIGESTIVE SYSTEM DISORDERS
SICKNESS AND DIARRHOEA: Occasional sickness is not a cause for concern in the younger dog. The dog is adapted to feeding from a wide range of different foods, and part of natural protection against food poisoning is the ability to reject unsuitable foods by returning them from the stomach via reflex vomiting. If there is a yellow coloration to the vomit, it means that the bile from the liver, which normally passes into the small intestine after leaving the bile duct, has for some reason been passed forward to enter the stomach. The bitter bile acids will cause reflex vomiting as soon as they reach the stomach wall, and will be sicked up, together with any food left in the stomach.

Repeated sickness, starting off with recognisable food followed by slime, or food followed by mucus alone, is a more serious sign. It may be associated with obstructions due to a foreign body, or to infection such as Pyometra or Hepatitis. Some outbreaks of diarrhoea will start with food being vomited, as this will stimulate the intestine. As soon as the food enters the small intestine, then the stomach empties itself reflexly, by vomiting any food remaining within the stomach. Sometimes a reversal of the normal flow of food will cause the appearance of a faecal vomit.

Diarrhoea is the passage of frequent loose or unformed faeces: it is associated with infections and irritation of the intestine. The rapid transit of food taken in by mouth means that water cannot be absorbed by the large intestine, and soft or runny stools result from the incomplete digestion and water reabsorption. When blood is present, it may appear as streaks from the large intestine. If blackish and foul-smelling, it means that the blood has come from the small intestine and been subjected to some of the digestive fluids. The condition is then known as dysentry.

Chronic diarrhoea is a condition in which the looseness of faeces lasts more than 48 hours. It may be associated with malabsorption, when the lining of the intestine is incapable of absorbing digested food. Alternatively, diseases such as food intolerances, bacterial overgrowth, lymphoid and other tumours may be the cause, or maldigestion, when there is a failure of the digestive juices to break down the food. Other causes include Exocrine Pancreatic Insufficiency (EPI), inflammatory bowel diseases, or any disturbance in gastric or liver function. Investigations by the veterinary surgeon will include blood tests and faecal laboratory examinations. These may be followed by X-rays or endoscope examinations.

The treatment of sickness and diarrhoea involves, firstly, withholding solid food for 24 hours, giving small quantities of replacement fluids as soon as the dog stops vomiting (proprietary electrolyte fluids are probably best), then introducing a highly digestible food in about one third of the normal quantity, fed on the second day of the illness. This amount should be increased slowly, until, by the fourth day, a full ration of food is given again. In the recovery period, fats should be avoided, as well as milk and dairy products, due to the dog's inability to digest lactose.

GASTRIC DILATION: This disease is better-known as Bloat, and 'torsion' can be a problem in any of the larger breeds. It is especially associated with feeding regimes in which a highly digestible food can be swallowed rapidly, combined with the consumption of large quantities of water which contribute to the development of the bloat. Feeding immediately after strenuous exercise has also been blamed. When a dog is fed in the late afternoon or evening, there is the chance of the dog lying down, so that abdominal movement associated with walking or jumping up does not allow for eructation, or the dispersal of gas from the stomach. Greedy feeders who swallow air as they gulp down their food are considered at greatest risk, but this problem does seem associated with flat slab-chest dogs, who have large deep chests and thus suspended stomachs.

The bloated stomach may rotate as a 'torsion' or volvulus, and become a Gastric Dilation and Volvulus condition (known as GDV), which means an acute emergency. The dog needs to be rushed to the veterinary surgery for treatment of shock and for deflation of the stomach. Affected dogs seem uncomfortable, become depressed and look at their flanks with expressions of disbelief. At first, the left side just behind the ribs is the only side to bulge, and tapping with the your fingertips will produce a drum-like resonance over the left rib cage edge, and over the distended abdomen behind. Within a few hours both sides of the abdomen appear distended behind the rib cage, the dog becomes more uncomfortable and lies down a lot as the pain increases. The gas-filled stomach presses on the diaphragm restricting the breathing, the colour of the tongue becomes more purplish and breaths are more frequent and quite shallow. Some time at this stage, the weight of the enlarging spleen attached to the greater curvature of the gas-filled stomach makes the stomach twist in a clockwise direction. The signs of discomfort become more noticeable as the stomach's exit to the oesophagus is pinched off by a 180-degree rotation. If a stomach tube is passed through the mouth down the oesophagus at this stage, the tube can be pressed down no further than just beyond the entrance level of the oesophagus into the abdomen. No gas will pass back up the tube, even though the stomach is still tight and filled with gas.

Emergency treatment at the veterinary surgery will usually mean setting up an intravenous drip to deal with the shock. Decompression of the stomach will be attempted, possibly first by using the stomach tube as described above, or, probably more successfully, by inserting a wide-bore (18 G needle) canula at the point behind the left rib arch that shows the most distension by gas. The finger should then be kept on the needle hub protruding through the skin, partially to hold it in place as the size of the stomach reduces, and partially to vent the gas out slowly or in 'pulses'. This ensures that the blood in the veins can start to flow towards the heart again, once the abdomen size returns to normal. Frequently, a laparotomy will be necessary to empty the stomach or to provide a means of fixing the stomach to the abdominal wall, so that an adhesion will make it less likely that gas distension will appear again.

CONSTIPATION: This disorder usually occurs either through your Labrador eating too many bones whose chalky residue clogs up the rectum, or, in older male dogs, it may be associated with enlargement of the prostate gland. Treatment with lubricants and enemas should be followed by high-fibre diets. Soluble fibre, as found in oatmeal, is thought to add to the moist faecal bulk and thus retain water from the large intestine lumen, so that the faeces are not bone hard and painful to pass. Allow exercise, or place the dog in the garden 30 minutes after feeding, as this will stimulate the reflexes for normal defecation.

BREEDING AND REPRODUCTION
There are no specific problems in the Labrador breed, and both mating and whelping should proceed with the minimum of trouble (see Chapter Ten: Breeding Labradors).

THE OLDER LABRADOR
GERIATRIC CARE: The Labrador is a relatively long-lived breed. Ten to 12 years of age is considered a good age for a working dog, but many Labradors may live to 15 years, provided they avoid accidents and injuries. The tendency for Labradors to overeat if food is available leads to adiposity and will significantly shorten

a dog's life. Some of the oldest dogs are also the leanest, so dietary control helps if you wish your dog to live longer. After about ten years of age, it may be advantageous to divide the daily ration into two small feeds to help absorption and digestion. Any tendency to overweight must be checked, and regular weighing helps to control dietary intake. The older dog will use up less energy in exercise and, if housed for most of the day, fewer calories will be burned up to keep the dog warm. Some reduction in calorie intake is desirable, and there are special diets prepared for the older dog which are higher in fibre and lower in calories than the diet for the younger dog.

Keep a careful watch on the condition of your Labrador's mouth, as breath odour is one of the first signs of dental disease or of decay of food trapped between the gums and 'ledges' of tartar that may have built up on the teeth. Labradors may have cracked teeth from chewing bones earlier in their life, and only in old age does the tooth root become infected, followed by the development of an abscess. The back upper molar teeth are often affected, and an abscess will show as a swelling immediately below the eye if the carnassial tooth has infected roots. Chewing as a form of jaw exercise is one method of keeping teeth healthy, but, when there is a build-up of plaque on the tooth surface, cleaning the teeth using an ultrasonic scaler, followed by a machine polish, is a better way of keeping a healthy mouth.

Monitor the length of your Labrador's nails, since less exercise and possible arthritis sometimes lead the older dog to put less weight on the affected leg, so that nail overgrowth occurs. Careful trimming to avoid cutting into the 'quick', or live part of the nail, will help many older Labradors. Elbows too should be inspected for calluses on their outer side, as dogs who are stiff do not move as often as they might to relieve their body weight on the surface they sleep on. The skin over the outside of the elbow has little padding from fat or muscle and bone lies just underneath, so leathery skin or a callus can easily occur. In extreme cases the callus develops cracks and fissures, and a bacterial infection is set up so that the surface becomes pink and oozing.

URINARY INCONTINENCE: This is one of the problems found in older dogs. Leakage from the bladder, resulting in damp patches on bedding overnight, may be remedied by removing the water bowl after 7pm to prevent evening drinking. Also effective is the possible use of one of the sympathomimetic group of drugs to promote bladder storage. A urine sample should be examined: sometimes mild cystistis and bacteria will be found in the urine, and treatment with an appropriate antibiotic will reduce bladder sensitivity and storage will be better. If large quantities of urine are being voided day and night, then investigation of urine concentrations and blood biochemistry tests is necessary to rule out major disease. Diabetes Insipidus or Mellitus, Cushing's disease and Nephrosis may all be first detected if a dog is incontinent when left shut up indoors. Blood tests are necessary to distinguish many of these conditions in the older Labrador.

16 *BREED ASSOCIATED DISEASES*

A number of diseases which are seen in Labradors will be dealt with in this chapter, as some are thought to have a genetic basis. Some digestive disorders probably spring from the fact that the Labrador is a working dog, bred through generations for retrieving game birds. When kept in a domestic situation, the breed may become more susceptible to diseases related to scavenging and eating whatever becomes available.

Other diseases such as Retinal Atrophy have a strong genetic basis, and can be progressively bred out, but a recessive gene is involved. The condition can be identified in the young dog, so affected animals can be stopped from being used in a breeding programme. There is a lot of inconclusive evidence about some of the conditions described, and the most common sorts of eye diseases now found in Labradors (Posterior Pole Cataract and Retinal Dysplasia) seem to cause very little disturbance to most working dogs' vision. It is important to recognise all these conditions and, whenever possible, breed from affected dogs only on a limited scale, until the puppies can be examined to see if the condition is more frequent or more severe in the next generation.

INHERITED EYE CONDITIONS
In the USA the control of eye disorders is supervised by CERF, and Diplomates of the Veterinary College of Ophthalmology are the only veterinarians authorised to certify that dogs are free of hereditary eye disease. The situation for eye certification in Europe is more complicated, as there is no one central body to issue a European certificate. The position of certification in countries such as Holland and Sweden is on a par with that of the UK. The UK scheme, administered by the British Veterinary Association and the Kennel Club, is based on certification by veterinary surgeons who have special certificates as eye examiners. In such countries as France and Germany the certification situation is more variable, and panels of eye examiners are often appointed by individual groups of breeders.

LENS DISORDERS
CATARACT (POSTERIOR POLE TYPE): The lens of the eye has a front surface that bends the light to focus it on the retina, and a back surface adjacent to the vitreous jelly which holds the retina in place. The type of cataract most often found in Golden Retrievers, and which also occurs in Labrador Retrievers, usually causes only a minor disturbance in vision. Known as 'pp' (posterior pole) cataract, it produces an opacity affecting the back of the lens at its centre – the part closest to the retina. Due to the multi-layered nature of a lens, the cataract just inside the lens capsule appears where the lines converge as an inverted letter Y. It seldom causes a total lens opacity, but is not infrequently seen when an ophthalmoscope is used by the veterinary surgeon to inspect the eye. In the guide dog breeding programme, despite attempts to totally eliminate pp cataract from the breeding lines, it is seen in both Labradors and in Golden Retrievers, and equally in first cross matings of the two breeds when working dogs are bred in this way purposely. Parents both

clear of pp cataract have produced puppies who develop pp cataracts later in life, so it would seem that a recessive gene with a late-onset factor in some individuals may be responsible.

HEREDITARY CATARACT: Congenital cataract, that is, a cataract seen at birth or soon after the eyes open, is not a Labrador breed problem. An opacity of the lens would be seen as a white reflective object in the eye, and a congenital cataract would be found soon after the puppy's eyelids open. A dominant gene for this form of cataract occurs in the Golden Retriever but is not found in the Labrador Retriever.

LATE-ONSET CATARACTS: Cataracts that appear in the lens of this breed later in life are less likely to be hereditary. An opacity in the lens may develop at any age, and may be due to an injury to the eye resulting from a blow to the face or a penetrating foreign body, such as a blackthorn. In a metabolic disease such as Diabetes Mellitus, cataracts may form in both eyes. They have a characteristic 'water cleft' appearance. Some toxic substances will damage the lens, while a nutritional deficiency may also result in cataracts. Other conditions affecting the rest of the eye, such as Glaucoma and Uveitis, may develop and cause a cataract as a complication.

RETINA DISORDERS
GENERALISED PROGRESSIVE RETINAL ATROPHY (GPRA): This type of eye disease, first described by Parry in 1953 as affecting Irish Setters, was commonly known as night blindness because it was in the dim light near to dusk that affected dogs were most likely to become lost. GPRA was successfully bred out in Irish Setters, as it was inherited through a dominant gene and with the small numbers then present in the breed it was easy to control. Once breeders knew how the disease spread, and they all stopped using affected dogs for mating, the condition became rare in litters of puppies. At the time, it was commonly known as 'PRA' and it was found that other breeds, such as Poodles, might develop a similar PRA. However, this

appeared later in life, so was more difficult to breed out. Later, specialists realised that there was yet another sort of PRA, so the term 'Generalised Progressive Retinal Atrophy' (GPRA) was used to describe the first type, in which the photoreceptors of the retina actually degenerate.

The Labrador has a late-onset form of PRA, which may be detected by the ophthalmoscope, well before the dog shows any signs of blindness at four to six years of age. There is a gradual degeneration of the photoreceptors that receive the light at the back of the eye, and the blindness develops very slowly. The condition is different from other forms of blindness, as the dog can still constrict the pupils when a bright light is directed at his eye, so there is never a total loss of response to light.

Detailed examination of the retina is made with an ophthalmoscope by a veterinary surgeon, and certification under the Kennel Club/British Veterinary Association scheme can be be made in the UK at three years of age in the Labrador breed. Re-inspection of the eyes every year is recommended, as some dogs do not exhibit GPRA until later in life.

CENTRAL PROGRESSIVE RETINAL ATROPHY (CPRA): This eye condition is a retinal pigment dystrophy of the epithelium. Unlike the other form of retinal atrophy, this one takes the form of daytime blindness. The centre of the retina, where the cones of light receptors are most closely packed, becomes damaged so the sight deteriorates in the brightest light conditions.

The disease is mainly seen in UK-bred dogs, and both Labrador Retrievers and Golden Retrievers can suffer from it. Fortunately, this form of eye disorder rarely progresses to total blindness. CPRA is becoming quite rare. Light brown spots on the reflective part of the retina are the characteristics the veterinary surgeon looks for. There is an inherited failure of the retina to get rid of waste products after light falls on its photoreceptor layer. Local antioxidant deficiency and abnormal lipid metabolism are other factors in the profile of this retinal disease. For this reason, it was associated with feeding dogs on tripe diets that are low in Vitamin E, and other protective constituents. When these waste products accumulate to excess, the cell dies and an area of the retina, usually near the centre, also dies and shows brown coloration. Dogs develop blindness only slowly from two to three years of age onwards, but they may have lost a considerable amount of vision by eight years of age before the owner really becomes aware of their partial blindness.

RETINAL DYSPLASIA: When examining eyes for the better-known hereditary diseases, small marks known as 'rosettes' are seen on the highly reflective retina. Sometimes, folds in the retina may also be seen at the back of the eye when ophthalmoscopic examinations are conducted. Some of these folds are seen as fine grey lines that seem to be of little consequence, but sometimes larger areas of brown discoloration are seen against the bright reflective surface of the tapetal fundus – the surface of the retina. Retinal Dysplasia may, later in the disease, display itself as detachments of part or all of the retina, and there may be near-total loss of vision. This detachment is very rare in the Labrador.

The two forms of Retinal Dysplasia which may be encountered in the Labrador Retriever are:

TOTAL RETINAL DYSPLASIA (TRD): This is the most severe form that develops early in life, and is recognised by the white pupil known as leucocoria. Puppies are blind from birth, but, when still in the nest, the fact that they cannot see is not immediately obvious. The retina at the back of the eye detaches, and becomes drawn forward like a loose tent behind the lens. One eye may appear bigger than the other, and nystagmus, an uncontrolled eye movement, can be easily noted along with the blindness. Often, the eye will develop a cataract after the retina detaches.

MULTIFOCAL RETINAL DYSPLASIA (MRD): The second type of Retinal Dysplasia is the one seen more frequently in Labradors during routine eye inspections with an ophthalmoscope. Folds in the retina, close to the optic disc, appear as grey streaks but do not affect the dog's sight. Often, as the eyeball grows, these 'stretch marks' tend to become less noticeable. MRD in the Labrador is not inspected for in the current BVA/KC certification scheme, as it has caused no eyesight problem in the breed.

GLAUCOMA
Glaucoma is a condition in which the inside of the eye over-inflates, with fluids causing pressure damage to the retina and the lens, as well as making the cornea opaque. Unless treated early in the disease, a permanent loss of sight may result. Presently under investigation in the British Veterinary Association /Kennel Club scheme is a primary glaucoma affecting the Golden Retriever breed, but the Labrador does not have an hereditary glaucoma.

CORNEAL LIPIDOSIS
This is seen as a white mark obscuring part of the front of the eye, but it seldom causes complete blindness and the dog seems to be able to see through or around the opacity without too much disadvantage. It is usually associated with a high-fat diet which causes the lipid material to pass out of the bloodstream and settle in the layers of the cornea. It is not known to have a genetic basis in Labradors.

EYELID DISORDERS
ENTROPION: The condition known as entropion may be an inherited defect of the eyelid structure. It is seen in some Labradors as an inturning of the eyelids. There may be excessive tear formation, and the overflow of tears is noticeable on the faces of light-coloured dogs. As the eyelashes are pulled on to the eye by a spasm of the eyelid muscle, abrasion of the cornea can result in a corneal ulcer. Once diagnosed, severe cases will need immediate surgery to evert the eyelid edge, while milder cases may be treated with lubricating eye ointments. In a growing dog, the skull conformation alters, so that turning-in of the eyelids may correct itself spontaneously. Small eyes were thought at one time to predispose a dog to entropion. It is true that, if there is a nutritional check or weight loss, the pad of fat behind the eye becomes less thick so that the eyeball sinks more into the skull's orbit. Smallness of the eye may be less

noticeable once the nutritional state improves and the eyeball becomes more protruding again.

ECTROPION: This looseness of the eyelids, with undue exposure of the pink lining of the lid, may be an hereditary disease in some breeds with loose skin on the head, but, in the Labrador, ectropion is usually the result of an eyelid injury and is not inherited.

BONE AND JOINT DISEASES WITH HEREDITARY INFLUENCES

HIP DYSPLASIA (HD)
The problem of Hip Dysplasia in the breed has been greatly over-emphasised in some books, but the problem is widespread and can be said to exist in any breed in which more than five per cent of the breed shows recognisable signs. The working guide dog is rarely disadvantaged by HD, as it does not affect the daily life of the dog. Such a Labrador walks at a slow pace, does not have to jump up and does not do agility work. Any pain or discomfort may be associated in the young dog with rupture of the round ligament of the hip that suddenly allows for subluxation with a short period of pain, or, in the older dog, pain from the disease of osteoarthritis that can develop secondary to an existing Hip Dysplasia.

The disease is not entirely an hereditary one, and environmental factors such as feeding, exercise and the position the young dog is made to sit in, may all be responsible for up to 60 per cent of the occurrence of the Hip Dysplasia changes as seen on X-ray. Fortunately, the extreme views once held by experts, who recommended not breeding from any dog showing any traces of hip dysplasia, have been moderated with time and experience. Some of the matings of 0/0 hip score dogs have produced litters of puppies with a hip score little better than the breed average of 16.22. With a hip score range of between 0 and 103 in the UK scheme, there would usually seem little justification for attempting to breed from stock with an above average score. This can be modified by breeding from higher-scoring bitches who may have other characteristics which could be of especial value

to the breeder in a programme to seek a particular type of dog.

In the USA, a similar scheme is operated by the Orthopaedic Foundation for Animals (OFA), and a high standard X-ray plate is needed for evaluation by the organisation's radiologists. Established in 1966 as the world's largest all-breed registry, a seven-point scoring system is used for hips ranging from 'excellent' to 'severe dysplasia'. Dogs must be at least two years old to receive a breeding number from the OFA, although preliminary evaluations will be made by the OFA on dogs younger than 24 months, to help breeders choose their future stock. A slightly different approach is taken by the University of Pennysylvania Hip Improvement Programme (PennHIP). Here, two views of the hind limb are required to measure the amount of displacement or 'joint laxity' in the hips. This method of evaluation overcomes the objection that some dogs appear to have very unstable hip joints, but when X-rayed in the extended position they appear to have normal hip structure. The third hip evaluation scheme is operated in the USA by the Institute for Genetic Disease Control in Animals (GDC). Similar open registries of blood lines are used in Norway and Sweden to help breeders select stock for mating. The normal dog can be certified at 12 months of age, and the information is then available on a progeny report held in a database.

GUIDELINES FOR HIP IMPROVEMENT
1) Score all stock using the BVA/KC scheme or similar schemes that are available outside the UK. This necessitates X-rays of all young breeding stock.
2) As far as practical, breed only from stock with a hip score better than the breed average.
3) Follow recommendations about feeding and exercise to avoid undue injury and stress to the growing hip joint.
4) Regularly review all inherited diseases in the dog group (e.g. in a kennels), and enquire about littermates or parents. Expect to get evasive replies when asking others!

OSTEOCHONDROSIS
Another disease with an hereditary basis, osteo-

chondrosis is seen in large and giant breeds of dogs. The Labrador is likely to suffer from Elbow Osteochondrosis and one or both elbows may be affected, as shown by forelimb lameness in the growing puppy. This lameness is most likely to develop between five and seven months of age. It will not be severe at first, but later one elbow may become so badly affected that the dog cannot fully bend the elbow and the muscles of the shoulder on that side become thinner, causing an imbalance as the dog walks. A veterinary examination will show that when the elbow is bent up, the dog pulls his foot away because of the pain. The joint may become more distended, and the leg feels thinner than the opposite foreleg, but over half the affected dogs have OCD in both forelegs to a greater or lesser extent. Dogs may show Osteochondrosis of the shoulder joint, and this seems to develop at a slightly younger age than the elbow form, so both shoulder and elbow joints of both legs should be X-rayed to ensure a correct diagnosis.

An X-ray under general anaesthesia is necessary to view the elbow joint from two different angles to show up the signs of osteoarthrosis, secondary to the OCD. Severely-affected parents should not be used in breeding programmes, but the rapid bone growth produced by some high-protein diets may make the condition worse, because the bone cartilage grows at too fast a rate to be converted into stronger bone to support a joint.

PANOSTEITIS

This can be a cause of sudden lameness, most often in a foreleg, but sometimes the lameness will alternate from front to back legs. The lameness is sudden and severe, apparently suggesting that a bone has been broken, but the X-ray will show no damage to the bone structure at all. Darker areas in the bone marrow region may be seen in the X-ray plate, and sometimes the periosteal bone appears thickened at the site of pain. It is believed that this is an auto-immune condition, as it does not appear until six months of age, and only infrequently does it cause lameness in the middle-aged or elderly Labrador.

Treatment involves resting the dog for a few days, then giving controlled exercise until the dog walks soundly again. Non-steroidal anti-inflammatory tablets can be given, and severely lame dogs may benefit from corticosteroid injections.

OSTEOARTHRITIS

This condition, which limits joint movement, starts as damage to the cartilage on the joint surface. Additional bone may then be laid down round the edge of the joint, possibly as a result of inflammation and an attempt to support the joint. The disease develops progressively, leading to lameness, pain, the grating feeling known as crepitus and then joint instability. The joint feels thickened from the outside, and there is limited movement when it is bent to stretch it or flex it. If a joint is not moving, then the muscles weaken, or atrophy, so that the leg becomes wasted. X-rays should be taken to assess the degree of new bone building up around the joint. A management plan for the dog can be drawn up, and pain control is the first priority in treatment. Osteoarthritis is particularly associated, in the older Labrador, with Osteochondrosis of the elbow and with Hip Dysplasia's after-effects.

CRUCIATE LIGAMENT RUPTURE

The stifle, or knee joint, is not robustly constructed and depends on a number of ligaments and cartilages to hold it together and give free movement. The stifle is used in jumping and for forward propulsion, so overweight dogs who are suddenly asked to perform tasks, even those as simple as jumping out of a Range Rover or estate car rear door, may land heavily and damage the ligaments.

The cruciate ligaments are those crossing the centre of the stifle joint, and there are two other collateral ligaments that support the sides of the joint. The kneecap, or patella, also has ligaments that run at the front of the joint and these can also fail to support the stifle joint, throwing a greater strain on the two ligaments at the centre. It is usually the front ligament in the centre of the stifle joint – the anterior cruciate ligament – that takes the greatest strain when the dog jumps or turns awkwardly, and this may tear or, at worst, break completely in half. The result is a very lame dog. Often the stifle joint is so unstable that the two bone ends forming the joint can be slid over each other. This instability is used in the 'draw forward' test.

Cruciate rupture usually happens suddenly during extreme exercise and does not improve with enforced rest, as with many other injuries. Heavy dogs the size of Labradors will usually require a surgical operation to repair the torn ligament. There are a number of techniques employed, but most require a ligament implant inserted through or around the joint. Provided the operation is done before arthritic changes develop in the joint surface, the results are very good, since the joint is stabilised again.

DISORDERS WITH A POSSIBLE INHERITED BASIS

SKIN COMPLAINTS

Many dogs scratch for a variety of reasons. Atopy now seems to be increasingly common in the Labrador breed, perhaps more so since mange has become rare and flea bites have become common. Housing dogs exposes them to house dust mites at an early age, whereas in former times most gundogs were reared in outdoor kennels and frequently spent a lot of their non-working time as an adult in a kennel. Atopic dogs are those who are genetically predisposed to dermatitis. Often it is the flea bite that first makes the dog itch, but the dog's own genetic make-up causes the irritation to persist and the skin condition worsens.

Some atopic dogs are seen with pink, itchy ears, some excessively lick at their paws which have dark orange saliva-stained hair, while others have pink skin on the abdomen and the perineum. Unfortunately, some dogs may then develop a severe generalised skin disease, and *Staphylococcus intermedius* as a bacterial infection produces a secondary bacterial dermatosis. Ear infections result from atopic ear irritation, and toenails scratching an itchy ear can transfer all sorts of organisms into a ear canal that seems to have a low resistance to infection, with colonies of organisms growing rapidly in the moist, warm ear tube.

Atopy is related to the type of allergic disorder seen in humans as asthma, hayfever and atopic eczema in babies and infants. Such diseases result from allergic response to allergens in the environment such as spores, pollens, moulds, house dust and other dust mites. House dust mites thrive in warm, unventilated houses, feeding on debris including human skin scales or 'dander'. They may well enjoy feeding on dog dander when this is shed in your Labrador's sleeping or lying area of the house. Fitted carpets are difficult to clean up to their edges, and may require environmental spray applications to control a problem.

Treatment of the atopy may partially correct a situation where a dog 'never stops scratching'. Attention to the sleeping area aimed at removing dust, total eradication of fleas from the house, and feeding a single-protein, low-allergenic diet all help to reduce the scratching threshold. Specific treatments with cortisone drugs provide immediate relief, but the benefit will fade if repeated use of steroids is called for. Alternative treatments for itching include trying to find an antihistamine drug that is effective, and the use of lipid products can be very helpful. Gamma linoleic acid, one of the constituents of Oil of Evening Primrose, is used in various formulae, but further refining the drug to increase the active constituent DLMG has shown promise in humans, and raises hopes for better veterinary treatments soon.

EPILEPSY OR FITS

Fits are rare in the breed. Hereditary epilepsy, although suspected to exist, has not been substantiated in the small numbers of Labradors affected with idiopathic epilepsy.

DIGESTIVE SYSTEM DISORDERS

BLOAT

Sudden accumulation of gas in the stomach will cause distress and, if left untreated, eventual death. Gastric dilation and torsion of the stomach (GDV) can be a problem in any of the larger breeds. It is especially associated with the Giant breeds and Setters, but it may be found in Labradors as an acute emergency. The feeding routine should be such as to avoid hungry dogs swallowing food rapidly, then being left unexercised and unobserved. The GDBA kennel routine is to feed in the morning, before the two work periods during the daytime, so that gas cannot accumulate in the stomach. Any dog with a tendency to Bloat will be seen at the earliest stage of discomfort, and often a silicone-base tablet can be given at this stage to stop bubbles of gas being held in the stomach. Dogs known to 'bloat' can be made to eat more slowly by supervising them and feeding them on their own, with no competition from other dogs stealing their food. The treatment of Gastric Dilation is dealt with in the preceding chapter.

DIARRHOEA FROM BACTERIAL OVERGROWTH

The condition now known as SIBO (Small Intestine Bacterial Overgrowth) is a disorder that may be the cause of persistent diarrhoea, increased appetite and weight loss. The previously-used term BOG was more appropriate to the problem of some dogs suffering from over-frequent defecation. Explained simply, SIBO is a disorder in which too many bacteria for the dog's good health are living in the small intestine. These bacteria take some of the most valuable nutrients out of the food eaten as it passes from the stomach to the small intestine.

Possible causes are defective acid secretion in the stomach juices, slow passage of food through the small intestine, Exocrine Pancreatic Insufficiency (EPI), or defective local immunity of the gut wall to bacteria. Diagnosis has to be confirmed by blood tests, then a month-long course of antibiotics, together with a modified low-fat diet, is usually sufficient to clear the disorder entirely. The diet may be supplemented with Vitamin B and trace elements such as are found in a number of pet health tablets available.

COPROPHAGIA

The eating of faeces is a habit acquired by dogs kept in kennels. Dogs who are adequately supervised at a time when defecation is about to occur will have little opportunity to explore the smells or the taste of recently-voided faeces. The flavouring agents and palatable residues found in faeces after prepared foods have been digested, apparently to a dog's satisfaction, must be blamed for the dog's subsequent nose investigation and ingestion. Efforts to break this behaviour pattern should be adopted. Deterrents such as garlic, paprika and even fresh pineapple have been used to curb a dog's desire to eat faeces. The habit may not be so revolting as first thought, since rabbits use the method of eating faeces from their own rectums as a way of further digesting cellulose for food. Many free-range animals will eat herbivores' faeces left on the ground as a way of obtaining extra Vitamin B.

EXOCRINE PANCREATIC INSUFFICIENCY (EPI)

This is most often associated with the German Shepherd breed, but about one third of all cases are found in other breeds and may be found in Labradors. The disease may not show up until middle age as chronic diarrhoea with weight loss, due to a failure of the digestive enzymes in the small intestine. The EPI blood test is used to confirm a diagnosis. Response to treatment, using supplements of digestive enzymes in dried pancreatic extract combined with drugs to lower stomach acidity, has proved to be good. Unfortunately, long-term treatment adds to the expense of medication.

BREEDING AND REPRODUCTION

DYSTOCIA FROM GROSS OVERSIZE OF A PUPPY

There are no specific breeding problems associated with the Labrador breed. Usually, litter numbers are large and the relatively neatly-shaped puppies are delivered by the bitch without human aid. If, for any reason, there are only one or two puppies carried, they will be normally-shaped but will grow relatively too large for the width of the bitch's pelvic canal. This problem may be seen in the older bitch, whelping when reproductive failure means fewer eggs are released from the ovary for fertilisation. A single oversized puppy presents the biggest problem of delayed birth. In the case of a five-year-old bitch mated for the first time, she may well develop dystocia with a dead puppy as a result.

DELAYED MATURITY

A few Labrador bitches come on heat for the first time later than the norm, which is to have a heat by ten to 12 months. Most of these slow-to-mature bitches will have their first heat by 18 months of age, and there is no reason why they cannot conceive and carry a normal litter in spite of this later-maturing tendency. Running these bitches with other bitches already on heat can sometimes stimulate reproductive activity. Pheronomes or 'smell hormones' may play a part, but some young bitches seem to resist all attempts to get them to breed until the time they are naturally mature.

CRYPTORCHIDISM

Before birth, the male dog's testes originate in the abdomen from a site near the kidneys, similar to that occupied by the mature bitch's ovaries. The testes normally descend from within the abdomen through the inguinal canals, and can be felt in the scrotum about 20 days after birth. Export pedigrees for dogs require a statement that both testes are present in the scrotum, and it may be difficult to be certain that both testes can be felt in the scrotum of the very young puppy.

Total absence of the testes (Anorchia) is very rare, while Monorchidism implies that only one testis has developed. The most usual abnormality is Unilateral Cryptorchidism, when one testis is retained in the abdomen and one can be felt in the scrotum. Unilaterally cryptorchid dogs are fertile, and have mated bitches, but it is a polygenic inherited defect and attempts to breed out the condition should be supported by not using affected dogs for stud. It is considered by some authorities that the litter mates may all carry the same genetic factor for cryptorchidism, so even the litter sisters of affected dogs should not be bred from if it is required to eliminate the condition more thoroughly than at present.

The problem of the testis retained within the abdomen is that, with the testis in the cooler site of the scrotum, the organ functions better. The higher body temperature within the abdomen seems to stimulate the cells within the testis to produce oestrogens.

Seroli cell tumours are thirteen times more common in cryptorchid males than in males with normal-sited testes. Other signs of the tumour are a bilateral hair loss in the older dog, a pendulous penis and attraction of other male dogs to the cryptorchid. Anaemia may develop, due to excess oestrogen production depressing the bone marrow. Castration to remove both testes is advised, but occasionally a request is made to leave one testis in the scrotum, and only have the retained intra-abdominal one removed.

HEREDITARY MYOPATHY

This recently-studied disease has been reported in the USA, UK, France and Australia. The cause of the disease is unknown, but it seems to be transmitted by an autosomal recessive gene. The disease is not fatal, but seems to appear as a muscle weakness in puppies between the ages of eight weeks and eleven months. The puppies may appear underweight, quite slim and hold the head lower than normal, due to the muscle weakness. The dogs tire easily on exercise and this seems worse in cold weather. A bunny-hopping gait is seen in many affected puppies and should be watched out for.